Rethinking World Politics

Rethinking World Politics
A Theory of Transnational Neopluralism

Philip G. Cerny

OXFORD
UNIVERSITY PRESS

2010

OXFORD
UNIVERSITY PRESS

Oxford University Press, Inc., publishes works that further
Oxford University's objective of excellence
in research, scholarship, and education.

Oxford   New York
Auckland   Cape Town   Dar es Salaam   Hong Kong   Karachi
Kuala Lumpur   Madrid   Melbourne   Mexico City   Nairobi
New Delhi   Shanghai   Taipei   Toronto

With offices in
Argentina   Austria   Brazil   Chile   Czech Republic   France   Greece
Guatemala   Hungary   Italy   Japan   Poland   Portugal   Singapore
South Korea   Switzerland   Thailand   Turkey   Ukraine   Vietnam

Copyright © 2010 by Oxford University Press, Inc.

Published by Oxford University Press, Inc.
198 Madison Avenue, New York, New York 10016

www.oup.com

Oxford is a registered trademark of Oxford University Press.

Library of Congress Cataloging-in-Publication Data
Cerny, Philip G., 1946–
Rethinking world politics : a theory of transnational neopluralism / Philip G. Cerny.
   p.   cm.
Includes bibliographical references and index.
ISBN 978-0-19-973369-9; 978-0-19-973370-5 (pbk.)
1. International relations.   2. World politics—21st century.   3. Transnationalism.
I. Title.
JZ1310.C47 2010
327.101—dc22   2009026458

9 8 7 6 5 4 3 2 1

Printed in the United States of America
on acid-free paper

For Ruthie, Ella, Joe, and Elwood—
may the twenty-first century
be good to you!

There is a tide in the affairs of men
Which, taken at the flood, leads on to fortune;
Omitted, all the voyage of their life
Is bound in shallows and in miseries.
On such a full sea are we now afloat,
And we must take the current when it serves,
Or lose our ventures.
—William Shakespeare, *Julius Caesar*, IV.iii.214–221

Contents

PART I: IDENTIFYING CHANGE

1   Introduction: Why Transnational Neopluralism?   3

2   Globalization and Other Stories: The Search for a
    New Paradigm for International Relations   24

3   Space, Territory, and Functional Differentiation:
    Deconstructing and Reconstructing Borders   40

4   Reconfiguring Power in a Globalizing World   64

PART II: DYNAMICS OF CHANGE

5   Multinodal Politics: A Framework for Analysis   85

6   Globalizing the Public Policy Process: From Iron
    Triangles to Flexible Pentangles   111

7   Embedding Neoliberalism: The Evolution of a Hegemonic
    Paradigm   128

8   The State in a Globalizing World: From *Raison d'État*
    to *Raison du Monde*   157

9   Institutional Bricolage and Global Governmentality: From
    Infrastructure to Superstructure   175

PART III: IMPLICATIONS OF CHANGE

10   Some Pitfalls of Democratization in a Globalizing World   195

11   The New Security Dilemma   217

12   Financial Globalization, Crisis, and the Reorganization
     of Global Capital   245

13   Rescaling the State and the Pluralization of Marxism   270

14   Conclusion: Globalization Is What Actors Make of It   289

Bibliography   307

Index   327

Part I

IDENTIFYING CHANGE

Chapter 1

Introduction

Why Transnational Neopluralism?

1. THE BASIC THEME: FROM *RAISON D'ÉTAT* TO *RAISON DU MONDE*

The theme of this book is that the fundamental underpinnings of world politics are being transformed in a globalizing world. Most work on world politics has either explicitly or implicitly taken for granted that there are two distinct yet coexisting political processes and sets of institutions at work simultaneously in the modern world—domestic politics and international relations (Hollis and Smith 1990). The first takes place within established nation-states, and the second takes place as nation-states as political units (or "unit actors": Waltz 1979) interact with each other. The state, as a set of political institutions, apparatuses, and processes, plays a unique role in linking and cutting across both levels. Therefore, the state—embodied in the "modern nation-state"—is seen to be what world politics is still all about.

However, since the early twentieth century, another paradigm has been at work in the study of politics, although mainly limited to the domestic field. That paradigm is pluralism. At the time of writing this book, we are celebrating—or not celebrating, as cultural memory is limited on this score—the publication of the first, seminal work in this area, *The Process of Government: A Study of Social Pressures*, by Arthur F. Bentley (Bentley 1908). Pluralism as a paradigm itself has a checkered history, challenged by Marxist class analysis, theories of elitism and corporatism, and the revival of sociological theories of the state in the tradition of Max Weber. For our purposes, the key development in the evolution of pluralism as a concept is the version called *neopluralism* (Lindblom 1977; McFarland 2004), which acknowledges the shortcomings in early versions of pluralist theory and proposes a more realistic version of the approach.

In neopluralism, the outcomes of various political processes are not determined in the last analysis by the a priori existence of cohesive, vertically unified nation-states as such. Rather, they involve a range of individual and collective (group) actors below, outside, surrounding, and populating the state. These actors have very different levels and kinds of power resources, understandings of how to use that power, material interests, normative values, political projects, and, of course, the determination to pursue their interests, values, and projects in a range of public and private arenas. In other words, such actors are not equal, but there are enough of them with competing interests and values, and there is enough fluidity in political structures and processes, to ensure that competition and coalition building among "groups," as they are known in the literature—a version has been called "group theory" (Truman 1951)—are the main source of both political stability and change, repression and freedom, stagnation and progress. Their most important characteristics for our purposes, however, are that they have *competing* interests as well as common interests, that there are several of them, and that they engage in processes of conflict, competition, and coalition building in order to pursue those interests.

In this pluralistic (and/or neopluralistic) political process, actors face a range not only of *constraints* but also of *opportunities* to shape political outcomes, depending on how they operate within those constraints or how they seek, successfully or unsuccessfully, to transcend and/or transform them. Of course, this sort of analytical approach can be a poor predictor of political behavior where the matrix of constraints and opportunities is relatively open and the matrix of conflict and coalition building more complex. Therefore, political analysis requires extensive ex post facto process tracing and a certain amount of educated guesswork as to future developments. In chapter 14, the concluding chapter to this book, I outline a few key scenarios of where the twenty-first century might lead. But all of them depend on the capacities of real-world, crosscutting "interest" and "value" groups to manipulate constraints, to identify and take advantage of opportunities, and to shape new directions through processes of competition and coalition building.

What is new, however, and forms the focus of this book, are the rapidly growing *transnational linkages* among groups and the emergence of those increasingly influential, even powerful, *cross-border interest and value groups* that are coming to dominate a growing range of crosscutting, uneven yet crucial, transnational political processes. These processes are not replacing nation-states. However, they are crystallizing into transnational *webs of power*. These webs and their interlocked strands of power and political action are continually and ever more rapidly expanding, intensifying, and consolidating, becoming more and more densely interwoven as the new century advances. States are themselves increasingly trapped in these webs.

Whether in terms of economic interdependence, including multinational firms and global financial markets, as well as production, distribution, and consumption chains; social interconnections, migration, and the movement of people; relationships of violence and force (including terrorism);

"transgovernmental networks" cutting across governments; problem-solving "epistemic communities"; technological change from the Internet to a growing variety of human activities; ideological conflict and competition; and a whole range of other deep trends, the most important movers and shakers are no longer simply domestic political forces, institutions, and processes. Rather, they are those actors who can coordinate their activities across borders, at multiple levels and multiple nodes of power; can convince and bully governments, other actors both public and private, and mass publics alike; and therefore can shape not merely transnational—even global—outcomes but also local and regional micro- and meso-politics too (Sassen 2007).

This book is therefore about both these actors and the shifting playing fields on which they operate. And although cross-border political processes may be converging around them, their diversity is growing, too. Political processes are becoming more open, not more closed. A new *world politics*—not "international relations"—is emerging, fitfully, unevenly, generally unexpected and poorly anticipated, through crisis and reaction more than rational, top-down planning. Nevertheless, it is leading to a new form of what the French social philosopher Michel Foucault has called "governmentality." Governmentality, short for "governmental rationality," is the ultimate political art of managing conflicting underlying structural realities and trends by internalizing relevant norms, rules, habits, and ways of doing things in people's everyday behaviors, rather than imposing them from the top down. In the twenty-first century, however, governmental rationality is changing. I argue that traditional governmentality, embodied in the notion of *raison d'État* or "reason of state" that has been at the core of political modernity, is being replaced with a transnational or world rationality—what I call *raison du monde*—that actors are increasingly taking for granted and using to guide their actions in this disorderly and as yet undomesticated new political cosmos.

2. DOMESTIC POLITICS AND INTERNATIONAL RELATIONS IN THE STUDY OF POLITICAL SCIENCE

The study of politics since the ancient Greeks has focused on three main, inextricably intertwined, strands of understanding. The first is power—who possesses power, how the competition and struggle for power plays out, who gets what out of the system, and how power is institutionalized in social structures, particularly the state. The second is justice—what is fair and right, how different conceptions and practices of justice in terms of personal relationships, moral standards, and the distribution of goods and

values are materialized in social, economic, and political life, and how it
might be possible to pursue justice normatively, as a moral or ethical goal,
in society. And the third is basic social concord—how to promote the peaceful coexistence, cooperation, and competition of a range of diverse and
potentially conflicting actors, groups, and interests around commonly
accepted rules of the game. For the most part, however, each of these dimensions has been seen in political philosophy—and also in empirical political
science—as limited in scope to the domestic politics of the family, the local
community, the city-state, and, in modern times, the nation-state. As
Aristotle wrote in the *Politics*, conceptions of "justice" and "friendship" had
purchase only within a limited political community or *politeia*; all other peoples were outsiders or foreigners. Senator Arthur Vandenberg famously
said, "Politics stops at the water's edge."

Most political theorists have taken these limitations for granted, either
explicitly or implicitly. Some, following the ancient Greek historian
Thucydides, have assumed that lacking the domestic social bonds of justice
and friendship, relations between such limited political communities—
most recently, of course, "states"—are predominantly, even exclusively, a
field reserved for purer forms of power politics and the external pursuit of
"national interests": wars, balances of power, diplomatic relations between
sovereign nation-states, and the like. These approaches are called "realist,"
because the bottom-line "reality" is ostensibly the struggle for power and
survival among autonomous states. Others, like the eighteenth-century
German philosopher Immanuel Kant and what have been called "idealist"
political theorists, have argued that states, too, can have fundamentally
peaceful—"positive-sum"—goals, and that states, like individuals, can
themselves potentially get together to create institutions and practices that
systematically stabilize and promote cooperation, rather than conflict,
among those states.

Nevertheless, the modern international system is widely seen by *both*
schools as fundamentally a "system of states," embodying limits and constraints on the development of "international society" that cannot be transcended unless some form of world state were to emerge (contrast Waltz
1979; Buzan 2004; Hurrell 2007). And despite the uneven emergence of
what has been called "global governance" (Diehl 2005) or even the "global
state" (Shaw 2000), international institutions and regimes remain not only
"intergovernmental" in structure—they can promote cooperative outcomes
only as long as their member states do not "defect" as a result of clashing
national interests—but also unevenly developed *and* fragmented by issue
area. In a system of states, while positive-sum outcomes or "absolute gains"
are not impossible to achieve in limited circumstances, they will nevertheless always be subordinated in the last analysis to national interests and

"relative gains," that is, who's up and who's down in the international pecking order or pyramid of power. The threat of defection constitutes the
"default" state of affairs.

In contrast, this book asks: To what extent, in the twenty-first century, is
this fundamental structural state of affairs eroding or changing? How is it
changing, and in what ways? What are the principal variables—the social
and historical forces, that is, not just underlying structural characteristics
but real-world *actors*—that might be seen to drive those processes of change?
Is that change likely to constitute a fundamental transformation of the very
system itself? And if so, are we likely to see a world emerging that looks
more and more like domestic politics rather than like traditional international relations? Are we moving toward a world in which the pursuit of
power and relative gains among states becomes subordinated to relatively
peaceful political competition—"politicking"—over interests and values
among crosscutting political groups, economic interests and market actors,
transnational value groups and social movements, and other individual and
collective actors that are primarily concerned with pursuing their own interests and values, without having to limit themselves either to working only
within the domestic political sphere or to subordinating their wider interests and goals to those of states ("national interests") and to the constraints
of a system of states? Or do the conflicts of interests and values among such
groups actually make transnational conflict *more* likely—but this time, not
reflected so much in interstate violence, on the one hand, as in violent conflict between those very transnational groups and actors, not to mention
among them and state actors trying to hold the ring, on the other?

In this quest, the core of this project is to ask whether what has come to
be called "globalization"—that is, the transnational overlapping, crosscutting, and interpenetrating of markets, communications, social and cultural
identities, common value goals, political processes, and the like—represents
such a fundamental underlying structural change, and, if so, what is globalization and who is driving it? As we will see throughout this book, my main
hypothesis is that globalization involves—and is driven by—a growing and
evolving process of the (so far uneven) interaction of actors and groups
stretching across national boundaries and state borders. This does not imply
the demise of the state as an institutional structure, but it does mean that
states are increasingly "enmeshed" (Hurrell 2007) in an expanding and
increasingly complex web of political, social, and economic relationships
cutting across the vertical borders between states.

Indeed, the borders characterizing this world are increasingly *horizontal*
borders between "interests," broadly defined to include material interests,
cultural identities, and social values—that is, economic sectors and markets; crosscutting social groupings, including classes and fractions of

classes, ethnicities, religions, and the like; diverse parts of a "disaggregated" state (Slaughter 2004) linked into "transgovernmental networks"; political pressure groups, value groups, and social movements; and myriad other social, economic, and political actors, both individual and collective, who increasingly operate on international, transnational, and "translocal" play-ing fields. In other words, the primary hypothesis I am exploring is that globalization both entails, and *is itself driven and shaped*, by a process of the still uneven, but increasingly crosscutting, pluralization of world politics. As I will argue, this is not a process that can be measured by quantitative indi-cators or proxy variables. It is an evolving, historical process that involves something fundamentally, essentially new and as yet both unrealized and unpredictable. It is a "black swan" (Taleb 2007).

Finally, ideological and paradigmatic worldviews are evolving toward more flexible forms that can be adopted and adapted by diverse groups to reflect this interaction between the pursuit of their interests and the grow-ing questions of scale and structural change represented by globalization. In this sense, ideology both "follows the election returns" and feeds back into the way politicking is carried out. It represents the interface of com-plexity and integration, of convergence and diversity, which characterizes world politics today. In this context, "neoliberalism" means different things to different people but has certain common features—most important, a recognition both that states are more and more constrained as "unit actors" and that power struggles and coalitions among groups are increasingly both diverse and interlinked across borders, whether through markets, networks, and/or hierarchies.

Neopluralism, then, is the term I adopt to characterize the overarching trend pattern in world politics. This "transnational neopluralism" is, how-ever, a work in progress, continually shaping political action and institu-tional change and, in turn, itself being reshaped in a range of inextricably intertwined ways. It is driven by the competition of increasingly crosscut-ting, transnational interests; internalized through the new governmentality of *raison du monde*; expanded by the new horizons of scale opened up by globalization; guided by the evolving norms and values of increasingly diverse "varieties of neoliberalism" (Soederberg, Menz, and Cerny 2005); and embedded by a political process called "structuration" (see chapter 5) that ultimately leads to institutional change, as well as behavioral change.

3. PLURALITY, PLURALISM, AND POLITICAL THEORY

As noted earlier, the year 2008 was also the centenary of the publication of Arthur F. Bentley's *The Process of Government*. That book, whatever its flaws (and there were many), revolutionized the field of political science in the United States and elsewhere. It did so in two ways. In the first place, the book argued that formal political institutions were not as important as they had been traditionally seen to be in the study of politics. Indeed, such institutions were little more than a playing field upon which a range of "interests"—loosely defined—competed over political power, influence, and policy outcomes.

In the second place, the real causal variables (as we would call them today) of politics were found not in the competition of political parties, the technical solutions of bureaucrats or judges, or a struggle of social classes, but rather in the interaction of myriad such interests, in a "great moving process" of competition and coalition building. "Interests" took many forms, including common material self-interest (the usual way the word is used), collective social and cultural identities, and shared philosophical and ideological values. Bentley and his later follower David Truman (Truman 1951), founded what came to be called the group theory of politics. For a while, in the middle of the twentieth century, group theory and its other label, pluralism, developed into what is often called a dominant or hegemonic "paradigm" (Kuhn 1962) in American political science and, by extension, elsewhere, particularly in Britain. Pluralism became, explicitly and implicitly, the principal way of examining the world and identifying basic causal explanations in politics.

Pluralism has since both declined and evolved as a would-be paradigm. As Sheldon Wolin wrote in the 1960s, in political philosophy there is no such thing as a dominant paradigm in the manner of Thomas Kuhn's seminal historiography of the philosophy of natural science (Wolin 1968). The history of political philosophy, Wolin argued, has at all times been one of multiple, competing paradigms—of alternative political philosophies, not only a range of normative philosophies setting out what should be but also competing empirical theories offering different causal explanations. And sometimes outright conflict, including violent conflict, over these alternative paradigms in the real world overshadows the more peaceful and stabilizing implications of traditional pluralism. So in the 1960s, for example, in an era of political doubt and confrontation reflected in the American civil rights movement, the Vietnam War, the Prague Spring and the subsequent Soviet invasion of Czechoslovakia, the "Events of May" in Paris, and the outpouring of critical theories on both right and left, pluralism was challenged by other paradigmatic claimants on both right and left.

Five of these claimants, in particular, have left their mark. One was a conservative reaction in the history of political philosophy under the influence of the antibehavioralist political philosopher Leo Strauss (Storing 1962). This strand was primarily limited to the academy—at least until the

1990s, when Straussians constituted a key grouping within the neoconservative movement in the United States, especially in the Project for the New American Century, founded in 1997, and later the George W. Bush administration. The second was more salient publicly—the renaissance of Marxist and neo-Marxist approaches not only throughout the social sciences, including political science and international relations, but also in myriad protest movements and radical politics, lasting well into the 1970s and beyond, especially outside the United States. In the 1970s and 1980s, however, neo-Marxist theorizing tended to be overtaken by a third claimant, including other critical approaches as postmodernism, poststructuralism, and deconstructionism, which saw the modern world as continually fragmenting and dividing rather than moving toward a new equilibrium or higher normative plane.

The fourth claimant, the opposite of postmodernism, involved the revival of interest in the state itself as an institutional structure in both comparative politics and international relations. This new statism revived not only the sociological theories of Max Weber, with his focus on bureaucracy and officialdom as the keystone of modernity, but also Marx's state theory, especially as taken from his pamphlet *The Eighteenth Brumaire of Louis Bonaparte* (1852), focusing on what came to be called the "relative autonomy of the [capitalist] state" (Jessop 1982; Holloway and Picciotto 1978; Poulantzas 1976). This uneven blend of neo-Weberian and neo-Marxist approaches has been particularly influential in the guise of the "new institutionalism" in history, sociology, and institutional economics—but especially in political science and international relations (Hall and Taylor 1996). Since the 1980s, however, the most influential analytical approach in American political science—the fifth claimant—has been public choice theory, also called rational choice and collective action theory (Olson 1965; McLean 1987). Along with formal economic modeling and mathematical game theory, from which it stemmed in part, as well as the employment of quantitative methods (already established in the so-called behavioral social sciences and parts of political science since the mid-twentieth century), this approach introduced a whole new language of equations, formal logic, and claims to predictive value, supposedly at least partly analogous to the methodologies of the natural sciences.

Each of these approaches called into question one aspect or another of traditional pluralism. On the one hand, the pluralist critique of institutional approaches was attacked as missing crucial structural variables that constitute the institutionalized playing field of politics and thereby inherently shape the action of individuals and groups, who must work within distinct configurations of structured constraints and opportunities. On the other hand, analysts questioned the pluralist assertion that groups were essentially autonomous from each other and relatively internally unified in pursuit of their particular interests, values, and identities; such assumptions were attacked as either missing wider solidarities, such as nation or class, or else underestimating the rationality of individual choices in the political marketplace. Pluralism thus came under attack from various different, inherently theoretically incompatible, sides.

Despite recent claims to dominant paradigmatic status by rational choice theory and its cognates, such as game theory and econometric modeling, pluralism has nevertheless remained analytically influential on an everyday level, evolving into different strands, primarily involving three mutations. First, the concept of the interest group has been partly unpacked, involving a wider range of phenomena—a more diverse plurality of actors and collectivities at various levels of analysis, from individuals to social movements, as well as a redefinition of "interests" around a larger universe of motivations. Second, the structure of the institutional playing field has also been unpacked, not only focusing on a wider range of "political opportunity structures" (including transnational ones) and how they both empower and constrain actors but also seeing state actors themselves as relatively autonomous in pursuing their interests both inside the state and in relation to nonstate actors, both within and across borders. Structural variables have therefore been somewhat more effectively, if controversially, internalized and institutionalized through an approach called "structuration," which we will encounter later. Third, Bentley's assumption that the competition and coalescing of plural interests is a relatively open process to which most groups have access has been replaced, as noted previously, by neopluralism. These issues appear and reappear throughout this book.

4. SOCIAL CONFLICT, STABILITY, AND GLOBALIZATION

These theoretical issues are particularly significant when examined in the context of globalization. The exogenous conditions usually associated with globalization alter the patterns of rewards and penalties—the payoff matrix—of group politics in such a way as to make the effective promotion of the interests of a growing and increasingly significant range of old and new groups dependent on their ability to pursue those interests on international and transnational levels, as well as through the domestic nation-state. This leads an increasing number of interest groups in turn to develop not only strategies and tactics for political action but also *institutional* strategies—that is, strategies for modifying the ways existing institutions work and even designing new institutions and less formal political structures to complement and/or substitute for existing ones.

Of course, this "institutional selection" process (Spruyt 1994) is never complete. The original consolidation of the modern nation-state and states system as the dominant organizational form of the modern world 400 to 500 years ago represented the locking in of earlier conjunctures, especially the decline of feudalism. However, this process was also one that for various historical reasons was profoundly *reinforced* not only by later historical changes—especially the Second Industrial Revolution, the emergence of modern Weberian bureaucracies, and the Clausewitzian organization of nineteenth- and twentieth-century warfare—but also by the activities of new interest groupings, such as trade unions and left-wing parties, industrial capitalist elites and mass right-wing parties, new middle classes, and catch-all parties, as well as old ones, such as aristocrats seeking to adapt to changes that would otherwise undermine their power and status (Mayer 1981).

Today, changes in a wide range of exogenous variables—exemplified by, for example, the physical environment (with the challenges of pollution, resource depletion, climate change, etc.), the changing economic structures represented by trade interdependence, financial globalization, post-Fordist production structures, transnational webs of economic power and influence, and the like, and globalizing sociocultural perceptions and norms enabled by the development of new information and communications technologies—are altering the payoff matrix within which both group activities and institutional structures must operate. It is this very complexity of exogenous, material, and quasi-material structural change, paradoxically, that is today creating increasingly permissive conditions for neopluralist interest groupings to exploit.

Globalization hypothetically involves the emergence and crystallization of new patterns of governance. Economic structural change, for example, is provoking dynamic responses of promotion, accommodation, and resistance to those changes. In this context, "power" itself is inevitably becoming more diffuse, refracted through an increasingly complex, prismatic structure of socioeconomic forces and levels of governance—from the global interaction of transnational social movements and interest or pressure groupings, multinational corporations, financial markets, and the like, on the one hand, to the reemergence of subnational and cross-national ethnic, religious, and policy-oriented coalitions and conflicts of the type familiar in domestic-level political sociology, on the other.

World politics as I define it here (namely, both domestic politics and international relations, taken together) is therefore being transformed into a "polycentric" or "multinucleated" global political system operating within the same geographical space—and/or overlapping spaces—in a way analogous to the emergence of coexisting and overlapping functional authorities in metropolitan areas (Ostrom, Tiebout. and Warren 1961; Brenner 2004).

The underlying governance problematic in such multilayered political systems is at least twofold. In the first place, it becomes harder to maintain the boundaries that are necessary for the efficient "packaging" of public or collective goods; in the second place, it becomes harder to determine what collective goods are demanded or required in the first place—that is, even to measure what is the "preferred state of affairs" (Brenner 2004: 832–835; cf. Cerny 1999a).

Furthermore, state actors themselves paradoxically act in routine fashion to undermine the holistic and hierarchical character of traditional state sovereignty, authority, or *potestas*—a "hollowing out of the state" (Jessop 1997). The result is a growing "privatization of the public sphere," not only by selling off or contracting out public services and functions but also in the deeper sense of reducing society itself to competing "associations of consumers" in which administrators are little more than buyers in competing corporations (Ostrom, Tiebout, and Warren, 1961: 839; cf. Lake 1999).

The international system of states as unit actors is thus being superseded by a much more diffuse, decentralized, and crosscutting structural pattern, based on a new version of Durkheim's division of labor (Durkheim 1893/1933: 405–406). Durkheim actually argued that there was no such thing as a genuine crosscutting international division of labor; he saw it as an almost wholly domestic phenomenon. However, as today's increasingly transnational division of labor expands, the kinds of things that states can do, and the constraints that derive from external pressures, are constantly changing and becoming more complex. Complex systems are characterized by "overlapping memberships" and "cross-cutting affiliations" (Truman 1951); in other words, different "groups" are often interconnected in complex ways that reflect diverse, even contrasting, identities and belongings, cutting across territory, class, gender, ethnicity, family ties, and the like.

But without the state and its authoritative capacity to enforce the rules of the game, transnational complexity would seem to imply instability. Traditional pluralist theorists argued that, paradoxically, pluralism was actually a key stabilizing factor in the modern world. For example, in Simmel's reformulation of Durkheim, pluralism and functional specialization are in the last analysis stabilizing, not destabilizing. In a "complex social structure," he argued, the roles and group memberships of individuals overlap with and cut across those of other individuals and groups—in the family, in employment, in friendships, in leisure activities, in communications, even in politics—creating a mutually reinforcing web of interactions cutting across potentially conflicting macrogroups such as economic classes (Simmel 1922/1955). Stability is therefore not derived simply from cooperation, consensus, norms, system equilibrium, economic modes of production, and other macrolevel phenomena. Rather, it depends on the overlapping and intertwining at the micro- and meso-levels of what would otherwise be destabilizing conflicts, mitigating them and even making them cancel each other out, as argued by Lewis Coser in his classic updating of Simmel (Coser 1956):

> Groups which are not involved in continued struggle with the outside are less prone to make claims on total personality involvement of the membership and are more likely to exhibit flexibility of structure. The multiple internal conflicts which they tolerate may in turn have an equilibrating and stabilizing impact on the structure....

> In flexible social structures, multiple conflicts crisscross each other and thereby prevent basic cleavages along one axis. The multiple group affiliations of individuals makes them participate in various group conflicts so that their total personalities are not involved in any single one of them. (Coser 1956: 152–154)

In today's globalizing world, overlapping memberships and crosscutting affiliations are spreading across an ever wider range of manifest and developed—complex, cohesive, differentiated, and so on—structural categories. This fluidity, identified by such analysts as Keohane and Nye (1977/2000) in the theory of complex interdependence, opens up further possibilities. It constitutes the basis not just for an international plurality of building blocks, but for the crystallization of new dynamic pluralist processes. Nevertheless, such uneven pluralization in a globalizing world can be destabilizing, too. This is an issue that runs throughout this book.

5. INTEREST GROUPS AND THE GLOBALIZATION PROCESS

In this changing environment, the stage is set for an increasingly active, accelerating, and open process of interest group adjustment—the "rearticulation of social and political coalitions," as Spruyt (1994) calls it—at multiple levels and in multiple settings or nodes. This adjustment process affects interest groups at several levels. In the first place, it affects the "underlying group formation" of society, that is, the interface between the socioeconomic structure and politics. At one level, the physical or material environmental bases of certain types of interest group association have been transformed by both technological change and greater awareness of the international and transnational interconnectedness of environmental and other issues. In particular, the multinationalization of industry, the expansion of trade, and the globalization of financial markets, along with the development of a transnational consumer society, have transformed many of what Bentley called "wealth groups" and V. O. Key called "sectional

groups" (Key 1953) into transnational groups involved in complex competition and coalition building with each other, with state actors and international institutions, and increasingly with mass publics. At another level,
values and consciousness are also being transformed in the context of
globalization.

Within and across states, too, bureaucrats, politicians, and other officials
or "state actors" have become more and more imbricated with groups of
their counterparts in other countries through transgovernmental networks,
policy communities, and the like. In the economic sphere, post-Fordist
forms of production based on flexibilization have transformed "techniques
of industry," labor markets, finance, and the like. And in an area that Bentley
tended to dismiss, the rediscovery of ideas not merely in terms of formal
arguments but even more so in terms of discourses—whether constructivist
discourses of institutional reconstruction or postmodernist discourses of
multiple circuits of power—has transformed the everyday content of what
he called "discussion groups" (as distinct from "organizational groups"), as
well as that of political actors and intellectuals.

However, the question remains whether we are yet at the stage where
"great cross-nation interest groupings," as Bentley called them, are becoming sufficiently well developed to "force [themselves] into the field and insist
on modifying the process of adjustment." Of particular importance is
whether the development of a range of "transnational opportunity structures" (Krieger and Murphy 1998) provides sufficient vital structural space
for key groups to act in potentially transformative ways, in turn increasing
the vulnerability and malleability of the system in feedback fashion.

At the same time, however, such changes also give rise to adaptive as well
as transformational modes of behavior. Therefore, the particular *shape* a
transformed international system is likely to take will be determined primarily by whether particular sets of groups—in particular, which competing groups led by "institutional entrepreneurs" or "change masters" (Kanter
1985)—are best able, either strategically or accidentally, to exploit the manifest and latent structural resources or political opportunity structures available to them most effectively in a period of flux. A key variable in explaining
group-led change is thus the presence of *strategically situated groups* in a
flawed and/or fluid structural context. Their presence constitutes a necessary but not sufficient condition of structural change.

The perceived inability of states to coordinate their responses to such
complex pressures in strategic fashion—and to be *seen* to do so by more
transnationally aware publics—is said to have several structurally significant consequences. This question is at the forefront of public consciousness
at the time of writing, when a range of poorly coordinated national responses
to the 2008 global financial crisis has raised fundamental questions about

the capacity of "global governance" to cope with the most pressing issues of the day. One consequence is the fragmentation of domestic state responses to political pressures—that is, the splintering of the state itself. Another is the necessity for such responses to be coordinated across borders, leading to an increasing process of institutional bricolage at the level of formal and informal transnational structures and processes. A third, linking the first two, is the development of transgovernmental networks among significant but internally fragmented state actors, often playing ad hoc games of catch-up to adjust regulation and government intervention to perceived new economic realities through such processes as competitive liberalization and regulatory arbitrage.

Within this context, key sets of groups that have in the past been closely bound up with the territorial nation-state are increasingly experimenting with new forms of quasi-private regulation of their activities, especially in the context of neoliberal ideology and approaches to governance. Just as in domestic politics, those interest groups that are best endowed are not only the most involved in globalization but also the most likely to succeed. And state actors themselves, once said to be "captured" by large, well-organized domestic constituencies, are increasingly captured instead by transnationally linked sectors that not only set state agencies and international regimes against each other—a process sometimes called "venue shopping" or "forum shopping"—in the desire to level the playing field for their domestic clients in the wider world, on the one hand, but also cause them simultaneously to try to network in an increasingly dense fashion with their peers in other states, on the other. Among the major losers are trade unions and other groups with few transnational linkages, although they are sometimes still in a strong position to demand and obtain compensatory side payments from national governments.

Alongside these economic developments has come a range of social and political developments. The impact of new technologies has intensified pressures resulting from the interaction of previously compartmentalized social and cultural categories, with an emphasis on the sheer speed of that interaction (Douglas 1999). The development of Marshall McLuhan's global village has been paralleled (or, for some, even superseded) by a postmodernist fragmentation of cultures and societies (Deibert 1997). In political terms, the reidentification of societies as "multicultural," emphasizing shifting identities and loyalties, is unraveling the consolidation of "national culture societies" (Znaniecki, 1952/1973) that was at the heart of the nation-state political project from Bismarck's *Kulturkampf* to postcolonial "nation-building" (Bendix 1964).

Major social movements and cause groups are increasingly focused on transnational issues such as the environment, human rights, women's issues, the international banning of landmines, opposition to the holding of political prisoners, promoting sustainable development, and eliminating poor countries' international debts. Uneven but growing pressures for migration, of both unskilled and highly skilled people, along with new possibilities for international communication, have led to the growth of active diasporas, as well as of "global tribes" (Kotkin 1992). The end of the cold war also unleashed a huge number of social and political demands that had previously been kept in ideological and political check. In this context, the notion of the public interest itself is being questioned, and perhaps being transformed, releasing groups from the rigid ideological categories of the mid-twentieth century.

The growing salience of a range of fault lines in existing domestic and international political structures has therefore, first of all, created *permissive conditions* for broad-based, paradigmatic structural change. In a deeper sense, however, the increasing salience of those fault lines and their interaction in complex, changing exogenous circumstances are themselves generating *causative conditions* for change. What kind of change and what kinds of new power relationships will actually emerge will, however, depend on the complex interaction of such conditions, on the one hand, and the way actors interpret and attempt to manipulate them in pursuing their interests, on the other.

Whether change overall is fundamental and far-reaching enough to become paradigmatic change—that is, *transformational* change—will depend on the balance of forces between sets of groups whose actions continue to reinforce existing structural forms and practices and those whose actions generate and reinforce new forms and practices. Furthermore, change will depend on the way the latter groups actually act in practice. Although they might be expected to act in ways that challenge the structure, they also may for various reasons—including cultural and ideological reasons, as well as calculations of short-term gains—not be able, or even not choose, to act in such ways. Routine, adaptive, or structure-bound behavior may in the end be the preferred course of action for many strategically situated groups.

And finally, those alternative outcomes—or "multiple equilibria"—that may exist in theory and in the minds of key actors may prove either too ambitious, on the one hand, or too amorphous and fragmented, on the other, to form an effective foundation for those groups' strategic or tactical calculations and for their pursuit of specific, coherent outcomes. Indeed, such potential outcomes are often only dimly perceived and may well be too unfocused to constitute a ground for effective strategic action. Nevertheless, as specific actors continually probe the potential for new ways to pursue their interests, it is likely that a more transnational form of rationality—*raison du monde*—will crystallize and consolidate.

6. THE STRUCTURE OF THE BOOK

This book addresses a wide range of issues critical for the development of a theory of transnational neopluralism. The book is divided into three parts. In the next three chapters of part I, I look at three fundamental elements of change and attempt to identify *what it is that needs to be explained*—the *explanandum*—by any new paradigm: globalization, the nature of borders, and the underlying configuration of power itself. Chapters 5–9 (part II) set out the basic framework of analysis developed in the book—the *explanans*—and look at the main political dimensions of change: transnational neopluralism itself, policy-making processes, neoliberal ideology, the state, and the embryonic institutions of transnational governance. Part III looks at some of the broader implications of change in specific contexts: the question of democracy and democratization in general and its relation to pluralism in particular, international security, the financialization of world politics, and the impact of these processes on critical theories, especially today's versions of Marxism. The concluding chapter considers the roles of key actors in an increasingly transnational neopluralist world and suggests four scenarios for the development of world politics in the twenty-first century.

In chapter 2, I look back at the question of paradigms (Kuhn 1962; Wolin 1968) in the study of politics—both domestic politics and international and global politics. I argue that the paradigms that have been dominant in political science and international relations, although they have served well up to a point, have been undermined by structural developments and patterns of political action over many decades, particularly since the middle of the twentieth century and increasingly as we get further and further into the twenty-first—what is generally referred to as the process of globalization. What Kuhn called "normal science" is continually being challenged and undermined by a fundamental transformation of what I (and many others) prefer to call "world politics." World politics not only crosses over between the international and domestic levels of analysis but also involves a process of interaction and semifusion of the two supposedly distinct levels, however uneven and continually evolving, that is fundamentally transforming the way we understand how the world works. In attempting to explain globalization, therefore, a new paradigm is needed—transnational neopluralism.

Chapter 3 is a reinterpretation of the way we understand the history and development of different forms of bordering and stratification, of territorial enclosure and the opening of crosscutting spaces, in this complex world— in particular, the relationship between social, economic and political processes, on the one hand, and geographical conceptions of space and territory, on the other. The increasing interlinking and interpenetration of "horizontal" forms of social stratification, economic markets, and political structures increasingly problematizes that traditional "container" of political systems and processes, the nation-state—not doing away with the state but enmeshing it in expanding webs of social, political, and economic identities, patterns of behavior, and political action that transform its role and function in the wider transnational and global context. Chapter 4 continues this questioning by identifying a range of ways the character of power itself is being transformed by the same processes.

Chapter 5 contains the core of the book's theoretical and analytical argument—namely, that a process of what has been called "structuration" has been unfolding, however unevenly, that puts transnationally linked, organized, and intertwined "interest" and "value" groups (although definitions vary) at the heart of the transformation processes. These groups play a crucial role in shaping what is a multilevel, multinodal process of politicking—of pursuing their collective interests and goals, of seeking to influence and control policy making, of shaping political processes and power structures, and of competing and forming (and breaking) coalitions in the pursuit of those goals. They seek increasingly to "capture the benefits of globalization" for their constituents, across borders and at different levels of action. Furthermore, they play a central role in the transformation of globalizing public policy-making processes at various levels, as argued in chapter 6.

Chapter 7 looks at what I argue is the key ideological shift at the heart of this transformation, both rationalizing and guiding it, but also evolving with it—neoliberalism. Neoliberalism is not simply a revival of laissez-faire economics but rather a political project aimed at reconfiguring relations between states and other governance structures, on the one hand, and markets and other economic structures and processes, on the other. Its key doctrines of flexibility and competitiveness, promoted and sustained by new forms of promarket regulation, are more compatible with economic internationalization and globalization than traditional forms of state intervention. The evolution of neoliberalism, in the wake of political transformation and crisis, has, however, increasingly involved a refocusing of policy on newer forms of regulatory, managed, and even social neoliberalism, reflecting the imperatives of adjustment not just to globalization but even more to the rise of transnational neopluralism.

Chapter 8 considers the continuing but also continually changing role of the state and of state actors in this context. I argue, in particular, that state actors, in having to operate on increasingly multilevel, multinodal playing fields, are less and less guided by the requirements of reinforcing, defending, and building autonomous states, and more and more guided by the need to politick, to network, to make effective policies, and to refashion state and international apparatuses themselves, not only to reflect global realities but also to pursue their own interests, values, and political projects more effectively. In other words, what the French social philosopher Michel Foucault called *raison d'État*—or "reason of state," the dominant governmental rationality of the modern world—is increasingly ceding primacy to *raison du monde*, "global reasoning," or a rationality rooted in globalization and transnationalization, whatever the playing field actors are operating on.

Chapter 9 continues the theme of governmentality, addressing the thorny problem of how international regimes, institutions, and other forms of so-called global governance fit into this picture. I argue that the ad hoc, trial-and-error, and issue-specific character of the development of these institutional structures—what anthropologists call bricolage—constitutes a fundamentally uneven, sometimes schizophrenic, and very often inefficient quasi superstructure for both the top-down tackling of global or transnational challenges and the bottom-up pursuit of those interests and values most highly prioritized by transnational (as well as domestic and local) interest and value groups.

Chapters 10 through 13 trace the process of the development of transnational neopluralism through four key issue areas: democratization, security, financialization, and capitalism. First of all, the attempt to spread democratic practices and institutions, whether in terms of building national democratic institutions where they have not existed before or especially by attempting to design and construct new forms of global democracy, raises a number of both old and new issues. In particular, I look at the relationship between pluralization and democratization, from the lessons of national democratic developments from the eighteenth through the twentieth centuries, to key issues in democratic theory, to the "governmentality gap" (chapter 10). Although democratization faces an extremely rocky road in a globalizing world, the development of transnational neopluralism enables the emergence of at least some potential for the consolidation of political processes that permit a minimal degree of bottom-up pressure, especially in particular circumscribed issue areas. However, pluralization is not a proxy for true democratization in the way it has traditionally been depicted, and it can morph into nondemocratic or only pseudodemocratic forms, too.

The pursuit of security, the subject of chapter 11, is undergoing a particularly radical transformation—the New Security Dilemma. States—and people—are no longer most threatened by interstate wars—that is, wars between nation-states—as was the case in the "modern" state system of the seventeenth through twentieth centuries. Violent conflict today overwhelmingly involves civil wars, ethnic and religious conflicts, cross-border wars, transnational terrorism, and the like. Indeed, attempts by states to provide international security through traditional state-based military modes and mechanisms are proving increasingly counterproductive in today's environment of complex economic interdependence, multiculturalism, and asymmetric power relations. At the same time, some states are increasingly prioritizing interdependent economic development, the promotion of global governance (despite its structural weaknesses), and "pooled sovereignty" rather than national sovereignty, national interests, autonomy, and the threat of defection. The model of "civilian states" (Sheehan 2008) and the "civilianization" of international relations is not only emerging as a viable alternative but also inextricably intertwined with the development of transnational neopluralism with its cross-border networks of interdependence—refocusing international politics on a different kind of "who gets what, when, and how," as Harold Lasswell put it, and therefore of a qualitatively different conception of security, one that looks more like policing than like traditional interstate warfare.

What would seem at first glance to be the most problematic issue area today, in the context of the current financial crisis and recession, is what has been called "financialization." This is the focus of chapter 12. The increasingly tight coupling of global financial markets, new forms of financial innovation, the politics of economic growth, and the process of economic development have led to a politics of regulatory change over the past three decades that was long believed to be stable but has proven deeply fragile (Nesvetailova 2007). The process of so-called financial deregulation was not only promoted by self-interested capitalists, although they were key players, but also by actors in the real economy seeking new forms of investment, regulators and bureaucrats at home and in transgovernmental networks, a wide range of interest and even value groups, political parties and leaders on both right and left, neoliberal intellectuals of various stripes—not just economists—and, of course, voters and consumers. For example, people wanting to own their own homes but lacking the resources to do so were an essential part of the complex set of causes of the so-called subprime mortgage crisis in the United States that started the process of unraveling.

Chapter 13 looks at recent developments in neo-Marxist theory, especially those varieties of Marxism that have, intentionally or inadvertently, introduced more pluralistic or neopluralistic factors into the analysis. The main focus of the chapter is on the version of neo-Marxism that looks at the "rescaling of statehood," that is, those authors who have addressed the problem of globalization by analyzing altered playing fields of various kinds—what has been called the search for a new spatiotemporal fix for capitalism. This version, and other versions, too, bring further into question some of the basic problems of the theory of capitalism itself, especially the Marxist version of the labor theory of value. Marxism may have been out of fashion in the late twentieth century and often ignored by academics, too, but the financial crisis and recession of 2008–2009 revived interest in alternatives to neoliberal globalization. Nevertheless, I argue that basic flaws in the Marxist critique continue make such attempts problematic.

In all of this, I argue that the most important changes in both domestic and international political economy—those that have led today to the deepest crisis since the Great Depression of the 1930s—have been the result of *imbalances* in the development of transnational neopluralism, which is why it is "neo"-pluralism, not just pluralism. In a globalizing world, states may be taking the lead on bailouts and economic stimulus packages, but a return to the corporatist welfare state of the post-Depression era is precluded. Financial globalization and neoliberalism require a reinventing of governance across borders, and thus far the outlines of such a process are not only vague and dim but also deeply problematic and bedeviled by the "governmentality gap" discussed in chapter 9. The eventual outcome will not be shaped primarily by states but by changing patterns of transnational neopluralism itself, as different groups jostle and bargain over policies, institutions, and economic theories.

In the conclusion (chapter 14), I will sum up by looking at some key categories of actors and possible scenarios for the development of transnational and global politics in the context of growing transnational neopluralism. In the last analysis, what might be called the "process of governance"—echoing Bentley's "process of government"—in a globalizing world is a highly contingent affair. It would be impossible to predict its outlines in any clearly defined manner. However, it is likely that at least some of the developments of the past three decades or more will prove to be resilient and lead to further developments more or less along the same lines. These developments nevertheless are not linear or unidimensional but may lead to a range of alternative outcomes or what economic theorists call "multiple equilibria." I therefore set out four alternative scenarios or trajectories for the future. Transnational neopluralism is indeed a new pathway or developmental trend that will not only continue but also increasingly shape the future in path-dependent fashion; however, that pathway still contains within it several significant potential variations.

7. CONCLUSION: A NEW BRANCHING POINT

We are at a complex branching point in historical and theoretical terms, and we need to conceive of a new way of looking at world politics that goes beyond the traditional distinction between domestic and international levels of analysis. We must not, of course, throw out the nation-state baby with the old realist bathwater. What we are seeing is not the disappearance of the state but the actual transformation of the state, its absorption into transnational webs of politics and power, and the reconstruction of the notion of "statehood" itself along multilevel, multinodal lines. The key driving force in this transformation and reconstruction will be transnationally linked group political actors engaging in crosscutting competition and coalition-building behavior, exploiting the growing institutional loopholes of global politics, constructing new power games, creating new networks, and changing people's perceptions of how world politics works by changing the parameters and dynamics of who gets—and should get—what, when, and how. Underpinning this transformation of political behavior will be the ideational shift from *raison d'État* to an evolving and expanding *raison du monde*.

This book has been in the works, in one version or another, for at least fifteen years and is the culmination of a lifetime professional project that includes, in particular, *The Changing Architecture of Politics* (Cerny 1990a). If I were to acknowledge and thank all the creative and supportive people who have added to my knowledge and understanding over the years (and decades!), who have read and commented on a wide range of the earlier articles and book chapters that I have mined in producing this book, or who have supported this project in less direct ways, it would require at least another chapter, not to mention a superhuman memory, which I do not profess to possess. Therefore, I will not name names, except for one. As an undergraduate at Kenyon College in 1965, I took a course on political parties with a young assistant professor called Leonard G. Miller. In this course, we got to know and discuss some of the classics of pluralist and elitist political sociology. Since then, I have regularly refreshed and expanded my familiarity with this literature while observing the emergence of globalization and evolving both academically, from comparative politics to international political economy and world politics, and politically, from a youthful libertarianism to social democracy to "social neoliberalism" (see chapter 7), with various stops in between. Otherwise, I would also just like to thank colleagues over the years in Research Committees 16 (Socio-Political Pluralism) and 36 (Political Power) of the International Political Science Association, the International Political Economy Group of the British International Studies Association, and the International Political Economy Section of the International Studies Association, for the lively debates and discussions under the auspices of these fora. The rest is history, and those of you who have shared your ideas with me know who you are. Thank you all so very much.

Chapter 2

Globalization and Other Stories

The Search for a New Paradigm for International Relations

> Globalization refers to a world in which, after allowing for exchange rate and default risk, there is a single international rate of interest.
>
> —Samuel Brittan, *The Financial Times* (6 June 1996)

> [W]e may best consider contemporary globalization in its most general sense as a form of institutionalization of the two-fold process involving the universalization of particularism and the particularization of universalism.
>
> —Roland Robertson, *Globalization: Social Theory and Global Culture* (1992: 102)

1. THE CONTESTED STORY OF GLOBALIZATION

A fundamental transformation has begun in the way we perceive world politics. In terms of the framework used by Thomas Kuhn (1962) in his examination of how analytical theories undergo major changes or "scientific revolutions," what has often been presented as four centuries of "normal science" in politics and international relations has been dominated by the Westphalian or realist understanding or paradigm of how the world is organized. This paradigm posits a priori that the paramount collective actors or "unit actors" in international relations are states. The interaction of states constitutes the bottom line of world politics, setting the rules of the game and determining the outcomes of the most significant games. Other potentially important actors—from individuals, social categories, and interest groups at the subnational level, to multinational firms, financial and other market structures, international regimes, and cross-border social or cultural groups at the transnational level—are not capable of altering the basic configuration of structural power that determines the dominant dynamics of the international system (Waltz 1979).

However, this approach is today being challenged across a sufficiently wide range of empirical findings that many theorists have started to search systematically for an alternative paradigm, initiating a process of rethinking the way we conceive of the world analogous to what Kuhn called "paradigm shift" (Kuhn 1962). Many theorists and analysts have focused on the concept of globalization, although the meaning and contours of globalization and the way it works in practice are ill defined and widely contested. In this book, globalization itself is seen to be not merely a description of what is happening but an essential feature of a deeply *political process*—a dependent variable with crucial feedback effects—that has been driven and shaped not so much by material variables such as economic conditions as by actors, that is, by transnational neopluralism.

Of course, there is much life in the old paradigm yet. Once institutions and social structures have crystallized, by definition they lock in patterns of behavior. Elements of social change, as Talcott Parsons (1964) noted, must reach a cumulative threshold before existing systems are altered. The state as an institutional structure is not withering away. Indeed, it can have new and often more complex and extensive functions in a more open and interdependent world, as I argue later in this book. States themselves are expanding their activities in some fields, such as regulation and environmental protection, while reducing them in others, like the public ownership of industries or monopoly provision of public services. In some issue areas, there is a race to the bottom, but in others, there is a race to the top (and many levels in between).

Furthermore, globalization is itself an elusive concept, deeply contested in terms of both actual existence and substantial form. To some observers (like Brittan), globalization is both bounded and well defined, with a simple, sometimes even unidimensional, core or driving force, like the convergence of interest rates and stock market prices or the information technology revolution. To others, however, it represents a qualitatively new stage in the development of human society—a set of ideas and perceptions revolving around how the world keeps getting smaller, so-called space-time compression (Harvey 1989; Douglas 1999). That, in turn, is seen to entail changes in the way human activities and institutions are organized, with a wider variety of transnational and even virtual spaces and a quickened tempo of everyday life empowering cross-border actors and laying the groundwork for the emergence and crystallization of new social, economic, and political structures that both undercut and transcend the state.

At the same time, the shape or internal structural form that globalization takes has all too frequently been assumed to be a process of convergence, a homogenizing force, with social, economic, and political structures becoming more and more alike in a shrinking world. Increasingly, however, other analysts are arguing that globalization is a fundamentally "heterogenizing"—even polarizing—phenomenon (Radice 1996). Instead of the interactions among states constituting the bottom line of world politics, that bottom line now consists of a range of multilayered processes of conflict, competition, and coalition building among a growing diversity of actors large and small, old and new. A globalizing world is complex in many ways, at many levels, developing within an *already* complex social, economic, and political context. Many varied dimensions of convergence and divergence can and do coexist, what economists call "multiple equilibria." Ecologists, among others, speak of "global localization" (sometimes called "glocalization"), as reflected in the well-known slogan: "Think globally, act locally."

In the economy, different markets, firms, and sectors are organized in distinct ways, whether because of the claimed benefits of different ways to govern the firm, especially the distinction between markets and hierarchies, in the name of economic efficiency—the new institutional economics (Williamson 1975 and 1985)—or as the result of the different social-structural histories and practices employed by key groups, the new historical or sociological institutionalism (Granovetter 1985 and 1992). For example, owners of more mobile forms of capital learn to arbitrage across these categories precisely because they are structured differently and provide different trade-offs of risk and return.

At the same time, social and political actors look for new ways to pursue their interests and goals in a globalizing world. The expansion of international and transnational economic and sociopolitical activities not only links the global and the local more directly but also does so without actually eliminating other intermediate levels such as the regional and national—indeed, sometimes even strengthening them. New layers of structure and activity are superimposed over old, thereby changing the configuration of world politics in tangled ways. Even more problematic are the complex subnational, transnational, and supranational ethnic cleavages, tribalism, and other often revived or *invented* identities and traditions that abound in the wake of the uneven reconfiguration of social relationships, economics, and government policies characteristic of the global era. Therefore, quite varying outcomes can be envisaged as this globalization or transnationalization process unfolds. Will the result be a new, benign pluralism or the crystallization of more intense conflicts and inequalities? Will the pattern be stable or unstable? Globalization can just as well be seen as the harbinger not of a new world order but of a new world *disorder*, even a new medievalism of overlapping and competing authorities, multiple loyalties and identities, prismatic notions of space and belief, and so on (Minc 1993; Kaplan 1994; Cronin and Lepgold 1995; Kobrin 1998; Cerny 1998).

Another contested dimension of globalization concerns the forces that drive the process itself. Globalization is usually seen as primarily an economic phenomenon, but the disciplines of sociology and anthropology have taken it firmly to heart as a cultural process, too, even a hegemonic one (Robertson 1992). Geographers increasingly question the nature of territory per se as it has constituted the physical and psychological field of state, economy, and society, speaking of the increasing restructuring of human life around complex virtual spaces in a postmodern world (Taylor 1996; Kofman and Youngs 2008), and some analysts regard the essence of globalization as "deterritorialization" (Scholte 2000). The pure and applied sciences, of course, have always been global in their essence, but this traditional universalism has been dramatically intensified through the information revolution and the ever more rapid diffusion of complex technologies and ideas. In international relations and political science, however, because states as both unit actors and political systems have constituted the raison d'être of the discipline itself, resistance to the notion of globalization has been greater.

Perhaps more important, however, how we conceptualize globalization is not just about whether it can be empirically identified, categorized, or verified according to particular measurable criteria such as the convergence (or not) of corporate forms, government policies, trade patterns, or social structures. Perhaps its most crucial feature is that it constitutes a *discourse*—and, increasingly, a quasi-hegemonic discourse that cuts across and gives meaning to the kinds of categories suggested previously. In this sense, the spread of the discourse itself alters the a priori ideas and perceptions that people have of the empirical phenomena they encounter. In so doing, the very idea of globalization leads people to seek out and try to adopt both intellectual and real-world strategies and tactics that, in turn, may restructure the game itself around a different governmental rationality, what I call *raison du monde*.

Globalization can therefore be made to mean many sometimes quite different things. For example, some say that "globalization" is fundamentally distinct from "internationalization"—or "inter-nationalization" (with a hyphen), as Hirst and Thompson (1999) argue. The former is often seen to entail the withering away of the state, and the latter leads to its reinforcement as the state takes on a more global reach through complex reciprocity among states and "pooling sovereignty." Others argue that internationalization is not a distinct phenomenon but actually an essential component of globalization, along with such well-known processes as "transnationalization" or below-the-state cross-border linkages or even "translocalization" (Spruyt 1994). Thus, globalization is an essentially contested concept. Given its complex, heterogeneous nature, globalization appears both sweeping and vague. An "additive" definition would say that the essence of globalization can be found only in the dynamic *interaction* of these disparate processes, producing a new and evolving form of path dependency that cannot be wholly or easily predicted in advance. Measuring trade openness, cross-border financial or information flows, or other proxy variables may suggest much but proves little.

At another level, however, this chameleon-like character of globalization is its strength. The concept of globalization can be plausibly marshaled to explain a wide range of distinct but inextricably intertwined phenomena in complementary and mutually reinforcing ways—as many strong religious, cultural, or ideological belief systems do. It is above all because of this wide applicability and interpretive power that globalization can today stake a claim to paradigmatic status. With the erosion of old axioms, a process of "paradigmatic selection" follows. As a result, the concept of globalization is increasingly shaping the terms of the debate about the future of world politics.

2. FALSE STARTS: NEOREALISM, NEOLIBERAL INSTITUTIONALISM, AND OTHER INTERDEPENDENCE STORIES

In the traditional realist paradigm, the distinction between the *intra* national and *inter* national domains has been at the heart of the discipline and practice of international relations since the seventeenth century, in several mutually reinforcing ways. The formal-legal organization of the international sphere has been based on treaties among sovereign states, and international law has emerged from the juxtaposition, convergence, and overlap of systems of domestic law and decision making; both are still seen as dependent on this rootedness for their force today. Furthermore, the very concept of an international political system has developed out of a historically evolving mixture of the voluntary association of states that retain the capacity to defect, on the one hand, and a process of locking in the outcomes of violent conflicts and/or the power resource differentials between states— the balance of power—on the other. Wars have structural consequences, and indeed, military force is seen as the bottom line of the realist interpretation. In contrast, domestic politics, despite deep internal conflicts, has been seen, in Easton's (1953) phrase, to derive from the "authoritative allocation of values" (Poggi 1978). At the international level, there is as yet no analogous source of authority nor any system of genuine or even potential "world government" capable of steering such a process—or of possessing the kind of political legitimacy that would be necessary to do so. The two levels of analysis may interact in mutually dependent ways, but for realists, they are both analytically and behaviorally separate and distinct.

Globalization involves quite different notions. The most fundamental premise cutting across and linking the different strands of globalization theory is that domestic and international politics are increasingly inextricably intertwined, not separate and distinct. Sometimes it is asserted that this intertwining has been present throughout modern history, sometimes that it represents a new phase of social and political structuration. Indeed, the venerable notions of state and nation are themselves frequently seen as historically circumscribed, time-bound, path-dependent social constructs that evolved out of the *global* conditions of an *earlier* era. The state itself was therefore a product of a first stage of incipient globalization. This earlier era was marked by the crisis and decline of European feudalism and the emergence of early capitalism around dynastic rulers, who had consolidated their territorial domains as the complex vassalage system of feudalism broke down and new structures of social identification and collective action were "selected" (cf. Tilly 1975; Anderson 1974; Anderson 1991; Cerny 1998; Holton 1985; Spruyt 1994; Wallerstein 1974). Once the institutional form represented by the European nation-state had been consciously and/or inadvertently constructed out of the outcome of power struggles and alliances among actors at the time, it was, as Granovetter (1992) writes about path dependency in general, "locked in, [and therefore] other possibilities were foreclosed." Time-specific stochastic outcomes hardened into durable institutional structures, both domestically and internationally.

The rigid application of the levels-of-analysis or "inside-outside" distinction has always been criticized by a wide range of analysts as merely partial, static, or worse. Idealists have long called for the construction of new institutionalized systems of international governance, but these have tended to bump up against the predominant interests of states. With the expansion of internationalization and transnationalization in the last third of the twentieth century, however, critics of the dominant levels-of-analysis view began looking for alternative ways of looking at the problem that could be *realistic* without being "realist" (e.g., Keohane and Nye 1977/2000). They were concerned with practical issues and social practices, not with imagined international communities.

What they focused on was complex interdependence. Now the terms "interdependence" and "globalization" are often used interchangeably, or at least seen as two sides of the same coin. However, "interdependence" in international relations terminology is generally taken, in the last analysis, to mean the interdependence of *states*. Thus, states were seen to remain the dominant actors even in an interdependent world—however sensitive and vulnerable they may be to what happens in other states and however intertwined their economies and societies. Interdependence analysts usually prefer the term "internationalization" to "globalization" for this very reason (e.g., Keohane and Milner 1996). They take the view that complex interdependence qualifies—but does not fundamentally undermine—the traditional, state-centric approach, in two ways.

In the first place, interdependence is seen to lead to the internationalization of *domestic* policy making within and by states. In the context, for example, of the convergence of world interest rates (Helbling and Westcott 1995) or of the growth of world trade and foreign direct investment, economic policies are increasingly constrained by what goes on elsewhere. This has been the case in the past, too, whether in Wallerstein's "modern world system" (1974) or in the era of the gold standard from the 1870s to the 1920s. However, although the density and complexity of such linkages increased dramatically in the late twentieth century because of economic, technological, and cultural changes, interdependence proponents tend to take it for granted that the main sociopolitical playing field nevertheless retains its traditional state-centric form. States still retain the capacity to internalize and manipulate the forces of globalization to their own advantage, if only state actors recognize the problem and approach it more effectively. What is more, this capacity is often *reinforced, not eroded,* by international economic interdependence, for example. The growth of new liberal international institutions and governance structures actually enables states to pursue their interests—especially where they coincide or overlap—even more effectively in an interdependent world by recognizing just how, for example, to use international regimes in a cooperative fashion to pursue national interests in a positive-sum, win-win fashion (Keohane 1984).

Second, given what has just been said, interdependence analysts by and large accept that the international political playing field is still rooted in the interactions of states primarily concerned with their *relative* power positions. It may be more possible to pursue common interests, but "relative gains" still trump "absolute gains," whether in the case of conflict between the two or where the interests of the more powerful states are in play. In this sense, writers like Robert O. Keohane, one of the coiners of the term "complex interdependence," retained dominant elements of Waltz's (1979) "neorealism" in his attempt at a synthesis he calls "neoliberal institutionalism" (Keohane 1984 and 1986). (Note that there is a definitional issue here with the word "neoliberal" that is addressed in later chapters.) States are therefore increasingly drawn into a process of constructing interstate institutions or regimes in the pursuit of their *national* interests (Krasner 1982), not through internationalist idealism. Patterns of collective action *by and among states operating as rational unit actors* in the international system, shaped by complex (mainly economic) interdependence, will lead, it is argued, to the formation of both informal and formal structures and institutions that can take on an autonomy of their own at the international level—that is, "international regimes."

Indeed, interdependence is sometimes said to be leading to a "new multilateralism" (Ruggie 1993a), but this time rooted in positive-sum games rather than zero-sum games. The traditional distinction between domestic and international levels of analysis may be altered, adapted, and manipulated, even rationalized and streamlined, but it is not fundamentally undermined. State actors are particularly privileged by this situation. They increasingly have the possibility of playing "two-level games" (Putnam 1988; Haggard 1990), coordinating their action across both levels of analysis, thus actually increasing the effectiveness of states. Interdependence theory thereby reconstitutes realism in a more effective form. It does not constitute an alternative paradigm.

3. GLOBALIZATION AND THE SEARCH FOR AN ALTERNATIVE PARADIGM: COMPLEXITY AND COHERENCE

In contrast, the concept of globalization focuses on levels of complexity that are often missed, dismissed, or ignored by interdependence theory. Globalization is not merely about the impact of economic interdependence on a combination of domestic political systems and the interaction of states. It is about reconceptualizing the very field of political science as a whole (and other social sciences, too) in ways that describe and explain *both* the historical power of states *and* the current dramatic crystallization of those complex social, economic, and political webs that constitute the changing world system today. Globalization is therefore not about the emergence of a borderless world or the decline of the state as such. Such arguments are profoundly misleading, and both intellectual debate and social discourse have suffered as a result. In fact, globalization is inherently complex and heterogeneous in at least three principal ways, ways that can, for the sake of simplicity, be labeled economic, social, and political.

A. The Economic Dimension: Complex Market Structures and New Sources of Competitive Advantage

In the first place, economic globalization does not necessarily denote convergence and homogeneity. It leads neither to the emergence of a homogeneous marketplace nor to the dominance of any one type of corporate organization, for example. Of course, pressures for convergence do exist, but so do pressures for divergence and diversity. What globalization does involve are conditions for the increased dynamic interaction and intertwining of deeper trends that are, if not contradictory in the strict sense, at least in profound tension with each other. There are multiple equilibria in play— alternative outcomes from the interaction of the *same* variables. Economic institutions, structures, and practices are increasingly in flux. Diverse pathways are opening up, and the shape of any future path dependency is not yet locked in. There is increasing room for actors to engage in what the French call "bricolage," picking and mixing from a range of different practices, some old, some new, in potentially innovative configurations.

In economic terms, globalization involves the expansion and multilayering of the playing fields within which different market actors and firms interact, transforming the international economy from one made up of holistic national economies interacting on the basis of *national* comparative advantage into one in which a variety of "competitive advantages" (a distinction elaborated in Zysman and Tyson 1983) can be manipulated in ways that are not so fundamentally dependent on the nation-state as a social, economic, and/or political unit and that are open to a wider range of pressures and activities. Previous constraints are less constraining, and the "opportunity structure" is more open and variegated. For example, contrary to popular belief in convergence, globalization has strengthened a range of different forms of corporate governance, from the American-style MNC (multinational corporation), to the so-called Overseas Chinese–type extended family firm, to the small niche firm operating translocally. It has reflected a varied range of optimal economies of scale in diverse industrial sectors, from local craft-style industries to global finance based on almost pure information technology. And it has linked together a range of different territorial and quasi-territorial bases, from "global cities" to subnational regions to nation-states to transnational and international regions to the world economy itself. Economic actors increasingly see globalization as a set of diverse opportunities rather than top-down constraints.

Different types of corporate organization, for example, once locked in, have a certain staying power *only so long as they continue to provide competitive advantages over time* in the particular markets and sectors in which they compete. Change will vary from sector to sector and from market position to market position. Some embedded "state-societal arrangements" (Hart 1992) may prove particularly vulnerable. As Japanese banks and firms in the late 1990s and early 2000s prepared to sell big chunks of their keiretsu-style cross-shareholdings, as stagnation and financial crisis in Japan deepened, and as the pressures of globalization bit harder, it would be wrong to see traditional corporate organizational forms as set in national tablets of stone. But at the same time, Japanese investors and managers were not merely adopting Anglo-American ways. They were looking to find new ways of keeping what they regarded as the positive features of the traditional Japanese model while adapting to the imperatives of transnational competition (Malcolm 2001; Cerny 2005b). The search for a "Third Way" in politics, too, is not merely limited to the United Kingdom, where the term originated, nor to Western liberalism or social democracy. It has led to an ongoing academic and practical debate over what I have elsewhere called "different roads to globalization" (Soederberg, Menz, and Cerny 2005: Introduction).

Globalization in this sense needs to be kept in historical perspective. Indeed, there was a kind of convergence associated with the catch-up industrialization of the late nineteenth and early twentieth centuries that in some ways was much greater than that of contemporary globalization. The 1930s saw the apparent culmination of a process of convergence of national political economies toward the model of autarchic nationalistic empires (Cerny 1990a: 212–216). The "new industrial state" analyzed by John Kenneth Galbraith in the 1960s, the "modern industrial enterprise" examined by Alfred Chandler Jr., and the concept of "industrial society" put forward by Clark Kerr all envisaged that what we now call Fordism and the Second Industrial Revolution, based on large integrated production processes and mass production for mass markets, not only were already embedded in path-dependent form but also would continue to be the wave of the future (Galbraith 1967/2007; Chandler 1990; Kerr 1983).

The interaction of convergence and divergence today is crucial. For example, a single rate of interest can coexist with a wide range of economic activities and market structures; it does not determine their form, even if it shapes a critical range of outcomes. What is significant about economic globalization, then, is that while there is at one level a much bigger, global playing field, this simultaneously contains and promotes a growing profusion of playing fields. Many of these playing fields (although not all, of course) are no longer coterminous with the traditional convergence between Second Industrial Revolution production structures, on the one hand, and the Weberian bureaucratic state, on the other, the interaction of which dominated the institutionalization of what we usually think of as "modern" national political economies and the modern nation-state itself. The complex world of contemporary globalization and the Third Industrial Revolution is far more fluid (Cerny 1995).

B. The Social Dimension: The Emergence of New Forms of Embeddedness

The second dimension of increasing global complexity is social. Those observers on both right and left who criticize the caricature of globalization described earlier take it as a given that if there is not one big market, there is no real alternative but to operate on the basis of the continuing centrality of the nation-state for regulating economic activity and promoting collective values and goals (Hirst and Thompson 1999). Economic activities are often seen in this literature as still being fundamentally embedded (with the exception, for some, of global finance) in national social structures. Of course, in the "modern" world, that is, since the eighteenth century, certain nation-states were eminently successful in creating ersatz forms of national Gemeinschaft along the lines of Bismarck's Kulturkampf in late-nineteenth-century Germany, and both modern liberal-democratic forms of government and industrial welfare states have been crucial aspects of this social restructuring, often referred to as "nation-building" (Bendix 1964).

Nevertheless, such national political cultures have, and always have had, serious weaknesses. Obviously nation-building in the postcolonial world has been a highly ambiguous process, as other social, territorial, and ethnic identities and loyalties have led to the collapse or near-collapse of a whole range of states from the fringes of Europe (e.g., the former Yugoslavia, Lebanon) through Africa, Asia, and Latin America. Even Canada seemed at one point to be about to divide between English-speaking and French-speaking regions. In almost all developed, mature nation-states in the north, the project of national integration has in recent years seen significant challenges from regional identities, ethnic minorities, and multiculturalist or radical pluralizing ideologies, including black nationalism, Islamicist movements, and radical feminism, sometimes leading to violent confrontation.

Wars today are rarely interstate wars (Rogers 2000). In 1995, according to the Stockholm International Peace Research Institute, all the world's serious wars were civil wars (*Financial Times*, 14 July 1996). The events of 11 September 2001 and their aftermath involve a complex hybrid of global, national, regional, and local political, religious, cultural, ethnic, and economic factors. Even the most recent attempt to revive interstate war, the American invasion of Iraq, turned into something resembling a complex, multisided civil war. Indeed, as the neomedievalists tell us, the true (ideal-type) nation-state as a social and cultural unit has really existed for only perhaps 100 to 150 years, since sometime in the mid-nineteenth century, and even then its form has been deeply and continually contested. The world is perhaps returning to its *normal* state of crosscutting, multiple loyalties and identities. In social theory terms, deconstruction and globalization paradoxically go hand-in-hand, opening the way for various projects of *re*construction.

There are many forms of embeddedness other than the state. Ethnic groups and religious movements provide deep identities—identities that both predate the nation-state and will undoubtedly continue to develop beyond, and in spite of, attempts to shoehorn them into national containers. Kurds and Hutus, for example, have virtually no stake in the extant nation-state form of organization as such. The territories of the former are split between three problematically constituted nation-states, Iraq, Iran, and Turkey, and the latter have been scattered by the triumph within the

Rwandan state of their age-old minority enemies, the Tutsi, even as they unsuccessfully tried to wipe out the latter through genocide.

Even more interesting is the as yet embryonic literature on better organized and more influential transnational cultural groups. The Overseas Chinese (ethnic Chinese living in other countries but maintaining their transborder networks) are a particularly salient case in point. They are said to constitute a closely interconnected network of groups active at the cutting edge of international (especially Asian) business, with close links to areas of China (mainly South Coast port cities and their hinterlands) but accustomed to operating internationally over several centuries, well adapted to communicating and undertaking transactions through cutting-edge technology such as the Internet, but at the same time the bearers of continually reinvented traditional values of collective solidarity (Seagrave 1995). Kotkin (1992) identifies several "global tribes" with widespread diaspora-rooted networks—Jews, whom he considers to be the original global tribe; the Anglo-American diaspora, with its individualist and internationalist capitalist culture (cf. Herman 2001); different (and competing) groups of Asians, including newer diasporas of South Asians, Southeast Asians, Japanese, and Koreans; as well, of course, as the long-established Overseas Chinese, and several "future tribes."

At the same time, social hierarchies and the class system are changing, too. If we look back at the history of social thought, we are reminded that specifying the identity of class and nation has always been highly problematic analytically. After all, Marx himself saw the nineteenth century bourgeoisie as an already internationalized class and called for "workers of all countries [to] unite" to overthrow it. Today, businesspeople, business schools, the financial press, and international elite gatherings and organizations, however nationally rooted they may remain in many ways, proclaim the virtues of global management styles and transnational profit-making strategies, and they see the problems of capitalism—as well as of their own firms and sectors—in global terms. The discourse of globalization has become increasingly hegemonic in the business world. Looking more to discourse formation than to instrumental power, Susan Strange (1990) wrote of an "international business civilization." At the same time, the concept of "epistemic communities," linking think tanks, academic analysts, policy makers and business elites, is the focus of increasing scrutiny (Haas 1992; Stone 1996; Higgott 1993; McGann 2009).

From another perspective, too, we once again live in a world where, as in the late nineteenth century, Marxist and other radical writers see the emergence of a transnational class system. Stephen Gill (1990) speaks of a new transnational elite rooted in such networks as the Trilateral Commission; Robert Cox (1993) writes about a "transnational managerial class"; Kees van

der Pijl (1995a) outlines a new "transnational historical materialism" organized around "globalizing elites" (1995b) and a "transnational cadre class"
(1994); Leslie Sklair (2000) writes of the "transnational capitalist class"; and
Michael Hardt and Antonio Negri (2000) see the emergence of a global
"empire" as the highest stage of capitalism. At the same time, however,
class itself is once again challenged, as before, by other forms of identity and
solidarity, such as religion, ethnicity, and culture. And there certainly is no
international working class to unite in revolution. Anticorporate movements
tend to be dominated by middle-class groups such as students, much like
the events of May 1968 in France (see Starr 2000). Indeed, the working class
in advanced capitalist societies is generally far more rooted in national structures than the middle and upper classes because of the greater immobility
of labor as a factor of capital; this is reflected by the limited development
of any new internationalism among trade unions. However, migration
and international wage competition are often thought to be eroding these
constraints.

Probably the main contribution provided by the more radical perspectives, however, is to remind us that the expansion of complex, crosscutting
forms of social embeddedness and the crystallization of an embryonic transnational class system do not lead to a homogeneous world business culture
based on a stabilizing, expanding, trickle-down form of capitalism, but to
division and polarization (Radice, 1996). As the author of the United Nations
Development Program's (UNDP's) 1996 Human Development Report,
Richard Jolly, stated, the growing divide between rich and poor—wherein
the combined assets of 358 billionaires exceeded the total annual income of
nearly half of the global population—is producing a world "gargantuan in
its excesses and grotesque in its human and economic inequalities"
(*Financial Times*, 16 July 1996). Added UNDP administrator James Gustave
Speth: "An emerging global elite, mostly urban-based and interconnected in
a variety of ways, is amassing great wealth and power, while more than half
of humanity is left out" (*International Herald Tribune*, 16 July 1996).

While the more aware establishment commentators argue that the main
issue facing American (and Western) foreign policy is "how to make the
transition from a closed society to the global market while maintaining
political stability" (Thomas L. Friedman in the *New York Times*, 18 July
1996), increasing inequalities and the resulting violent conflict and break-
downs of order are likely to create conditions that cannot be controlled by
any one country or even by the developed world as a whole—what Kaplan
(1994) called "the coming anarchy." How such conflicts evolve and are managed, how coalitions emerge, are broken, and reemerge—that is, transnational neopluralism—will be the crucial factor in shaping "global" society in
the future.

C. The Political Dimension: The Competition State
or the Splintered State?

Finally, the heterogeneity of globalization is reflected in political changes. The state itself—although still the most important single organizational level and institutional structure in the world—has been transformed by and through the globalization process. Indeed, the state has paradoxically been one of the major driving forces of globalization, reacting to the more complex structure of constraints and opportunities characteristic of the new environment. This transformation involves a fundamental shift of organizational goals and institutional processes within state structures themselves, as the industrial welfare state has been replaced by the Competition State (see chapter 8). This shift is creating a new role for the state as the enforcer of decisions that emerge from world markets, transnational "private interest governments," and international quango-like regimes. (The term "quango"— Quasi-autonomous National Government Organizations—was coined in Britain in the Thatcher era to denote mixed public-private agencies given an authoritative role in overseeing, regulating, and/or implementing particular public policies and administrative processes.)

The essence of the post–Second World War national industrial welfare state lay in the capacity state actors and institutions had gained, especially since the Great Depression, to insulate certain key elements of economic life from market forces and at the same time promoting other aspects of the market (Polanyi 1944). This did not mean only protecting the poor and helpless from poverty and pursuing welfare goals like full employment or public health but also regulating business in the public interest, fine-tuning business cycles to promote economic growth, nurturing "strategic industries" and "national champions," integrating labor movements into corporatist processes to promote wage stability and labor discipline, reducing barriers to international trade, imposing controls on "speculative" international movements of capital, and the like.

But this compromise of domestic regulation and international opening, what John Ruggie called "embedded liberalism" (Ruggie 1982), was eroded by increasing domestic structural costs—the "fiscal crisis of the state" (O'Connor 1973/2001)—as well as by the structural consequences of growing external trade and, perhaps most important, of international financial transactions (Block 1977; Strange 1986). The crisis of the industrial welfare states therefore lay in their decreasing capacity to insulate national economies and thus nationally based interest groups from the global economy and from the combination of stagnation and inflation in the 1970s—or today, stagnation and deflation—that resulted when they tried to do so.

Today, rather than attempt to take certain economic activities *out* of the market, to "decommodify" them as the industrial welfare state was organized to do, the Competition State pursues increased marketization—"commodification"—in order to make economic activities located within the national territory or otherwise contributing to national wealth more competitive in international and transnational terms. But the rapid rise of the Competition State has given rise to a further paradox. As states have attempted to promote competitiveness in this way, they have—seemingly voluntarily—given up a range of previously crucial policy instruments. The debate rages over whether, for example, capital controls can or should be reintroduced (Abdelal 2007), or whether states are still able to choose to pursue more potentially inflationary bailout and stimulus policies without disastrous consequences—a key issue in the light of the financial crisis and recession of 2008.

The nation-state, of course, is therefore not dead. But its role has changed. States are less and less able to act as "strategic" or "developmental" states (Zysman 1983; Johnson 1982) and are more and more like "splintered states" (Machin and Wright 1985). At the same time, state actors and agencies are increasingly intertwined in "transgovernmental networks"—systematic linkages between state actors and agencies within particular jurisdictions and sectors, cutting across different countries and including a heterogeneous collection of private actors and groups in interlocking policy communities (Slaughter 2004). The functions of the state, although still located at a structural crossroads where diverse forces and trends most often interact, are becoming increasingly fragmented, privatized, devolved, and extraterritorialized, and interest groups are evolving to cope with changing political constraints and opportunities.

In international terms, states, in pursuing the goal of competitiveness, are increasingly involved in what John Stopford and Susan Strange (1991) called "triangular diplomacy," the complex interaction of state-state, state-firm, and firm-firm negotiations. More broadly, complex globalization involves not merely two-level games, *pace* Putnam, but (at least) *three-level games*, with third-level—transnational—games including not only "firm-firm diplomacy" but also transgovernmental networks and policy communities, internationalized market structures, transnational interest and cause groups, and many other linked and interpenetrated markets, hierarchies, and networks.

In this sense, the amount of government imbrication in some aspects of economic and social life can actually *increase* while the power of the state to control other activities continues to *diminish*. One example is the way financial globalization and deregulation have raised the pressure for governments to increase monitoring of financial markets, criminalization of insider trading, and the like, pressure that has increased exponentially during the current financial crisis. Whether we are talking about bailouts of financial firms, new forms of regulation to deal with liquidity crises, restructuring regulatory agencies, radically increased government spending to reflate an economy that has seized up financially, or the quasi nationalization of banks in country after country, the role of the state has been dramatically raised once again to the forefront of daily politics. The admission by former U.S. Federal Reserve Chairman Alan Greenspan in October 2008 that his faith in the market to solve the problems of the global economy was tragically misplaced simply demonstrates the paradoxical expansion of procompetitive regulation in a complex market economy. The growth of overlapping and competing authorities does not reduce interventionism; it merely expands the range of possibilities for splintered governments and special interests to carve out new fiefdoms, both domestically and transnationally, and for other groups to compete for influence and control on these emerging hybrid playing fields.

4. CONCLUSION: GLOBALIZATION AS PARADOX

The paradox of globalization, or the shift of a crucial range of economic, social, and political activities to a global scale, is that rather than just creating one big economy or one big polity, it also divides, fragments, and polarizes. Convergence and divergence are two sides of the same coin. Globalization is not a single discourse but a contested concept giving rise to several distinct but intricately intertwined discourses. However, the power of the *concept* of globalization itself as both process and discourse—its main advantage in an accelerating process of paradigmatic selection—lies in this very complexity.

It remains to be seen whether the forces of convergence create a complex but stable, pluralistic world based on liberal capitalism and the vestiges of liberal democracy, or whether the forces of divergence and inequality create a more volatile, neomedieval world. Whatever the outcome, however, globalization will involve a recasting of previously embedded forms of path dependency and a new flowering of multiple equilibria. Hard political choices will have to be made, and creative solutions sought. In this context, the scope for politics and the potential significance of the role of innovative agents and "institutional entrepreneurs"—the core of transnational neopluralism—will be greater than at any time since the emergence of the states system itself.

Chapter 3

Space, Territory, and Functional Differentiation

Deconstructing and Reconstructing Borders

1. INTRODUCTION: VERTICAL AND HORIZONTAL BORDERINGS

Politics and society have been seen, ever since Plato's *Republic*, as involving two kinds of bordering and structural differentiation. The first or "vertical" dimension is one of geographical place—of situating and rooting political systems and communities in particular *physical* or *territorial* locations. These "hard" geographical places provide the material conditions for the development of the face-to-face contacts, knowledge-sharing networks, resource agglomerations, and organizational synergies necessary for effective collective action. The second or "horizontal" dimension is one of *social stratification* or *functional differentiation*, of evolving and rooting that collective life in a division of labor and function among different human tasks, roles, and activities. Although often thought of as "soft" or "virtual" spaces, the latter define the boundaries of human life at least as much as hard geographical spaces. They are complex and multidimensional, reflecting the myriad dimensions of politics, economy, and society more closely than mere geography.

Through most of human history, political actors have sought, whether for political, economic, and/or sociocultural reasons, to fuse these two distinct kinds of bordering within the same *multifunctional* social and organizational unit—the *politeia* or political community, whether that be at the village, regional, city-state, nation-state, or imperial level. The multifunctionality of macrosocial institutions, however constituted, has since the birth of human society been perceived as a necessary, if not sufficient, condition for political, ideological, and administrative effectiveness. Nevertheless, deep tensions between these two distinct forms of differentiation (and cooperation) have always constituted a profound source of political instability, economic inefficiency, organizational disorder, and social conflict. The process of transnational neopluralism is causing people to reconstruct the relationships between these two sorts of borders, as they have developed in the modern world, in fundamental ways.

Historically, those tensions have increased, the larger the physical scale of the territorial unit involved and the more complex the economic and political life that was meant to be contained within that unit. Multifunctionality and size together bring increased costs as well as benefits. Two sorts of limiting processes are always at work. On the one hand, looser, more diffuse forms of extended political organization, such as traditional empires and feudal systems, suffer from both local and external centrifugal forces pulling them apart; on the other hand, more localized, city-state types of units cannot benefit from the military and economic economies of scale and scope potentially available to larger units. However, over the past three-and-a-half centuries—a developmental trend usually dated to the Peace of Westphalia of 1648, at the end of the Thirty Years War, the second of the great postmedieval religious wars that plagued Europe—political actors have labored to bring about that multifunctional fusion at the level of the nation-state, while relations among nation-states have been seen as the bottom-line structural building blocks of the international system.

Nevertheless, the role of nation-states as building blocks has always been analytically and politically highly problematic. The modern nation-state has been a political project rather than a fait accompli. It has continually been manipulated, undermined, and reshaped, politically, economically, and culturally—both from above by formal and informal empires (Subrahmanyam 2006) and Kotkin's global tribes (Kotkin 1992), on the one hand, and, of course, from below, by class, ethnic, and political divisions, on the other. But today's challenge is not merely one of degree; it is one of kind. The particular form of organizational fusion that has constituted the modern state is increasingly cut across and challenged *systematically* from both above and below by transnationalization and globalization, which bring pressures from both above and below together across territorial borders. Out of globalization has come a new, *post-nation-state political project* of complex, flexible, multilevel fusion, a project in which multifunctionality is pushed increasingly into the background, and a project with its ideological foundations in the spread of neoliberalism, itself driven and shaped by transnational neopluralism. Instead of the state with its *raison d'État*, multifunctionality is increasingly embodied in neoliberalism, with its transnational flexibility, the internalization of *raison du monde* governmentality, and, above all, transnational neopluralist political processes.

2. EMBEDDING THE NATION-STATE AND THE STATES SYSTEM

The concept of nation-state is itself an uneasy marriage between two equally problematic concepts: the "nation," denoting a supposedly socially coherent, large-scale, solidaristic, territorially defined social whole; and the "state," denoting a supposedly organizationally coherent, quasi-hierarchical, relatively efficient system for collective action, systematic decision making, and policy implementation. However, both of these underlying concepts are problematic in themselves. In traditional realist thinking, politics, economics, and society have been bifurcated between an "inside" and an "outside." The "inside" is seen as relatively civilized (or civilizable), characterized by some as hierarchical and by others as an arena for the pursuit of collective action and collective values such as liberty and social justice. The "outside," in contrast, is seen as either an ungoverned semiwilderness characterized as anarchical and ruled entirely by power balances and imbalances among states mainly constructed through war or as a quite different sort of society, a semigoverned but often fragile "society of states." In both cases, the inside and the outside are seen as fundamentally distinct, dissimilar, and even mutually contradictory or schizophrenic, both normatively and empirically. And yet they are increasingly inextricably intertwined and interdependent.

This conceptualization of world politics is credible only because the *actors* who have created, consolidated, and built upon the nation-state have seen— and constructed—the nation-state itself as a crucial, Janus-like structural axis of this system. Political actors are compelled by the system's structural imperatives to be concerned *at one and the same time* with pursuing projects of political, social, and economic improvement at home—what Foucault has called "biopolitics" (Foucault 2008)—while also paying attention, first and foremost, to constructing and defending the structural bottom line of sovereignty, that is, securing and defending the homeland from external threats and pursuing national interests abroad. In this latter task, they must be willing and able to put survival of the nation-state first and to be ruthless in confronting external enemies, even when this apparently contradicts and undermines the domestic political and social goals and values they would otherwise swear by. Reconciling these two tasks is at the core of the concept of multifunctionality and *raison d'État*.

The underlying pseudomaterial foundation of this schizophrenic political balancing act is territoriality, or what Bob Jessop and Neil Brenner have called the "spatio-temporal fix" (see chapter 13). Without relatively fixed territorial borders—boundaries or "containers" (see Brenner, Jessop, Jones, and MacLeod 2003) that simultaneously enclose and order a range of fundamentally disparate human activities—the modern world could not exist. Village and tribal societies were too small to have such formalized and defended boundaries, although the periphery of the village itself was certainly defended. Nevertheless, especially in hunter-gatherer, slash-and-burn, and nomadic societies, the space between villages was not the precise property of the particular society but something between a dangerous no-man's-land and a quasi-heavenly open space belonging to the gods. It could be either good or evil, like Greek gods, but it was not *possessed*. In feudal, early trading, and most precapitalist imperial societies, too, boundaries were both fluid and multilevel. They involved not rigid borders but shifting "frontiers," where "civilization" met "barbarians" and where different castes and noble ranks interacted in a continual confrontation-cum-bargaining process involving different rights and privileges in the same or overlapping territorial spaces. Political power in the periphery of empires—the institutional form of choice in the premodern world—was uneasily managed through suzerainty rather than sovereignty, and the frontiers of suzerainty were eminently fungible the farther one got from the center. Warlords, merchants, priests, and bureaucrats coexisted uneasily, shifting allegiances when it suited them and when they could get away with it, with priests and bureaucrats in particular serving whomever they thought possessed the most power at the time, like the legendary Vicar of Bray.

Political power on land was more like sea power, where despite claims that Rome or Britain might rule the waves—"mare nostrum"—the vast mass of geographical space was without clear ownership or control, continuously contested but ultimately fluid. Of course, the difference with the sea was that land-based political centers could be controlled and organized through geographically fixed fortifications and social as well as physical habitats. Eventually, the military and political power of these centers enabled them to spread their organizational control across land and even across the sea, as in the various European empires after 1492. These empires were much more than nation-states, including within them multilevel and even internally contradictory forms of governance, but they ultimately served the purposes of the "metropole," the dominant nation-state (or "empire-state") at the core (Subrahmanyam 2003 and 2006). The collision of these land empires and their seaborne extensions provided the means to carve up the world into "nationally" controlled territories. Eventually, with the decolonization of the European empires in the 1950s and 1960s, the whole globe was ostensibly carved up into discrete nation-states with supposedly clear, internationally recognized territorial boundaries—the last gasp of nation-state development before the current wave of globalization.

Thus the emergence of world politics in the seventeenth through nineteenth centuries actually meant attempting to organize the political architecture of the planet *as a whole* around discrete, sovereign, and mutually recognized states with clear boundaries. This was paradoxically true of empire-states, too. The ideology of nationhood at the core of—and justifying—empire was a key element of what the French called their *mission civilisatrice* and the British called the "white man's burden." Furthermore, the nation-state, as well as being problematic in and of itself, was also always an *unfinished* project, with structural contradictions that have deepened with globalization. Revolutions, national rebellions, irredentist movements, population transfers, class conflicts, civil wars, and the like were key moments that could make or break nation-building projects—as Barrington Moore Jr. pointed out with regard to the American Civil War and other upheavals (Moore 1966). Indeed, the racial divisions, hatreds, and distrust that were spawned by American slavery—part of a huge transnational phenomenon of the eighteenth and nineteenth centuries—are still the most potent cause of domestic conflict and instability in the United States, and in much of Africa and Latin America, too.

Nevertheless, the construction of nation-states also created national identities, foreign policies, and state apparatuses with ever-growing social and economic functions—industrial and welfare states in particular, both authoritarian and democratic. In the process, the construction of nation-states also reconfigured world politics, creating an international (interstate) relations system that depended on the balance of power to maintain peace and stability yet paradoxically was wracked by widening wars and by the 1940s gave way to total war. The subsequent nuclear confrontation of the cold war—and its eventual culmination in the superpowers' development of what Mary Kaldor (1981) called a "baroque arsenal"—was indicative of the underlying instability of this interstate system and its potential vulnerability to nuclear holocaust.

Nevertheless, the project of establishing single, unidimensional boundaries for human societies was a deeply flawed project in the first place. It was always crosscut by transnational conflicts, cleavages, and connections, whether by political empires, alliances, and ideologies; by an increasing economic division of labor as capitalist modernization progressed; or by cross-border social bonds, patterns of communication, migration, and social movements—indeed, by all three in complex feedback circuits. It was therefore eminently (a) vulnerable to being whipsawed between the spatial as well as the social and functional requirements of different human activities and (b) prone to continual warfare, oppression, and the imperative of hierarchical control to keep it from meltdown. Political processes proliferated, both domestically and internationally, simply to keep the system in place and working and to keep those boundaries from being holed below the waterline—while also lighting those problematic beacons of liberty and social solidarity that fed and intensified the momentum of its development. The modern political imperative of shoehorning multidimensional human life into nation-state boxes required eternal vigilance and a thick-skinned resistance to that natural complexity.

That project could only be taken to its highest level—the "high modern" nation-state of approximately 1850–1950—because it coincided and fit together with the other great organizational project of the modern world, the Second Industrial Revolution. This structural congruence of Weberian bureaucratic politics and Fordist economics—the coming of modern, large-scale hierarchical organizations in both politics and economics—squared the circle of territoriality. As Eric Hobsbawm argued in his classic *Industry and Empire*, the British-based First Industrial Revolution of the late eighteenth and early nineteenth centuries was not only too early but also too fragmented—what we would today call "modular" and "incremental"—to take up the ensuing challenge of catch-up industrialization in the United States, Germany, and Japan from around the 1870s onward (Hobsbawm 1968; Gerschenkron 1962; Kemp 1969). This surge of "late industrialization" came at a time of huge technological change and the growth of economies of scale in such industries as the railways, steel, chemicals, communications, and later automobiles—the source of the term "Fordism." It was only when such large-scale industrial organization—what Chandler (1990) called the "modern industrial enterprise," something that passed Britain by at the time (Kemp 1969)—came into being that the fusion of Clausewitzian military-bureaucratic statism, economic-industrial statism, and welfare statism could take place. It also fostered two world wars started by autarchic national empires.

The seventeenth-century France of Louis XIV's minister Jean-Baptiste Colbert may have been the original prototype of the modern nation-state (Anderson and Anderson 1968; Spruyt 1994). However, French economic and political development was too sporadic and diverse to develop into a quasi-organic national industrial welfare state, despite the best efforts of Napoleon III (Marx 1852/1987), until that model was already in its later stages of decay after the Second World War (Cerny 1982). At the turn of the twentieth century, however, Germany and Japan were becoming the leading prototypes of new powerful, industrializing, mainly authoritarian nation-states seeking empires, with Russia (and later the Soviet Union) constituting an alternative, pseudosocialist authoritarian version. Democracy took a nationalist turn from the French Revolution onward, while Marx's call of "Workingmen of all countries, unite!" increasingly fell on deaf ears as Lenin, Stalin, and others reshaped communism into a nationalist and statist form of authoritarian socialism.

At the same time, the United States, because of its special conditions—extensive domestic natural resources and available land; a rapidly growing internal market; huge investment flows from abroad (especially Britain); a large middle class and growing working class rooted in the flow of ambitious, hardworking immigrants; a strong educational system and technological infrastructure; and a liberal political tradition (Hartz 1955)—was rapidly rising to economic as well as political preeminence. And the welfare state, from Bismarck to Lloyd George to Franklin Delano Roosevelt (not to mention its role in fascism and communism, as well as in the democracies) created the crucial popular base for this modern state form by incorporating the working classes into both national consciousness and the growth of the national economy. But this apparent institutional hegemony of the nation-state form was to prove shaky as the next wave of globalization grew in the late twentieth century.

3. THE SEEDS OF CHANGE

What went wrong with this integrated, territorially bounded nation-state/ interstate model? Was this not the survival of the fittest institutionally? Why do we today, instead of the "strong state" so imperative for the working of the modern Westphalian model, have not only weak states but also states that in some ways apparently limit their own power, whether through neo-liberalism at home or globalization abroad? And why do apparently militar-ily dominant states get stuck in foreign quagmires and undermined by transnational social movements, ethnic and religious conflicts, civil wars, and terrorism? To find an answer to these questions, first looking back at the nation-state itself as a long-term political project and political construct is crucial. Indeed, in some ways, it is difficult to understand how such a model could have been so successful over time. As pointed out earlier, the requirements for the kind of boundary setting necessary for nation-state building were extremely rigorous.

Boundaries had to enclose or contain three basic types of variables: politi-cal, economic, and sociocultural. The first requirement was development of a state apparatus and a political process that could at least to some extent be effectively sovereign: not only an organized bureaucracy, especially a mili-tary and police bureaucracy that could impose order (Weber's "monopoly of legitimate violence") and the rule of law, but also a policy-making process that sought to shape and ostensibly improve the lives of the people enclosed within those boundaries (Foucault's "biopolitics"). Perhaps even more important was the capacity to get different interests, factions, groups, classes, and ethnicities to accept a set of common rules of the game in order to transform their potential for conflict into relatively peaceful competition. The development of political institutions, political systems, and, in particu-lar, widely accepted legal systems required a holistic, centripetal form of organization that benefited particularly from territoriality.

Second, the boundary-setting process required establishing *national economies*—production and market systems to a significant extent rooted and contained within national borders. Indeed, this aspect of the process became highly problematic once trade and capital movements took society beyond the relative parochialism of precapitalist, localized agricultural production. It was not until the late nineteenth century and even the twentieth century that the political apparatuses and processes of the most developed statelike polities moved beyond being competing empires with fungible frontiers to being *economically* relatively sovereign nation-states, albeit still with empires to feed their need for raw materials and to absorb their simpler consumer goods. And it was only when the economic bureaucracies of large-scale capitalism developed and when industrialization and economic growth became the main objectives of government policy with the Second Industrial Revolution that state and industrial bureaucracies partly fused (Lenin and Hilferding's "finance capital": Lenin 1917) and partly mimicked each other (Galbraith's "new industrial state": Galbraith 1967/2007) and that a range of key economic activities—not all of them, of course—could be enclosed behind national borders and integrated with the political processes discussed previously. At the same time, this growth process created sufficiently large economic surpluses that governments could skim off enough in taxes (Schumpeter 1918/1991) to build the foundations of industrial welfare states, further integrating a range of domestic groups and interests into the political process and giving them stakes in the bordered nation-state (Gallarotti 2000).

Third, of course, was the challenge of creating sociocultural enclosure. Popular nationalism was a key bulwark against internationalist liberalism and socialism, as well as subnational and local particularism. The Kulturkampf (i.e., the government-led "cultural struggle" to inculcate a nationalist spirit) in 1870s Germany was not merely a Bismarckian invention but an inherent part of a much longer term process everywhere, although it took quite different forms (Curtius 1932/1962). With regard to religion, the original 1648 Peace of Westphalia was an essential agreement and symbol of the subordination of religious institutions to the authority of the national state, with other aspects of sovereignty an afterthought. However, the establishment of national religions became a running battle in many areas that continued to undermine state holism, with the centuries-old Irish question, for example, still undermining the otherwise highly centripetal British state. Linguistic integration has been a running battle, too.

Probably the most important cultural factor in creating a sense of belonging to the nation-state has been war, especially after the advent of the *levée en masse* (mass conscription) following the French Revolution and industrialized warfare in the nineteenth century (Clausewitz 1832/1989). Industrialized warfare brought together bureaucratic political organization, economic organization, and cultural organization into one cataclysmic experience for ordinary people, fusing them into a technologically advanced fighting force and centralized support system, and forging them into seeing themselves as a "people" united in deadly conflict, where their other experiences were still much more fragmented (Pursell 1994).

Probably the other most important factor in creating cultural enclosure was, of course, democratization—although it tended to appear later in almost all countries. Democracy ostensibly fused political institutions and processes with economic processes (economic growth, capitalist firms, the welfare state) and the sense of belonging or ownership of the nation-state from the bottom up. Paradoxically, however, these changes often reflected the dynamics of top-down political mobilization more than spontaneous bottom-up national consciousness (Nettl 1967) and promoted a sense that the national state somehow represented the public interest or the common good.

Nevertheless, as can be seen from even a cursory critical glance at the three dimensions of the boundary-setting process, the whole project was riddled with exceptions and structural weaknesses. The domestic political development of various countries was often more centrifugal than centripetal in its underlying dynamics, as conflicting groups sought to suppress each other, exclude their opponents, and demand their complete defeat rather than include them, as in the Iraqi notion of *sahel* (Wong 2007). Fear of defeat on the part of particular groups, whether hegemonic or subaltern, led to vicious spirals or negative-sum games where no one was willing to compromise. All factions were fearful of defeat and ruthless in victory. In many cases, in fact, only severe authoritarian measures enabled the enclosure process to move ahead. Democratization often proved dysfunctional rather than functional—leading not to internal compromise on political processes but to intensified conflict between entrenched and excluded groups—until some protostates reached a later stage when national integration had *already* developed by other, generally top-down, means or, indeed, had had it forced on them through defeat in war by already democratized powers.

However, as historians like Kennedy (1987) and Spruyt (1994) have pointed out, what really made the political enclosure process work was its reciprocal, *mutually interactive* character among states internationally, where states either imitated, or were forced to imitate, each other in order to survive. This process of imitation-imposition started in Europe, and Europeans either imposed it directly on the rest of the world through imperial expansion or caused non-Europeans to try to imitate it, the better to resist it, as with Japan in particular.

But in Europe, and later in the rest of the world, it was the *failure of empire* to establish itself *within* the European continent as a whole—despite the best efforts of Charlemagne, Napoleon, and Hitler—that led to the sorts of interstate conflicts that institutionalized exclusive national boundaries. Postmedieval dynastic rulers in Europe did not intend to create nation-states. Indeed, many of them wished to reestablish the Holy Roman Empire, a sprawling, feudalistic, multicultural concoction that was nevertheless culturally, economically, and socially highly successful in its day. The Ottoman Empire that succeeded it in the east had a somewhat analogous structure but was never as economically successful (Mazower 2004). What created postmedieval, "sovereign" nation-states were (a) the *increasing impossibility for absolutist rulers to actually subdue and conquer rival dynasties* and (b) *subsequent attempts to prevent other dynastic rulers with imperial pretensions from undermining one's own power.*

The kind of unidimensional national boundaries characteristic of the later nineteenth and twentieth centuries were not the result of some inside-out or bottom-up intention of preformed "nations" or "peoples" to create something like modern effective nation-states, although nationalism did become a potent if unstable ideology. They were ultimately, and ironically, the by-product of the *clash of failed imperial projects within Europe itself*—the top-down constructions of absolutist monarchs whose intra-European imperial ambitions were stymied by the state-building successes of their continental rivals. As Spruyt (1994) has so cogently argued, certain quasi empires—Bourbon France being the prototype—succeeded by doing two things at the same time: simultaneously creating strong domestic organizational structures ("arenas of collective action") *while also* defending themselves effectively against external predators (allowing them to make "credible commitments" with regard to other states). Once the French monarchy succeeded, the others had to imitate it if they were to survive and prosper. What might facetiously be called "keeping up with the Bourbons" became the bottom line of success. Europe was carved up into states, frontiers were increasingly enclosed, and the three dimensions, political, economic and sociocultural, became mutually reinforcing as the modern state grew. Eventually, of course, empires became counterproductive and rebellious, but that is to jump ahead in our story.

This, of course, did not dampen more frontier-like imperial ambitions, ambitions that were driven by the limitations of surplus extraction and economic development within state borders. To retain power, absolutist monarchs required new sources of income and economic growth to buy off rising demands from the very urban and rural sectors of the population they increasingly needed to court to maintain and strengthen their regimes in the face of economic structural changes—the advent of capitalism and eventual industrialization—and external threats. Despite occasional failed attempts to resurrect the European imperial project (most notably Napoleon and Hitler), the most successful nation-building projects within Europe were precisely those where state actors effectively *diverted the imperial project outward* to the rest of the world. Unable to expand domestic production and markets beyond the relatively narrow geographical limits of their own increasingly circumscribed portions of Europe, the imperative of continually keeping up with the Bourbons (and the Tudors, Stuarts, Habsburgs, Hanoverians, Hohenzollerns, etc.) required the conquest of overseas empires in order to generate economic surpluses. So at one very fundamental level, nation-states sought to transcend the limits of their enclosed boundaries by going elsewhere, thrusting outward, and paradoxically spreading the combined nation-state–empire model to the rest of the world. The first wave of globalization was therefore not about states in general, but about the increasing power and impact of "empire-states" in particular (Subrahmanyam 2003).

As the European-generated nation-state system first consolidated within Europe and then spread by imposition and/or imitation to the rest of the world through these empire-states, the conditions for the later decay and undermining of that system began to grow, too. While nation-state borders were increasingly being defined, embedded, and reinforced politically, economically, and socially within Europe, so also were the broader, global trends that would ultimately challenge that emerging and consolidating border-setting process. The territorial stalemate in geographical Europe was only deepened by continual warfare, leading to two world wars and to the ultimate stalemate that was the cold war, rooted in nuclear deterrence. To this was added the ever denser and more profound internationalization of the once-European nation-state system, not only through European empires but also eventually by Europe's position at the interface of the competing American and Soviet empires (Deporte 1979)—the legacy of an ideologization of politics into capitalist democracy versus state socialism/Soviet communism, which, like nationalism, also started in modern Europe.

This confrontation of capitalism and communism also replaced the political and social values maintained through enclosed nation-state borders with those of *universal values*—transnational images of freedom, equality, and social justice—undermining the unstable, inward-looking, nationalistic, nation-state synergy that had begun with the British, American, and French revolutions. At the same time, the entropy characteristic of many of the new postcolonial nation-states of the third world demonstrated that imitation does not bring success if the political, economic, and social preconditions of border setting are not in place. What would later be called globalization increasingly eroded modern nation-state boundaries from both above and below, outside-in and inside-out, along all three of the dimensions identified earlier.

The development of the nation-state and the states system was therefore a schizophrenic affair, its very success implanted from the very start with seeds of decay. On the one hand, the convergence of political, economic, and social boundaries led to an embeddedness of territoriality at the nation-state level, a sense that the locality of human activities had shifted to a higher scale and that village, local region, or city-state institutions and the sense of belonging that had characterized family- and kinship-based societies—what sociologists call Gemeinschaft (Tönnies 1887/2003)—had effectively been transferred upward to the level of the nation-state. On the other hand, the development of a capitalist world economy, the ideologization of politics around universal values, and concepts like social "modernization," "individualization," "functional differentiation" and the like—not to mention extended notions of "freedom" and "social justice"—created a wider framework of understanding, within which the nation-state–interstate system would increasingly have to be legitimated and evaluated. This would prove to be beyond the capacity of nation-states to achieve by themselves.

4. DECONSTRUCTING THE NATION-STATE PARADIGM

The boundary-setting process, always contingent—always inherently a sociopolitical project-construct, set up and moved forward by political, economic, ideological, and institutional entrepreneurs—therefore contained the seeds of its own decay, as with all Kuhnian paradigms. Nevertheless, that process of decay has not thus far smashed the nation-state as such. Rather, it has *enmeshed* the nation-state and the states system in crosscutting webs of governance and of transnationally embedded social, political, and economic processes, creating complex *nonterritorial—functional— boundaries*. Deconstruction and reconstruction together constitute a dialectical politics of reinventing space in a globalizing world—a politics that has come to be characterized and shaped by neoliberalization.

The deconstruction of the modern nation-state–states system has proceeded rapidly along all three of the dimensions discussed earlier. In the first place, a trial-and-error process of developing international institutions and regimes has been in place since the late nineteenth century in a range of issue-areas and policy domains, starting with communications (the International Telegraph Union), taking a major if problematic leap with collective security (the League of Nations), and, after the Second World War, extending to a whole gamut of issues. By the end of the twentieth century, a new term, "global governance," was being applied to such regimes taken together. Although for the most part such institutions remained "intergovernmental," that is, subordinated to negotiations among their member governments, they increasingly achieved a certain autonomous legitimacy and authority, given that governments found it more and more difficult to act independently and were, in turn, subjected to the imperative of seeking cooperative outcomes (Ruggie 1993a).

At the same time, issues of public policy increasingly came to reflect a range of often asymmetric complex interdependencies across borders. Macroeconomic policy, partially shielded from international pressures during the postwar period of embedded liberalism and the expansion of the welfare state, became progressively subjected to "embedded financial orthodoxy" (see chapter 12), and priority was given to anti-inflationary policy, deregulation, and privatization (see chapter 7). Trade policy was, of course, a particular focus, linking the politics of domestic interest groups, elite and mass, with the process of reducing trade barriers. The collapse of the Bretton Woods exchange rate regime in the early 1970s accelerated the internationalization of financial markets and a process of regulatory arbitrage and competition among governments to retain and attract investment, leading further to discussions of the concept of an "international financial architecture."

The crisis of the welfare state in the 1970s inaugurated a painful process of restructuring social policy around market and business types of organizational principles (Clayton and Pontusson 1998; Evans and Cerny 2003). Direct outcome-oriented state intervention in the economy was progressively replaced by process-oriented, "arm's-length" regulatory policies, public-private partnerships, and the promarket approach of the Competition State. Transgovernmental networks among policy makers and bureaucrats expanded, cutting across state hierarchies, and processes of policy transfer deepened (Evans 2005). Of course, although these trends began within and across the more developed states, they also spread rapidly to "transition" (i.e., postcommunist) and developing economies, both through the demonstration effect and through pressure not only from the core states of the Group of 7 but also from international economic institutions such as the World Bank, the International Monetary Fund, and the Organization for Economic Cooperation and Development.

The political dynamics of mass politics and interest group politics have also been transformed. Business interests are increasingly dominated not only by the interests of multinational corporations but also by those of small and medium-size enterprises whose upstream and downstream operations require foreign markets, external sources not only of raw materials but also of component parts and basic consumer items, overseas labor resources, and footloose sources of investment capital. People are more and more aware of the constraints of international economic conditions on interest rates, consumer prices, changing labor markets, and the like, leading to new patterns of demands and voting. Indeed, it is argued that in the broad spectrum of political inputs, producer groups, long dominant through business pressure groups, trade unions, and similar groups, are being overtaken by more diffuse, broad-based *consumer interests*. Consumers may, indeed, be the main drivers of economic globalization, as well as of political liberalization (see also chapter 13). Finally, political debate and party competition are increasingly dominated by the issue of how to deal with so-called global realities.

Up to the end of the twentieth century, then, it was possible to see domestic political systems as increasingly becoming a terrain of conflict, competition, and coalition building between groups, factions, and parties that favored more globalization and neoliberalization on the one hand, and those opposed—those more in favor of the traditional "modern" national-level politics of protection and redistribution—on the other. Today, however, that competition has come to be characterized by an *embedded neoliberal consensus* in which protection and redistribution are relegated to the periphery, and mainstream discourse focuses on the need to "capture the benefits of globalization" for purposes of rebuilding and rearticulating coalitions, on the one hand, and on the promise to move toward a more "social neoliberalism" or "globalization with a human face" on the other (see chapter 7). Traditional boundaries between left and right, so deeply embedded in the nation-state and the states system, have not so much been left behind as given a new salience and urgency as political actors seek to adapt popular, electoral, and pressure group politics to new interdependencies.

Along the second dimension discussed earlier, the economic dimension, the blurring and enmeshing of boundaries is even more obvious. There is no need here to expand at length about the roles of international financial markets, trade growth and interdependence, international production chains, multinational corporations, and the like in deconstructing the economic borders so painfully erected in the process of nation-state building in the nineteenth and twentieth centuries. National markets and economic sovereignty are increasingly a fiction. Economic effectiveness, for either the private sector or governments, today means the capacity to manipulate international economic conditions to improve the profitability, productivity, and competitiveness of domestic firms and economic activities vis-à-vis foreign and/or transnational competitors and to obtain benefits from market interdependencies for domestic consumers.

Where economies of agglomeration (or location) occur, as they do in a number of key sectors, those locational advantages have less and less to do with nation-states as places and spaces per se (big factories, immediate access to raw material supplies, nationally integrated consumer markets, etc.). In contrast, they increasingly involve craft industry synergies, knowledge clusters, and the like—spaces and places that, like "world cities" and regions like Silicon Valley, possess *locational advantages that derive not from where they are physically located within a national territory but from how they are plugged into the international economy*. Post-Fordism and the flexibilization of a range of industrial processes, along with marketing and the rapid expansion of service sectors, imply synergies of "glocalization"— the interaction of processes of globalization and localization—across geographically disconnected spaces, not exclusive embedded spaces within discrete, contiguous national territories. Of course, the political clout of ideas such as protectionism and domestic populist redistributionism is still powerful among certain voters and pressure groups. Nevertheless, the shift of public policy and political discourse from outcome-oriented state intervention to process-oriented arm's-length regulation and the promotion of competitiveness (along with compensating losers), as discussed in chapters 6 and 7, represents a further entrenching of the embedded neoliberal consensus.

Along the third dimension, the sociocultural, the embeddedness of the nation-state and the states system is perhaps more robust. We are all brought up in a world of identity and belonging that privileges national-level social bonds, perceptions, and discourses. People in developed nation-states do indeed see themselves primordially as American, English (but perhaps not British), French, Japanese, and so on—although tribalism, class and ethnic conflict, and the like have stymied nation-state consolidation in much of the developing world. Nevertheless, other bonds, perceptions, and discourses are increasingly overshadowing the national in ways that are growing in salience and intensity. This social transformation is even reflected in the rapid disillusionment with foreign military adventures that has been characteristic of recent decades. As with the Vietnam Syndrome, the Soviet adventure in Afghanistan, and the American war in Iraq, empires and potential hegemons are being undermined just as much by opposition at home as by military defeat in the field—the body bag syndrome.

Furthermore, immigrants, diasporas, and other mobile individuals and groups are no longer cut off from their networks of origin. The Internet, for example, creates virtual spaces for transnationally connected people to maintain their identities in ways that represent *neither* the national space of their origins (where they may well have been minorities) *nor* that of their destination country as such, but instead more complex spaces where both are inextricably intertwined. These are exemplified by remittances, which constitute an ever-increasing form of development funding. The nation-state

alone is too confining and counterproductive a source for identity formation, although no clear and dominant alternative focus has yet emerged.

In this context, transnational multiculturalism clearly transforms, and
occasionally undermines, the exclusive, painfully constructed, and often
incomplete or counterproductive national cultural boundaries so important
to people's identities in the modern nation-state. Liberal states may adapt
relatively better by resorting to more complex strategies of reconciliation
among contending groups, whereas nonliberal states and state actors may
engage in attempts at crude assimilation, repression, or even ethnic cleans-
ing. However, in both cases, national identities are increasingly crosscut
and transnationalized in the process.

Although we may not be in a full-blown postmodern era of fragmentation, disorientation, and virtual spaces, nevertheless, the deconstruction of
modern national and ideological cultural narratives is leading to myriad
attempts at identity *re*construction that privilege, at both global and local
levels, the kind of crosscutting and overlapping notions of group membership that were so crucial to mid-twentieth-century pluralist thinking at the
domestic level. Sociocultural boundaries are no longer between fixed physical territories but cut right across individual identity, too, like a more complex version of those who were once derided as "hyphenated Americans."
Multiple hyphenation of identities along different virtual or "soft" borders
(locational, ethnic, religious, gendered, occupational, orientation to "liberal"
or "monistic" politics, etc.) is the norm today (Mostov 2008).

But it is not merely multiculturalism that is at issue here, whether within
particular national spaces or within groups and individuals, but a partial
simultaneous transnationalization and localization—glocalization—of culture itself. At the local end of the spectrum, some circumscribed but highly
self-conscious communities like the Zapatistas of Chiapas in Mexico do not
merely make claims on behalf of their own unique political, economic, and
social autonomy (although many ethnic groups and tribes do). Rather, they
increasingly claim a *universal* right for such communities to demand autonomy from what they see as the oppressive centralization of state-building
elites and the onslaught of multinational corporations. At the global end
of the spectrum, increasingly geographically dispersed groups—Kotkin's
global tribes, not to mention major religious groupings and transnational
epistemic communities of experts and professionals—play a crucial role
across the world in spreading transnational and global knowledge and organizational forms. Of course, much of the present-day analysis of the phenomenon of terrorism, along with the virtual elimination of interstate wars
and the ubiquity of below-the-border, cross-border, and civil wars, takes
both its novelty and its significance from examining the organizational flexibility that derives from terrorism's transnational, nonstate character (Cerny

2005a). The New Security Dilemma (see chapter 11) is rooted in the failure
of the states system to cope with these nonstate security challenges.

5. DECONSTRUCTION AND RECONSTRUCTION, FUSION AND
COALITION BUILDING: THE ROLE OF NEOLIBERALISM

Political, economic, and sociocultural borders are therefore in a growing
state of flux and deconstruction, while de facto and experimental reconstruction projects increasingly dominate institution building and institutional
reform, political discourse and competition, public and economic policy
making, and social and cultural politics and policy. These reconstruction
projects are profoundly shaped by cross-border functional differentiation
and by the transnationalization of a range of political processes and groups.
In this context of transition and change, world politics (i.e., domestic, international, transnational, translocal, etc., taken together) in the twenty-first
century are increasingly dominated by a range of policy and institutional
strategies rooted in neoliberalism—a flexible and fungible paradigm that
nevertheless involves and makes sense of the uneasy and uneven interaction of convergence and diversity of a globalizing world.

Boundaries, especially economic boundaries, are less and less about distinctions between territorial units and constituencies and more and more
about those between:

- different *economic sectors* with different asset structures (discussed
  later)
- crosscutting *sociocultural networks and interest groups* that span the
  local and the transnational
- *state agencies* (and public-private organizations) with competing
  clienteles and crosscutting, cross-
  border—transgovernmental—connections
- new groups of social and economic *winners and losers*

What is emerging, therefore, is a range of attempts to *politicize*—that is, to
(re)claim for the theoretical as well as the practical realm of politics (and
political science)—what has been seen up to now as an ineluctably economic
image of globalization. This involves a reinvention of the social dimension
of politics through new policy and coalition "spaces" populated by a wide
range of new, and old, political actors in both the developed and developing
worlds. Although technological and economic structures can alter the
parameters and payoff matrix of the playing field of politics and public policy, in the last analysis, outcomes of the interaction of politics and economics

in a transnational political context are primarily determined by political action and not merely by economic-structural variables.

6. CONSTRUCTING NEW BOUNDARIES

These new political processes are differentiated more by sector and issue-area than by physical, geographical, and territorial space. They therefore involve the construction of *new boundaries between issue-areas*—a horizontal restructuring of institutions and policy domains. Although at first glance these new boundaries seem like virtual boundaries when compared with territorial borders, they are just as real for the actors bounded by them. In many cases, they are even *more* real, with impacts on people's core interests in fundamental, behavior-determining ways: through the distribution of economic opportunities, costs, and benefits; through the construction and reconstruction of social bonds, ideologies, cultures, and identities; and through changing patterns of politicking, policy making, and pressure group activity—indeed, in the most crucial aspects of everyday life.

Three kinds of bordering dimensions, taken together, differentiate these issue-areas and distinguish the forms of governance most likely to develop in each—what are sometimes referred to as "policy domains" (Arts, Lagendijk, and van Houtum 2009). The first is a mainly economic-structural dimension, developed primarily in the field of institutional economics—that of *asset structure* (Williamson 1975 and 1985). Williamson's key hypothesis is that where a particular economic activity or process is characterized by assets that cannot easily be disconnected or disentangled from other assets—in other words, where they are only fit for a specific purpose and lose value if redeployed for other purposes ("specific assets") and where it is difficult or impossible to determine their prices through a standard, market-based price-setting mechanism—then they are usually more effectively organized and governed through hierarchical structures and processes, namely, decision-making or governance processes that determine the uses for those assets by authoritative pronouncement or *fiat* or "long-term contracting." However, where an activity or process is characterized by assets that *can* be separated out and/or divided up without losing value, especially where there are other uses to which they can be easily redeployed—where they can be bought and sold freely and where there is an efficient price-setting mechanism at work ("nonspecific assets")—then they are likely to be more efficiently organized through *markets* or "recurrent contracting." It should be noted that spatiality is a key element in this equation, as physical location and economies of agglomeration are among the most significant specific assets.

   In purely economic terms, this means that firms with extensive specific assets are more efficiently organized through quasi-monopolistic, hierarchical governance structures. In *public policy* terms, this means, on the one hand, that where a particular industry or activity is characterized predominantly by specific assets—for example, a large, integrated, Fordist production process with nondivisible technological assets like large integrated factories and production lines, low marginal costs, and high economies of scale based on economies of agglomeration (traditional cold rolled steel production, for example)—then direct government intervention, whether through public ownership, direct control, subsidization, and/or traditional hands-on forms of regulation, is more likely to lead to relatively efficient outcomes than privatization or marketization, which would lead to private monopolistic or opportunistic behavior. On the other hand, where an industry or activity is characterized predominantly by nonspecific assets—say, a flexible, post-Fordist steel minimill or an Internet firm—then not only will it be more efficiently organized through private markets but also in public policy terms, arm's-length regulation concerned with setting general, process-oriented rules for market transactions, ensuring price transparency, and preventing fraud in an otherwise privately organized market setting, will be more efficient. This distinction becomes crucial in the context of globalization, especially when applied to intermediate forms such as networks (Thompson, Frances, Levaçić, and Mitchell 1991).

   If globalization does indeed involve increasing flexibilization and post-Fordist production and distribution processes, and if a larger (global) market means that more assets can be traded on liquid transnational markets, this implies in economic terms that the specific asset-dominated Second Industrial Revolution model of domestically based monopolies is increasingly likely to be replaced by a marketized, nonspecific asset-dominated Third Industrial Revolution model of industrial organization and governance more generally. Public policy, in turn, is likely to shift its general orientation away from outcome-oriented, direct intervention of the traditional type associated with the industrial welfare state toward process-oriented regulation and reregulation. However, it also implies that public policy itself needs to become more flexibilized and marketized, moving away from what has been called a "one size fits all" hierarchical bureaucratic form of intervention toward *promarket* regulation, privatization, contractualization, and the like (Osborne and Gaebler 1992), if it is to be effective in such a transnational setting. Although globalization does not imply the increasing dominance of pure markets, it does involve a shift away from corporatist hierarchies to intermediate forms that are more difficult to regulate and control at the national level.

In this sense, globalization, flexibilization, and neoliberalism actually open up more *spaces* for transnational political actors to conflict, compete, cooperate, and build coalitions. The traditional interventionist state becomes not only a "regulatory state" (Moran 2002) but also a Competition State seeking to maximize returns from globalization. In turn, rather than being restricted to the nation-state container, the reconfigured boundaries among economic sectors and issue-areas in a globalizing world open up a wide range of complex spaces—some new, some reconfigured old spaces as political behavior adjusts to the more complex global playing field—for transnationally linked political actors, especially interest groups that define those interests in their global context.

The second dimension therefore concerns the *configuration of interests* characteristic of the industry or activity concerned. For example, where people involved in a particular industry are concentrated in a discrete geographical area and where the impact of competition (whether domestic or foreign) affects the whole interest group and not merely some subgroups, then there will be direct pressure, whether through lobbying or electoral behavior, for governments to promote or protect that industry through traditional outcome-oriented means. However, where those people affected by the fate of an industry are geographically dispersed—indeed, this refers mainly to producer groups, as consumer groups are usually geographically dispersed anyhow—then political actors will have a wider set of policy options to deploy (Frieden and Rogowski 1996). What appear to be the geographical boundaries of the firm or sector become transformed into boundaries between concentrated losers from market competition, on the one hand, and both dispersed losers and winners, on the other. Political coalitions between the two latter categories can often resist demands for protection from even the most concentrated losers, although this is highly variable, and in extreme recessionary conditions such as those prevailing at the end of 2008, bailouts have returned to the agenda in a dramatic way—although trade protection is still off the table. In either case, neoliberal political coalitions can be constructed on a quasi-cross-class basis.

Patterns of cross-border *sectional or economic-utilitarian politics* of, say, specific agricultural sectors will be very different from those of a rapidly changing steel industry, varied high-tech sectors, textiles and other consumer goods, or the commercial aircraft industry, based mainly on their asset structures (specific or nonspecific) and on their cross-border geographical integration and interdependence. And at another level, new forms of *value politics* on a range of globalizing noneconomic issue-areas like AIDS prevention, poverty reduction, criminal law, and the like have been growing, where transnational pressure groups, advocacy coalitions, and nongovernmental organizations (NGOs) seek new ways to compete and cooperate in the quest for political influence, economic clout, and social relevance (Lipschutz 2005).

The third dimension concerns the relative *sensitivity and vulnerability* of the industry or activity to international or transnational economic trends, in particular, export potential, import vulnerability, position in an international production chain, and exposure to internationally mobile capital. There are two main aspects of this dimension: the mobility of physical capital and cross-border price sensitivity. When an industry or activity is insulated from such factors, then lobbying pressure and "iron triangles" in that sector are likely to favor traditional protective and/or redistributive policy measures. However, where firms and sectors are highly integrated or linked into such structures and processes, especially where there is a world market price for a good or asset that determines local prices, then lobbying pressure from firms in that sector and from industry organizations is likely to be organized through "flexible pentangles"—coalitions that include transnational actors from outside the national container that operate at a transnational level to influence global governance processes—and to push for neoliberal outcomes (see chapter 6).

In the light of these three dimensions, I would argue, first of all, that the growing marketization of assets—that is, the structural shift caused by flexi-bilization and the globalization of markets, when added to the increasing dispersion of losers and the growing sensitivity of sectors to international markets—means that public policy in general and the political coalitions that support it are likely to shift over time in a more and more transnational as well as neoliberal direction, challenging the traditional boundaries of the nation-state. However, what is perhaps more important in portraying processes of change is to argue that certain key sectors, sectors that constitute structurally significant nodes of economic activity and thereby have an impact on a wide range of other sectors, "go transnational" first, creating a domino effect on others, even where they are characterized by more nonspecific assets, geographical concentration of interests, and low sensitivity and vulnerability.

Finance is a particularly crucial sector, linking together and acting as a crossroads issue-area and policy domain where most of the others meet (see chapter 12). Regulatory changes and regulatory arbitrage in the financial sector are key triggers for wider neoliberalization, especially as they have direct knock-on effects on the availability and cost of capital, as well as the regulation of accounting standards, consumer protection, fraud prevention, corporate governance, and the like. Indeed, neoliberal, promarket reregula-tion started with financial regulatory reform, and that continues to be the bottom-line focus of public policy innovation. This is the case not only in developed countries but also indeed in developing countries, where it forms the core of both the so-called Washington Consensus and, in a more complex manifestation, the post-Washington Consensus, with its increasingly regulatory focus (Guha 2007), reinforced by the development of international "capital rules" favoring international capital mobility (Abdelal 2007).

These dimensions might potentially be applied to assess the likelihood and shape of neoliberal policy innovation and coalition building across a range of contrasting, differently structured issue-areas and policy domains, and the actors that populate them, including:

- financial systems and regulation
- international monetary policy and exchange rate management
- macroeconomic—fiscal and monetary—policy
- microeconomic and strategic industrial policy
- public and social services
- trade policy
- corporate governance
- labor markets
- welfare states
- the most informal, diffuse, and unorganized—but nonetheless increasingly marketized—issue-area of all, consumption

This reconstruction of space implies a wide range of options for policy innovation in different issue-areas and policy domains, even *within* the parameters of an "embedded neoliberal consensus." In some cases, traditional policies of subsidization and redistribution will be appropriate, too, especially in times of crisis. However, it is ultimately the *mix* of policy measures that is at the core of the new transnational political process and neoliberal coalition building. And it is, furthermore, crucial to examine the process of interaction among these and other issue-areas and policy domains. As pointed out earlier, the politics of certain key issue-areas like financial regulation can play a distinct catalytic role in reshaping global economics and politics *as a whole*, imposing their particular market and policy structures on other sectors and issue-areas, too.

Finally, the reconstruction of such horizontal borders is, I argue, *overdetermined*. The actors and institutions that make up the galaxy of multilevel governance and multinodal politics in the twenty-first century can all be seen as pushing more or less in the same direction, that is, toward more transnationally interconnected political processes and market structures. In one sense, this means that there is a holistic, fusion aspect of the transnationalization process that transcends national borders, although not the centripetal multifunctionality of political institutions and processes characteristic of the ideal-type nation-state. But it also means that the constellation of variables all play distinct, if complementary, roles in this process. In the first place, as argued earlier in this chapter, political actors—politicians and bureaucrats, policy and institutional entrepreneurs, interest groups, and even ordinary voters—have been key actors in this process. For example, state actors today, in pursuing traditional goals of economic growth and development, tend to prioritize using public policy to promote and enhance the international competitiveness of firms and sectors that also play significant roles in the domestic economy—the Competition State again. In this role, they increasingly construct broad yet neoliberal coalitions such as New Labour in the United Kingdom (Cerny and Evans 2004), the current Christian Democrat–Social Democrat coalition in Germany under Angela Merkel, or even, despite nationalist electoral rhetoric, the quasi-neoliberal majority of Nicolas Sarkozy in France.

At the same time, international economic institutions and other structures and processes of global governance base their own legitimacy and authority on neoliberal coalition building, whether in shoring up their own financial support from donor states, developing their own institutional autonomy, and/or attempting to ensure compliance through quasi-voluntary conditionality among client developing states. The Washington Consensus and, indeed, its post-Washington Consensus successor can be characterized as coalition-building projects to legitimize, as well as control, the development process to ensure that it proceeds in a broadly neoliberal direction (Cammack 2004). The role of the United States in international negotiations, although at times erratic, has also been one of the main factors pushing for trade and financial liberalization over the past seventy years, although the European Union and other international organizations have also played a key role in transnational rule making (Abdelal 2007). Indeed, it has been argued that the United States benefits from a "globalization premium" in that the internal organization of the American economy and policy have given not only the American state but also *American nonstate actors* key roles to play through domestic and transgovernmental coalitions in spearheading liberalization processes.

7. CONCLUSION: THE NEW SPATIALITY, OR FROM CONTAINERS TO STRAINERS

Nevertheless, the key to understanding the new horizontal stratification of transnational politics lies not in the hard or soft power of the United States or other nation-states as such, nor in the development of global governance per se. The key is the political flexibility, fungibility, and transnationality of globalization itself, at both elite and mass levels. In today's globalizing world, neoliberalism reaches the parts—the spaces and places—other discourses and political projects no longer reach, as we will see in more detail in chapter 7. The oversimplified view of modern space and territoriality as requiring exclusive, multidimensional, territorial borders needs to be replaced with a paradigm of complex linkages across space and time and the reordering of governance and politics along multilevel and multinodal lines—including, but going beyond, the notion of networks to a more complex range of institutional forms, economic structures, social processes, and patterns of politicking. States are no longer containers of politics, economics, and society, but "strainers," through which each issue-area is sifted into the complex politics of a globalizing world.

A key dimension of this process is to bring actors back in. The new world politics requires not domination and rule but what Preston has called "orchestration" and "political choreography" (Preston 2000)—a ratcheting upward of Foucault's art of governmentality to complex translocal, transnational, international, and global levels. Political and institutional entrepreneurs must learn new skills, especially the skills of operating on several asymmetric playing fields at one and the same time—playing fields that can be within, cutting across, above, and below old-fashioned national borders. This will require an increasing focus on new institutional strategies and institutional entrepreneurs, as well as new policy strategies and policy entrepreneurs. World politics is approaching a new branching point or tipping point—one that will deconstruct those boundaries, reconstruct them, and construct new ones, connecting issue-areas and policy domains across borders, producing a proliferation of innovative roles for actors in transnational neopluralist political processes, and creating a new spatiality for the twenty-first century.

Chapter 4

Reconfiguring Power in a Globalizing World

1. THE CONCEPT OF POWER IN WORLD POLITICS

The concept of power as developed by realist theorists has been seen as the key factor, variable, driving force, or "currency" in the relations among states, derived originally from the thought of such political theorists as Machiavelli and Hobbes and central to the nineteenth-century German concept of Realpolitik. In this understanding of the world, there is no agreed, overarching political forum in which individuals, economic interests, and social groups can systematically and effectively express their views and pursue their goals—in other words, engage in collective action—other than through the level of the state and of those international regimes or global governance institutions and less formal processes licensed by sovereign states, and they are ultimately constrained by them in terms of the basic structural dynamics of the system. In the words of Aristotle, "justice" and "friendship" on a social level can exist only *within* the *politeia* or political community. All other people and communities are by definition *outsiders*—foreigners—and relationships with them, even if they are relatively peaceable most of the time, are in the last analysis, when external threats to the polity are perceived, dominated by asocial relations of force.

As a result, such goals as justice, fairness, equality, democracy, and redistribution are ultimately seen to be trumped by power rivalries and stabilized only by *balances of power* among states (Little 2007). Power *as such* in the international arena concerns the relative power of different states, rooted in relations of force. Higher ends like social justice, economic welfare, or even civil peace itself are subordinated to the underlying requirements of survival, national self-interest, and "self-help" (Waltz 1979). Those higher ends are not forgotten, but are only effectively operationalized domestically through the state itself and internationally through the medium of state action, where they are subordinated to underlying relations of force (Morgenthau 1949; Pin-Fat 2005). Indeed, the dominant power imperative of world politics therefore prioritizes and privileges qualitatively different kinds of ends from those of domestic politics, requires quite different means, and justifies radically different standards of conduct by actors—such as killing and repressing enemies—from government leaders down to ordinary people, especially, but not exclusively, when they become soldiers.

However, this traditional conception of power has always had a range of critics:

- believers in transcendent religious, spiritual, moral, and/or ethical values, whether metaphysical or humanistic
- economic liberals, who see market forms of exchange as entailing imperatives of growth, efficiency, and prosperity that ultimately expand onto a transnational or global scale
- Marxists, who, in contrast, see the very same capitalism as creating ever-evolving means for an internationalized ruling class to expand its domination, and ultimately look to its replacement by socialism
- liberal democratizers who seek to expand democracy not only within a growing number of nation-states but also across borders in more democratic and/or pluralistic institutions, legal principles, and political processes (see chapter 10)
- political science pluralists and neopluralists who see political behavior as increasingly driven by transnational interests, values, and identities, rather than merely domestic ones, as I do in this book

Each critique also carries with it an underlying understanding of how the structure of the international system has been undergoing fundamental change and transformation over time—particularly in the light of globalization. All sorts of economic, political, and social relationships that cut across borders are today seen from a range of diverse perspectives as undermining—or at least potentially undermining—the realist inside-outside distinction that has been constituted historically not only through international relations theory but also through practices of war, diplomacy, economic competition, and the like.

In these critiques, the world is seen as being constituted more and more through revived, emerging, and even hegemonic crosscutting linkages and loyalties of friendship, justice, class, economic self-interest, identity, and/or belonging—the traditional stuff of domestic political philosophy and politicking, now crystallizing and consolidating across borders. These increasingly densely structured linkages do not merely constrain the actions of states but, more important, *enable* social, economic, and political actors to develop modes of transnational action. They create webs of collective action that are different not only in degree but also in kind from the crude relations of force characteristic of traditional international relations. States are being cut across, run around, manipulated, and reshaped by complex transnational and "glocal" linkages that are transforming state behavior itself.

Earlier modes of all of these trends have existed since time immemorial. Indeed, the era of a clearly defined states system and of the "high nation-state" from the mid-nineteenth to the mid-twentieth century has been relatively short in the *longue durée* of history. However, in the global era, these trends are taking new forms that can be interpreted as heralding a fundamental structural transformation of world politics and society. The very nature of power in world politics is being transformed into something much more closely resembling the traditional domestic version but spread not only among states "inter-nationally" but also transnationally among cross-border economic interests and "global civil society," and translocally among world cities, ethnicities, economic "clusters," aficionados of Internet social Web sites, and the like. We are approaching a "tipping point" (Gladwell 2000).

2. THE TRADITIONAL CONCEPTION OF POWER
IN INTERNATIONAL RELATIONS

There are four main ways in which power is seen as different in the international context from power in domestic political systems. All four of these ways can be seen as distinct dimensions of what is often called the inside/outside distinction, which forms the core of the realist paradigm but is important for the other approaches as well. In Roman times, this distinction—and the inherent yet schizophrenic connection between the two levels—was symbolized by the god Janus, the god of the city. Janus, whose statue was placed at the city gates, had two faces, looking in opposite directions—one looking inside the city, seeking to nurture social bonds, solidarity, and community, and the second looking outside, prepared to fight invaders and pursue the city's external interests against aliens by force. This division of world politics into inside and outside requires a dual role for the state and state actors—the city-state in Greek times and the nation-state in modern times. This dual role is today often called "two-level games" (Putnam 1988).

A. The International Authority Vacuum

The first of the four main dimensions of the inside/outside distinction derives, as noted previously, from the observation that there is no world government, no overarching authority structure, and no autonomous international political process to define norms, make decisions, and impose sanctions on those transgressing those norms or defying those decisions. States and state actors cannot appeal to a higher authority, either to pursue their own goals or to prevent others from pursuing theirs. As in Thomas Hobbes's state of nature, the international world is a potential "war of all against all," in which what is today called "defection"—the willingness and incentive to opt out of cooperative arrangements when a state's fundamental national interests are seen to be threatened—is the default state of affairs. Self-defense and what Kenneth Waltz, the leading theorist of the neorealist school of international relations, calls "self-help" constitute the bottom line of world politics (Waltz 1979).

This kind of self-regarding imperative is indeed said to be the only *legitimate* course of action in a world made up of sovereign states accountable only to their own "people." In this world, there is no use trying to appeal to a higher authority, whether supernatural or supranational; states are the bottom line because in the last analysis, that's all there is. Indeed, because of the primordial priority of power as force, such appeals can be dismissed either as hopeless idealism and impractical romanticism, on the one hand, or as a mask for ulterior motives of external (or even domestic) power seeking, on the other. In the words of Samuel Johnson, "Patriotism is the last refuge of a scoundrel." For realists, however, it is the espousal of supranational idealism that marks the real scoundrel. Only actors who effectively pursue the genuine national interests of their states can be truly moral as well as practical (Morgenthau 1949; Pin-Fat 2005).

B. The Legitimacy of State Power

The second dimension, which follows from the first, is that the goals states pursue will be fundamentally different on the "outside," international level from those that state authorities and political actors pursue "inside" the domestic political system. In particular, in this context, it is not only exceedingly difficult but regarded as *illegitimate* for states to impose their social values on other independent sovereign states. Pursuing and enforcing norms of social and economic justice, the distribution and redistribution of wealth or other resources, and furthering elemental social bonds among the people can be done only within states, unless there is a process of alliance, emulation, or interactive economic growth among states themselves, in which other states *voluntarily* adopt the same values. The issue of spreading democracy is a particularly thorny conundrum in this context, involving a version of Rousseau's notion of "forcing people to be free."

This dimension therefore rests on an apparent philosophical paradox. Each state is in theory entitled to possess a different internal moral, ethical, and socioeconomic system, although the extent of this autonomy is historically uncertain. Indeed, in this context what one might call moral realists like Morgenthau have argued paradoxically that peace could only be promoted through noninterference and mutual recognition of the ultimate sovereignty of states to determine their own priorities and national interests. The existence of a plurality of different kinds of states with different values and interests can therefore be seen to guarantee a kind of state-centric pluralism, based on mutual recognition of those differences (Hurrell 2007)—almost a kind of vertically containerized international multiculturalism. The Peace of Westphalia was, in fact, fundamentally a religious truce between Protestant and Catholic European monarchs after centuries of religious warfare and complex institutional conflicts between monarchs (and between them and the papacy), with each agreeing not to interfere in the others' choice of religion within their "own" states. This principle was later extended to other choices, including modern ideologies—except, of course, that in the twentieth century in particular, those ideologies have themselves become internationalized.

Nevertheless, such sovereign autonomy has often masked desires for conquest, as demonstrated by the history of European imperialism and colonialism, while Nazis, Fascists, and Communists attempted to spread their values forcefully by conquering or promoting revolution in other states. In this sense, therefore, the notion of power as sovereign autonomy, on the one hand, and power as the use of force to pursue national interests, on the other, has always represented a complex dialectic or contradiction within the traditional conception of power in world politics—one which was summed up by the Roman writer Vegetius in the famous maxim: "If you want peace, prepare for war." However, preparation for war often leads to the vicious spiral known as the "security dilemma" (Herz 1950), potentially leading to arms races and the unintended outbreak of war. Thus the history of the modern world has been an unstable dialectic of war and peace stemming directly from the clash of national interests—interests that cannot be fully insulated from external factors, even without full-blown globalization— and outwardly oriented, even universalistic, ideological goals, on the one hand, and the unstable foundations of the interstate system in relations of force and balances of power, on the other.

C. The Dualistic Organization of Power

The third dimension, again following from the first two, is that power is *organized* differently within the state's internal domain from its external environment. Neorealists in particular label inside politics as "hierarchical" in the sense that there is some sort of vertical, centralized, or at least centripetal state structure that can be either authoritarian or liberal democratic—with all shades in between. In principle, however, more domestically liberal and pluralist forms of this centripetal state allow competing actors to coexist, relating and interacting through a range of horizontal processes such as elections, shared and/or competing economic interests, and multiple social institutions, including churches and families. Different groups, factions, individuals, and interests, whether pursuing their economic self-interest or attempting to further social values—what V. O. Key called "sectional" and "value" groups (Key 1953)—accept (at least up to a point) common rules of the game, and conflicts are resolved through common procedures and processes, whether through political institutions and parties, courts and the legal system, rule-governed bureaucracies, and/or shared social norms.

Nevertheless, whether hierarchical or pluralistic—domestic polities are always a complex mix of the two—the role of power *within* a state tends to concern the use of power as a means to a higher end rather than an end in itself, that is, the "public interest" or "common good." Although power struggles, corruption, and domination by particular individuals and groups over others are ever crucial to domestic policy processes and institutions, one of the main trends of the past few centuries in the developed countries, and today increasingly in developing countries (although there are always steps backward, too, as in Kenya in early 2008 and the ongoing disintegration of Zimbabwe), has been the *institutionalization* of power as a stabilizing force. Power has moved from the foreground—where it has been when tribal elites, medieval nobles, mafias, and warlords of various stripes have used brute force for the direct expropriation of wealth and the assertion of control—to the background. This process is an essential part of what is generally seen as progress, modernization, or development. Naked exercises of power are seen in this context as normatively illegitimate, and power is seen as legitimate only when it is applied in the service of social stability, development, social values (both individualistic and collectivist), and the public interest. In this context, as Weber argued, what keeps the state together is its "monopoly of legitimate violence," but the key word here is "legitimate"—constitutionally constituted forms such as the "police power," courts, and political institutions.

However, as noted earlier, politics of this sort are nevertheless said to stop at the water's edge. Because the international system is, in contrast, "anarchical"—a description accepted by a range of different approaches to international relations, meaning not chaotic and disordered but simply without an effective overarching system of government or governance—the state is *obliged and even compelled by the imperatives built into the international system itself to act as if it were a single, fused unit* in foreign policy. The "outside" state needs to act *as if* it were genuinely organized vertically—as if it were at one and the same time both an effective "container," bottling up internal politics and preventing it from spilling over into the international sphere, on the one hand, while constituting a genuine, relatively efficient command-and-control system for coordinating and mobilizing potential domestic material and human resources and capabilities for the pursuit of power on the international level, on the other.

Therefore, not only is the state, to use Waltz's term, *required* by the structural imperatives built into the interstate system to act as a "unit actor" vis-à-vis other states analogously organized but also leading politicians must act like "statesmen" representing a holistic "national interest," and the outward-facing state is organized through command hierarchies like armed forces, intelligence agencies, and foreign policy makers, rather than through competitive political processes or economic markets. This capacity for unified action has often been seen as stronger in authoritarian than in democratic states—as reflected in Vladimir Putin's address to the Presidential State Council of Russia on 8 February 2008—and stronger in states with strong, autonomous executives, as in the unitary executive theory of the George W. Bush administration, especially as espoused by then Vice President Richard Cheney (Savage 2007; Gellman 2008). Nevertheless, this view has been contested throughout history; see, in particular, Pericles' oration to the Athenians as reported by Thucydides. It is also at the core of contemporary debates about transatlantic relations, summed up in the statement that "Americans are from Mars; Europeans are from Venus" (Kagan 2003; contrast Sheehan 2008).

The result, as noted by Rosenau, is to separate in organizational terms domestic policy making—left to "parochial" interests and actors—from foreign policy, which is effectively the preserve of "cosmopolitan elites" (Rosenau 1961). Of course, this means that foreign policy can be—and often is—manipulated for domestic purposes (Cerny 1980). More important, however, it means that there is a continual tension within even the most democratic of polities between accountability and transparency, on the one hand, and control and secrecy, on the other. The effect is to create a kind of dual state, reflecting the Janus image mentioned earlier. Centralized command powers—legitimated, as noted before, by perceived external imperatives and the logic of solidarity (i.e., the dialectic of threats and national interests, of wanting peace but preparing for war, etc.) rather than by social values and the logic of peaceful individual and/or group competition within a relatively acceptable set of rules of the game—are thus structurally hegemonic whenever a serious perceived threat arises, leading to a dispute between the supposed imperatives of "national security," on the one hand, and "civilian" values, on the other.

D. Power as Capability in a World Where Force Rules

The fourth dimension, then, that of raw power—the use of force and violence—is the ultimate arbiter of international relations, the "currency" of world politics. The influence of a particular state depends on its basic stock of potential power resources or capabilities, its ability to mobilize people and resources to fight, and its capacity to use—or threaten—force to impose its will beyond its borders. The concepts of "resources" and "capabilities" in this context are extremely fungible, however. As the Russian Empire learned in 1905 and 1914, having the biggest fleet and the largest army are not much help against a better organized and more highly motivated opponent. "Hard" capabilities themselves are often difficult to assess and measure except in actual battle situations, sometimes even leading decision makers to go to war simply to test their capabilities. Guerrilla warfare has classically been able to counter much larger conventional forces, the apparent technological superiority of American forces in Iraq and Afghanistan today is sometimes said to be an actual disadvantage against the improvised methods of insurgents, the might of the Israeli army failed faced with Lebanese resistance in 2006, and major weapons systems like nuclear missiles may be useful only to the extent that they are *not* used, as in the doctrine of deterrence and mutually assured destruction (MAD).

Even more problematic are the "soft" capabilities of strategic planning, tactical skill, efficient organization, communication, and the general psychological state of the armed forces. However, these are themselves dependent on the existence not only of an economic infrastructure that can provide the required finance, technological, and production capabilities, workforces, and so forth to supply the armed forces with effective equipment and weaponry but also of a social and human infrastructure—the sense of identity, loyalty, and belonging to the nation rather than to ethnic, family, or religious ties, warlords or mafias, particular subnational or cross-national geographical region and the like. And political resources are necessary, too—reliable and effective leadership, legitimate and efficient political institutions, and inclusive political processes. Solidarity must exist from the bottom up, not just from the top down.

The effective building, marshaling, and use of traditional forms of power are therefore highly problematic. In the traditional understanding of international power relations, the international system itself is defined as a structure of relative power based on (a) how many strong or weak states there are, or the polarity of the international system, and (b) how great the disparities are among them, or the degree of hierarchy of the system (Waltz 1979). A system with three or more strong powers is multipolar, a system with two dominant powers is bipolar, and a system with only one hegemonic power is unipolar. Alliances are precarious; an oft-quoted Chinese proverb has it that "The enemy of my enemy is my friend." In this context, the main stabilizing—and potentially destabilizing—mechanism is a balance of power among states (Little 2007).

However, balances of power are ultimately contingent. They emerge from wars, and conditions change over time. Old powers decline, new ones arise, and various kinds of reequilibration occur. In the last analysis, even when there is relative peace and stability, those conditions emerge from and are maintained by underlying relationships of force. And these relationships depend on the effectiveness of states in being capable of developing, continually modernizing, and using force—as well as *not* using it in circumstances where the very use of force has counterproductive effects, that is, where miscalculated aggression leads to defeat; where overambition leads to "imperial overstretch" (Kennedy 1987); where "planning for the last war" proves useless in the face of technological and organizational advances; where the very use of force triggers multiple layers of conflict, such as civil, cross-border, and ethnic wars; where domestic opposition to particular wars leads to defeat at home; and where the very structure and foundations of the state are threatened with destabilization, disintegration, and state failure in case of defeat. Furthermore, as I argue later, all four of the traditional dimensions of international power outlined here are increasingly coming under pressure in a globalizing world.

3. BEYOND ANARCHY AND HIERARCHY: CROSSCUTTING FORMS OF POWER IN THE WORLD ORDER

The traditional realist conceptualization of power as described here has been challenged at many levels. "Idealists," "liberal internationalists," and "liberal (or sometimes neoliberal) institutionalists" argue not only that growing interdependence among states since the First World War has led to the uneven development of a range of institutions such as the United Nations and the World Trade Organization but also that a raft of smaller specialized regimes, along with transgovernmental networks, together constitute an important and relatively autonomous superstructure that increasingly leads to cooperative outcomes (Keohane 1984; Ruggie 1993a; Slaughter 2004). Marxists have, of course, long argued that the inherently internationalized infrastructure of capitalism, rooted in the relations of production, constitutes an authoritative sociopolitical superstructure, too—a superstructure that in the era of globalization takes on an even more transnationalized form, which Gill calls the "new constitutionalism" (Gill 2003).

New critiques have also arisen to challenge the image of the inside/outside structuring of international power relations. Postmodernists perceive a fragmentation of traditional narratives of the state and the states system, but with no emerging alternative conception of power except the interaction of micro-"circuits of power" (Foucault 1980). Economic liberals and neoliberals argue that transnational market forces and new forms of market-friendly regulation at multiple levels—transnational, regional, national, and local—are creating a range of norms, practices, policies, and institutional reforms that spin new webs of power within and below—as well as across—borders.

Indeed, the global is sometimes not seen as a distinct level at all, but one that is immanent and embedded in the local, whether in terms of the organization of geography and space (Brenner, Jessop, Jones, and MacLeod 2003) or in terms of the dynamics of social and political relations at the microlevel (Sassen 2007)—the macrocosm within the microcosm. Transnational neopluralists assert that those interest groups that have the most clout today are those that can coordinate a range of multilevel transnational linkages. And constructivists and other ideas-oriented theorists argue that transnationally oriented ideologies, especially neoliberalism, are becoming increasingly embedded and hegemonic, shaping globalization, on the one hand, but also engendering potential resistance, on the other (Gills 2000).

In all these cases, analysts argue that the traditional inside/outside distinction and the vertically organized forms of power intrinsic to it are being not only eroded but also systematically crosscut by horizontal linkages, organizational forms, and power relationships, whether political, social, or economic, in increasingly complex forms of transnational interdependence. Whether this rapidly evolving state of affairs leads to or constitutes a coherent system of global governance is, of course, highly contested (Prakash and Hart 1999). But this increasingly multilayered, multilevel, or multinodal structure requires a reconfiguration of our very conception of how power is structured and how it is wielded by actors in practice—the structure and dynamics of power or, indeed, what is power in the first place? This reconfiguration involves all four dimensions of power discussed earlier.

A. Governance without Government?

In terms of the first dimension of power, debates among academic political scientists, international relations theorists, and international political economists—as well as among practitioners, policy makers, politicians, international bureaucrats, economic and financial commentators, military experts, and others—focus more and more on whether, as noted previously, some sort of system of global governance is in fact emerging. This does not constitute the equivalent of world government, of course. Indeed, the very concept of governance as it was previously used in political theory connoted not formal institutionalized structures and processes, but informal practices, indirect processes of social control, and loose and fungible structures of power, such as the "self-organizing networks" analyzed by policy network theorists (Rhodes 1996), economic sociologists, marketing specialists, and political economists (Thompson, Frances, Levačić, and Mitchell 1991; Castells 1996; Henderson, Dicken, Hess, Coe, and Yeung 2002).

It is certainly true, of course, that the underlying structures of these institutions and processes are still highly intergovernmental. They are set up by states, their decision-making members are appointed by states, and their voting arrangements most of the time reflect the relative power of states—often as determined by funding arrangements that give disproportionate power to the largest donor governments. Indeed, governments are often not bound by their decisions and have at least some sort of powers of veto and/or are able to dilute and avoid complying with institutional decisions. Nevertheless, the crystallization of new formal and informal structures, institutions, and processes is widely seen to enable the development of cooperative arrangements that are not as subject to defection as in the case of direct intergovernmental relations, not as dominated by purely national interests as unmediated foreign policy-making processes, and not as dependent on self-defense and self-help as neorealist unit actors would be (Keohane 1984).

In some cases, institutionalized processes have become relatively independent from the control of states, especially where autonomous legal processes give decision makers formal insulation from governments (Ruggie 1993a). Probably the most advanced of these regimes is the World Trade Organization (WTO) Dispute Settlement Mechanism. Of course, even here there are limitations. Only member states have legal standing to bring actions against other states for violating the requirements of membership by imposing trade protection measures, and there is no process for directly compelling compliance with the decisions of WTO panels—the only sanction is to permit the injured party or parties to impose retaliatory measures. However, outside groups and organizations are widely consulted in the dispute-settlement process—for example, some international organizations have formal observer status—and compliance can usually be negotiated rather than imposed, often *before* a formal adjudication is reached (Wolfe 2005). The result is a semiautonomous political process that pursues the goal of freer trade, for better or worse, depending on your viewpoint, on as close to a supranational basis as it is possible to reach in a world of still formally sovereign states. The clamor of states to join the WTO beyond the original 123 who participated in the Uruguay Round negotiations, including

China, and with Russia and the Ukraine among several waiting in the wings—there were 153 members as of January 2008—indicates that there is a strong consensus among the overwhelming majority of states that the benefits of membership and compliance with the rules significantly outweigh the costs.

Of course, most international regimes are less inclusive, more constrained by member governments, and/or much narrower in their remits. States often engage in venue shopping and forum shopping to find the organization they think is most likely to support their national position. But the fact that they participate in such processes on a regular basis and formulate strategies and tactics around such international and transnational rules of the game is a strong indicator that states and state actors themselves generally act to reinforce rather than undermine the process. Thus, many analysts argue, there are several characteristics that lead to the conclusion that the development of international regimes has reached some sort of critical mass in developing toward a more coherent form of global governance with significant supranational potential, at least in specific, but often structurally important, issue-areas. The resistance of the George W. Bush administration in the United States to join certain organizations such as the Kyoto Protocol on climate change has been widely seen across the world as the deviant behavior of an arrogant, warmongering regime—behavior that is, however, likely to change under the Obama administration.

The main variable propelling this process of change is usually seen to be the nature of the *policy issues and challenges* that face both states and international organizations today, challenges like global economic growth, climate change and pollution, cross-border civil and insurgent wars, increasing relative inequality, and the growing public salience of poverty and uneven development—not to mention a range of significant issues concerning particular transnationally networked economic sectors, crosscutting transportation and infrastructure issues, technological changes with global implications such as governing the Internet, and the like. The enmeshing of public and private-sector organizations, especially in issue-areas requiring international regulation, further reinforces the formal and informal roles of international regimes. Also the development of regional organizations, especially what many analysts would regard as the semisovereign European Union (EU), has taken regime development and institutionalization to a very high level on a range of issues, rules, and practices. Nevertheless, despite the EU's relatively high level of integration, not only are some of the same questions we have asked of other international regimes still relevant—especially the role of EU member states in key decision-making processes—but also other regional organizations have proved much weaker and more internally conflict-prone, making regionalization a rather uneven process in the global context.

These characteristics of a wide range of international regimes are therefore widely thought to be leading to ever-increasing potential "absolute gains" for participating actors, rather than the zero-sum "relative gains" of autonomous nation-states pursuing their national interests in the traditional way. In this context, the question of absolute versus relative gains is not merely an issue of state preferences for one or the other, the main traditional perspective (e.g., as reflected in the debates in Baldwin 1993), but rather involves the role of structured constraints and opportunities in the organization of a growing system of regimes, sometimes referred to as "neoliberal institutionalism" (Baldwin 1993; Keohane 1984 and 1989). In addition to the development of a complex if often fragmented international decision-making superstructure, then, new if still embryonic forms of transnational *quasi authority* are seen to be emerging that are increasingly rooted in crosscutting, postnational forms of legitimacy that are less rooted in national structures of accountability (see chapter 9; also see http://www2. warwick.ac.uk/fac/soc/csgr/activitiesnews/conferences/conference2007/ for a range of papers on the issue of legitimacy).

However, global governance advocates would also accept that operating in such a changing world is leading to new problems of management and control, what Lake has called "the privatization of governance" (Lake 1999; Kahler and Lake 2003), and the increasing importance of "private authority" in international affairs (Cutler, Haufler, and Porter 1999; Ronit and Schneider 2000; Hall and Biersteker 2003). Institutions and processes of global governance do not, of course, have the direct sanctioning power that has been at the core of state development and power in the modern era—especially in the form of Weber's "monopoly of legitimate violence," whether domestic or international. Their sovereignty is to some extent "pooled" rather than compromised by the development of these institutions and processes. Nevertheless, the inside-outside distinction is being increasingly—and systematically—transgressed in many significant ways, and nation-states themselves are being enmeshed in such transnational webs of semi-institutionalized power despite the ad hoc and fragmentary nature of the process.

B. New Forms of Transnational Legitimacy

In terms of the second dimension of power, the goals of social, political, and economic actors increasingly reflect normative values beyond just national defense, the pursuit of national interests, or the position of the state in an international pecking order as determined by relations of force and balances of power. The key to this change lies in the same driving force that is reinforcing the practical impact and quasi authority of international regimes—that is, the changing nature of the crosscutting challenges that states, regimes, interest groups, value coalitions, private sector actors, and the like face in the global era.

The increasing integration of transnational economic markets has led to the emergence of cross-border interest groups, both formal and informal, including groups representing such economic or sectional interests as multinational corporations; financial market actors, banks, accountants, auditors, investors, bondholders, and today social groups affected by the U.S. subprime mortgage crisis; coalitions of farmers, small businesses, and the like affected by the need to operate in global markets; and even trade unions and other social groups affected by global economic change. Furthermore, international awareness of and concern about issues of social justice, poverty, and the power of abusive and/or corrupt elites have led to the rapid growth of "value" groups (Key 1953) or "transnational advocacy coalitions" (Keck and Sikkink 1998), now widely referred to as "global civil society," often with close relationships with more socially oriented international regimes.

Among the most potent themes of global civil society groups are human rights and human security. In other words, these groups have been successfully redefining two of the most important social and political issue-areas of the modern world for the traditional legitimation of nation-states themselves—stemming from the Enlightenment—as having a primordially international and even global dimension. Human rights—the international equivalent of civil rights, one of the most important value issue-areas where democratic states have in the past claimed to represent the most elemental underlying interests and values of their citizens—are now being internationalized. And security, since time immemorial, the overwhelmingly predominant rationale for the state to retain and pursue power, especially military power, in the international arena, is being reclaimed for the world as a whole—a qualitative leap beyond the rather crude and often stalemated twentieth-century notions of collective security represented by the League of Nations and the United Nations. And perhaps most salient of all, given the recent growth of concern with issues like climate change and the increasingly obvious effects of global warming, have been environmental groups. These groups have come to occupy a particularly central place in the claim to represent people in general across borders, not only transcending the nation-state but also calling for global solutions to deal with a growing, imperative crisis.

Crosscutting forms of power and influence are therefore being, and will continue to be, used more and more to pursue goals of fairness (Kapstein 2006), transnational economic regulation (Jordana and Levi-Faur 2005),

"green" environmental policy (Kütting 2004), human rights, multiculturalism, corporate governance (Gourevitch and Shinn 2005), criminal behavior
by governments (e.g., the International Criminal Court), excessive use of
force (e.g., the Ottawa Convention on the Prohibition of the Use, Stockpiling,
Production and Transfer of Anti-Personnel Mines and on Their Destruction),
and many others, in a cross-border, transnational context. The pursuit of
social justice and even social and economic redistribution is no longer limited to the arena or container of the nation-state, and new forms of political
and social action requiring the linking of local, national, regional, and international interest and value groups across borders (Tarrow 2005), along with
the building of transnational coalitions to push for transnational policies
and solutions, are becoming increasingly significant. Political, social, and
economic power is being harnessed transnationally in ways previously disqualified by the inside/outside distinction.

C. Reorganizing Power

In terms of the third dimension, therefore, power is clearly increasingly
being *organized* in crosscutting, transnational ways. In addition to the proliferation and expansion of international regimes and global governance—
the most obvious but problematic public face of this reorganization
process—transnational circuits of power are increasingly organizing
around sectors and issue-areas rather than around holistic national interests. Of course, many of these organizational trends are still embryonic, and
actors based in nation-states still play key roles, but the general direction of
change is clear.

In economic sectors characterized by the growing significance of multinational or transnational corporations, the ability of these corporations
to coordinate their own actions across borders—in pressing for regulatory
changes, playing off tax jurisdictions, and so on—is just the tip of the iceberg. Even small firms that seem ostensibly local are not immune, being
dependent on foreign raw materials, export markets, investment finance,
migrant labor, and the like, and increasingly form nodes of wider networks and coordinate their actions. As a result, in addition to the journalistically salient phenomenon of the offshoring of jobs and its impact on
local employment in downsized firms, people of all social classes and
groups are becoming enmeshed in increasingly complex and subtle ways
in international production processes, technological developments, markets, and consumer preferences. In other words, the organization of the
world of work—once embedded in the Fordist factory system—increasingly depends on flexible, complex transnational economic activities and
circuits of political-economic power. Ordinary people in everyday life are

growing more and more aware that their fates depend not so much on decisions taken at the national level but on wider developments and trans-formations at international, transnational, and translocal levels (Hobson and Seabrooke 2007).

Less formal networks and more formal interaction among firms, "private regimes," "alliance capitalism," and the ability of nonstate actors in general to develop a range of formal and informal interconnections, both economic and political, have led to significant degrees of policy transfer both across states and in terms of shaping the evolution of global governance more broadly (Higgott, Underhill and Bieler 1999; Evans 2005). The linking of financial markets and institutions across borders has led to far-reaching changes in market organization, including cross-border mergers and con-vergence of market practices. Financial crises have played a large part in catalyzing these organizational changes, as demonstrated by global fallout from the subprime mortgage crisis in the United States. Significant issue-areas such as accountancy, auditing, and corporate governance have led to ongoing negotiation processes among firms; private-sector organizations representing particular industrial, financial, and commercial sectors; and governments and international regimes to reconcile conflicting standards and move toward a more level playing field (Mügge 2006).

Not only have government agencies redefined their aims and objectives in the light of transnational experience—interacting increasingly through transgovernmental networks among governmental agencies and public and private policy communities—but also value-oriented and sectional pressure groups organized across borders have, as noted previously, come to the fore in a number of key issue-areas, such as the attempt to expand "corporate social responsibility" agreements and standards (Lipschutz 2005). These processes are uneven but ongoing. In this context, the organi-zation of power is increasingly *horizontally stratified according to issue-area*, mainly structured through economic and social linkages across borders, and therefore less amenable to control and centralization through the state. Indeed the "splintered state" (Machin and Wright 1985) or "disaggregated state" (Slaughter 2004) is characterized by horizontal cross-border power relationships, too.

D. Changing Forms of Force and Violence

The fourth dimension—the use of force and violence—has also undergone fundamental change (see chapter 12). The end of the cold war did not result so much from the breakdown of a particular balance of power as from the increasing ineffectiveness of interstate balances of power generally to regu-late the international system. Both cold war superpowers became weaker in systemic terms because traditional forms of power could not cope with the challenges of the late-twentieth-century international order. This change has entailed not merely the replacement of interstate competition for military security by new forms of interstate competition, such as for economic security or even what Nye has called "soft power," which is merely a mode of projecting traditional national forms of state power by different means (Nye 2004). Rather, it involves a much more far-reaching realization that *security based on the simple interaction of unitary nation-states itself is becoming a cause of even greater insecurity.* This risk is represented not only from above, by a general threat of uncontrollable nuclear annihilation—the core problematic of the bipolar balance of the cold war itself—but also from below, by the rise of civil wars, tribal and religious conflicts, terrorism, civil violence in developed countries, the international drugs trade, state collapse, and more.

The very provision of security as a public good—the raison d'être of the Westphalian states system—can no longer be guaranteed by that system. Changing payoff matrices are creating a range of incentives for players—especially nonstate players—to defect from the states system itself unless restrained from doing so by the constraints of complex interdependence. Attempts to provide international and domestic security through the state and the states system are becoming increasingly dysfunctional. Such attempts both lead to increasing "imperial overstretch" and provoke severe backlashes at both local and transnational levels—what has been called "blowback" (Johnson 2004)—creating a double bind for states seeking to exercise traditional forms of power. These backlashes interact with economic and social processes of complex globalization to create overlapping and competing cross-border networks of power, shifting loyalties and identities, and new sources of endemic low-level conflict. According to Gallarotti, they even lead to what he calls the "power curse": that states with extensive traditional capabilities are turning into Goliaths in a world containing a growing range and diversity of Davids (Gallarotti 2009).

A combination of economic interpenetration and low-level conflict—along with the post-Vietnam "body bag syndrome" in the most powerful countries (including the United States in the wake of the Iraq War), leading to popular revulsion at more ineffective forms of state-based military action—is taking over the kind of systemic regulatory role played by interstate conflict and competition in the Westphalian system. These factors increasingly constrain and counteract traditional forms of power projection—without, however, replacing them with an effective mechanism for resolving the problems of ethnic conflict, state failure, local or regional economic crises, and the like in the developing world. "New wars" and low-level conflicts can escape or undermine the constraints of balances of power, big power intervention, UN peacekeeping, and formal international borders (Kaldor 1999). Emerging mechanisms of stabilization are therefore highly uneven, riddled with structural tensions, and suboptimal in terms of effective governance, although in quite different ways from traditional balances of power and the old interstate "security dilemma" (Herz 1950).

The future of military force as the bottom line of power is itself being questioned once again, but in a rather different way from earlier forms of extragovernmental pacifism and antiwar protest. As noted previously, a rather different model of the pursuit of different kinds of power *by states themselves* has potentially been emerging as the result of long-term change in and experience of international war and power relations over the past fifty to a hundred years. In particular, there has been a transformation in European attitudes and foreign policy across the board as the result of having been the cradle of two devastating world wars and the geographical epicenter of the cold war. This transformation involves a shift toward a combination of demilitarization and multilateralism—reinforced by the regionalism of the European Union but primordially rooted in the experiences of European nation-states—as the new, core organizing principles of the international system (Sheehan 2008; Moravcsik 2007).

Europe's identity as a new model "civilian superpower" (Galtung 1973), reflected not only in the foreign policies of Germany and other states but also in the attitudes of elites and mass publics (Harnisch and Maull 2001), is an expression of a widespread and expanding normative perspective that the use of force in international relations is just as immoral and counterproductive for both society and individuals as is the use of force by private actors domestically. There is as yet no equivalent of Weber's "legitimate monopoly of violence" at the international level, and yet at the same time, the use of traditional forms of power by states is becoming increasingly delegitimized. For example, the counterproductive use of force by the United States in the "global war on terror" in the name of state security and the *heimat* (homeland) has paradoxically been a catalyst in expanding calls for what might be labeled the "domestication of power" in the international system. For example, it is widely held outside the United States— and increasingly inside, too—that terrorism is fundamentally a "law and order" question that is best addressed by domestic-style police powers and legal methods, rather than by labeling terrorists as "enemy combatants" and pursuing them militarily as if they constituted a traditional statelike international threat. The drive for American hegemony and empire that was represented by the George W. Bush administration may prove to be the last hurrah for the use of traditional state-based methods of power and force in the international arena.

4. CONCLUSIONS: THE FUTILITY OF FORCE
AND THE ASCENT OF POLITICS

Power at the international level has traditionally been seen as constituting the underlying structural dynamic of the international system—beyond and outside the bounds of domestically rooted relationships of "friendship" and "justice," and ultimately manifested in the real or latent use of force, that is, through war or the threat of war. Power in this traditional sense has been embodied by and embedded in nation-states, the fundamental building blocks and unit actors of international relations. That conception of power has been seen as stemming from or reflecting the lack of world government and therefore the "anarchy" of a system within which the highest authorities have been states themselves, pursuing their national interests and seeking to affirm their place in the international pecking order. It has involved a limited form of power—power in and of itself, organized by states, rooted in the use of force—rather than as a means to a higher collective end.

Today, the international system is undergoing a fundamental process of structural change that is transforming the way power is conceived, shaped, built up, organized, and used. This process of the reconfiguration of power increasingly cuts across state borders and is embedded in new but still embryonic forms of global governance, reflecting the sort of "higher" normative values that domestic actors have always pursued at home, shaped by transnational interests and global civil society rather than interstate conflict, organized through transnational and transgovernmental networks rather than unified foreign policy elites and military command structures, and informed by a growing sense that the use of force is becoming increasingly counterproductive in an international system characterized by complex interdependence—and, indeed, that international power must be increasingly civilianized and domesticated to be both effective and legitimate in a globalizing world. Given the increasingly counterproductive and delegitimized character of power in a globalizing world, transnational actors linked across borders are not merely taking advantage of new permissive conditions but are driving further change, both proactively and in feedback fashion.

Part II

DYNAMICS OF CHANGE

Chapter 5

Multinodal Politics

A Framework for Analysis

1. WHY MULTINODAL POLITICS?

Today a number of factors, including ethnic and religious ties, multiculturalism, transnational communities, and the internationalization of production, consumption, and finance, have fostered the emergence of a vast range of alternative sources of economic advantage, political influence, and social identity. These varied processes of change, usually brought together under the label of globalization, include the development of denser relations among states ("internationalization"), growing below-the-border dealings cutting across states ("transnationalization"), denser interactions among localities and regions ("translocalization" or "glocalization"), and the transformation of social, economic, and political relations and processes at the domestic and local levels themselves—the macrocosm within the microcosm. More important than any one of these levels, however, are the *interaction effects* among them, which is where transnational neopluralism is most significant in shaping change.

This overall process of transformation, I suggest, has three main interlocking dimensions. The first and most obvious involves a change in the character of the state's domestic "functions"—that is, its tasks, roles, and activities. This involves, first and foremost, the way so-called public goods are perceived, pursued, and provided (Cerny 1999a). In particular, the aim of social justice through redistribution and protectionism has been challenged and profoundly undermined by the marketization and transnationalization of the state's economic activities (and of the state itself) and by a new embedded financial orthodoxy. These changes not only constrain the state in its economic policies but also alter people's understanding of what politics is for, thereby challenging the political effectiveness of the very national liberal-democratic political systems that are supposed to represent what the people want.

The second dimension involves a fundamental reorientation of how states interact economically. State actors are increasingly concerned with promoting the competitive advantages of particular production and service sectors in a more open and integrated world economy—the Competition State—not only to produce collective economic gains but also to build new coalitions and expand the scope and reach of their own power and influence. In pursuing international competitiveness, state agencies closely linked with those economic sectors most closely integrated into the world economy increasingly accept, and indeed embrace, those complex interdependencies and transnational linkages thought to be the most promising sources of profitability and economic prosperity in a rapidly globalizing world.

The third dimension concerns the relationship between structure and agency in general, in other words, people—that is, between constraints embedded in existing structural and institutional rules, existing patterns of the distribution of resources and power, and existing practices and ways of doing things, on the one hand, and those individuals and groups who make tactical and strategic decisions, day-to-day or over the long term, that can alter or break those rules, patterns, and practices, directly or indirectly, intentionally or unintentionally, on the other. Rather than continuing path dependency, these effects generate multiple equilibria, creating the possibility of new branching points and thus opening the way to potential path modification and reconstruction of the system itself. It is crucial to identify these structural faults and explore the potential constraints and opportunities that actors may face in attempts to manipulate and reshape the structure of the system.

This process does not merely concern those global ideologists in business studies, important as they are, who declare that we live in a borderless world, or just the rapid growth of transnational cause pressure groups like Greenpeace who focus on the problems of "the planet." It also involves strategic action across both public and private domains, not only for more concrete competitive advantages in the world marketplace but also for reshaping social and political processes and institutions to reflect both new distributions of power and resources—"distributional effects"—and new ways of looking at the world or "social epistemologies" (cf. Ruggie 1993b; Deibert 1997).

In this process, for example, the focus of the economic mission of the state has shifted considerably from its traditional concern with production and producer groups to one involving market structures and consumer groups, and from its understanding of the role of the state in general as a "decommodifying agent" to that of a "commodifying agent"—that is, con-ʳned with making markets work better and more efficiently rather than ᵕcing them with authoritative allocation mechanisms. In this context, ᶜtors have found their roles changing as the state itself has become more splintered and disaggregated. Indeed, the density and complexity of state actors' interactions with other political, social, and economic actors has also increased, together with the density and complexity of the objects of their concerns. These include the dramatic expansion of transnational socio-economic interpenetration; the immediacy of global economic, social, environmental, and security challenges; the evolution of transnational communication and norms; and the limits of traditional forms of national power projection.

Nevertheless, the state will not wither away. Indeed, in some ways it will continue to expand and develop its tasks, roles, and activities. The crucial point, however, is that those tasks, roles, and activities will not just be different; rather, they will lose much of the overarching, macroauthoritative, and superior normative philosophical character traditionally ascribed to the effective state, the good state, or the just state. All of these concepts have assumed a level and quality of internal coherence and of difference from the external "other" that the state's most essential—and most ideologically and culturally legitimate—task has been to protect. Future structural developments, however, will be the product of an increasingly transnational, cross-cutting structure of micro- and meso-interdependencies, partially mediated through the state but with their own autonomous—neopluralist—dynamics, too. In the long run, state actors must adapt their own strategies to both perceived and material global realities, while other kinds of actors, economic and social, will play key roles, too, in restructuring the political arena.

2. RESTRUCTURING THE POLITICAL ARENA: THE PROCESS OF STRUCTURATION

In this context, it is crucial to be able to explain not only the political behavior of groups and actors but also wider and more long-term structural change. Most theories of globalization have privileged material explanations of structural change. The prevalent image is that of a shrinking world. Changes in exogenous conditions are seen in turn to alter human behavior in ways that are broadly predictable because their patterns are determined by the underlying material or ideational morphology of those exogenous conditions per se. Exogenous structural variables promoting globalization include the infrastructure of travel and transportation, competitive imperatives facing the multinational corporation, the abstract and all-pervading character of international finance, the flexibility of post-Fordist production techniques, the innovation and spread of information and communications technology, a general speeding up of the tempo of life and consciousness, the development of a cultural global village, and the indivisible ecology of the planet. Nevertheless, attempts to extrapolate future world orders from such structural changes are highly problematic. They never really capture the range of possibilities—possibilities that are shaped by actors.

In contrast, most agency-centered approaches, particularly constructivism, have shied away from grappling with the structural or material aspects of globalization. They go too far in the other direction. Constructivists' overemphasis on the potential autonomy of ideas and institutions, in particular, has paradoxically turned the attention of scholars away from broad paradigmatic change and focused discussion on limited debates about the ideational character of existing institutions, incremental changes within the existing states system, and/or the possibilities for resistance within the current world order. Much of today's constructivism in international relations, far from reflecting the transformational epistemological vision of Berger and Luckmann's original "social constructivist" critique of functionalist social theory (Berger and Luckmann 1966), seems content to challenge the hard material-structural character of neorealism with a soft classical realism of a more historical and ideational type (e.g., Wendt 1992), while nevertheless allowing national actors greater scope for international regime-building within that context (Finnemore 1996). In addition, postmodernism, poststructuralism, and postpositivism, while taking a more critical stance, have nevertheless had little to say about the globalization process except as a potential negation of modernism and positivism.

In contrast to both the determinism of structuralism and the indeterminacy of constructivism, this chapter starts from the structurationist view that structure and agency are mutually constituted in an ongoing process that simultaneously both (a) consolidates and yet fractures structures and (b) constrains and yet empowers agents, in a reciprocal, interactive process over time (Giddens 1979). The concept of structuration has been interpreted in various ways, and critics often tend to see it as breaking down when operationalized. In other words, structuration-based approaches are usually said to end up either privileging *either* structures *or* actors or, indeed, reifying the process of interaction between them. Nevertheless, a more modest application of structuration as an analytical concept can be a useful starting point for process tracing. In this context, actors are conceived of as acting within (unevenly) structured *sets of constraints and opportunities*, as in Michel Crozier and Erhard Friedberg's concept of "structured fields of action" (Crozier and Friedberg 1977). At the same time, however, those sets of constraints and opportunities are themselves conceived of hypothetically as the *cumulative products of agency* and, in different ways, vulnerable to political action in an ~ngoing interactive process.

'o construct a preliminary simplified representation of the structuration 's, some typological distinctions are useful. Structures, whether static or

Table 5.1 Structuration Processes

* Structural Coherence Actor Orientation	Tight	Loose
Structure-bound	Type 1: Routine adjustment	Type 2: Incremental adaptation
Transformative	Type 3: Punctuated equilibria	Type 4: Articulated restructuring

changing, can be characterized as either uneven and loosely held together, on the one hand, or tightly woven and homogeneous, on the other. Agents, in turn, can act either in structure-bound or merely adaptive ways, on the one hand, or in entrepreneurial and potentially transformational ways, on the other. In this sense, I would suggest a stylized heuristic typology of *four ideal-type structuration processes*, as represented in the two-by-two matrix in table 5.1

This typology is based on four interrelated hypotheses, each represented in one of the ideal-type structuration processes set out in the table.

- In the first place, where structure-bound actors are situated within a tightly woven structural context (Type 1), the interaction between structure and agency would tend to be of a fairly static, *routine* kind, predominantly leading to passive or merely reactive *adjustment* to exogenous structural changes. Indeed, such changes should be robustly predictable from knowledge of its exogenous sources.
- Second, where structure-bound actors are situated within a loosely articulated structure (Type 2), a form of *incremental adaptation* analogous to certain kinds of traditional Darwinian random selection might be anticipated. However, actors would be likely to have some limited opportunities (wiggle room) for creative adaptation and institutional bricolage, especially in the face of exogenous changes but in reaction to consequent endogenous changes as well.
- Third, where change-oriented or transformative actors—those whose understandings, visions, and knowledge enable them to transcend existing structural constraints in developing their strategies and tactics—are situated within a tightly woven structure (Type 3), one might expect an uneven structuration process in which both exogenous and endogenous pressures for change would build up over time and lead to *punctuated equilibria*. The result would be

unpredictable conjunctural upheavals—"black (or gray) swans" or "fat tails" (Taleb 2007)—the outcomes of which can take a variety of different forms from reequilibration to structural degradation to revolutionary change.

- Fourth, where transformative or change-oriented actors are situated within a loosely held-together structure (Type 4), possibilities for actor-orchestrated, purposive *articulated restructuring* would be greater. Such opportunities for transformative change would be accompanied, however, by increased uncertainty about how controllable different component parts of the structure might be (especially under strong exogenous structural pressures); managed change can give way to instability and volatility.

With the partial exception of Type 1 structuration—routine adjustment—therefore, even the tightest exogenously led processes of structural change generate multiple equilibria that actors can, to some extent, manipulate or reshape. Indeed, even routine adjustments can sometimes build up incrementally into wider changes. Meanwhile, endogenous processes of change become more central to the process; it is not merely exogenous independent variables that cause change and transformation, but endogenous ones as well. In this context, globalization entails not only *permissive conditions* for change—not restrictive ones, despite (or because of) increasing uncertainty—but also *causative conditions*, especially in terms of actors' values, goals, strategies, and tactics, assuming that actors themselves are capable of conceiving of and pursuing their goals and strategies in conscious and psychologically autonomous fashion. Structuralism and constructivism, material and ideational variables, and actors located within more or less manipulable sets of constraints and opportunities are in constant interaction and inextricably intertwined in ongoing historical processes.

3. THE FIVE STAGES OF STRUCTURATION: POSTFEUDALISM AND GLOBALIZATION IN COMPARATIVE PERSPECTIVE

To put this approach into perspective, I next now outline a five-stage model of change, adapted from a format originally developed by Hendrik Spruyt in the context of the European transition from feudalism to the sovereign nation-state (Spruyt 1994). Spruyt actually identified three stages of transition, which I expand to five. He calls this process one of "institutional selection," the core of which is the identification of multiple equilibria—in other words, the existence of multiple alternative potential future developmental pathways generated by the decline of the feudal system. He identifies three of these alternative pathways: the city-state on the Venetian model; the city-league, based on the Hanseatic League in northern Europe; and the sovereign nation-state, based on the centralizing Bourbon monarchy in France. Had the early, relatively centralized French state not been as bureaucratically and economically strong as it was in the fourteenth through seventeenth centuries as the result of factors unique to its previous historical development—plus the innovative, transformative actions of key state and socioeconomic actors like Colbert—other models might have proven more resilient, leading to either the continued coexistence or concurrence, whether stable or unstable, of diverse postfeudal succession models in Europe, as had been characteristic of the so-called Dark Ages or, indeed, to the dominance of one of the other models.

However, the ability of French state actors in particular to pursue a more centralized economic development strategy at home and to make reliable and durable contractual arrangements, formal and informal, binding on other domestic groups, on the one hand, and to deal effectively with external actors internationally through a coherent and unified foreign and security policy, on the other, reinforced and enlarged the dual capacity of the French state as (a) an arena of collective action domestically and (b) a source of credible commitments. The effectiveness of these developments, along with the size of domestic French resources in its economy and population, in turn led to a process of emulation by dominant groups in other protostates in order to ensure their survival, prosperity, and political power. Thus the nation-state itself as an institutional construct was reproduced and imitated by actors seeking to defend and promote their own interests and values in a fluid, unsettled, and complex set of historical circumstances. This process is identifiable with hindsight but was relatively open and extremely unpredictable within the ebb and flow of events and choices at the time—until, at a later stage, the system of states crystallized in Europe itself and eventually spread outward through empire and emulation.

This developmental route did not, of course, emerge and crystallize in a vacuum. Previous elements of the old feudal system remained, although their position was altered, often for the worse, but sometimes finding new sources of power and influence—for example, the Roman Catholic Church and the aristocracy (Mayer 1981). But many new trends were already in place, too, such as:

- urbanization and the migration of former serfs from the countryside
- the development of new productive technologies, including artisan manufacture with innovative tools, machinery, and contractual relationships between managers and workers, especially in the expanding cities

- the growth of broader social organizations such as guilds rooted in those emerging forms of production, along with local governments representing such new corporatist interests
- the development of consumer demand, along with demands for more influence on the political and social front from a variety of groups—more affluent nobles, the growing urban middle classes and *lumpen proletariat*, increasingly independent sectors of the peasantry, and merchants involved in burgeoning long-distance trade (what Spruyt calls "translocal trade" to indicate that it was not yet fully "international"), among others
- the development of the common law in England and the rediscovery of Roman law on the European continent, both of which put intergroup relations on a more formal and organized institutional footing
- new forms of warfare, more efficiently organized and controlled from the top down, first by France and then by Prussia on land, and by the Netherlands and England on the sea

Indeed, the transition from feudalism to the nation-state laid the groundwork for a first phase of globalization led by the most powerful states themselves, through their later frustration at the territorial carving up of Europe and consequent quest for overseas empire.

Five stylized stages of this process can be distinguished. Of course, these phases do not succeed each other neatly; they are uneven, overlapping, often largely concurrent, and inextricably intertwined. The first involves what Spruyt calls *exogenous independent variables*—although these, too, were the result of earlier developmental processes and multiple equilibria. In this case, typical exogenous independent variables included:

- the emergence of artisan manufacture
- the growing monetization of labor and exchange
- new forms of transportation such canals, long-distance roads, and bigger, faster sailing ships
- technological developments like early mechanics
- the expansion of translocal and long-distance trade
- the rapid growth of food production in the late feudal era before its decline and economic crisis, and its later revival (Anderson 1975; Tuchman 1978; Holton 1985)
- the development of long-distance financial relationships (Kindleberger 1984)

In other words, European feudalism in its later stages itself underwent accelerating and increasingly dramatic changes analogous to globalization today, as the political structures and institutions of medieval society were overtaken by the transformation of the socioeconomic infrastructure (Anderson 1974 and 1975). Patterns of production, trade, finance, and labor—what today are often taken for proxy variables for economic globalization, and sometimes globalization tout court—were being transformed across Europe, pointing to the emergence of what would prove to be a set of *permissive preconditions* for the fundamental social, political, and economic transitions that were about to take place. It is crucial to remember, of course, that these exogenous independent variables were themselves not truly "exogenous" with regard to their own development. They were not the emanations of some sort of underlying, spontaneous, material structural change. Rather they resulted from the interactions of various actors at various stages of the development of the feudal system itself.

The second stage in my list (i.e., linking Spruyt's first stage and my third stage, which follows and is also Spruyt's second stage) flows from the first stage and concerns key *distributional changes*. In other words, this stage stems from the exogenous independent variables listed previously as mediated by and through key groups of actors. In particular, structural changes like those just outlined lead to, and are inextricably intertwined with, changing distributions of resources, and therefore of power and influence, during the period of transition—shaping yet more distributional changes further down the line.

Two sorts of distributional changes can be identified, although they are again often intertwined in practice. The first concerns the partial, but highly significant, ways that the amount and distribution of political power and material resources previously commanded by actors embedded in the old system are adapted and converted by those actors into new forms of power and influence—both in the period of transition and in the succeeding phase of consolidation, whether the nation-state is in the postfeudal period or in the emerging global (dis)order of the twenty-first century. In the postfeudal transition, such "old" groups as nobles and religious hierarchies increasingly bureaucratized and monetized their holdings, especially through the development of private property rights in land and the marketization of their products. Leading nobles sought to increase and entrench their power through the development of centralized monarchies and through more highly organized forms of taxation and warfare. And peasants sought greater control over their work and rewards from their labor, whether in the fields or through migration to the newly expanding cities.

Second, of course, "new" groups emerged and sought to develop innovative ways to increase their wealth and power. Urban entrepreneurs and internationally active merchants were able to control the rapidly growing productive sectors of the economy, obtain greater profits, and invest in new forms of production, distribution, and exchange. Bankers and financiers became increasingly crucial to the translocalization of production, trade, and consumption. Urban laborers, although usually at the sharp end of any direct confrontations, became increasingly able to use new skills and the capacity to vote with their feet to live better—at least better than they had as serfs—and to seek upward social mobility. And a petty bourgeoisie of shopkeepers, clerks, supervisors, bureaucrats, and what would later be called the intelligentsia became more and more central to social change and economic development.

Most important, however, were the political consequences, as these groups in transition—both "old" and "new"—sought more influence over entrenched feudal elites and over the outcomes of political and legal processes, especially through the expansion of private property rights, regulatory backing and protection from market failure, the opening of overseas markets, and, most important—the source of the British, French, and American revolutions of the seventeenth and eighteenth centuries, not to mention the many more since—more "voice" in governmental processes.

Absolutist monarchies lasted only so long as they promoted and reinforced these trends. They were eventually overthrown when they were seen as not doing so by large enough coalitions. This was not democracy yet, but it was a new embryonic pluralism. It is this second stage that I argue constitutes the closest analogy to globalization today, rooted in corresponding distributional changes at the transnational level. In particular, the shift from traditional forms of political and economic hegemony of sectors of society who made their living from the land, to those who increasingly made it through early industrial production and translocal trade is not dissimilar to today's shift from the hegemony of those groups whose power and influence derived from their domestic dominance, whether national-level corporations, national bureaucracies, or national trade union organizations, to those whose political and economic clout and muscle derive from the transnational scale and scope of their activities and networks, whether multinational producers, financial market actors, consumers, or, increasingly, workers. Nevertheless, elements of the third, fourth, and fifth stages are not far behind.

The third stage, deriving from the second, is what Spruyt calls the *rearticulation of social and political coalitions*. This represents the heart of the pluralist political process itself. The fluid and volatile distributional changes just described in turn lead actors to seek new ways of pursuing their interests and furthering their values through shifting alliances and seeking new forms of influence in both public and private arenas. In the transition from feudalism to the nation-state and the states system in Europe, this rearticulation of coalitions concerned in particular the ability of the following groups to expand their influence:

- Rising urban classes challenged the monopoly of power of the aristocracy.
- Various sections of the aristocracy, old and new, forged alliances with sections of the bourgeoisie to convert their previous power resources to ones more relevant to changes in the economy, in the growing bureaucracy, and in emerging nation-state-based practices of diplomacy, warfare, and imperialism.
- Monarchies converted their power bases from personal ties of feudal obligation to more formal bureaucratic hierarchies, especially for taxing and spending and for modernizing military hierarchies, and sought new forms of support for these changes, sometimes from sectors of the aristocracy, sometimes from the new middle classes, and sometimes even from the emerging masses, through patriotism, religion, or national "defense of the realm," as well as economic expansion.
- Value groups, whether religious, liberal, or revolutionary, interacted more and more systematically with (and against) each other and a range of diverse competitors and collaborators.

As newspaper editor Charles Dudley Warner famously said in 1870 (following Shakespeare): "Politics makes strange bedfellows"—especially in times of transition and change. It is this process of the rearticulation of social and political coalitions that lies at the heart of Barrington Moore Jr.'s magisterial *Social Origins of Dictatorship and Democracy* (1966) and Theda Skocpol's *States and Social Revolutions* (1979), chronicling how diverse groups competed for control and influence in the consolidating nation-states of the seventeenth through nineteenth centuries. Today, analogous alliances among diverse transnationally linked groups, cutting across private and public sectors, involving both sectional groups pursuing common material interests and/or those value groups often referred to collectively as "global civil society," are increasingly driving the globalization process.

The fourth stage, again inextricably linked and overlapping with the third, involves a shift from the emergence of reactive and adaptive forms of competition and coalition building in the context of structural change to new *proactive strategic and substantive forms*. This stage is characterized by the uneven but sometimes rapid, and increasingly imperative, search for the stabilization of more successful experiments in resource and influence building, for more regularized control of reconfigured policy-making processes, and for new, more systematic policy agendas. In particular, during the long transition to the nation-state and the states system, European political, economic, and social actors experimented with new ways to:

- promote economic growth and ultimately industrialization
- entrench property rights
- regulate trade and finance
- develop new police powers to control urbanization and protest
- resolve conflicts through more elaborate and autonomous legal mechanisms
- deal with growing problems of mass society through labor regulation and embryonic forms of welfare
- pursue economic and social as well as security goals in the new, highly competitive international system of state consolidation and imperial expansion

These new forms of competition and coalition building involved attempts not only to gain power or pursue interests within a system in transition but also to reform and reinvent various aspects of the system itself, however incrementally, in order to entrench those interests and goals. Crucial to all of these developments was innovation in different forms of government intervention in the economy and the reinforcement at both ideational and organizational levels of what Foucault calls *raison d'État*. Today, political competition over—once again—economic growth (and decline) not only of the system as a whole but also of particular sectors and regions; over regulation of trade, finance, labor, and migration; and over the nature of political bonds themselves is bringing into question basic assumptions of social belonging and legitimacy; the distribution of resources, power, and influence; and the increasing hegemony of *raison du monde* in a rapidly globalizing world.

The fifth stage—Spruyt's third stage—is what he calls *institutional selection* proper. It is not enough to rearticulate social and political coalitions, to develop new policy agendas, or to reform the system in an ad hoc way in the context of such far-reaching change. It is necessary to rethink and reconfigure the very institutional superstructure of society and politics itself more systematically. In the transition from feudalism to the modern nation-state, and in the development of the modern state itself, this meant building a more centralized (or centripetal) state, reflecting both Waltz's distinction between the "anarchy" of the international arena and the "hierarchy" of the domestic state, on the one hand, and Foucault's *raison d'État*, on the other.

These two dimensions were mutually reinforcing. In the nation-state era, to make credible commitments, pursue national interests, and project state power on the international stage, it was necessary to develop central military command-and-control systems; promote and build up industrial production and economic autonomy more generally; expand infrastructure for transportation, communications, and weapons production; and construct more efficient taxation and national banking systems to provide funding. All of these developments went alongside a redefinition of citizenship, the promotion of patriotism and loyalty to central institutions—not merely personal fealty to the monarch or nobility—and, eventually, the expansion of popular forms of legitimacy through parliamentary representation and ultimately the mass franchise. Crucial to all of these were the development of constitutionalism and of mechanisms of state economic intervention and the institutionalization of legal systems and the rule of law in general.

Today, of course, we are in a relatively provisional stage of the development of international institutions and regimes, a stage in which different regimes and agencies are often set up for distinct issue-areas and the political processes associated with them are weak, as well as divided. There is no overarching authoritative, supranational institutional structure. The United Nations, in particular, is hobbled by its highly intergovernmental structure. International, transnational, and global institutions are in the midst of a process of institutional bricolage—that is, a combination of ad hoc experimentation in a fluid institutional context and, in particular, conjunctural circumstances, on the one hand, with a combination of pragmatic adjustment and strategic action, on the other. This institutional bricolage is similar to what I have elsewhere called, following Foucault, *governmentalization*. I return to this theme in more detail in chapter 9.

Today's process of institutional selection is nevertheless at the core of the development of so-called global governance. "Governance" is itself a contested concept, originally consisting of informal practices, networks, and power structures. On one level, however, in the context of international institutions and regimes, global governance has been redefined to include more formal institutions, such as the International Monetary Fund, the World Bank, the World Trade Organization, and a range of others, although usually restricted to particular issue-areas. However, the coherence, capacity, and control span of such institutions and processes are seen to be tentative, uneven, and open to a wide range of multiple equilibria over the coming decades. On another level, too, institutional selection is also at the heart of the transformation of the state itself into a Competition State. Nevertheless, the institutional selection process is still in an embryonic and fluid state overall.

4. THE PROBLEM OF PUBLIC GOODS AND THE NOTION OF THE "PUBLIC" IN A GLOBALIZING WORLD

The process of structuration today is therefore a complex one in which different kinds of existing—and transformed—structures and institutions interact with an expanding and increasingly diverse set of actors seeking to pursue their interests and values. There are two fundamental structural shifts to be considered here. In the first place, the state has traditionally been perceived to be inextricably intertwined, even coterminous, with the very concept of the "public," in terms of both the classical notion of the "public interest" and the contemporary quasi-economic concept of "public goods." I argue that the constitution of the public itself is being transformed in the context of political (as well as economic and social) globalizing trends. Second, I address the institutional framework and the changing roles of the state.

Broadly speaking, however, the power structure of a globalizing world is inevitably becoming more complex and diffuse over time, diffracted through a "prismatic" structure of socioeconomic forces and levels of governance (Riggs 1964). World politics is consequently being transformed into a polycentric or multinucleated global political system, operating within an increasingly continuous geographical space and/or set of overlapping spaces. In these conditions, it becomes harder to maintain the boundaries that are necessary for the efficient "packaging" of public or collective goods. Indeed, it becomes harder to even determine what collective goods are demanded or required in the first place—that is, to measure what is called the "preferred state of affairs" (Ostrom, Tiebout, and Warren 1961). State actors themselves paradoxically act in routine ways to refashion and even undermine the holistic and hierarchical character of traditional state sovereignty, authority, or *potestas*. The result is a growing quasi privatization of the public sphere, not only by selling off or contracting out public services and functions but also in the deeper sense of reducing society itself to competing "associations of consumers" in which administrators are little more than buyers in competing corporations (Ostrom, Tiebout, and Warren 1961: 839). This combination of structural trends is, in turn, triggering a reassessment of the way public or collective goods themselves are conceived of in a globalizing world.

Collective or public goods in theory are those (a) that are difficult to divide up into marketizable commodities because of their characteristics as "specific assets" (Williamson 1975 and 1985) and therefore require centralized managerial control and funding through authoritative means like fees and taxes rather than the price mechanism and (b) from the enjoyment or use of which insiders cannot be excluded, requiring authoritative mechanisms for identifying insiders who can be made to pay the costs of such goods, versus outsiders who cannot be made to pay, in order to exclude the latter, who would otherwise be free riders, from enjoying benefits without having to pay their share of costs. In other words, true public goods are characterized by *indivisibilities of both production and distribution*. The provision of public goods has thus been a classic task of hierarchical governments (states) (Cerny 1999a).

The first condition, concerning the structure of production, is referred to as *jointness of supply*, or the indivisibility of the production process. This concerns the extent to which technological economies of scale in production, plus the structure of transaction costs, mean that large factories, long production runs, and the like make collective provision through hierarchical management structures (usually seen in political terms as involving an existing governmental structure, i.e., municipal, regional, or national) more efficient than private or free-market provision—as is said to be the case with so-called natural monopolies. In a globalizing world, however, such calculations become more complex. In some industries, goods that once may have been most efficiently produced on a collective basis (especially on a national-territorial scale) may nowadays be more efficiently organized along lines that imply larger, *trans*national optimal economies of scale, making national public provision unacceptably costly and uncompetitive. In other cases, technological change and/or flexible production may actually reduce optimal economies of scale, turning such goods effectively into private goods. Indeed, these are increasingly produced and traded in a global rather than a national marketplace, with a greater structural fragmentation, rather than jointness, of supply. The fates of traditional Fordist mass production industries, such as steel in the 1980s Rust Belt, are emblematic of the first, and today's flexible, relatively small-scale steel minimills represent the second (Reich 1983; Zysman and Tyson 1983). This distinction can be seen in the debate in the United States over steel tariffs in the early 2000s, when declining Rust Belt firms clamoring for tariff protection came into conflict with internationally competitive minimills that opposed it.

With regard to consumption, economists refer to the criterion of *excludability*, or the indivisibility of the consumption process. Public goods are by definition nonexcludable, which means that collective provision has to be organized to prevent nonpaying users (free riders) from making the provision of the good too expensive for the rest; that is, such goods must be financed through forced payments (taxes). Again, in a globalizing world, it has become increasingly difficult to exclude nonpaying users (free riders) from both inside and outside national boundaries from benefiting from nationally provided collective goods in ways that appear costly in terms of domestic politics and public policy, as shown in contemporary debates on immigration and free trade agreements (Cerny 2008). The rapid growth of transnational private regulation (Mügge 2006), transnational network forms of organization, both private and public (Slaughter 2004), and legal convergence and extraterritoriality is again symptomatic. Thus with regard to both production and consumption, it is becoming more and more difficult to maintain the sort of public or collective boundaries necessary for efficient domestic state provision of certain crucial public or collective goods.

Different categories of collective goods have different kinds of normative and economic characteristics. I refer elsewhere to four such categories: regulatory, productive, distributive, and redistributive collective goods (Cerny 1999a, where I adapt the categories developed by Lowi 1964). Each of these categories has been transformed by the structural changes associated with globalization and with the other economic and political trends that are inextricably intertwined with globalization. With regard to regulatory public goods, in a world of relatively open trade, financial deregulation and reregulation, and the increasing impact of information technology, property rights and other basic rules are increasingly complex for states to establish and maintain. In this context, the ability of firms, market actors, and competing parts of the national state apparatus itself to defend and expand their economic and political turf through activities such as transnational policy networking and regulatory arbitrage has both undermined the control span of the state from without and fragmented it from within.

With regard to productive collective goods, the advent of flexible manufacturing systems and competing low-cost sources of supply—especially from firms operating multinationally—has been particularly important in undermining state-owned and parapublic firms, for example, in the crisis of public ownership and the wave of privatization of the 1980s and 1990s. Competitiveness counts for far more than maintaining an autonomous, self-sufficient national economy, in both the developed and developing worlds (Haggard 1990; Harris 1986). The same can be said for more traditional forms of industrial policy, such as state subsidies to industry, public procurement of nationally produced goods and services, or trade protectionism, as demonstrated by the example of steel mentioned earlier.

In contrast to productive collective goods, distributive collective goods are characterized less by their technical indivisibility—economies of scale and transactions cost economies deriving from *hard* production systems— and more by potential *soft* scale and transactions cost economies deriving from their management structures, on the one hand, and from the collective characteristics of their consumers rather than their producers, on the other. Policy-oriented economists have come to consider a much larger range of such goods as being appropriate for market or quasi market provision. Many of the basic public services and functions, such as the provision of public health, education, garbage collection, police protection, and certain kinds of transport or energy infrastructure, which have been at the bureaucratic heart of the modern industrial welfare state, are being disaggregated and commodified in a range of ways that have become common but remain highly controversial (Osborne and Gaebler 1992; Dunleavy 1994).

Redistributive collective goods are even more fundamentally political, with their public and collective character deriving typically from political decisions about justice and fairness rather than from the economic efficiency (or inefficiency) of those public allocation mechanisms they engender. Today, for example, neocorporatist bargaining and employment policies are under challenge everywhere in the face of international pressures for wage restraint and flexible working practices. Although developed states have generally not found it possible to significantly reduce the overall weight of the welfare state as a proportion of gross domestic product, there has been a significant transformation in the balance of how welfare funds are spent—from the maintenance of freestanding social and public services to the provision of unemployment compensation and other "entitlement" programs, and from maintaining public bureaucracies to devolving and privatizing their delivery (Clayton and Pontusson 1998). And the most salient new sector of redistributive public goods, environmental protection, is particularly transnational in character; pollution, climate change, and the rape of natural resources do not respect borders.

These changes not only increase actors' options but also prioritize strategic and tactical flexibility, increasing overall openness to change and empowering actors who can take advantage of a range of specific changes and manipulate them tactically and strategically (Raffel, Leisink, and Middlebrooks 2009). Oligopolistic and mass production industrial sectors that have been incorporated into state-led and/or "neocorporatist" structures must become internationally competitive to survive; technological changes diffuse quickly across borders; even defense industries and other "strategic" sectors are no longer immune from foreign competition and transnational linkages (Latham and Hooper 1995); macroeconomic policy is increasingly vulnerable to cross-border shifts in demand, supply, and financial flows; small businesses and the service sector increasingly have to compete; and even the welfare state and employment policy can no longer be insulated from external economic pressures for marketization and restructuring in the name of greater efficiency and "choice."

In this context, the nature of political debate is changing in fundamental ways. In political-theoretical terms, the idea of what is "public" is essentially normative. In the economic theory of collective goods, in contrast, the main issue is material-structural indivisibility. Normative issues are subsumed into technical economic debates about indivisibility. Paradoxically, however, these debates, in fact, acquire their credibility from the a priori presence of an overarching hierarchical state structure or container that ostensibly embodies the public in primordial fashion. In a globalizing world, however, the normative character of the public becomes manifest once again. The heart of political debate today is therefore about choosing among competing conceptions of what should be treated as public and what should not. For example, you can "throw money" at various industries and sectors, but it is increasingly difficult to control the way that money is used and the way those sectors develop and change—a problem faced in dramatic terms by public policy makers attempting to counteract the current financial crisis and recession.

In terms of the transformation of public policy and policy making, therefore, several types and levels of state activity are significantly affected and even transformed by the globalization process, opening new avenues for actors to reshape and even transform political and policy-making processes and their outcomes. The interaction of transnationalization, internationalization, and domestic restructuring has pushed at least four specific types of policy change to the top of the political agenda:

1. a shift from macroeconomic to microeconomic interventionism, as reflected in both deregulation and industrial policy
2. a transformation in the focus of that interventionism from the development and maintenance of a range of "strategic" or "basic" economic activities (in order to retain minimal economic self-sufficiency in key sectors) to one of flexible response to competitive conditions in a range of diversified and rapidly evolving international marketplaces, that is, the pursuit of dynamic "competitive advantage" as distinct from the more static "comparative advantage"
3. an emphasis on control of inflation and neoliberal financial orthodoxy—supposedly translating into noninflationary growth—as the touchstone of state economic management and interventionism, despite exceptions in time of crisis
4. a shift in the focal point of party and governmental politics away from general maximization of welfare within a nation (full employment, redistributive transfer payments, and social service provision) to the promotion of enterprise, innovation, and profitability in *both* private and public sectors

These fundamental policy changes form the core of the notion of the Competition State (Cerny 1997 and 2000a; chapter 8).

In this context, there have been some striking similarities, as well as major differences, among both developed and developing countries (Soederberg, Menz, and Cerny 2005). Trade policy, monetary and fiscal policy, industrial policy, and regulatory policy are all moving to a more differentiated repertoire of state responses to the imperatives of growth and competitiveness—what I call "embedded neoliberalism" (see chapter 7). Underlying all these changes is the uneven transnationalization of issue-areas, a question we return to later. State actors and their different agencies are increasingly intertwined not only with transgovernmental networks but also with transnationally linked nonstate actors in complex cross-border policy networks, such as epistemic communities of experts and policy makers in a range of technical issue-areas.

Complex globalization, as I have already argued in chapter 2, has therefore to be seen as a process involving (at least) *three-level games*, with third-level—transnational—games including not only firm-firm diplomacy but also transgovernmental networks, transnational policy communities, internationalized market structures, transnational pressure and interest groups (of both the "sectional" and "cause" varieties), and many other linked and interpenetrated markets, hierarchies, and networks. These changes increase the opportunities actors face in reacting to such changes, including manipulating the possibilities inherent in the multiple equilibria that result, deconstructing and reconstructing coalitions, developing wider strategies for change, and transforming institutional structures—engaging in institutional bricolage—to reshape longer lasting power configurations. In particular, contrary to the popular image of deregulation, the growth of competing authorities with overlapping jurisdictions does not reduce interventionism. Rather, it expands the range of possibilities for splintered governments and competing groups of actors to challenge old fiefdoms and attempt to develop new patterns of influence and power, both domestically *and* transnationally.

5. PLURALISM AND NEOPLURALISM

In this context, it is primarily the capacity of a wider range of actors to manipulate and reshape the distribution of power and resources, alter the rules of the game, transform political practices, and redefine the concept of the public and the public interest that will determine the evolutionary pathway and shape of the globalization process. In the context of the structural shifts outlined previously, this capacity privileges those actors whose interests and values allow them to build transnational coalitions in particular issue-areas, spilling over into a broader process of system transformation.

Pluralism is an approach to political sociology that can be normative, empirical (positivist), or both. It is rooted in the following propositions. First, the key independent variable in explaining the operation and outcomes of political processes is the role of the actor or agent. Structures are important in that they constitute the playing field on which actors operate, but, as argued before, such playing fields are not set in stone. Of course, they constrain actors' behavior in key ways, but under certain circumstances—see the prior discussion of structuration—they are complex and often somewhat, or even highly, fragmented, manipulable, vulnerable to structural crisis in particular conditions, and, most important, open to the production of multiple equilibria or alternative outcomes. Therefore, the capacity of particular actors to manipulate, dominate, ignore, break out of, transcend, reshape, and/or reconstruct those patterns of structural con-straints and opportunities is highly *variable*. The goals and the capacities (or, indeed, the lack of ability) of different actors to "work" or transform the institutions will determine the substance of political outcomes, as to whether they are institution-bound or structure-bound, on the one hand, or recon-structing and/or transformative, on the other.

Second, actors may be individuals, and individuals may be reactive or proactive, mixed-motive, or strategic "political (or institutional) entrepre-neurs." But most of the time, actors normally cluster in collective action units, traditionally called "groups." Groups are said to represent "interests," and, as noted earlier, those interests reflect common material self-interests (sectional groups), common social, ideological, or philosophical values (value groups), or both. Groups, in pursuing their interests, seek to gain influence and power through bargaining, competition, and coalition build-ing among themselves and with relevant state actors. In this context, it is crucial for there to be alternative possible outcomes—multiple equilibria—depending on the state of the bargaining, competition, and coalition-build-ing processes involved, that is, the balance of power, resources, and influence among those groups themselves.

In this situation, state actors such as bureaucrats and officials may either act as surrogates for particular groups ("capture theory") or maintain a cer-tain—debatable—level of "relative autonomy" wherein they represent either their own personal interests (as usually posited in rational choice theory) or what they see as the wider or higher interests of "the state" as a collective actor or institutional structure (Nordlinger 1981) or, indeed, of "the public" in the sense of a perceived interest of the collectivity in general. Thus state actors may also constitute a distinct interest group or set of interest groups across different parts of the state. Groups are not monolithic and are them-selves composed of competing subgroups and factions. "Who rules" is a relatively fluid process, never fully closed, static, or hierarchical.

Third, however, the concept of pluralism has been widely criticized as both normatively and empirically deficient. In modern liberal societies, the recognition of the legitimacy of plural claims on the political and social system is seen not only by Marxists and radicals but also by domestic as well as international realists and conservatives as overly optimistic, inten-tionally misleading, or even suffering from false consciousness—that is, as apt to obscure the real, harder power structures of state, violence, and/or class that determine the most crucial outcomes. As the result of these criticisms and of a range of empirical investigations over time, the kind of mid-twentieth-century pluralism reflected in the "end of ideology" and, more recently, the "end of history" literatures has been, to a large extent, supplanted by neopluralism. Neopluralist approaches emphasize more than their pluralist predecessors the fact that some actors and groups are, over time, more able to marshal resources, make and interpret rules, and embed practices in ways that privilege their own interests over others. In other words, to paraphrase Orwell, all groups in the pluralist universe may be equal, but some are more equal than others.

There are three *caveats* to this claim, however, that are crucial to maintaining the distinction between traditional elite theory and class analysis, on the one hand, and neopluralism, on the other. The first is that relatively powerful and influential groups often have conflicting interests among and even within themselves and therefore will clash over outcomes, so no permanent hegemonic coalition is likely to emerge. Second, therefore, powerful groups must rely on coalitions with less powerful groups, which therefore have at least some power and influence over outcomes. And third, the configuration or balance of power among a range of diverse groups will depend to a large extent on the kinds of issue-areas in play—and, of course, on complex historical circumstances. Different groups may well have conflicting interests in different issue-areas and therefore must make a range of partly complementary, partly conflicting coalitions and bargains over time and across the political system as a whole. Whether there is a ruling class than can rule in a coherent fashion is highly questionable in this context—a debate that has also characterized the development of neo-Marxist theory in recent decades (Holloway and Picciotto 1978).

McFarland takes on board both the early neopluralist approaches of Lindblom and Dahl and contemporaneous debates on the relative autonomy of the state and places them in the context of an evolving "research sequence," leading from pluralism to neopluralism (McFarland 2004; cf. Lindblom 1977 and Dahl 1989). He identifies three main—familiar—categories of actors: producer groups (similar to Key's sectional groups), social movements (similar to value or cause groups but with a wider "movement" dimension), and institutional actors and state officeholders. In identifying the basic dynamic of the political process as a pluralist one, McFarland, like Lindblom, denies that any one coalition analogous to a social class in Marxist class analysis has the coherence and muscle to monopolize rule within the system. As noted previously, however, the key to understanding how neopluralism works in practice is the way the *power dynamics vary from issue-area to issue-area.*

In some cases, oligopolistic economic sectoral interests can be allied with prominent legislators and key bureaucrats in what have been called iron triangles—a key instance of which was traditionally the Second Industrial

Revolution steel industry, thus the label. In other issue-areas, however, outcomes can be more open and bargains more uncertain, in which case there are likely to be a range of competing groups (both sectional and value), alternative points of access to relevant policy-making processes, conflicts among state actors themselves in different institutional branches and agencies, and multiple potential policy agendas and instruments that can be competed and bargained over (see chapter 6).

6. TOWARD TRANSNATIONAL NEOPLURALISM

The central hypothesis entailed by the transnational neopluralist approach is that those actors who will be most effective at influencing and shaping politics and policy outcomes are those who possess the most transnationally interconnected resources, power, and influence in a globalizing world—namely, those who:

a. perceive and define their goals, interests, and values in international, transnational, and translocal contexts, that is, what might be called the *ideational matrix*

b. are able to build cross-border networks, coalitions, and power bases among a range of potential allies and adversaries, or the *political-sociological matrix*

c. are able to coordinate and organize their strategic action on a range of international, transnational, and translocal scales in such a way as to pursue transnational policy agendas and institutional bricolage—the *institutional matrix*

Globalization in this sense not only constitutes a set of permissive conditions for the development of transnational pluralism and neopluralism but also is itself increasingly constituted by the very political processes identified here. Jessop calls this aspect of political life "strategic selectivity" (Jessop 2002). The strategies and tactics adopted by actors to cope with, control (including damage control), manage, and restructure political institutions, processes, and practices determine what sort of globalization we get. These strategies and tactics unfold at three levels.

The first level, the *base*, concerns such factors as the distribution of resources in society; the kind of processes of production, distribution, and exchange prevalent therein; the state of consciousness or the perception of interests, values, and possibilities of the various individual and group actors; and the sorts of basic solidarities and alliances of a more political nature that emerge from all of these taken together.

The second level concerns what de Tocqueville called the character of *intermediaries*, or the openness or closure of political processes and coalitions that transform the raw material of the base into more specific political and economic resources within a narrower political process—sometimes called the power structure. How open or closed are elites? Do interests interact systematically with politicians, bureaucrats, and the like in a corporatist or neocorporatist fashion? What embedded alliances have evolved over time, and how open or flexible are they? Is public policy made by iron triangles, closed policy communities, wider policy networks, or transparent, competitive, pluralistic processes?

The third level concerns the structure of the *institutional playing fields* themselves, whether concentrated or diffused, unitary or fragmented, and the sorts of rules and practices that have evolved to coordinate different levels and/or pillars of the political system. Although some writers talk about the emergence of a global "public sphere" (Germain 2001), the main thrust of the literature on globalization is that globalization makes such publicness more problematic, thereby creating a need for a new politics of reshaping multilevel governance around various "new architectures" that will re-create the "public" either at a higher level or through a more complex network structure. At the same time, however, as noted earlier, globalization also involves the uneven multiplication of points of access and control, which, allied with plurality, pluralistic practices, and pluralism-promoting strategic actors, entail the evolution of a new kind of transnational neopluralism, however uneven. Do such changes support genuine competitive pluralization, or do they merely entrench new forms of political oligopoly or monopoly at a transnational and/or global level?

In the global economy, shifting patterns with regard to economies of scale and scope do not provide conclusive evidence either way. Of course, multinational corporations hold a privileged position, as do financial market actors in an integrated, twenty-four-hour global financial marketplace. But small and medium-size enterprises also increasingly operate on a transnational scale, and it is even argued that globalization is leading to a long-term Ricardian process of the equalization of wages across the world (Kitching 2001). Only where particular industries, such as commercial aircraft, possess overwhelmingly global economies of scale are oligopoly and monopoly clearly dominant (usually with state support), whereas in nearly every other industry, new entrants have been proliferating.

"Old" groups have in many cases been able to parlay their existing resources into new profits by developing new investment strategies, restructuring and "flexibilizing" enterprises, and the like. Perhaps more important, however, has been the emergence of "new" groups of entrepreneurs, whether in countries that have traditionally encouraged such groups, like the United States, or in those that have in the past suppressed or inhibited their activities, like China and India (Baumol, Litan, and Schramm 2007). The power of latent or potential groups or categories has been growing as well. Perhaps the most important of these is consumers, whose role in the allocation of resources has dramatically increased in contrast with that of more traditional producer groups (see chapter 13). New categories of losers have been created as well, although in some cases these are groups that have already long been disenfranchised, suppressed, or subsumed in authoritarian social hierarchies such as tribes or clans. Nevertheless, existing hierarchies are everywhere being challenged by new coalitions, whether coalitions seeking greater participation in global capitalism and economic growth or those seeking to resist change, such as traditional kinship hierarchies, anticapitalist movements, or religious fundamentalists.

A dialectic of fractionalization and reorganization is therefore taking place that is analogous to the "rearticulation of sociopolitical coalitions" that Spruyt identified with regard to the earlier transition from feudalism to the nation-state. The control of politics by preexisting iron triangles, corporatist blocs, or other dominant domestic policy coalitions is everywhere being challenged by diverse, more fluid coalitions at different levels of aggregation and organization. The single most important change in developed countries has probably been the growing predominance in economic policy making of transnationally linked interest and value groups and the decline of nationally based, protectionist politics, despite the pressures of the current financial crisis. Although it is always possible for geographically concentrated groups whose position is worsened by economic globalization, such as workers displaced by import competition or by outsourcing, to organize resistance up to a point—and often to receive media and political attention for doing so, as in the 2007 presidential election in France and in the run-up to the 2008 presidential election in the United States—the increasing imbrication of both small and large businesses in international markets, production chains, and strategic alliances has tended to diffuse such effects more widely across the economy.

Together with the combination of the deskilling and reskilling of the workforce, and along with the flexibilization of production methods and the long-term decline of national trade unions, it is becoming more and more difficult to organize politically effective resistance to globalization as such. Meanwhile, the restructuring of financial markets has drawn more sectors of the population into marketized finance, whether directly or indirectly through institutional investors such as pension funds, while traditional banking institutions have themselves become more marketized (Litan and Rauch 1998). In other words, the sociopolitical balance between what were once called "national capital" and "international capital" has both blurred and shifted. There is little purely national capital left—a problem that has been exposed ever more starkly by the 2008–2009 financial crisis.

The blurring of these traditional lines between what once formed the basis for the left-right divide at national level has switched the focus of group politics toward other kinds of linkages, whether the translocal restructuring of influence around multiculturalism and/or mutually exclusive but cross-border religious and ethnic identities, diaspora communities, world cities, and the like, on the one hand, or the transnational/global reorganizing of businesses and market structures around more extended networks, the development of epistemic communities of scientists and experts, the rapid growth of transnational advocacy coalitions and networks (nongovernmental organizations, civil society, environmentalism, etc.), on the other. "Left" and "right" are not opposites today but are characterized by new forms of "diversity within convergence." They are not only crosscut by convergent varieties of neoliberalism—new "valence issues" or common values held across the left-right divide (Campbell, Converse, Miller, and Stokes 1960)— but are also divided within themselves over how to interpret, pursue, and implement diverse goals. Certain dimensions of public and economic policy have increasingly become embedded and overdetermined: the reduction of barriers to trade and cross-border finance, the shift of government policy away from direct intervention toward regulation, the transformation of the state from the welfare state to the Competition State, the expansion of mixed governance and the outsourcing of traditional governmental functions to private and/or mixed public-private providers, and the flexibilization of labor markets, among others (see chapter 7). And across borders, more and more policy issue-areas are debated, competed over, and reregulated in various mixed arenas of transnational regimes, global governance, and transnational groups of private sector actors.

In this context, actors themselves increasingly need to be able to operate on the basis of flexible response, shifting coalition building, and variable geometry in terms of both choosing short-term and/or long-term allies and developing policy strategies that involve the coordination of policy making across borders. Long-term left-right blocs are giving way to mixed, complex, and looser coalitions. Indeed, this process is running well ahead of consciousness of the implications of such changes, leading to political cognitive dissonance and, at times, to strange alliances that can distort preferences rather than effectively pursue them—as reflected in the support for the Republican Party in the United States by less well-off "social conservatives" since the Reagan era of the 1980s (Frank 2004). Pluralism is particularly relevant to a context where such parameters are in flux; it is, after all, as Bentley contended, itself a "great moving process."

Pluralism and neopluralism are not static; they are plastic. The changing constellation of actors in a globalizing world *plus* the increasing complexity of the structured field of action create opportunities for reactively and/or proactively restructuring the political playing field itself, as particular problems and issues are confronted in practice, at all levels—micro, meso, and macro. New patterns of influence and control are generated—from the fractionalization and recasting of old alliances to the emergence and consolidation of new hierarchies, control mechanisms, and unequal power structures. Globalization in its ideal type, end-state form is fragile, because it is never realized in practice and depends on political practices and institutional rules of the game for its stabilization and continuity. At the same time, however, globalization is inherently dynamic, and the very plurality of groups in a changing structural context gives it a critical fungibility in a fluid world.

These processes of change will not be smooth or self-regulating. There will inevitably be the development of new inequalities, conflicts, and destabilizing events, interacting with old inequalities, conflicts, and destabilizing circumstances inherited from history, in a heady brew represented in its more extreme form by cross-border ethnic and religious conflicts and terrorism. The evolution of globalization, however, unlike Darwinist evolution, is not a random process of natural selection. It involves conscious actors, whether individuals or groups, who can creatively interpret structural changes, multiple equilibria, and opportunities; change and refine their strategies; negotiate, bargain, build coalitions, and mobilize their power resources in ongoing interactions with other actors; and—both in winning and in losing—affect and shape medium-term and long-term outcomes. I believe we are currently somewhere in the late second or early third stage of the structuration process as outlined earlier, at a critical moment when alternative avenues of transformation are opening up. The globalization process will continue to develop and expand, but it will be shaped more and more by the interaction of an expanding, pluralistic, yet unequal constellation of actors operating across increasingly diverse, multinucleated transnational spaces, opening up a range of alternative outcomes and multiple equilibria.

Chapter 6

Globalizing the Public Policy Process
From Iron Triangles to Flexible Pentangles

1. THE LIMITS OF TRADITIONAL APPROACHES TO PUBLIC POLICY

Most academic discussion of the public policy process treats the international and global levels of analysis as exogenous. This reflects a general tendency in social science to see domestic political systems as the paramount playing fields where political actors interact and pursue their goals. Today, however, the politics of the policy process increasingly cuts across borders, as well as domestic socioeconomic categories, becoming less hierarchical and bureaucratic and more and more marketlike and networklike. Whereas statist, neopluralist, and new institutionalist critiques of pluralism of the 1970s and 1980s sought to reinsert domestic hierarchical structures—namely, the state—into American-style political science, today analysts of transnational markets and globalizing civil society are suggesting a new multilayered multipolarity, on at least three levels:

- the emergence of a new, more complex pecking order of groups cutting across and linking socioeconomic as well as political hierarchies
- a transnational rearticulation of social and political coalitions, as actors attempt to cope with and control the globalization process
- the development of more complex and fluid governance structures or quasi-institutional playing fields through which these factors interact

These new playing fields reach down to regional and local levels, too. They increasingly subsume domestic-level policy processes and incorporate domestic actors into wider, crosscutting arenas. This multilayered web of governance is linked and articulated through a complex of public and private processes and institutions; the exemplar is global finance, rooted in markets and networks. This web undermines more traditional state-embedded hierarchies and overlays them with new kinds of pluralist and neopluralist groups, interests, and forms of political behavior that often do not fit easily into traditional notions of politics in the domestic arena. These newer forms of politics and politicking not only enable new political forces to influence the policy-making process across borders but also generate innovative combinations of old and new pressures and interests domestically, from the bottom up.

Globalization therefore involves *differential* patterns of politics in which interest groups, political parties, and political entrepreneurs seek to use different parts of the policy process to benefit from globalizing trends in specific issue-areas. Diverse actors face divergent cost-benefit calculi. At one level, the policy process becomes a terrain of conflict and coalition building between those actors and interests that believe they would benefit on the whole from globalization, on the one hand, and those that believe they would be disadvantaged, on the other. But at another level, globalization (especially globalization as discourse) itself becomes a bargaining process among groups that are characterized by different kinds of payoffs. This process benefits primarily those groups that are transnationally linked and networked, providing them with what Thomas Friedman (1997) has called a "globalization premium." The notion of the policy process in general therefore needs to be reconceptualized for a globalizing world. In this chapter, I suggest some modest ways to develop a new model of the policy process to reflect this changing environment.

2. THE FIRST-ORDER PROBLEM: ENDOGENIZING THE GLOBAL

The model outlined here is based on two fundamental propositions. The first is that mainstream analytical approaches to policy analysis are not inherently restricted to understanding what goes on in the domestic arena. Most are rooted in methodological assumptions and practices that are quite easily translated onto the international or transnational level. Pluralism, neopluralism, democratic elitism, and some forms of neocorporatism are common to much of the empirical, taxonomic, and model-building literature in public policy. All can be applied in a transnational context. Within international relations, too, a range of nonrealist approaches, traditional as well as critical, already put analogous pluralistic or quasi-pluralistic processes of conflict, competition, and coalition building at the center of their analyses.

The second proposition is that globalization develops out of complexity and breeds further complexity, opening up a widening range of international and transnational playing fields and arenas. There is not just one end state of an integrated, globalized world, but rather a number of distinct trends involving both convergence and divergence, occurring at a number of levels, across a range of distinctly organized sectors, issue-areas, and social processes (Hülsemeyer 2003). Of course, these trends do not occur in isolation from each other. They generate interaction effects in both time and space. To point out a key aspect of this interaction process that has often been misunderstood by analysts, what Paul Hirst and Grahame Thompson call "inter-nationalization"—with a hyphen, indicating that they are referring to traditional inter-state or intergovernmental relations among states (Hirst and Thompson 1999)—is not so much a separate and distinct process from transnationalization; rather, the two are inextricably intertwined processes that, when combined with other crosscutting structures and processes such as translocalization, together produce the complex outcome called globalization.

Indeed, these interaction effects further alter the distribution of resources across different groups, sectors, and issue-areas, thereby change the pecking order or distribution of resources and authority in society, and, in turn, reshape the ways people interact, make sense of, and attempt to manipulate the world through politics and policy making. Whether we are talking about integration of global financial markets, internationalization of production, or the emergence of intergovernmental institutions and transnational regimes, both new and transmogrified constraints and opportunities transform political action in unanticipated ways. Trial-and-error and tit-for-tat approaches often trump both older embedded patterns and preconceived proactive strategies. Thus globalization can be seen as opening up a wider—but more asymmetric—transnational opportunity structure.

Various studies have attempted to cross these boundaries in specific issue-areas, potentially creating a small Kuhnian revolution. One area concerns European public policy, which focuses on the development of an intermediate institutionalized playing field, the European Union, and the system of "multilevel governance" it has spawned (Marks, Hooghe, and Blank 1996). Another area involves epistemic communities and transnational policy networks, focusing mainly on issue-areas where high-level knowledge is a crucial element—for example, environmental protection (where scientists, informed intellectuals, and nongovernmental organizations [NGOs] play a key part), the role of think tanks, studies of the Internet and other aspects of technological interpenetration, and policy transfer, where key elites copy policy techniques seen in other countries (Evans 2005). Furthermore, the study of transnational advocacy networks and other interest and pressure groups capable of a kind of variable geometry in seeking out points of access at a variety of levels has grown rapidly, reflecting the flexibilization of interest group politics in a globalizing world. An important academic development in this context is the ascendancy of the transdisciplinary academic field of international political economy, especially in issue-areas like trade, production, money, financial services, central banking, immigration, and some aspects of macroeconomic policy. None of the work in these more specialized subfields of study, however, has yet led to the development of an overall analytical framework for the policy process.

Probably the most robust concept in the traditional policy literature—if often criticized as far too limited—is that of *iron triangles.* Iron triangles lie at the heart of wider and more complex notions of issue networks, policy networks, and policy communities (Heclo 1978). Iron triangles are not unproblematic. As Anthony King has written: "Within the federal government in Washington, the old iron triangles...have given way to much more amorphous issue networks, to the description of which a simple Euclidian geometry is no longer appropriate" (King 1978). Nevertheless, the image they convey is still much clearer in terms of discourse and language than those of the wider, if still domestically rooted, frameworks they spawned. The notion that relatively narrow coalitions of actors, both in and out of governments, linked around specific issues and distributions of resources, and brought together by regularized professional (and often personal) contacts would settle many ongoing outstanding issues—especially routine issues—and negotiate potential conflicts through bargaining among themselves is a commonsense one.

In iron triangles, the policy process consists mainly of three broad categories of actors:

1. relevant elected officeholders—members of legislatures, party officials, ministers in parliamentary governments, and the like, as well as officeholders in key lower level institutions such as American states and provincial governments—whose policy-making responsibilities and clout in terms of resource allocation are concentrated in specific issue-areas (e.g., membership of congressional or parliamentary committees)
2. bureaucrats employed in agencies that regulate, control resources for, propose and implement policy toward, or otherwise deal with those same issue-areas
3. nonofficeholding actors, mainly in the private business and voluntary sectors (and those that cut across the public-private divide), who have (a) particular objectives they wish to pursue with regard to those same issue-areas, whether as unorganized interests or as organized pressure groups, and (b) some combination of relevant mobilizable resources, including specialized knowledge, direct economic interests, elite network contacts, financial and other material resources, a popular or group base, and ideological affinity, that can enable them to influence government policy through their regularized interactions with (1) and (2)

Actors in each of these categories are conceived as operating first and foremost within a national playing field. There are several good reasons for this. In the first place, *politicians* in liberal democratic systems are widely seen to be primarily concerned with staying in office and managing sufficient institutional and material resources and prestige to gain not only regular reelection but also promotion on the basis of existing career ladders within institutions like legislatures and executives, hierarchies such as parliamentary committees and advisory bodies, and, of course, political parties. Their priorities, even when dealing with transnational issues, are focused first and foremost on their colleagues and, in particular, on voters, whose field of reference is predominantly national. Second, appointed *bureaucrats* are seen to be concerned primarily with expanding the scope and scale of their empires (turf, prestige, and pay), as well as rising in the bureaucratic hierarchy. Nevertheless, they want a quiet life and not continual conflict with politicians, colleagues in other agencies, or private-sector actors. Third, relevant *nongovernmental actors*—whether those with direct material interests in the outcomes of particular policy processes, from individuals or firms to highly organized special interest groups or other pressure groups, whether pursuing sectional interests or causes, or even informally linked groups of electors connected to the issue-areas in question—are seen to be concerned primarily with maximizing outputs from the national governmental system. And it has to be recognized from the start that of the four main types of public policy outlined in the previous chapter—regulatory, productive, distributive, and redistributive—national governments are still the main providers of immediate material outputs, as has become abundantly clear in the various responses in different countries to the 2008–2009 financial crisis.

Nevertheless, these actor categories are still particularly useful to our model. Indeed, two of them, bureaucrats and interest groups, can be directly translated onto the transnational plane. The main exception concerns elected political officeholders; it is highly problematic to extrapolate their roles transnationally. In liberal democratic systems, such officeholders always see themselves as almost exclusively beholden to domestic voters and interests in domestic politics, or else as embodying the unified state in international affairs. Even when operating on an international or quasi-diplomatic plane and attempting to find cooperative ways to tackle international and global issues, they will fiercely avoid acting in a manner that might be seen by their domestic constituencies as contrary to national interests or, indeed, to the interests of key groups of voters or those special interest groups that helped put them into office. Of course, this incentive structure can shift significantly where elected officeholders—especially legislative officeholders—must deal on a regular basis with transnationally crosscutting interests and/or transgovernmentally linked bureaucrats; in such cases, however, their actions can be seen predominantly as dependent variables. Normally, however, their international and transnational roles are highly circumscribed by their embedded state locations, whether as domestic policy players or traditional foreign policy actors.

In contrast, domestically appointed bureaucratic actors are frequently in a position relative to their agencies' concerns and to the interests of their main sectoral constituencies—particularly with regard both to transnationally linked economic interests and to advocacy coalitions (cause groups)—where they can internalize vital international and transnational dimensions into their evaluation of a range of policy issues and potential solutions. Furthermore, they also become enmeshed in transgovernmental networks around specific issue-areas where those issue-areas are structured transnationally, as increasingly is the case. This is particularly true where they are part of a bureaucratic hierarchy—for example, an independent central bank or a securities regulator—that is relatively insulated from direct political pressures, or where a relevant and relatively autonomous domestic policy network or epistemic community exists to support transnationally innovative approaches. Finally, increasing linkages at private-sector and NGO levels can pull interest group and advocacy coalition actors into the international and transnational arenas, often interacting with both domestic and international or transnational bureaucratic actors on a regularized basis. The iron triangles of the past are being overlaid, supplemented, and even replaced, I argue, by *flexible pentangles* at the center of complex webs of governance.

However, while the image of iron triangles symbolically represents giant Second Industrial Revolution steel industries with their national markets and close corporatist relationships with the state (and often with trade unions), that of flexible pentangles evokes global financial markets, international financial institutions, complex multinational corporations, transnational production chains, contemporary information and communications technologies such as the Internet, and, most directly, post-Fordist industries. The growth of international capital flows, cross-border price sensitivity, and related technological developments has driven economic globalization and shaped policy responses along more market-oriented lines, leading to the emergence of an *embedded financial orthodoxy* in public policy making (Cerny 1994a and 1994b).

Flexible pentangles therefore represent, in highly stylized fashion, a *five-sided policy process* analogous to the three-sided iron triangles. The first three sides of the former are the same three categories represented in iron triangles: domestically based politicians, bureaucrats, and interests, broadened, however, by the endogenization of international and transnational actors and crosscutting structural factors, as described in earlier chapters, not only to include a wider range of actors but also to give more *domestic* influence and clout to transnationally linked groups. The abstract, nonspecific character of financial markets in particular—the fungibility of money across economic sectors and socioeconomic categories, as well as the increasingly dematerialized, electronic infrastructure of finance—creates structural pressures for actors to accept the transnational rules of the game, indeed, to continually forge amended and new rules that conform to the imperatives of profitability and innovation in global finance. Their global scope and their ability to bypass and constrain state actors in turn create growing pressure for liberalizing and marketizing a range of sectors beyond the financial sector per se.

The fourth of these five sides, or actor categories, of the pentangle involves those more formalized or highly institutionalized public or quasi-public activities undertaken by the International Monetary Fund (IMF), the World Bank, the World Trade Organization (WTO), the Bank for International Settlements (BIS), the International Organization of Securities Commissions (IOSCO), the G7, the G20, and many more—the *transnational public sector*. The fifth category is made up of the universe of interlocking transnational webs of governance constituted by mixed public-private sector quasi institutions (markets in the active sense) and nonstate actors that are able to coordinate their activities across borders—the *transnational private sector*, broadly speaking. As with interest groups or pressure groups in the traditional pluralist literature of American political sociology, increasing weight in a globalizing world must be accorded to cross-border nongovernmental structures and actors, from transnational markets to civil society. Cutting across and linking the transnational public and private sectors with the three traditional domestic actor categories are Slaughter's (2004) transgovernmental networks.

3. HOW THE POLICY PROCESS IS CHANGING

Although such inside/outside linkages have existed since time immemorial, the pace, density, and complexity of change today are unprecedented. Furthermore, globalization is not merely an economic process but a *political* process. It involves building coalitions and developing institutional strategies for coping with and controlling the globalization process around not only material self-interest but also criteria such as justice, fairness, and the effective provision of public goods, as noted in the previous chapter. These developments are intermediated through a range of increasingly salient issue-areas that present unfamiliar challenges and opportunities, as well as creating new constraints, for policy actors. These issue-areas run the gamut of different types of public policy, both domestic and international, traditional and emerging, as indicated in this brief provisional list.

- Foreign economic policy is perhaps the most obvious area where a range of cooperative intergovernmental practices, institution-building processes, transgovernmental networks, and transnationally linked sectional interest groups have led to new arrangements and practices on a trial-and-error, often ad hoc, basis. These new arrangements have been seen as necessary to cope with and promote such innovative policy trends as trade liberalization, financial deregulation and harmonization, energy policy, environmental policy, and aid policy. National economic interests are increasingly impossible to disentangle from the interdependencies of the contemporary world. It must also be emphasized that many aspects of security policy, too, have been affected by globalization, leading to a New Security Dilemma (chapter 12).
- Macroeconomic policy is also increasingly intertwined with international and transnational processes. Fiscal policy, interest rate setting, money supply control, and other measures to fine-tune—and today, also bail out—the domestic economy must increasingly be adjusted in ways that take into account the interests of transnationally linked producers, investors, consumers, and the like, as well as international economic institutions and other governments. Aggregate demand management, in particular, can only work if coordinated transnationally, whether formally or informally. The dilemma of national governments today in attempting to develop neo-Keynesian responses to the current financial crisis reflects their need—but not yet their effective capacity—to develop internationally coordinated stimulus and bailout packages in the short term, as well as design future strategies. Nevertheless, macroeconomic policy will continue to be partly coordinated by default, given the tight couplings and interdependencies that exist. Convergence will be more by "demonstration effect" than coordination.
- Domestic regulatory policy, especially deregulation and other forms of market-friendly regulatory reform, is conceived and implemented today not merely through domestic policy processes but increasingly through transgovernmental networks, institutions, and informal governance processes. Indeed, this is one of the thorniest aspects of global financialization and management of the current financial crisis. Sometimes government officials take the lead in marketizing regulatory regimes in order to benefit from greater international openness, and sometimes they are pushed and pulled toward change

by the rapid growth of international capital mobility, cross-border price sensitivity, and various forms of arbitrage, both economic and political, engaged in by private-sector actors across a range of relevant issues, most notably financial liberalization. Policy convergence in the field of financial regulation today is at the forefront of both formal and informal policy convergence *and divergence* among states, as demonstrated by the November 2008 summit meeting of the newly prominent G20 group of states.

- Patterns of microeconomic and mesoeconomic policy-making are also changing in response to global marketizing pressures. Political actors and governments no longer consider taking whole issue-areas out of the market (decommodification), as they once did in the past with regard not only to the welfare state but also to the promotion of particular industrial sectors, the pursuit of domestic self-sufficiency in sectors like energy, and the subsidized provision of long-term investment or "patient capital." Declining sectors are increasingly allowed to run down rather than be protected, and welfare and other public services increasingly are meant to work according to quasi-market principles—the new public management or reinventing government discussed earlier. Winners are no longer directly picked through traditional forms of industrial policy. Instead, governments prioritize the creation of a market-friendly and competitive regulatory environment applicable to all firms rather than a selected few—except in conditions where emergency bailouts are resorted to, and those are meant to be temporary and self-correcting over a relatively short period of time.

- Domestic political coalitions still retain a range of options for "domesticating" globalization, and those options are prioritized in a crisis. Nevertheless, those options are both narrower and in some issue-areas quite different from earlier periods. Thus, even where Keynesian fiscal and monetary tools are used in a crisis, the aim is to return protected sectors to the marketplace as quickly and efficiently as possible. And in the crucial area of welfare policy, for example, policy makers are increasingly challenged to find alternatives to traditional options of state-led policies of redistribution and public service provision without sacrificing its traditional goals of social justice.

- Moreover, key patterns of coalition building are changing. Political actors are led more and more to adopt approaches that prioritize capturing the benefits of globalization. This potentially allows the creation of new material and political resources for rebuilding decaying bases of support and attracting new constituencies, mass as well as elite, in a period of shifting identities, allegiances, and class structures in a globalizing world. Conservative coalitions pioneered this form of realignment in advanced industrial countries in the 1970s and 1980s, through Thatcherism and Reaganism in particular, while on the center-left, the notion of the Third Way that was adopted in the 1990s by New Democrats in the United States, New Labour in the United Kingdom, and the Social Democrats' Neue Mitte in Germany was explicitly conceived as a response to globalization—as was the concept of "change" as developed in the 2008 electoral campaign of President Barack Obama.

4. HOW THE POLICY PROCESS WORKS IN A GLOBALIZING WORLD

Just as with iron triangles, of course, some issue-areas will be dominated by only a subset of the basic actor categories. Rarely will an issue-area be characterized by an ideal-type, balanced five-node pentangular policy process as such. A number of more specific hypotheses can be suggested in this regard. The following are some typical but by no means exhaustive examples.

With regard to foreign economic policy making, for example, traditional foreign policy actors (diplomats and foreign ministry officials, members of national executive branches and their advisors, etc.; Rosenau 1961) and those involved in intergovernmental processes are likely to benefit from their positions in the domestic state hierarchy to exercise disproportionate influence. Furthermore, such actors are more likely to be able to resist pressures from parochial domestic interests and will see their primary role in a traditional, somewhat insulated diplomatic context; they still resemble Rosenau's category of "cosmopolitan" elites (Rosenau 1961). Nevertheless, such actors have always interpreted a major part of their role as promoting the interests of domestic firms abroad.

Today, however, that role is far more complicated as economic interest groups become increasingly transnationalized. It is thus difficult to disentangle national economic interests as pursued by these state actors from the special interests of multinational corporations, cross-border market organizations in sectors like finance, and cosmopolitan elites. Foreign economic policy making is likely to be caught in an expectations trap, where proclaimed domestic priorities are incorporated and subsumed into wider transnational policy considerations.

With regard to macroeconomic policy making, economic experts, central banks, treasury departments, and actors closely connected with particular phases of the legislative process and legislative-executive bargaining, such as members of parliamentary budget or banking committees, will benefit to some extent from similar advantages in terms of policy independence. However, they are increasingly likely to see their roles as an attempt to lead or respond to international market conditions, privileging such criteria as market confidence and stabilization. Convergence of interest rates has been a well-known feature of monetary policy in recent decades, and tax competition between national authorities, as well as regional and local authorities, has eroded the capacity of governments to fine-tune economies through tax advantages and other fiscal measures vis-à-vis international competitors. Tax competition can be effective for short periods where there are first mover advantages for specific tax breaks, but it is unlikely to provide long-term benefits, and the same is true of budget expenditure beyond short-term stimuli in crisis conditions. Indeed, the latter can lead to throwing good money after bad, as with Japanese spending on infrastructure in the 1990s; these limits are at the forefront of policy responses to the current financial crisis and recession.

With regard to regulatory policy, close links between particular regulatory bodies with transgovernmental links, specialized private-sector interests often with transnational links, elected officials with particular expertise in such fields, and international institutions form a complex system of ongoing bargaining and reform, especially with regard to so-called regulatory arbitrage between different national regulatory systems. This is the essence of Slaughter's (2004) "new world order." In particular, the more transnationalized the sector and issue-area, the more pressure for convergence and for leveling the international playing field rather than pursuing regulatory comparative advantages at the domestic level, which would in any case be eroded by regulatory arbitrage. Regulatory convergence is one of the most striking examples of a process where transnationalized special interests and transgovernmental networks have increasingly become enmeshed in bargaining processes where the splintered or disaggregated state is continually playing catch-up with transnational pressures and conditions.

In microeconomic policy, domestic economic interests, especially producer and consumer interests, have a much greater role to play. However, increasing interpenetration of transnational markets for a widening range of goods and assets can dramatically alter the perceptions of such actors and lead to a partial internationalization from below, along with demands for compensation for losers. The economic position of small businesses, workers, and consumers is increasingly dependent on international market conditions, so protection for particular groups and economic activities is likely to give way to the extension of side payments to those groups rather than to resurrecting trade barriers or capital controls. The unwillingness of consumers to prefer domestically produced consumer goods when imports are competitive on price and/or quality is a particularly robust obstacle to reviving traditional industrial policies. Declining industries are less likely to be propped up in the face of international competition, and picking winners is increasingly problematic in a world where firms and production processes are more and more transnationalized. Transnational policy measures, most notably the merger of Fiat and Chrysler as I write, have increasingly become part of the solution rather than part of the problem. Even in the issue-area most characterized by populist protectionism at the present time, scapegoating immigration has little real effect on migratory patterns and on the ongoing expansion of migration, especially where potential migrants are pushed by economic and political conditions to leave their regions of origin and employers seek cheap, mobile labor in regions of immigration (Schain 2009).

And finally, coalition-building strategies are likely to involve a much wider range of latent and manifest groups. As I have already pointed out, although class, regional, sectional, and other patterns of voting and interest group behavior still exist and can be extremely influential at election times, they are increasingly crosscut and rearticulated into competing "associations of consumers" in that even more multinucleated political system that is created in the process of globalization. Therefore, a number of different networking patterns or subsets—dyads, triads, quads, or even full-blown pentangles—are likely to develop within different issue-areas, although the development of a theory of how this will happen is premature. The literature is likely to be built from the bottom up as empirical case studies are carried out and compared.

Nevertheless, the substantive content of the policy process in different issue-areas is likely to vary in relatively systematic ways. In particular, adapting the framework applied to demands for protectionism developed by Jeffry Frieden and Ronald Rogowski (1996), it can be hypothesized that the relative concentration and diffusion of costs and benefits for different groups of actors in contrasting issue-areas are likely to lead to substantively different outcomes. Where locational advantages are particularly concentrated and correspond with national territorial boundaries, and where pressure group patterns are well developed, state actors will be under greater pressure to pursue traditional protectionist policies; however, as pointed out before, these are more and more likely to be substituted by side payments as markets and production processes become increasingly transnationalized. Nevertheless, patterns of action are likely to vary substantially across issue-areas, as Eric Helleiner, for example, has shown in his contrast between the politics of trade and finance (Helleiner 1994). Trade openness, he argues, depends on multilateral action, over which state actors and domestic interests may have a veto, whereas financial openness can effectively be pursued unilaterally by state actors responding to market developments and are therefore less constrained by pressures for domestic protection—pressures that are themselves increasingly transnationalized.

Perhaps the most obvious distinction shaping the content of the process is that between those groups and actors who represent or are otherwise linked with economic sectors characterized predominantly by nonspecific assets, on the one hand, and those characterized by specific assets on the other (see Cerny 1995 for a more extended analysis). In this context, the main hypothesis is that the endogenization of international and transnational elements into previously predominantly domestic policy processes is likely over time (a) to further privilege those sectors and actors in the former (nonspecific asset) category in terms of agenda setting, bargaining, and obtaining preferred policy outcomes *and* (b) to force those in the latter (specific asset) category to adopt strategies that are based less on protectionism and more on side payments. The latter needs to be bought off rather than featherbedded. In both cases, the center of gravity of the policy-making process in terms of setting the policy agenda, the payoff matrix for the bargaining process itself, and the range of feasible outcomes is shifted toward conditions that are broadly liberalizing or globalizing, in a feedback process that reinforces transnationally intertwined interests and actors and progressively marginalizes what used to be called "national capital."

Indeed, the proportion of economic sectors and activities that is characterized by nonspecific asset structures is growing, for two reasons. The first is that even large-scale manufacturing industries find it more difficult to establish and maintain monopolies, oligopolies, formal or informal cartels, and the like at international and transnational levels than at national or local levels. The world economy is too big for even the biggest economies of scale to lead to market dominance, despite the claims of prominent critics like Naomi Klein (2000). "Natural monopolies" may be significant players at the national level, but such sectors as the electricity industry, a classic natural monopoly, are not only being marketized domestically by government-led privatization and regulation but also increasingly vulnerable to takeovers by foreign firms in the process of becoming multinationals. I am aware of only one large-scale industry that is characterized by extensive *international* oligopolization to any great extent, the commercial aircraft industry. However, even here the evidence is ambiguous, and governments (including the European Union) have been assiduous in attempting to impose compensatory regulation. *Generally speaking, globalization promotes increased competitiveness in most sectors.*

The second reason is that many industries are in the process of restructuring to reflect technological changes that make them more flexible in terms of production processes, management and organizational systems, marketing, and the use of new information and communications technology—what is often called the Third Industrial Revolution or post-Fordism. Flexible structures are by definition more marketizable and therefore structurally nonspecific. The shift of the steel industry everywhere from large-scale plants (often now called Rust Belts) to minimills is typical, despite the fact that governments often have to pander politically to older large-scale firms for electoral reasons. The current crisis of the automobile industry—of course, the poster child of traditional Fordism—is a key example of how sectors once thought to be natural oligopolies or monopolies because of their specific assets, such as technological economies of scale, long-term contracting, and strategic positioning in production, distribution, and consumption chains, are being forced by global market conditions to flexibilize and marketize not just to remain competitive, but simply to survive. Furthermore, at the time I am writing, such changes are being demanded by governments, too, for example, as a condition for bailing out the automobile industry.

In this changing structural context, globalization alters the cost-benefit calculus away from the promotion of domestic self-sufficiency or insulation and toward adjustment mechanisms that integrate or endogenize internationalized and transnationalized agendas, bargaining situations, and policy outcomes. The capacity to form protectionist or quasi-protectionist coalitions is thereby increasingly circumscribed as *fewer actors—and, more important, fewer economically heavyweight and/or politically significant actors—have a direct economic or political interest in such mercantilist policy measures.* Broadly speaking, globalization compels actors to seek neoliberal solutions because only by accepting such solutions is it possible to form sufficiently large coalitions to gain tolerable compensatory benefits from the policy process in the medium to long term.

Nevertheless, there are important exceptions to this general rule, three of which are particularly salient as I write. The first involves exogenous shocks where previously negotiated policy and/or institutional outcomes prove to be counterproductive and the pressure of unfavorable events shifts the underlying pattern of coalition building away from what was previously agreed either into a reshaped bargaining process or toward the limbo of an empty core—that is, lack of sufficient a priori common ground for agreement—among former coalition partners, as with the current financial crisis. Previous financial crises in Mexico (1994), Southeast Asia (1997), Russia (1998), Argentina (2001–2002), and Turkey (2002) dramatically undermined domestic coalitions based on cushioning domestic industrial development through the manipulation of currency exchange rates and other traditional policy measures (see the special issue of the *Review of International Political Economy*, vol. 16, no. 4 [August 2009]). An illustrative example was the collapse of Argentina's peso-dollar convertibility policy (also known as the "currency board") in 2001–2002—a laboriously won settlement that after five years of relative success in the mid-1990s unwound dramatically (Datz 2009).

Furthermore, the 2008–2009 global financial crisis is a once-in-a-lifetime example of how such shocks can spread and rapidly undermine existing regulatory, fiscal, and monetary policies—in this case, how the beating of the wings of a relatively small financial butterfly, the subprime housing market in the United States, became the shot heard round the world. In this case, the distinction between endogenous and exogenous shocks melts away because of the tight coupling not only of international markets but also of a huge range of financial and industrial sectors, especially through the mushrooming of financial derivatives, once thought to be stabilizing instruments (Bryan and Rafferty 2006; Tett 2009).

The second involves negative reactions to particular liberalizing measures on the part of "concentrated" domestic interests, namely, those groups and actors that are able to mobilize a well-defined sector of the electorate, in particular, geographical regions such as traditional industrial zones, where particular industries dominate the local economy, and social categories such as workers in large factories, where elections are tight and can be swung by political action. An example of this is the Bush administration's agreement to impose tariffs on several categories of steel imports, especially from Europe and Japan, in March 2002. The American steel industry had already become divided between traditional firms and large Second Industrial Revolution production processes, on the one hand—the firms that had become uncompetitive and benefited disproportionately from the tariffs— and smaller, more flexible firms that remained competitive and regarded the tariffs as subsidies for their own *domestic* competitors, on the other. However, this latter group had become increasingly dominant and profitable in the steel sector. It organized a lobbying counterattack that succeeded in overturning this attempt at trade protectionism, which backfired. The tariffs were scaled back.

The third, in this case only a partial (and, at first glance, paradoxical) exception, is the spread—and often the transnational transfer—of tighter and stricter, rather than looser and apparently more "liberal," policy measures, such as increasingly strong environmental regulations, health and safety regulations, and financial regulatory reforms. An example of the last, still in the making, is the pressure to tighten up on auditing and accounting standards, not only in the wake of the bankruptcy of the Enron Corporation in late 2001 but also in the context of quasi-private regulatory arbitrage and competition for financial and other business between different global financial centers, especially London and New York. But this third exception may be the exception that proves the rule, as it is to a large extent the transnational policy transfer of such regulatory measures that is driving the development of the regulatory state and the Competition State.

Globalizing the policy process, therefore, although it is likely to lead to more neoliberal outcomes over time—given the altered balance of interests, groups, actors, and other entities involved in that process—is unlikely to lead to a disarming of the state as such. Rather, it is leading to a reallocation of state resources and authority away from insulated domestic agendas toward policy measures that promote coalitions among:

- actual cross-border interests, usually economic but also social and political
- those domestic interests that are not merely vulnerable to international and transnational conditions but also seeking to benefit from wider competitiveness
- domestic interests seeking compensatory side payments

In this context, furthermore, two additional trends can be identified. The first is the attempt (or strategic decision?) on the part of a growing number of political entrepreneurs, whether on the right or the left, to focus on facilitating such bargaining processes. Domestic populist politics are increasingly seen as marginal and unproductive, while the discourse of globalization as an inherent feature of political "modernization" is increasingly hegemonic.

The second is the emergence of an awareness in a number of countries, and in the IMF, the World Bank, and the WTO as well, that political bargains entered into in this context have a wider political or ideational dimension. If the types of shift of policy agendas, bargaining processes, and policy outcomes discussed here are to be seen as *legitimate* in the future, they will increasingly be presented as representing wider social and political values, as I argue in the next chapter. Margaret Thatcher's saying that "You can't buck the markets" is being challenged within the political mainstream *not* by the re-creation of the mid-twentieth-century industrial welfare state, the state of the iron triangles, but by the notion of "globalization with a human face" (Bill Clinton) or what I call "managed neoliberalism" and/or "social neoliberalism," including the official promotion of poverty-reduction approaches by the World Bank or the need for a "global safety net." Indeed, even outside that mainstream, today's antiglobalization protesters are increasingly aware that the nation-state no longer constitutes an effective arena for protest and that opposition to economic globalization itself requires the globalization of protest from below (Starr 2000; Lewis 2001).

Finally, in terms of the inclusiveness or exclusiveness of the policy process in transnationally linked issue-areas, mass-based or voter-oriented groups would at first glance seem less likely to participate proactively than in traditional domestic policy processes. However, this rule of thumb falls away when the issue-area concerned becomes clearly perceived in popular consciousness as being inherently or structurally international, transnational, or global. Thus environmental protection increasingly involves mass input, mobilized through transnational pressure groups like Greenpeace; at the same time, transnational epistemic communities in this issue-area have managed to keep their central role through their specialized scientific expertise, turning a latent transnational interest grouping into a manifest one. Trade, too, as an issue-area has from time to time mobilized mass groups, as in the wake of the so-called Battle of Seattle in 1999, although results are limited and mainly symbolic at this stage. And in the current economic crisis, awareness of the tight coupling of financial and other markets has started to spill over into mass consciousness, not only focusing blame but also making bailouts and economic stimulus packages a much more widely disseminated topic of popular debate.

5. CONCLUSION: TRANSNATIONALIZING THE POLICY PROCESS

At the core of this model of flexible pentangles, then, is an apparent paradox. For the most part, the addition of our two additional categories of actors—the transnational public sector and the transnational private sector—to the original iron triangle model tends to give an even larger agenda-setting role to elite groups because they are more likely to be transnationally linked than traditional domestic categories. The global "democratic deficit," the weakness of organized labor, constraints on the welfare state, and the like give increasing structural and relational power to the more mobile sectors of international capital (Reich 1991). At the same time, however, expansion of the number of relevant categories of actors also increases the possibilities for competition among various groups at different levels and makes it less possible for a closed or monolithic national state—or even some sort of emerging "global state" (Shaw 2000)—to result. The process is thus neopluralist rather than either fully pluralist or fully elitist. Globalizing the policy process involves the continual and growing interaction of both old and new elements of the political opportunity structure, giving political entrepreneurs considerable scope to shape that evolution. It strengthens the hand of transnationally linked interests and actors and shifts the balance of agenda setting, policy bargaining, and policy outcomes toward globalizing coalitions and protocoalitions. Indeed, the current financial crisis has brought home its centrality to all public policy making in the twenty-first century, domestic *and* international combined, increasingly inextricably intertwined in contemporary world politics.

Chapter 7

Embedding Neoliberalism

The Evolution of a Hegemonic Paradigm

1. INTRODUCTION: FROM ECONOMIC LIBERALISM TO NEOLIBERALISM

As I have argued throughout this book, neoliberalism since the 1980s has evolved into a complex, flexible, fungible, and increasingly variegated set of discourses that have proved particularly useful to a diverse range of actors in a globalizing world. It has become the ideological glue of transnational neo-pluralism. When it was adopted as a label for a new form of nationally rooted transatlantic conservatism in the late 1970s and 1980s, neoliberalism was seen to be embodied primarily in the politics and economic policies of Prime Minister Margaret Thatcher and the Conservative Party in the United Kingdom and of President Ronald Reagan and the Republican Party in the United States. It is often thought to entail a revival of what has sometimes been called "classical liberalism" or "nineteenth-century liberalism"—that is, a return to purer laissez faire principles and the ideology (and economic theory) of the self-regulating market.

However, this is an oversimplification. Neoliberalism in its three main varieties—"free market conservative, neoliberal structuralist and neoliberal regulationist" (Plehwe, Walpen, and Neunhöffer 2006)—paradoxically involves *an active role for the state in designing, promoting, and guaranteeing the free and efficient operation of the market*, a kind of imposed laissez faire somewhat analogous to Rousseau's image of people being "forced to be free" (cf. Foucault 2008).

Although the laissez faire interpretation of neoliberalism arose originally in the specific conditions of the British and American political economies during the recession of the 1970s, and was intertwined with the new assertive nationalism represented by its main advocates—in other words, it originally appeared to be primarily a phenomenon at the nation-state level—its rise also coincided with a range of structurally transformational transnational and globalizing developments: pressures for trade liberalization, the shift of the international monetary system from fixed to floating currencies, the explosion of international capital mobility and integration of global financial markets, the expansion of multinational corporations, the growth of transnational production chains and network forms of business organization, and vast technological changes, especially in information and communications technologies.

The scope and significance of neoliberalism has been transformed not only into the political and ideological manifestation of economic structural change and public policy innovation at national level but also into the ideational driving force behind the politics of globalization. Supporters and critics of globalization alike either attribute neoliberalism with promoting economic growth and efficient, transnationally open, free market capitalism, on the one hand, or attack it for justifying new forms of capitalist oppression, blinding elites and masses alike to the worsening inequalities and crisis tendencies engendered by globalization (Klein 2007), on the other. Neoliberalism has increasingly come to frame intellectual and political debates in recent years as economic doctrine, public policy agenda, descriptive framework, analytical paradigm, and social discourse. It has become deeply embedded in twenty-first century institutional behavior, political processes, discourses, and understandings of socioeconomic realities.

In this way, neoliberalism has superseded "embedded liberalism" (Ruggie 1982) as the key "shared mental model" (Roy, Denzau, and Willett 2007) of the evolving "art of governmentality" in a globalizing world (Burchell, Gordon, and Miller 1991; Foucault 2008). Embedded neoliberalism has become the Aristotelian or Gramscian "common sense" of the twenty-first century—that is to say, what people expect and take for granted. Nevertheless, the very embedding of neoliberal discourse and practice is in turn transforming neoliberalism from a relatively closed doctrine associated with particular individuals, governments, interest groups, political parties, international organizations, and even academic schools of thought like the Mont Pèlerin Society into a hegemonic concept that is seeping into and co-opting the whole spectrum of political life. In this process, the concept itself has been undergoing considerable evolution, especially in two main ways.

In the first place, neoliberalism is not a seamless web doctrinally and discursively. It is not only a contested concept in theoretical terms but also a highly internally differentiated one, made up of a range of politically linked but potentially discrete and freestanding subcategories and dimensions. These can be manipulated and orchestrated in different ways by political actors, leading to a much larger spectrum of strategic options, policy prescriptions, and de facto practices than the original conservative version would suggest—including what are here called regulatory, managed and social neoliberalism. In this way, a wide variety of interest and value groups, as well as political actors, can latch onto specific parts of the package and claim them for diverse political projects. Neoliberalism is proving to be eminently flexible and politically adaptable—a discourse that increasingly reflects the processes of transnational neopluralism.

Second, as argued throughout this book, the global political process itself is opening up to a much wider range of political, economic, and social actors. These include economic actors involved in transnationalizing firms, market structures, and networks, along with business school academics concerned with developing global strategies, actors in transnational organizations, state actors in both traditional policy-making bureaucracies and transgovernmental networks, cross-border ethnic and religious groups, workers in high-technology sectors, ordinary people linked through the Internet who do not need to move physically to participate in transnational society, and consumers whose preferences are for transnationally produced goods and assets. All are co-opting neoliberal discourse in a variety of ways suited to their political goals, resources, alliances, strategies, and tactics—manipulating and transforming it to fit, justify, and legitimate their own daily actions and long-term goals (Harvey 2005).

This chapter first examines neoliberalism as a contested concept; then traces how it has come to be embedded within the globalization process; deconstructs the concept into its different subcategories and dimensions; identifies some of the key actors who have co-opted neoliberalism into their own frames of references, strategies and tactics; and concludes by suggesting some of the forms that arguably might be expected to characterize its evolution in the medium term.

2. NEOLIBERALISM AS A CONTESTED CONCEPT

Neoliberalism is a relatively recent concept and is open to several often conflicting interpretations. Its widespread adoption reflects the fashion that appeared in the late cold war period for affixing the prefix "neo" to well-known political labels. This trend ostensibly signified that outdated ideological frameworks and/or historical paradigms were being, if not transcended, at least adapted and reshaped for a late modern or postmodern world. In the study of politics and international relations, other well-known examples of such neologisms have been neoconservatism (Mann 2004), neorealism (Waltz 1979), and neomedievalism (Cerny 1998). In a world where the very concepts of international relations and world politics are becoming more fluid and fungible, where the inside/outside distinction is being challenged, and where debates on globalization are increasingly framing our understanding of world politics, neoliberalism has moved center stage in an attempt to identify, locate, and define the complex character of politics and political ideology in the twenty-first century.

A. The Two Meanings of Liberalism in the United States and Europe

It is important to clarify how neoliberalism fits into the traditional spectrum of political doctrines. Neoliberalism in the study of international relations and international political economy has taken on two primary distinct—and partly contradictory—definitions, reflecting the historical ambiguity of its main precursor, "liberalism." Liberalism is itself a complex mixture of meanings, reflecting the ambiguity of its central referent—the notion of freedom or liberty and, in particular, the centrality of the individual as the main constituent or building block of society. "Classical" liberalism has always been rooted in both normative and methodological individualism. Liberalism can (and originally did) imply free-thinking, indicating that a liberal is of a critical bent of mind, as in Enlightenment philosophies. It can also refer to support for those civil freedoms and human rights that were central to the Enlightenment. Furthermore, it can mean the necessity or desirability of free and/or liberal democratic political institutions, rooted in individual consent rather than collectivist ideologies. Freedom of religion, and indeed a critical attitude toward the social role of religion, is also a major issue for liberals, reflected in the demand for the separation of church and state. Finally, economic liberalism is traditionally associated with market capitalism, implying an uneasy and fungible combination of laissez faire economics, especially the protection of private property, with promarket economic regulation.

Clearly, there has been much room for conflict among these meanings, depending on which dimension or dimensions are seen as taking philosophical and practical priority. For example, rights to life, liberty, and property, as in the seventeenth-century political philosophy of John Locke, can often conflict with each other in practice. In continental Europe, where the notion of liberalism has tended to retain much of this fundamentally antistatist meaning, the term is applied mainly to the political philosophy of the capitalist right—although its individualist core is obviously in conflict with more organicist right-wing ideologies, such as the elitism of Pareto and Mosca, certain forms of social Catholicism, or fascism in the late nineteenth and early twentieth centuries (de Ruggiero 1927). In the United States, this sort of liberalism is often called "nineteenth-century liberalism" or "classical liberalism," and indeed has much in common with Anglo-Saxon "conservatism."

This usage contrasts with the way the term "liberalism" has been used in the United States since the early twentieth century. American liberalism, paradoxically, has become a label for the moderate center-left, derived by writers such as Walter Lippmann and political actors like Woodrow Wilson from the nineteenth-century Progressive tradition in the United States, but tempered to be more inclusive and mainstream (Lippmann 1982). In this latter sense, American-style liberalism came to be somewhat analogous to moderate social democratic views in continental Europe; however, in Europe the development of social democratic ideology and party identification was sufficiently strong to resist being subsumed into liberalism, which retained its right-wing connotations.

Today, American conservatives and neoconservatives, following presidential candidate (and later President) George H. W. Bush in the 1988 election campaign, acknowledge that their own approach is rooted in what they call "nineteenth-century liberalism." However, they have also demonized twentieth-century American liberalism as the "L-word"—ostensibly entailing a dogmatic left-wing approach, and attempting to deny it the center ground sought by Lippmann, Wilson, and their liberal successors like Presidents Franklin Delano Roosevelt and John F. Kennedy (not to mention Barack Obama). In Australia, this center-left version of liberalism is referred to as "social liberalism." In the United Kingdom, liberalism, at least in the approach of the Liberal Democratic Party (formerly the Liberal Party) is seen as trying to combine the best elements of both conservatism and social democracy while emphasizing individualism. Identifying the political content of liberalism is thus problematic; it means what contrasting traditions say it means. The same, as we argue later, can be said for neoliberalism today.

B. Liberal Internationalism and Neoliberal Institutionalism in International Relations

In the study of international relations and international political economy, too, liberalism—and, today, neoliberalism—can be seen as having two distinct meanings, analogous to the distinction between "nineteenth-century liberalism" and "social liberalism" just discussed. The first of these derives from the quasi-idealist tradition of "liberal internationalism" associated with the legacy of Woodrow Wilson and the League of Nations. Liberal internationalism involved the construction of international institutions made up of sovereign states, the provision of collective security, and the expansion of international law along relatively liberal lines. The United Nations Universal Declaration of Human Rights is seen as a key document in this tradition, along with UN sponsorship of development, health, food, and housing programs. The establishment of the Bretton Woods system of international economic institutions at the end of the Second World War is also seen to represent international economic liberalism through the promotion and regulation of increasingly open international trade (through the General Agreement on Tariffs and Trade, now the World Trade

Organization), an international monetary system (through the International Monetary Fund), and economic development (through the International Bank for Reconstruction and Development, long since known as the World Bank). John Gerard Ruggie called the postwar system one of "embedded liberalism"; however, his analysis went further, linking international economic liberalism with American domestic liberalism (or European social democracy) through Keynesian macroeconomic policies, full employment, and the welfare state (Ruggie 1982).

In this context, Robert O. Keohane has referred to what he calls "neoliberal institutionalism" (Keohane 1984 and 1989; cf. Baldwin 1993). This usage has until recently been prevalent in the academic study of international relations in the United States, although it has rarely been adopted elsewhere. Neoliberal institutionalism was a concept developed out of regime theory. It posited that the development of the international system since the Second World War was characterized primarily by a broad but rather ad hoc proliferation of international regimes, whether of the broad, overarching kind discussed by Ruggie—the "regime of embedded liberalism"—or the narrow sense of specific, quasi-autonomous, problem-solving institutions dedicated to specific issue-areas, like the International Monetary Fund, the General Agreement on Tariffs and Trade (GATT), the International Labor Office (ILO), and specialized organizations for the law of the sea, shipping, intellectual property, and the like.

This definition of neoliberalism was constructed to distinguish it from the "neorealism" of Kenneth Waltz, also hugely influential in the American academy, which had brought the autonomous nation-state—seeking power and motivated primarily by relative gains rather than absolute gains—back to the fore as the only genuine "unit actor" in an "anarchic" international system (Waltz 1979; Keohane 1986; Baldwin 1993). Neorealism in turn gave rise to "hegemonic stability theory," which, following the collective action theories of Mancur Olson, argued that in an anarchic system—where "self-help," defection, and free riding were the default positions and international cooperation a fragile reed—only an overwhelmingly well-resourced great power or superpower could provide the public goods of international stability and security by paying the costs of those goods unilaterally and not depending on other actors to inject key resources. In essence, the presence of free riders was tolerable as long as the hegemon could provide essential international public goods by itself.

Keohane, in contrast, argued not only that international regimes had proliferated in the empirical sense from the 1940s to the 1980s but also that their widening scope of influence and control over increasingly significant and salient issue-areas gave them institutional autonomy and engendered habits of intergovernmental cooperation that were refocusing international cooperation on absolute gains and reducing the emphasis on neorealists' relative gains. Indeed, in this context there was no longer a systemic or structural imperative for the hegemony of a particular state or group of states; neoliberal institutionalism was taking over "after hegemony" (Keohane 1984). Nevertheless, Keohane's analysis still considered international regimes and neoliberal institutionalism to be intergovernmental constructs that to a large extent maintained the inside/outside distinction between domestic and international politics. Neoliberal regimes in this sense were not a substitute for liberal domestic politics but were broadly in the tradition of liberal internationalism, tempered by a certain amount of neorealism. Andrew Moravcsik went one step further by suggesting a "liberal theory of state preferences" that incorporated a wider range of domestic actors—and therefore international and transnationally linked domestic interests—into state behavior (Moravcsik 1997). Such an approach would accord state actors a wider repertoire of cooperative options without undermining the fundamentally state-centric character of international politics.

In this sense, both neoliberalism and neorealism can be contrasted with approaches that posit fundamental structural change in world politics or that would erode the inside/outside distinction, such as globalization. Despite common reference points, especially the growing interaction among international regimes, multilevel governance, and global civil society, neoliberalism in Keohane's sense is fundamentally distinct from, even opposed to, the idea of neoliberalism as a hegemonic, globalizing political doctrine and discourse cutting across the inside/outside divide.

C. Economic Neoliberalism in International Political Economy

The third use of the term "neoliberal" is quite different from Keohane's and is derived from the continental European version of liberalism, namely, "nineteenth-century" or "classical" liberalism. This usage focuses primarily on *economic* liberalism/neoliberalism, with its emphasis on the primacy of market mechanisms, but it has much wider political and social implications, too. It has also become more widely accepted and has increasingly supplanted "neoliberal institutionalism" as the main way the word is used not only in academic but also in policy-making and journalistic circles, even in the United States. The key to this way of thinking about neoliberalism is the assertion that the economic market should form the core institution or ordering/organizing mechanism of modern (capitalist) societies, and that both domestic and international politics are—and should be— increasingly concerned not only with helping markets to work freely (and therefore, in theory, efficiently) but also with making markets work well through procompetitive regulation, preventing and/or compensating for market failure, and so on. In this sense, neoliberalism, like classical liberalism before it, is essentially a normative/prescriptive doctrine and discourse, a framework for formulating and implementing public policy at both international and domestic levels. Unlike classical liberalism, however, neoliberalism does not assume that markets necessarily work in an efficient, spontaneous, and automatic—self-regulating—manner, unless they are strongly embedded in promarket rules, institutions, and politics. This overriding set of policy goals has several component parts, but those parts have a common normative logic.

In the first place, it is seen as necessary to design and establish institutions and practices that are market-based and market-led, both domestically and globally. This objective is seen as crucial not only in more developed capitalist countries, where social democracy and American-style liberalism are believed to have distorted markets ever since the New Deal and to have led to "creeping socialism" and, in particular, stagflation and recession in the 1970s, but also in so-called transition (i.e., ex-communist) states and in the developing world, where doctrines such as import substitution industrialization (ISI) by both left-wing and right-wing governments from the 1950s to the 1980s led to hyperinflation, overbureaucratization, and problematic levels of international indebtedness (Kaldor, Holden, and Falk 1989; Kemp 1983).

Second, it is seen to be crucial to instill a culture of individualistic, market-oriented behavior in people of all social classes, counteracting the "dependency culture" of the Keynesian welfare state that was blamed for the slump of the 1970s, for example, by "ending welfare as we know it" (Bill Clinton) and deregulating the labor market—what Bob Jessop calls the "Schumpeterian workfare state" (Jessop 2002). International regimes, too, have pursued similar goals, for example in the so-called Washington consensus of the 1980s and 1990s (Williamson 1990). Governments, and international institutions, too, it was argued, should be imbued with market-friendly attitudes and practices—"reinventing government," privatizing social and public services, promoting international competitiveness, deregulating and liberalizing specific markets or sectors, and/or using international aid to promote marketization through "conditionality." The concept of "governance"—or "good governance," with priority given to establishing and sustaining workable market systems—should replace that of "government."

Third, barriers to international trade and capital flows should be progressively dismantled. The most efficient markets, in theory, are those with the largest numbers of buyers and sellers, so that an "efficiency price" can be established that will "clear the market" (Williamson 1975; Lindblom 1977). (Clearing the market means that all the goods offered for sale will be purchased at a mutually acceptable price.) In theory, then, the most efficient markets ought to be global markets, because they are the markets with the most players. In this new era of globalization, then, nineteenth-century economic liberalism in its neoliberal guise has become the natural normative point of reference for classical and neoclassical economic theorists, public policy makers, and informed publics alike. Its political and social ramifications are huge, as were those of British economic liberalism in the middle of the nineteenth century with the shift to freer trade and the gold standard.

3. AN "EMBEDDED NEOLIBERAL CONSENSUS"?

This third strand of economic neoliberalism developed out of the return to fashion in academic economics of the theories of free market economists, like Milton Friedman in the United States and intellectual policy makers like Sir Keith Joseph in the United Kingdom (Joseph 1974), and came to dominate the domestic "conservative" (i.e., neoliberal) policy priorities of successful politicians such as Thatcher and Reagan. But the real springboard for its newfound intellectual and political success was the experience of crisis in the post–Second World War economic order, both domestic and international, especially in the recessionary era of the 1970s.

A. Neoliberalism, Crisis, and Change in the Global Political Economy

The 1970s crisis had several dimensions. The most important ones for our purposes include the following:

1. *The "fiscal crisis of the state"* (O'Connor 1973/2001), in which the budgetary costs of social policies, public services, nationalized industries, and bureaucracies were seen to grow faster than the tax base. This dimension of the crisis at first led to increasing attempts by governments in developed capitalist states to increase provision for those services through a combination of deficit spending and inflation, which fed into a vicious circle of budgetary crisis and an endemic inflationary spiral, especially in the United Kingdom. In a second phase, conservative (neoliberal) politicians, economists, and public policy makers increasingly proposed reducing tax rates and cutting back government services with the aim not only of reimposing budgetary discipline but also of producing additional economic growth that would result in higher tax payments despite lower rates—so-called supply-side policies.

2. *The partial breakdown of "social partnership" or "neocorporatist" arrangements*—usually tripartite, state-supported institutions or negotiating fora bringing together management, labor, and bureaucrats—that had become increasingly important in the 1960s for negotiating wages, working conditions, and hiring and firing of workers (Lehmbruch and Schmitter 1982; Goldthorpe 1985; Eichengreen 2006). The "stickiness" of wages and the slowdown in investment attributed to these arrangements were blamed in Britain and the United States, but elsewhere, too, for economic stagnation (Middlemas 1979).

3. *International and domestic economic conditions*, raising fears of a vicious circle of economic stagnation and decline. These conditions ranged from the reduction in the growth rate of world trade (and an actual brief decrease in 1982), along with an alarming rise in the "new protectionism," mainly through the introduction of nontariff barriers, on the one hand, and to increasing "stagflation," or simultaneous stagnation and inflation, on the other. There was a fear of a return to the vicious circle like the beggar-thy-neighbor protectionist and domesticist policies that were seen to have deepened the Great Depression of the 1930s.

4. *The breakdown of that part of the Bretton Woods system concerned with maintaining the "adjustable peg" system of managed exchange rates* known as the "dollar standard" or the "gold exchange standard"—often, at the time, confused with the wider system of Bretton Woods institutions themselves (which survived and retooled). Endemic exchange rate crises that had led to the end of the dollar's link to gold (1971–1973) were dramatically exacerbated by the Yom Kippur War of 1973–1974 and the fourfold rise of oil prices that resulted, starting a process that led to further rises in inflation, interest rates, and third world debt that regularly erupted during the 1970s and early 1980s, entrenching the deepest recession since the 1930s (Strange 1986).

B. New Conflicts and the Paradoxical Emergence of a Neoliberal Political Consensus

The experience of the recession of the 1970s at first led to various country-specific crises, differing somewhat from region to region, of what has been called the postwar consensus around domestic Keynesianism and/or "indic-ative planning" and the welfare state. Once Keynesian macroeconomic fine-tuning had failed to prevent stagflation and neocorporatism came to be seen as a major source of rigidity preventing businesses from responding to these crises, major sections of the postwar coalitions in most developed capitalist countries began to defect. The ideological and cultural glue of Ruggie's embedded liberalism—reinforced by the long boom from the early 1950s to the early 1970s and accepted even by most conservative parties in the 1950s, 1960s, and early 1970s—dissolved. Various middle-class groups and even fractions of the working class began to vote for parties and leaders promoting the new brand of economically liberal "conservatism"—or what would come to be called neoliberalism.

At the same time, however, attempts to shift from organized capitalism and neocorporatism to neoliberalism in Germany, Austria, Scandinvia, and elsewhere were mixed, given the historical path development of political institutions and the variation of political coalitions and economic structures in different advanced industrial countries, reinforcing long-divergent patterns among different "varieties of capitalism" (Hall and Soskice 2001). However, academic and political debates have raged over the significance of those variations in the context of increasing transnationalization and complex interdependence (Keohane and Nye 1977/2000; Hülsemeyer 2003; Soederberg, Menz, and Cerny 2005), including extensive debates on the fate of the welfare state (Offe 1984; Pierson 1994; Clayton and Pontusson 1998; Rhodes 2007).

Nevertheless, neoliberalism made increasing inroads into the politics and economic policies of a range of countries and across the political and sociological spectrum. In Britain, 42 percent of trade unionists voted Conservative in the key election of 1979 that brought Thatcher to power, and in the United States the Reagan Democrats also became part of the new neoliberal consensus. In the 1980s and 1990s, both the British Labour Party and the Democratic Party in the United States moved distinctly to the right in order to recapture the center ground, with labels like "New Labour," the "New Democrats," and the "Third Way." The failure of much of the supposedly "socialist" program of French President François Mitterrand, elected in 1981, to pull France out of the slump led to his administration partly reversing course and then giving way to "cohabitation" with rhetorically neoliberal conservatives, although much of French statism remained (Cerny and Schain 1984). Germany and Japan are still in the midst of this transformation (Yamamura and Streeck 2003; Hook 2005). The European Union has been seen as a driving force of neoliberalization, too, not only in terms of competition policy and the development of the single market after 1985 but also through the evolving discourse of European integration (McNamara 1998).

This process was not limited to the developed world. Much worse stagnation in the 1970s and 1980s in Soviet Bloc countries alienated many of the same groups—leading to the protests that brought down the Berlin Wall in 1989 and ended the cold war and thereafter to a wide variety of neoliberal experiments throughout the transition countries (Kaldor, Holden, and Falk 1989; Robinson 1999; Rutland 2000). And bureaucratic authoritarian governments in the developing world, especially those mired in the debt crisis of the early 1980s, found their quasi-nationalist, quasi-socialist coalitions dissolving in hyperinflation and crony capitalism. The rapid industrialization taking place in many transition and developing countries, fueled by globalization, created a demand for neoliberal policy innovations, broke up old corporatist sociopolitical coalitions, and laid the groundwork for new coalitions to emerge seeking to mobilize both existing and potential new supporters. Pressure from international financial institutions and from advanced industrial countries—the Washington Consensus referred to earlier—led to a first round of restructuring, while financial crises and shocks in Mexico, Southeast Asia, Russia, Argentina, and Turkey led to a wholesale shake-up of their financial systems. Today, while domestic political systems diverge, foreign policies compete, and economic reforms vary, neoliberalism has nevertheless become the economic policy program of choice in China, India, Brazil, and South Africa, the main middle-income developing countries, as well as in the Asian Tigers—and increasingly in poorer countries, too.

C. Conflict, Crisis, and Consensus in the Neoliberal Trajectory

Not all disillusioned groups bought the whole neoliberal package, but the politics of most countries increasingly revolves around the conflict between resisting neoliberal policies to preserve social values or entrenched positions, on the one hand, and capturing the benefits of globalization by internalizing neoliberal prescriptions, on the other (Soederberg, Menz, and Cerny 2005). Severe social disruptions have often resulted, especially when particular socioeconomic groups have become unemployed and/or impoverished—whether in developed countries or, more sweepingly, in those developing countries that suffered most from overextended and/or collapsed states, deteriorating terms of trade (especially the "commodity trap," whereby raw materials declined in relative value), or political divisions along communal or class lines. "Antiglobalization" protests did not take that ostensible form until the 1990s, but the rise in internal violence, civil wars, cross-border wars, terrorism, and the like is widely imputed to the negative effects of neoliberal globalization. Endemic financial and economic crises from the Latin American debt crisis of 1982 to today's global financial crisis demonstrate that adjustment to neoliberal policies can be a painful and politically divisive experience.

At the same time, alternatives to neoliberalism have also been ineffectual and often incoherent. Prime Minister Thatcher famously said that "there is no alternative" (TINA) and that "you can't buck the markets." In the light of such increasingly influential and politically successful perspectives, the key debates—both political and academic—about neoliberalism have revolved around whether globalization in its neoliberal manifestation is inevitable and whether there is a long-term process of convergence taking place across the world, one that cuts across the levels of analysis distinction and affects domestic and international politics alike. Within this process of convergence, embedded neoliberalism has been identified as the main ideational concept not only for explaining the dynamics of change but also for framing and designing public policy. Such an approach is proactively built around a range of market-promoting and market-enhancing policy measures—measures that are themselves rooted in the integration of domestic and international politics and the systematic restructuring of domestic politics around the successful insertion of the domestic into the new world politics. These explanations and policy prescriptions cluster around several distinct dimensions of neoliberalism.

4. DIMENSIONS OF THE NEOLIBERAL CONSENSUS

At least four main dimensions can be distinguished, although it is possible to identify more. There is increasing consensus among both national and international policy makers that these dimensions constitute component parts of a coherent package of policies that are seen to be "necessary" in the light of increasing interdependence and "global realities." However, the precise combination of policies and the degree of convergence along each dimension in different geographical areas—especially with regard to national political systems—depends on the configuration of existing domestic institutions and practices, the stances of interest groups both national and international (and the transnational linkages among groups across borders), and the impact and interpenetration of the growing international and transnational public and mixed private-public sectors. In a globalizing world, these dimensions are increasingly fungible in practice, especially in the context of financial crisis, thereby increasing the opportunities for actors to influence and shape outcomes.

A. Toward a More Open World Economy: Reducing Barriers to Trade and Capital Flows, and the Internationalization of Production

The first dimension, the one most directly related to the development of the post–Second World War international political economy, concerns the reduction of barriers to trade and capital flows. Trade barriers were blamed for the decline in world trade that deepened and extended the Great Depression of the 1930s, and the establishment of the General Agreement on Tariffs and Trade in 1947 led to several rounds of tariff reductions and, from the 1970s, attempts to tackle nontariff barriers too. The transformation of the GATT into the World Trade Organization in 1994, along with the negotiation of a range of regional and bilateral trade agreements, indicates that, despite great unevenness and some backward steps, free trade is in many ways the core building block of both embedded liberalism and later neoliberalism.

There has developed a growing consensus that trade barriers lead to a vicious circle of retaliation, leaving all participants worse off—whereas free trade, so long as it does not lead to serious short-term structural disruption, seriously "unfair trade," and the like, is a long-term, critical public good benefiting poor as well as rich countries by creating a virtuous circle of economic development and growth. Although free trade, uneven as it is—especially in areas like agriculture, textiles, services, and intellectual property—has been criticized for "going too far" (Rodrik 1997), even antiglobalization protesters today accept the need for lowering trade barriers on products on which poorer countries have a comparative advantage, rather than calling for more protectionism.

Furthermore, since the collapse of the postwar adjustable peg exchange rate regime in 1971–1973, several factors have led to a multiplication of cross-border capital flows. In particular, the combination of floating exchange rates, the globalization of financial markets, and the failure of import substitution industrialization and international aid regimes to foster effective development has led to the widespread reduction of capital controls. Developed countries, led by both government deregulation and the increasing clout of internationally linked market actors in both banks and securities markets, seriously began to reform their financial systems in the 1970s, while the IMF, the Bank for International Settlements, and other international regimes, including the OECD, pushed for liberalization and established a range of standards and benchmarks for doing so, such as the 1988 Basel capital adequacy standards and the more recent Basel II agreement (Baker, Hudson, and Woodward 2005; Abdelal 2007).

Meanwhile, formerly third world countries—today called "emerging markets," especially the larger middle-income developing economies—not only are increasingly able to attract foreign sources of capital, both foreign direct investment and international portfolio investment, but also are building reserves that are being lent back to chronically deficit countries in the advanced world, the United States in particular. Despite frequent financial crises and the acceptance that some limited and targeted capital controls may be useful for encouraging longer term investment (Chile) and for preventing capital flight in a crisis (Malaysia), the debate on international capital mobility today focuses chiefly on how to institute effective financial regulatory systems at national, regional (European, North American, and Asian) and international levels in order to smooth adjustment to an open global capital markets regime.

Another aspect of economic globalization, the internationalization of production, linked to both trade and financial liberalization, concerns the increasing acceptance of a leading role for multinational corporations (MNCs; Henderson, Dicken, Hess, Coe, and Yeung 2002). Although the project for a multilateral agreement on investment that would have established international rules protecting MNCs from state intervention was dropped in the late 1990s, along with various other rule-making projects in the face of growing opposition, developed and developing states alike, along with the major international economic institutions (Abdelal 2007), have come to see the internationalization of production—despite widespread fears of exploitation and market distortion—as a desirable and necessary, if not sufficient, condition for economic growth. Freer trade, financial liberalization, and the internationalization of production are today widely accepted as core drivers of both domestic and international economies, and they form the cornerstone of the neoliberal project at both national and international levels.

B. Embedded Financial Orthodoxy and the Neoliberal State

The second key dimension of neoliberalism is the reform of national finances, what has been called "embedded financial orthodoxy" (Cerny 1994a). The central feature of this process—its bottom line—has been the control of inflation. Inflation, especially in the form of hyperinflation, is seen as having in the 1970s undermined both the long boom in the developed countries and, even more starkly, development in the third world. Indeed, anti-inflationary policy has been the key touchstone of neoliberalism. Inflation has been seen not as just one instrument of fine-tuning the economy, as was thought to be the case in the 1960s and early 1970s (the "Phillips Curve"), but rather as the inevitable beginning of a vicious cycle of economic mismanagement, leading to recession and decline. Defeating inflation therefore became the first priority of neoliberalism.

This vicious inflationary cycle was seen to be at the heart of the crisis of the advanced economies during the 1970s, when political demands by powerful—corporatist—interest groups were seen, especially by the conservative right, to lead not only to a worsening "wage-price spiral" but also to "overloaded government" (Rose 1980). This analysis was at the heart of the Thatcherite critique of the postwar Keynesian consensus. Inflation was seen to be increasingly entrenched, with government expenditure pushed upward at every stage—what Sir Keith Joseph called the "ratchet effect." In the early years of neoliberalism, the harsh medicine employed focused on undermining such entrenched interests, especially trade unions—key symbolic targets included coal miners in Britain and air traffic controllers in the United States—on the one hand, and a combination of economic deregulation and austerity, especially punitive interest rates, on the other, what was called "monetarism." Inflation had to be "wrung out of the system" before markets could be freed up to work efficiently.

With regard to developing countries, this inflationary cycle of decline was even more complex (Kemp 1983), involving overdependence on import substitution policies; bloated, uncompetitive, and featherbedded industries, both nationalized and private, producing expensive and poor-quality products for a stagnant domestic market; state-owned or supported banks providing cheap loans to such businesses, often with a government guarantee and little hope of repayment; overextended and overstaffed government bureaucracies; a declining tax base; crumbling welfare states and public services struggling to counteract rising discontent from workers and poor people hit by rising prices on the one hand and falling incomes and state benefits on the other; and authoritarian superstructures, especially military regimes, trying to keep the system from collapse, often in the face of popular guerrilla movements—not to mention corruption. Defeating inflation therefore often involved fundamental regime change.

Beyond basic anti-inflationary policies, embedded financial orthodoxy has entailed a shift away from Keynesian macroeconomic demand management to a more market-oriented approach to fiscal and monetary policy. With regard to fiscal policy, both personal taxation—especially at higher rates—and, increasingly, corporate taxation rates have been widely lowered with the express intention of freeing up private capital for investment (supply-side policy). The role of tax reduction for consumption has been more controversial and unevenly applied, but lower taxes have become a key part of the neoliberal consensus on both right and left and in some countries, especially the United States, have been the centerpiece of vote-winning strategies. For example, tax cuts legislated by the George W. Bush administration were criticized by Democrats as a tax cut for the wealthiest, whereas presidential candidates Bill Clinton in 1992, John Kerry in 2004, and Barack Obama in 2008 spoke not only of rescinding tax cuts for the rich but also of legislating in the future for tax cuts for the "middle class" or the "99 percent of taxpayers" who did not benefit from the Bush program.

Balanced budgets are, in theory, another central tenet of embedded financial orthodoxy, although they are often more honored in the breach than in reality. In the United States, deep tax cuts under the Reagan administration

(1981–1989) and the George W. Bush administration (2001–2009), along
with increased spending, especially for defense and various wars, led to historically unprecedented budget deficits, well above the 3 percent standard
seen as tolerable by economists today. Indeed, the most rigorous budgetary
discipline occurred under the Democratic Clinton administration (1993–
2001). The European Union's Growth and Stability Pact limits national budget deficits to 3 percent of gross domestic product, although this has
constantly come under strain, especially in the current crisis, with higher
deficits tolerated in return for promises of future reductions. International
Monetary Fund and World Bank aid has increasingly become subject to
conditionality that requires recipient countries to run primary budget surpluses. In contrast to the United States, political leaderships of both left and
right in many developing countries, for example, Brazil, have adopted tight
budgetary discipline. Today, of course, balanced budgets have flown out the
window, as governments rush to bail out banks and big firms and to adopt
emergency economic stimulus programs. Keynesianism is back in fashion,
although at the core of the discourse is the claim that bailouts now will actually enable a return to budgetary rigor after the crisis has passed.

Another aspect of embedded financial orthodoxy has been the drive to
reform state ministries and agencies in order to reduce waste and make
them operate according to the same sort of efficiency standards used in successful businesses. Also, the mechanisms by which governments and state
agencies manage the money supply have been increasingly subjected to
supposedly nonpolitical disciplines, including the manipulation of the
money supply through open market operations, the trend toward making
central banks independent of political control, and the establishment of
sophisticated government debt management offices (DMOs) (Datz 2009)
and sovereign wealth funds. Finally, macroeconomic management is generally carried out more through monetary than through fiscal policy, although
that, too, is under pressure in the current crisis. Embedded financial orthodoxy, which is at the heart of neoliberal economics and ideology, is a key
component of what is called the "financialization" of both business and
public policy.

C. From Outcome-Oriented Interventionism to the Competition
   State and the Regulatory State

The third dimension of neoliberalism is a sea change in the character of
domestic state intervention. Traditionally, both socialist and social democratic approaches to economic intervention could be characterized as "outcome-oriented," and in the postwar period, the key objectives of public policy
were economic growth, promotion of industrialization, full employment,

and limited redistribution of wealth and income through the tax system and the welfare state. With this package came a broad commitment to greater equality—often, however, observed in the breach in both capitalist and ostensibly socialist societies. The goal of greater equality was particularly significant for social policy. Even center-right and right-wing parties once had to pay lip service to this objective, especially in the wake of the Great Depression and the Second World War (Offe 1984).

Increasingly, however, such substantive, more direct interventionist goals have given way to regulation and the regulatory state (Moran 2003; Jordana and Levi-Faur 2005). The concept of regulation is a general one that mixes together two distinct modes. The first concerns direct or indirect public control of sectors of the economy and of social and public services that, left to themselves, were seen to operate in ways that might potentially run counter to the public interest. Regulators, whether in government departments or relatively independent agencies (the latter was the case especially in the United States), often had considerable discretion to design and run services and set conditions—including some elements of planning—for the operation (wages, working practices, prices, outputs, mergers, etc.) of various industries including energy, infrastructure, and sectors considered strategic to the national economy. In France, the state promoted "national champion" firms meant to become major competitors in international markets and to dominate domestic markets, too (Zysman 1977).

The second meaning of "regulation," one that developed mainly in the United States, involves what has been called "arm's-length regulation": the role of regulators by definition is not to intervene to produce particular outcomes, but rather to establish and enforce general rules applicable to a particular sector, industry, or service to make it work more efficiently in the economic sense of the term. The ostensible purpose of these rules has been to prevent fraud, promote competition and restrict monopolistic and oligopolistic practices, counteract "market failures," enforce contracts and property rights, and generally provide a quasi-legal environment for actors— mainly private market actors—to operate in an efficient market fashion. Although the effectiveness of such an approach has been criticized in the light of scandals such as the 2001 Enron bankruptcy and the failure of regulators to check the financial bubble of 2004–2008, policy makers have ostensibly been trying to make regulation work better, not replace it altogether. The latter conception is at the core of the neoliberal project. As the authors who coined the phrase "reinventing government" wrote: "Governments should steer but not row" (Osborne and Gaebler 1992). Ideally, they argue, governments should not run industries or provide services directly but rather provide a working framework of rules and procedures—like those of an auction—for market actors to follow.

However, neoliberals are divided on one key aspect. Some neoliberals in the 1970s and 1980s, especially neoclassical economists, argued that government should stop intervening in the economy almost entirely. The concept of deregulation originally meant just what it said: repealing rules that caused market participants to behave in any way not dictated by their own self-interest or "utilities" and that thereby distorted markets and made them inefficient. Markets, it was argued, would be automatically efficient and self-regulating—the "efficient market hypothesis"—if left alone. At the same time, other neoliberals argued that it was the *type* of regulation that mattered and that arm's-length "prudential" regulation, the second type listed previously, was necessary to promote efficient market behavior. Deregulation, in effect, was never really deregulation; it increasingly replaced outcome-oriented and discretionary interventionism with new market-friendly regulations—ideally, a form of promarket or *procompetitive reregulation* (Cerny 1991). Indeed, in many cases the new regulations were more complex and onerous than the old type. A well-known example is insider trading regulation in financial markets, almost unknown (except in the United States) before the 1980s. Insider trading regulation, intended to prevent price-fixing among insider groups trading securities and engaging in mergers and acquisitions, requires a robust legal and supervisory superstructure to be effective. Thus promarket regulation can paradoxically be more intrusive than traditional forms of direct government intervention.

The arm's-length regulatory model is increasingly used to restructure public and social services. Cerny and Evans (2004) refer to the "Post-Welfare Contracting State," and Jessop refers to the "Schumpeterian Workfare State" (Jessop 2002). Moran argues that the culture of hyperinnovation characteristic of the new regulatory state is more intrusive and centralizing than ever (Moran 2003). The core of the regulatory approach is contractualization and "*ex post*" regulation—that is, behavior is not constrained a priori (or *ex ante*) but is agreed on a contractual basis and then subject to later litigation when and if rules are broken. *Ex post* enforcement includes both judicial and quasi-judicial procedures, especially through independent regulatory agencies, or "agencification." The primary purpose of such regulation is ostensibly the promotion of competition, seen as the central mechanism of efficient market behavior or what Adam Smith called the "invisible hand" of the market, although its secondary purposes—often given precedence in political discourse—are claimed to be prevention of fraud, protection of consumers, and avoidance of contagion from market failures.

Such rules-based systems nevertheless require extensive *ex post* monitoring and surveillance to determine whether agreed performance indicators or targets have been met, rather than the exercise of discretionary *ex ante* control. Ever more aspects of economic life are today subject to extensive regulation of this sort imposed by governments of both left and right in both developed and developing worlds. Indeed, a main role of the IMF, the WTO, and the World Bank today is to proselytize the regulatory creed and spread their version(s) of best practices throughout the world. Thus, although neoliberalism is rooted in a belief in the superiority of efficient markets, most neoliberals today would agree that many markets require extensive new regulatory regimes to make them work efficiently—although which markets need more regulation and which need less is a major bone of contention. Indeed, a whole new academic industry is emerging around the analysis of regulation in a global context, both critical and problem solving (Jayasuriya 2005; Jordana and Levi-Faur 2004). Today, beyond the immediate Keynesian matter of bailing out failing firms and adopting short-term economic stimulus packages, debates are heating up about what sort of new arm's-length regulations will be required to stabilize and streamline financial markets in the future.

D. Reinventing "Governance"

The fourth core dimension of neoliberalism concerns the role of the private sector and its complex interaction with public-sector institutions and mechanisms in a range of contexts. Rather than reinventing "government" as such, this involves a wider process of reinventing the fundamental relationship between the private and the public sectors that is supposed to maximize synergies between them, a process Rhodes calls "governance" (Rhodes 1997). At one level, for example, neoliberalism has always involved the privatization of many public and social services and experimentation with mixed public-private productive and distributive goods. However, the emphasis has shifted from the direct sale of government-controlled industries to the private sector, as in Britain under the Thatcher government, to contracting out services, the development of public-private partnerships (PPPs), and the use of private sources of finance for public purposes, for example, the British Private Finance Initiative (PFI) for the construction and sometimes operation of schools, hospitals, prisons, and the like (Dunleavy 1994).

Proponents argue that structural changes in the economy, especially the development of information and communications technologies (ICT), have fundamentally transformed how firms work and shifted the boundaries between public and private sectors—not merely reinventing government but also reinventing governance. Opponents argue that such services have a public character that is undermined by privatization. A key example cited is the privatization of aspects of military and defense provision, from suppliers of matériel at home to the use of private military contractors (PMCs) to support military activities in the field—as has been highlighted by the recent controversy over the role of Blackwater and DynCorp in Iraq—or even to substitute for them, as with mercenary forces in Angola, Sierra Leone, Fiji, and elsewhere (Cowen 2007; Leander 2007). Another objection is that cost savings have not, in fact, materialized, and governments have assumed private contractors' financial risks where cost overruns and quality deficiencies have occurred, as with Halliburton's (and other firms') activities in Iraq.

This dimension is linked with the shift to arm's-length regulation. Contractualization, the use of financial performance indicators, and *ex post* enforcement—rather than direct government control and/or provision— are at the heart of the system. It also involves the development of hybrid forms of governance around special-purpose bodies such as development agencies and quangos at local, subnational-regional, national, supranational-regional, transnational, and international levels. Indeed, the use of the word "governance" instead of "government" took its original inspiration for Rhodes not simply from the traditional distinction between government as formal institutions and governance as informal processes, especially policy networks, but also from international regime theory as discussed previously (conversation with author, 1993). Neoliberalism involves the substitution, where deemed appropriate (a matter for debate among neoliberals), of purpose-built regimes for the organization of public life, regimes that straddle the public-private divide and involve market participants directly in the authoritative allocation of resources and values. In this sense, neoliberalism, like neomedievalism, involves the semifragmentation of government into crosscutting and overlapping institutions and processes—the "splintered" or "disaggregated" state discussed earlier.

5. WHO'S DRIVING CHANGE? NEOLIBERALISM FROM TOP DOWN, BOTTOM UP, INSIDE OUT, AND OUTSIDE IN

The emerging neoliberal consensus is not simply developing "from below," as market forces and transnational interpenetration constrain institutions and actors to behave in particular ways. It is a political construction promoted and shaped in real time by political entrepreneurs and interest groups who design projects, convince others, build coalitions, and ultimately win some sort of political legitimacy. It is difficult to attribute either neoliberalism itself or its various component parts to a single causal factor like globalization. In the last analysis, it is the capacity of actors to co-opt, manipulate, and reframe neoliberalism around a range of diverse goals that enables embedding to proceed.

A. The Overdetermination of Neoliberalization

What is remarkable about neoliberalism, like embedded liberalism before it, is that it would appear to be overdetermined. In other words, several interacting factors and independent or quasi-independent variables are pushing *in the same direction*. Scholars will debate the relative significance and independence of these variables in embedding neoliberalism, but virtually all categories contribute to the increasing discursive and practical hegemony of neoliberalism. In this section, we look briefly at several types of categories—policy challenges and institutional responses, patterns of interest articulation and aggregation, and patterns of actor behavior cutting across and linking the first two—and suggest how they each contribute to the neoliberalization process.

Policy Challenges and Transnational Institutional Responses

In the first place, structural and institutional trends at both domestic and transnational levels have reinforced the embedding of neoliberalism. The scale of problems faced by political, economic, and social institutions has shifted upward and outward, making the traditional tools of the modern nation-state problematic to apply. Macroeconomic policy is increasingly constrained by the integration of international markets, leading to a convergence of monetary and fiscal policies and policy-making processes, including tax competition, the convergence of interest rates, and the trend toward politically independent central banks. Regulatory policy is increasingly affected by regulatory competition or arbitrage. Industrial policy has been transformed by the transnationalization and flexibilization of production and is increasingly targeted on niches that must be internationally competitive to survive—including many small and medium-size firms. Barriers to cross-border trade and capital flows are reducing, however unevenly. Social policies are being both marketized and reoriented toward compensating losers. And perhaps most salient of all at present, environmental problems such as climate change can be tackled only through extensive cooperation, often honored in the breach, thus constituting a crucial challenge to national policy autonomy that states are having serious difficulty adjusting to, given their other policy priorities.

In this context, traditional statist and mercantilist policy and institutional responses have been the main losers, despite attempts from time to time to resurrect them on the basis of resource wealth. Early, more rigid economic liberal and neoliberal responses have proved inadequate, too. The Washington consensus, the structural adjustment policies (SAPs) imposed by the World Bank in the 1980s as conditions for loans to developing countries, the lifting of capital controls, and attempts to shrink the welfare state have given way to the post-Washington consensus—attempts to innovate in areas such as poverty reduction, good governance, and regulatory reform and innovation. Although the development of international regimes and global governance institutions is still partial and fragmented, the World Bank, the IMF, the WTO, the Bank for International Settlements, the G7/8, the G20, the International Labor Office, and many more are not only rooted in a neoliberal rationale but also inherently bound up in a trial-and-error evolutionary process. Neoliberal discourse and normative principles have proved a particularly flexible resource in an institutionally complex and even messy world for policy experimentation and policy articulation and networking among a range of institutional levels.

Interest Articulation and Aggregation

Second, interests and interest groups are less rooted in domestic society and more locked into transnational and international patterns. Insulated domestic political solutions are increasingly impossible to design in an open, interdependent world. It is not only multinational corporations that have to define their interests in transnational fashion but also small businesses dependent on some combination of exports, imported inputs, investment from markets and institutions themselves dependent on globalized circuits of capital, and changing consumer preferences that pressure institutions and policy makers to pursue neoliberal policies. The resurgence of international migration and the challenge of multiculturalism are transnationalizing the very perception society itself. And technological change, in particular the rapid evolution of information and communications technology, makes cross-border linkages routine among ordinary people as well as decision makers.

Of course, such changes provoke backlashes from those at the sharp end. Protectionist and nativist pressures are constantly at the forefront of political debate and the news media (e.g., Buchanan 2006; *Lou Dobbs Tonight*, Cable News Network). In the short term, such pressures can seem very strong. However, what is perhaps most striking is that these backlashes rarely alter the wider trend toward openness. Even the American-led "War on Terror," with its restrictions on cross-border movement such as the Patriot Act and increased surveillance, looks increasingly temporary as political and legal opposition mounts and a new administration takes office. Attempts to impose stricter immigration controls around the world appear toothless in the face of economic incentives for people to move where employment and upward mobility seem available.

In this context, it can be argued that we are witnessing a rearticulation of social and political coalitions in the context of globalization. Traditional sectional groups such as businesses, trade associations, and trade unions (Evans 2007) seek to develop active, organized cross-border networks. Both sectional and cause or value groups are also increasingly associating through nongovernmental organizations and global civil society to pursue their wider goals (Edwards 2004). The most effective groups are those that can proactively articulate their activities on a multilevel basis, for example, coordinating local-level and grassroots-type organizational activities with pressure on provincial authorities, media campaigns, traditional methods of influencing national governments, legal action through courts and quasi-legal administrative bodies, recourse to and coordination with international regimes, and pressuring and negotiating with multinational businesses at the same time. Groups cannot merely call for authoritative action by hierarchical governments. They must also appeal to consumer interests, formulate innovative regulatory proposals, seek private-sector solutions such as corporate social responsibility guidelines (Lipschutz 2005), and promote neoliberal principles of good governance that can be applied in flexible, market-friendly, internationally open ways. Thus interest groups constitute a second fundamental variable in determining—and overdetermining—the trajectory of neoliberalism and neoliberal globalization.

Patterns of Actor Behavior and Framing Discourses

The changes just outlined represent fundamental structural shifts to which neoliberal policies and discourse appear to be the most appropriate response. At the core of both trends, however, is the role of actors. Set into an evolving institutional and distributional context, it is the ability of key actors—not only political entrepreneurs but also ordinary people in their daily lives—to adjust, adapt, refashion their understandings of the world, and develop strategies and tactics to deal with trends that will shape real-world developments. All sorts of different actors—economic, political, and social—are finding neoliberalism a more suitable vehicle for framing problems and developing strategies for pursuing their objectives.

Economic actors are not merely dependent variables in a process of economic change. Involvement in transnationalizing firms, market structures, and networks also generates a different kind of economic consciousness, which does not see the world as simply divided into national economies but as cut across by transnational sectors, strategic alliances, skills that are transferable across borders, and a concept of economic efficiency and profit that links the individual with the global context. As Stopford and Strange point out, countries don't compete, firms compete (Stopford and Strange 1991), and the very conception of competition is changing as actors—loosed from their national moorings—alter their horizons and refashion their businesses to stay ahead of the curve. The fact that business schools around the world pass on these global values, approaches, and strategic orientations in the very formation of actor understandings is crucial to the development, if not of a borderless world, then at least one in which borders are being continually deconstructed and reconstructed along functional lines (see chapter 3). Trade unions, too, are reorienting their strategies around such global values (World Commission on the Social Dimension of Globalization 2004).

Political actors are also reshaping the way they frame the world and approach both policy issues and sociopolitical restructuring. Most important are political entrepreneurs or institutional entrepreneurs, whether at local, provincial, national, or international levels—especially where they play pivotal roles linking the different levels of what has come to be called "multilevel governance." In this context, state actors—politicians, bureaucrats, political parties, and the like—are particularly crucial in formulating new public policies designed to overcome the legacy of the "overloaded state," stagflation, and similar problems and in breaking up old political coalitions and building new ones at both elite and mass levels to win elections or control and reshape bureaucracies in order to promote marketization and competitiveness.

In the 1970s, neoliberal state actors were primarily of the right, like Reagan and Thatcher. Today, with the exception of Hugo Chavez, Kim Jong-Il, Mahmoud Ahmedinejad, and Vladimir Putin, most state actors on both right and left are fundamentally neoliberal. The Competition State, whether in the United States, Europe, China, Singapore, or Brazil, is itself shaped by neoliberal state actors, often in the teeth of traditional left-right divisions and backlashes. One key trend constantly mentioned in this book involves transgovernmental networks of regulators, legal specialists, legislators, and other politicians and bureaucrats who regularly interact and share problems and views with similar actors in other countries. For example, financial regulators are likely to have far more in common with their interlocutors in other financial regulatory agencies, financial services regimes, and trade associations in terms of norms and understandings of how to deal with financial globalization than they will with politicians and bureaucrats in other parts of their own state apparatuses (Baker, Hudson, and Woodward 2005). Slaughter's "new world order" (2004) is profoundly neoliberal, too.

Another way political actors are important in spreading and entrenching neoliberalism involves political and economic power differentials among states. This is especially true of the role of the United States and the American model, with its inbuilt "globalization premium"—its neoliberal political culture, multilevel federal institutions, marketized economy, arm's-length regulatory culture, and free market ideology (Friedman 1997). American hegemony, it can be argued, is not fundamentally the top-down hegemony of the American "state" as such, but the bottom-up, infrastructural hegemony of the American model of society—popular in many parts of the world, even where American foreign policy is despised and resisted (Cerny 2006b).

A third way, of course, involves political actors with the expanding range of diverse international organizations, regimes, and other organs of global governance. These are staffed by people who see themselves as having an inherently more global perspective than those who work in national governments. It is not merely that they take on nonnational identity, but more that they seek to make those institutions increasingly autonomous of their formally intergovernmental sponsors. To the extent that such actors are able to entrench their positions, especially through espousing neoliberal goals that can reconcile their strategies with transnational private-sector actors and state actors, they will be able to both protect and expand their organizational turf while further embedding neoliberalism as the common sense of evolving global governance.

Social actors are perhaps the most transnational category of all. Issues of global inequality, environmental degradation, and challenges to the welfare state have mobilized a wide range of actors, including transnational value groups and global civil society; cross-border ethnic and religious groups, linked through migration, the expansion of diasporas, and the Internet; and ordinary people linked through the Internet who do not need to move physically to participate in transnational society. Interestingly, the antiglobalization movement, which has had a number of media and political successes, such as the demonstration outside the 1999 World Trade Organization meeting in Seattle, has transformed itself into the "alter" (or alternative) globalization movement, working through the World Social Forum and similar platforms. More important, however, is the way local and global actors interact through the development of "global microspaces," "transnational circuits," and "shifting spaces" (Sassen 2007). In all of these cases, actors have sought to craft new ways to navigate among the different levels of "glocal" action through "translocal civilities," "global nomadism," "global cosmopolitanism," and the like. In reconstituting their multilevel action frames, developing complex transnational-yet-local identities, and developing strategies dependent not on hierarchical state spaces but on flexible marketlike—yet socially aware—policy alternatives, these actors are actively reconstituting neoliberalism in a fluid yet fungible environment that goes beyond mere structural change.

B. The Politics of Neoliberalism: Innovating across Issue-areas and Multilevel Governance

Therefore, in the evolving world of embedded neoliberalism, the dominance of the discourse of neoliberal ideas—their ideological acceptability and centrality—gives actors who participate in the embedded neoliberal consensus greater ability not only to proactively design creative quasi-neoliberal responses and solutions but also to entrench, through socialization, a priori anticipated reactions that internalize neoliberalism in the way people frame political and economic issues. Neoliberal public policies, whether at national, regional, or international levels, do not only constrain but also bring opportunities. Contemporary politics entails both a process of choosing between different versions of neoliberalism and the attempt to innovate creatively *within* the new neoliberal playing field. Although open trade and capital flows, embedded financial orthodoxy, the regulatory state, privatization and hybrid forms of governance, and the postwelfare contracting state are the bottom line of neoliberalism, their implications vary dramatically by policy issue-area.

Of course, economic globalization and the new neoliberal politics and public policy it has engendered have involved a reshuffling of the pack. New groups, interests, and political entrepreneurs have emerged; old interests and coalitions have either declined or adapted; and the pecking order of influence and clout has been profoundly altered. But the need for stabilization and social integration has also forced such actors to innovate not only in different issue-areas but also simultaneously across the complex, multiple levels and nodes of governance that characterize the twenty-first century. There are several kinds of socially significant policy innovations that are being experimented with in different issue-areas and at different levels. These innovations at first glance seem quite disparate, but they all involve initial responses to the challenge of "reinventing the social" in a neoliberal world.

In the first place, we have witnessed almost everywhere a shift to regulatory and microeconomic industrial policy, with an increasingly dominant international dimension—the promotion of competitiveness. This shift is increasingly significant not only for multinational firms but also for small and medium-size enterprises in an open world economy. Along with a rhetoric of entrepreneurship, free trade, and a commitment to fostering structural change while compensating losers, this dimension of neoliberalism means that basic economic activities have been reframed and resituated in the global (or glocal) context rather than simply the nation-state. The promotion of competitiveness can also be, and often is, linked with side payments to loser groups.

In turn, conceptions of how to improve welfare have partly shifted to the transnational level, too. Linking trade opening to environmental and labor standards gives additional leverage to a kind of extraterritorial social policy, although the inclusion of such standards in multilateral and bilateral trade agreements has proved controversial—not least because countries with a comparative advantage in labor costs have resisted their inclusion. Paradoxically, and contrary to predictions a decade or two ago, welfare spending has not significantly dropped, and a range of welfare reforms have in some instances actually expanded and improved welfare services, especially in developed countries seeking to compensate losers. Neoliberalism is no longer seen as incompatible with welfare, but provision of welfare is increasingly framed in a global context. Political leaders like Presidents Fernando Henrique Cardoso and Luiz Inácio Lula da Silva in Brazil have sought in both domestic and international forums to reinvent domestic social policies (Cardoso 2001), and former United Nations Secretary General Kofi Annan's proposal for a Global Compact seeks to develop a kind of transnational neocorporatism through collaboration with business to promote social goals.

The stress put by neoliberalism on arm's-length regulation has actually helped increase the demand for, and supply of, regulation across the world by redefining regulation as a cross-border phenomenon. Demands for stricter and more accountable international rules and procedures for corporate governance, accounting standards, bond rating agencies, private mediation and arbitration procedures, antitrust regulation, and the like are reshaping government-business relations. Financial crises have reshaped international financial governance. Developed countries, particularly the United States, have not been immune either, as the recent subprime mortgage crisis has demonstrated. A neoliberal approach to a fluid, multilevel "international financial architecture" is today seen to be preferable to the kind of regulatory unilateralism represented by, for example, the U.S. Sarbanes-Oxley Act of 2002, widely regarded to have helped undermine the leading role of Wall Street in world financial markets.

As pointed out earlier, international regimes and global governance institutions have not only sought more autonomy but also transformed their policy goals to a more complex, evolved neoliberal approach. For example, the World Bank's shift in the mid-1990s to giving priority to poverty reduction goals over harsh structural adjustment policies changed the discourse of global governance toward more socially oriented goals, although how far it has changed the substance of policy is hotly debated. At the same time, the major international economic institutions, the leading developed states, and many NGOs increasingly emphasize good governance and democratization as necessary for stability and growth. Indeed, some analysts would include these as a fifth dimension of the embedded neoliberal consensus. Similarly, the World Social Forum and other nongovernmental platforms have shifted the focus of advocacy group debate from antiglobalization to alternative approaches to globalization. And despite U.S. withdrawal, the Kyoto Protocol, the International Criminal Court, the Ottawa Convention on

Landmines, and a range of other international agreements may prefigure a new kind of incremental public legal internationalism.

6. CONCLUSION: TOWARD "REGULATORY," "MANAGED," AND "SOCIAL" NEOLIBERALISM?

The evolution of neoliberalism over the past thirty years has therefore transformed it from a relatively dogmatic, enforced, pseudo-laissez faire doctrine into a kind of common sense for the twenty-first century. Embedded neoliberalism involves an acceptance that we live in a multilevel, more open, and marketlike globalizing world in which informal and negotiated policy processes do not merely complement relations among nation-states but constitute a complex, fungible, pluralized political game that is drawing in ever more actors. Furthermore, globalization has generated a range of multilevel, interlocking playing fields on which actors have increasing scope to experiment and innovate policy approaches in practical situations and engage in bricolage. Neoliberalism, with its mixture of free-market liberalism, arm's-length regulation, institutional flexibility, and international openness, has proven to be a relatively manipulable and fungible platform for actors to use to reconstitute their strategies and tactics.

Attitudes toward these changes, and toward the use of the term "neoliberalism" itself, of course, vary considerably. Although these developments and innovations, I argue, add up to a virtual range of *alternative neoliberalisms*, competing politically with and increasingly winning out over the original, more laissez faire neoliberalism of Thatcherism and Reaganism, still the process of discursive evolution is often uneven and unacknowledged. Paradoxes abound. Some commentators who are otherwise aware of the downside of neoliberalization nevertheless see it as spreading benefits widely (e.g., Coyle 2002). Others who put forward incisive criticisms of 1980s neoliberalism and reject the very concept can end up proposing policy changes that fit well with the sort of regulatory, managed, and social forms that neoliberalism is taking (Chang and Grabel 2004). This process of evolution and reinvention is therefore leading to the crystallization of better defined varieties of neoliberalism, articulated around negotiated transnational regulatory mechanisms—"regulatory" or "managed" neoliberalism—and a new, as yet embryonic "social neoliberalism" that a few years ago would have seemed like a contradiction in terms. Neoliberalism, far from being a monolithic creed, is a flexible doctrine that fits well with transnational neopluralism and is applicable in the context of the multiple equilibria characteristic of today's globalizing world. It is continually evolving as both old and new actors redefine it and internalize it in their increasingly transnational political projects.

Chapter 8

The State in a Globalizing World

From *Raison d'État* to *Raison du Monde*

1. THE NEW GOVERNMENTALITY OF THE COMPETITION STATE

Debates about the nature of the contemporary state and its changing role in the context of globalization and the emergence of transnational neopluralism are nevertheless still at the heart of political life and political theory as we begin the second decade of the twenty-first century. After thirty years or more of what Susan Strange called "the retreat of the state" (Strange 1996) at the crossroads of globalization and neoliberalism, academic, political, and journalistic observers have recently been beating the drum about "the return of the state" (Plender 2008). This is true as far as it goes, but it does not go very far. The argument in this chapter, revisiting my previous development of the concept of the Competition State (Cerny 1990a, 1997, 2000a, and 2005c), is that the state never left. Indeed, the state has constituted the primary structured field of action for the key actors in the transnational neopluralist process that is the focus of this book. Both neoliberalism and globalization have fundamentally depended for their promotion and embedding on the central role of the state for the interest groups that matter the most in this process. Nevertheless, I argue that the state that is supposedly "returning" to the heart of economic life is fundamentally different from its pre-1980s form.

The Competition State, born in the 1970s and 1980s and honed by both right and left in the years since, is not only evolving but also becoming ever more embedded and institutionalized. The Competition State reflects the most recent manifestation of what Michel Foucault calls "the art of governmentality" in a more open world (Foucault 2008). Nevertheless, he still saw this impact as the latest manifestation of the long evolution of *raison d'État*, as he interpreted it—a rationality embedded in and driven by the primacy of stabilizing, developing, and expanding the role of the state, albeit in a context where that role was becoming more and more "self-limiting." That is still partly true today, given the strategic position of the state at the crossroads of neoliberalism and globalization. However, *raison d'État* is increasingly giving way to *raison du monde*.

As observers from Keohane and Nye (1977/2000) to Bill Clinton in his speech to the 2008 Democratic National Convention in Denver have emphasized, we live in a world of increasingly complex interdependencies. Managing those interdependencies depends on the capacity of institutions, processes, and actors—whether at local, nation-state, transnational, and/or global levels—to develop solutions that further imbricate states and political processes into developing a relatively stable world, characterized first and foremost—as the German and Swiss *Ordoliberals*, the precursors of today's neoliberals, prescribed from the 1930s onward—by *economic growth*. As Foucault pointed out, for *Ordoliberals* and neoliberals, "there is only one true and fundamental social policy: economic growth" (Foucault 2008: 144). All else derives from that. And the key for both of these inextricably intertwined groups for the effective promotion of economic growth is the state-supported promotion of competition as the most fundamental foundation stone of successful capitalism.

> In other words: [the first principle of this revolution within liberal governmentality is] a shift from exchange to competition as the principle of the market…; the problem of competition and monopoly is much more [important for the success of capitalism] than that of value and equivalence. [However], *competition is not the result of a natural interplay of appetites, instincts, behavior, and so on.* (Foucault 2008: 116–120, emphasis added)

> …pure competition is not a primitive given. It can only be the result of lengthy efforts and, in truth, pure competition is never obtained. Pure competition must and can only be an objective, an objective thus presupposing an indefinitely active policy. Competition is therefore an historical objective of governmental art and not a natural given that must be respected.…There will thus be a sort of complete superimposition of market mechanisms, indexed to competition, and governmental policy. *Government must accompany the market from start to finish.* (Foucault 2008: 120–121, emphasis added)

Thus the role of the Competition State today increasingly turns on its head the *raison d'État* that characterized, in different ways, both postmedieval sovereignty and nineteenth- and twentieth-century liberalism. The substance of the mid-twentieth-century industrial welfare state was about dealing with market failure by taking economic activities out of the market and replacing them with authoritative hierarchies oriented toward social goals and productionism, often called "decommodification," at the national level. But the Competition State today is new in two inextricably intertwined ways. In the first place, it embodies the *Ordoliberal*/neoliberal state—rooted in procompetitive, promarket regulation rather than in command planning or direct intervention. But in the second place, it extrapolates that competitive imperative to the transnational and global levels. The Competition State, as I have envisaged it, is even more important, both politically and analytically, than the mere neoliberal state, because it embodies this global dimension.

The state and state actors have, in effect, become key promoters of globalization and therefore of global competition as the primary requirement for the achievement of economic growth for all states (in principle, at least), enabling the development of promarket social policies, too (Evans and Cerny 2003). This *raison du monde* has become the hegemonic paradigm for major political actors, even though it is still resisted by so-called realists and neorealists in the academic field of international relations. The underlying aim of state intervention in the twenty-first century is therefore not to replace the market, but to make it work more efficiently. Government promotion of competition—making it into spontaneous as well as regulated behavior and internalizing "enlightened self-interest" in everyday behavior, thereby enabling Adam Smith's "invisible hand" to work properly (the key to Foucault's notion of "biopolitics")—is the most fundamental and indispensable means to this objective.

Governmentality in its various historical guises and contemporary manifestations is essentially about managing the central contradiction of the modern era, that between top-down bureaucratic organization or Saint-Simonianism, on the one hand, and individual market and civil society-type group interest-oriented behavior and values, on the other—that is, between "totalization" and "individuation." Both of these taken together, while in constant tension, are inextricably intertwined, constituting the central and most essential elements of modernity. Understanding this tension was the gift to modernity, according to Foucault, of the Scottish Enlightenment and the Utilitarians (Burchell, Gordon, and Miller 1991; Foucault 2007 and 2008). In this context, governmentality involves not only biopolitics, neoliberalism, and the self-discipline of self-regulation but also, most essentially, the skills required to walk the tightrope between totalization and individuation, of being able to balance, reconcile, and mediate their contradictory concerns in real-world situations and to pass on those skills to others so that they become internalized in everyday life.

The progress of capitalism, and its essential "disciplinarity" in Foucauldian terms—that is, its capacity to influence and shape human behavior—consists in and is constituted by the ways actors continually and constantly make decisions and develop processes, institutions, and, most important, "practices" that enable this divide to be crossed, and its inherent tensions reconciled in practice, in both old and new ways and in changing external circumstances. This new form of governmentality is especially critical in times of fundamental structural crisis, turning problematic conjunctures into processes of structuration. The modern world, therefore, is deeply and extensively the result of a trial-and-error process of institutional, regulatory, and pragmatic bricolage in Lévi-Straussian terms—an art rather than a science—on the part of both state and private actors. Those actors today are busier than ever shaping and *constructing* the globalizing, neoliberalizing Competition State and internalizing the self-limiting, self-regulatory (rather than deregulatory) practices that are necessary for its survival and effectiveness.

Neoliberals, in the guise of the Mont Pèlerin Society of the 1940s and the new Hayekianism of the Thatcher era, as I have pointed out in the previous chapter, had little faith in laissez faire—despite their ideological façade of neoclassical economics—and saw state regulation as the key guarantor of the competitive marketplace. Deregulation in this context was not the removal of rules, but a form of reregulation, promulgating even more complex promarket and procompetitive forms of regulation, as we saw for example with the Big Bang in London and its aftermath (Cerny 1991). The industrial welfare state has therefore been transmogrified into the Competition State or the "regulatory state" (Moran 2003; Majone 1996), its modus operandi being one of pursuing more effective commodification rather than its opposite, and with an increasing focus on financialization as the core process—the infrastructure of the infrastructure.

In addition, of course, there has been a scale shift. With globalization, it has become more and more necessary to develop transnational and transgovernmental cooperative regulatory practices, whether in the public sector, such as the Basel Committee of the Bank for International Settlements, or in the private sector, as with negotiations on accounting rules or the influence of self-regulatory bodies like the International Swaps and Derivatives Association. The International Organization of Securities Commissions (IOSCO) is an exemplar of this intertwining of public and private or trial-and-error rule making—a process of institutional or regulatory bricolage, accelerated at times of financial crisis. The governmentalization of world politics is as yet fragile and embryonic, as the next chapter shows, but that is the challenge of governmentality as it shifts from *raison d'État* to *raison du monde*.

We are therefore not merely talking about the return of the old kind of state. The return of the state is not the sort of return of top-down control of the market by the national state in the way most observers like Plender (2008) seem to think. Rather, the ongoing and rapidly developing and evolving state they identify is a *multilevel* one, domestically and globally, of what I have called managed neoliberalism. It also involves a crucial dimension of social neoliberalism, with increased political awareness of the need for compensating losers. However, this involves not traditional welfare Keynesianism or macroeconomic demand management in the longer term—although some Keynesian measures are crucial in crisis circumstances, whether bailing out mortgage defaulters, extending guarantees to a wider range of financial institutions ("welfare for the banks"), and constructing fiscal and monetary stimulus programs. Rather, it involves the insertion or reinsertion of such groups and institutions, especially subaltern groups, into the market process through education, training, and so on. This sort of social neoliberalism, characteristic of Third Way policies in Britain or the New Democrats in the Clinton administration, as well as a whole swath of emerging market countries like Brazil, China, and India, is both an economic and a political—electoral—imperative in today's Competition State. Keynesian policies for combating financial crises and recession are not to be made into an ongoing process analogous to the postwar consensus after the Second World War. Instead, they are intended to enable markets to recover, and then to empower them once again to generate growth, in a policy environment designed to promote competition and therefore more efficient market behavior leading to *global* economic growth.

2. FROM THE INDUSTRIAL WELFARE STATE TO THE COMPETITION STATE: A POTTED HISTORY

In the last four centuries, states have come, to a large extent, to dominate and subsume other traditional forms of territorially based political organization, such as empires, cities, feudal structures, tribes, and villages. This organizational predominance of the state rests on two analytically distinct but inextricably intertwined foundations. In the first place, the state, as an organization or institution, is embodied in particular factors, including a set of generally accepted rules of the game, the distribution of resources in a particular society, a dominant ideology, and the capacity of the state to use force, whether through "the monopoly of legitimate violence" or a range of legal, economic, and social sanctions, to impose particular decisions and ways of doing things upon both individuals and the society as a whole. In the second place, the state, like other organizations and institutions, is in effect itself a *social entity* populated by a range of state actors within and around the state apparatus. These state actors make decisions and impose authoritative outcomes on nonstate actors. In other words, the state is both a structured field of institutionalized power and a structured playing field for the exercise of social (or personal) power.

The most important organizational characteristic of states, in both these ways, is that they are, sociologically speaking, said to be "differentiated" organizations (Hinsley 1966). In other words, states are organizationally distinct from families, churches, classes, races, and the like; from economic institutions like firms or markets; and, indeed, from nonstate political organizations such as interest and pressure groups or social movements. They are in legal and philosophical principle (and to a lesser extent in practice) both discrete and autonomous, in that they are not subordinate to, incorporated within, or morphologically determined by (structurally subsumed into) other organizations, institutions, or structures. The state stands on its own.

The state is nevertheless a *contested* category, both conceptually and in practice. The predominant modern state, as it has evolved in recent centuries, has often been taken for granted, a given of political, social, and economic life. However, it is more useful to see it as *problématique*—as a starting point or puzzle for analysis and debate. The very notion of the state is what philosophers call a "reification"—that is, seeing an abstract concept as if it were a material thing. But states, like ideas, have real consequences. The core of that reification involves whether, and how—or if—the state is genuinely differentiated from other forms of social organization with which it is inextricably intertwined in complex ways and what this imbrication means for understanding how the state works.

The concept of the state can be seen as contested on at least three levels. First, the state is an economically contested organization. As noted in earlier chapters, it is organized around relationships of power, as well as political ideas such as fairness and justice, whereas economic organizations like firms and markets are organized in principle around material relations of profit, exchange, and economic efficiency. However, firms and markets involve inherent relationships of power, too, and states and state actors have been increasingly involved over the long term in trying to promote economic growth and modernization. The umbilical organizational relationship between state and economy has been the subject of intense debates and conflicts, both academic and political, private and public. In the economic sphere, therefore, the idea of the state as a differentiated organization is continually under pressure, and complex linkages between state and economy tend to erode key aspects of the organizational distinction between the two.

Second, the state is a socially contested organization. States are not natural, spontaneous emanations from a taken-for-granted, preexisting society, people, or public. States are political superstructures that are historically constructed by real people around and over—and sometimes under—often deep divisions such as class, ethnicity, geography, gender, and ideology. People are regularly forced or indoctrinated into acquiescing to the rules, ideas, power structures, and policy decisions of the state. Citizens are made, not born, and this often entrenches deep conflicts of identity and interest within the state. States are ongoing political works in progress, always incomplete, and inextricably intertwined with complex social hierarchies

and networks. The notion of organizational differentiation is highly problematic here, and disentangling state and society is one of the central analytical debates in the social sciences and history.

Third, the state is a politically contested organization. States are politically constructed in the first place, and inherently controlled and/or fought
over by political, social, and economic actors—from absolutist monarchs
and national revolutionaries to various bureaucrats, officials, patrons, and
clients; from corporate elites to popular movements; and from religious
movements to warlords, corrupt cliques, and even criminal gangs. On the
one hand, some states can be organizationally strong in the sense that they
can be rooted in widely accepted social identities and bonds, or that their
institutions are effective and efficiently run, or that their writ runs throughout the territory. They can also be powerful internationally. On the other
hand, states can also be weak on all these levels. All states have particular
strengths and weaknesses, generally cutting across not only the society/
economy/polity frontier but also the so-called inside/outside distinction.

Nevertheless, what is most distinct about states in the modern world—
that is, as historians would say, since about the seventeenth century—is that
the state form of political organization has, at least until recently, *prevailed
historically* over other forms. The combination of hierarchical power inside
the state and the spread of the state form of organized governance across the
globe—along with the rise of modern political ideologies and the strategic
and tactical focus of political, economic, and social actors on gaining power
and influence *within* the state—has led to the widespread assertion that
states are somehow inherently "sovereign." The concept of sovereignty is
rooted in the notion that power and rule, to be effective and legitimate, must
stem from a particular source that is identifiable and (ultimately, in theory)
accountable, whether to a god—the concept of the "divine right of kings"—
or, in the modern world, to the people, as in "popular sovereignty" or "democratic sovereignty" (Weinert 2007). Thus state organizations in the final
analysis are said to represent a holistic concentration and centralization of
generalized, overarching political power that is unique among organizations—what the political philosopher Michael Oakeshott called a "civil association," as distinct from an "enterprise association" that has specific
purposes and a limited remit (Oakeshott 1976)—and central to what
Foucault called *raison d'État*.

The sovereignty of the state also has two dimensions, inside and outside.
In the first place, at the *international level of analysis*, there is no international
"state" or authority structure that has the kind of legal, political, social, economic, or cultural reality or claim to primacy or sovereignty that the state
possesses. The international system of states—that is, the claim that the
international system is itself composed of and constructed by (and for?)

states above and beyond any other institutions or structures—is seen as the norm. The international balance of power, the territorial division of the world, and international law are all constituted by and through relations among states. The international system is therefore constructed in principle on the foundation of states that are not only distinct domestically but also relatively autonomous *from each other*. Each state is in principle, in international law, founded on a unique base—a specific geographical territory, a specific "people" or recognized group of citizens, a specific organizational structure or set of institutions, a specific legal personality, and a specific sociological identity. As Aristotle argued, political communities or states ("polities") are rooted in common conceptions of justice and friendship that delineate and separate the "us" within the state or policy and the "them" or the barbarians outside.

This inside/outside distinction is in principle therefore *mutually reinforcing*, both historically and in terms of contemporary political action. On the one hand, the capacity of the state to stabilize, protect, psychologically foster, and economically develop the domestic or internal state and society requires the assertion of independence from external would-be conquerors or rulers ("noninterference"), the ability to defend and maintain the integrity of the national territory, the capacity of state actors and institutions to enforce their decisions on the populace in an effective manner, and the potential for the state to project power externally in the pursuit of its national interests. On the other hand, the ability of the state internationally to remain independent, defend itself, and pursue national interests in an often hostile world depends in turn on the capacity of the internal state to exact loyalty, develop economic strength and domestic prosperity, build and maintain an efficient military (and civilian) bureaucracy, and evolve into what is often called an effective "arena of collective action"—and vice versa.

3. BLURRING THE INSIDE/OUTSIDE DISTINCTION

Therefore, both dimensions of the inside/outside distinction are rooted in the *organizational capacity* of states—that is, the ability of states (and state actors) to act autonomously in both the context of the interaction of states in the international system, on the one hand, and the context of domestic politics on the other, *at one and the same time*. Historians usually focus on tracing the development of these dual capacities of states over time as being part of a wider process of modernization in the world system. Political scientists often focus on this process as explaining the parameters of strategic or "rational action" by political, social, and economic actors operating on modern domestic and international playing fields. However, the inside/outside distinction has always been problematic, as I have pointed out in previous chapters, and is becoming more so in an era of globalization. This is the case in two main ways.

On the one hand, various international, transnational, and global structures and processes have *always* competed with, cut across, and constrained—as well as empowered—states and state actors. The most successful European states throughout the early modern and modern periods were ones whose power and prosperity were rooted in international trade and imperial expansion, as well as domestic consolidation, including the United States once it had expanded across the American continent. Indeed, globalization itself has often been seen as the externalization of British and later American patterns of open capitalism, trade liberalization, monetary and financial hegemony, and military success in defeating more authoritarian and state corporatist states like Germany, Japan, and even the Soviet Union in the cold war (Mead 2007). But in working to expand and extend such patterns globally, state organizational power has paradoxically boxed itself in by promoting its own subsumption in the globalization process. (On the relationship between *raison d'État* and the eighteenth- and nineteenth-century European balance of power, see Foucault 2007.)

States and the states system thus do not exist in a vacuum, but are cut across by a range of complex interdependencies. Globalization theorists suggest that these interdependencies constitute a rather different structure of the international or global, one based on crosscutting linkages that states have both ridden on the back of and struggled to control—whether multinational corporations, international production chains, the increasing international division of labor rooted in trade interdependence, globalizing financial markets, the spread of advance information and communications technologies (the "global village" of McLuhan's theory of the modern media), rapidly growing patterns of migration and diasporas, or the emergence of diverse forms of global governance and international regimes, not to mention the rapidly evolving field of international law.

In particular, the vital core or bottom line of domestic state power—what is called in legal terms the "police power"—is becoming more and more problematic in this changing world, where formal interstate borders are often helpless in controlling the movement of people, information, goods, and ideas. These highly structured crosscutting linkages and patterns of behavior have encompassed and shaped the ways states are born, develop, and operate in practice—and they are becoming increasingly institutionalized. They have their own organizational characteristics, power structures, and actors that shape the world in ways even apparently strong governments must work harder and harder to catch up with. They may not exhibit the same holistic, hierarchical institutions and processes that are associated with developed states, but they are often more structurally mobile and organizationally flexible than states in general. In the twenty-first century, therefore, states are increasingly seen as the organizational equivalent of the Maginot Line—the useless fortifications the French built between the two world wars to stop German invasions—of global politics.

On the other hand, states are rapidly evolving in their role as arenas of collective action at the domestic level in ways that are—in the mirror image of the traditional inside/outside distinction—inextricably intertwined organizationally with complex interdependence and globalization rather than autonomy and force. Paradoxically, the world as a whole was finally divided up into nation-states only in the middle to late twentieth century, just as globalization was starting to change the organizational parameters of the world: in the 1950s and 1960s, when the British and French empires shed their final colonies, and in the 1980s and 1990s, when the Soviet Union lost its Eastern European empire and itself dissolved into the Russian Federation and other post-Soviet states. Furthermore, many newer states, as well as older states that had in the past been part of quasi-imperial spheres of influence, like that of the United States in Latin America, have not "developed" into bureaucratically effective, politically unified, socially homogeneous, or economically more prosperous and/or fairer societies. Some have thrown in their lot with regional organizations, especially the European Union, some have stagnated and become more corrupt, and some have become "failed" or "collapsed" states, like Somalia.

States are therefore not equivalent in organizational capacity. Some are effective and efficient and/or powerful, and others are weak, collapsed, or failed. Even in relatively developed and powerful states like the United States, a combination of economic problems and the increasing difficulty of controlling external events has led to what the historian Paul Kennedy called "imperial overstretch" (Kennedy 1987). These developments do not only involve the lack of capability to project military and economic power abroad but also include what in the Vietnam War was symbolized by the "body bag syndrome," the unwillingness of the American public to see American soldiers die for either unwinnable or inappropriate foreign adventures—a syndrome revived by the war in Iraq. James Sheehan has argued that precisely because of its extreme experience of war in the twentieth century, Europe, that cauldron of international imperialism and warfare in the modern era, has simply lost its taste for war and evolved into a grouping of "civilian states," more concerned with promoting transnational economic prosperity than seeing their survival and success as bound up in warfare and the external projection of power (Sheehan 2008).

States are also endogenously organizationally diverse. They consist of a bewildering variety of institutions and practices—democratic, authoritarian, egalitarian, exploitative—that have diverse consequences both for their inhabitants or citizens, on the one hand, and for other states and their inhabitants or citizens, on the other (Hurrell 2007). At the same time, no state can fail to be ensnared in the global web in one way or another. Each state combines with and internalizes globalizing trends in different ways, sometimes enabling them to exploit opportunities presented by the opening of international markets, for example, the BRICs (Brazil, Russia, India, and China), but sometimes finding their international linkages exacerbating problems at home, aggravating social or ethnic conflicts, hindering or even reversing economic development, or undermining political stability, leading to violent conflict, civil wars, and terrorism.

4. THE EVOLVING ROLE OF THE STATE
IN "INTERNATIONAL RELATIONS"

Nevertheless, states do remain the central and predominant political organization of the modern era—compared with all the others, at least. Markets and other economic organizational structures are concerned with material outcomes, not basic social or political organization. Ethnic groups pursue their own cultural goals, whether inside or outside existing political structures and processes. Only in theocracies do religious organizations claim full political sovereignty, and even in the leading theocracy of the twenty-first century, Iran, religious claims to political authority are contested at various levels. International regimes are fragmented and lack sanctioning power, despite neoliberal hegemony. As a result of variables like these, therefore, the role of the state is increasingly contested both inside and outside. States are the conventional product of history and social forces, not a given or a natural phenomenon, and their organization is continuing to evolve in a more open and interdependent world.

It is possible to identify a range of organizational issues crucial to any understanding of how states work both internally and externally (and in between) in this more complex environment. The first of these is what some international relations theorists call "capabilities," a term that originally covered mainly military resources but has been extended more and more to social and economic organization and, in particular, to the ability to maintain those military resources over time. States that could marshal concentrated military power to defend their national territories and, especially, conquer or exercise effective influence over other states and/or power sources have, over the course of modern history, been likely to exercise disproportionate influence over outcomes at the international level, as well as the domestic level. Such powerful states could use their organizational capacity to control other states and the evolution of the international system in general, whether through alliances or by more direct forms of domination. However, such states were also very vulnerable to complex shifts in the balance of power and often found that others could "balance" against them by forming alliances, too. Technological changes, for example, new generations of weaponry, as well as technologies of command, communication, and control, can also upset such existing balances or relations of capabilities. And diplomacy or international bargaining and politicking among states could constrain or effectively alter existing balances as well.

Although the possession of such capabilities has been the main underpinning of national strength or power in the modern era, today it is often seen that other forms of capacity or effectiveness are far more important. As noted before, people, especially in liberal democratic states, are more aware, because of the development of the global village, of the downside of military involvement in other parts of the world. Paradoxically, this globalization of awareness has led to a growing unwillingness to get involved in military operations abroad unless they are relatively costless and there is a clear exit strategy, as reflected, in particular, in the Powell Doctrine, put forward by then-General (later Secretary of State) Colin Powell when he was chairman of the U.S. Joint Chiefs of Staff at the time of the First Gulf War in 1991. Historians usually see the Tet Offensive by the Vietcong against American military forces in Vietnam starting in January 1968 as the most significant cultural watershed here, for the United States in particular, when, for the first time in history, images of battles apparently being lost (although military historians disagree on who won or lost Tet) were viewed on television over the breakfast table in the United States and around the world by ordinary people, helping to fuel an already rapidly growing mass movement against the Vietnam War.

More important, the costs of war, like the costs of empire in the 1950s, are increasingly seen by economists and policy analysts to be counterproductive for economic development, growth, and prosperity—in other words, a severe drain on the state (and the country) in terms of both wealth and power, rather than a benefit. Debates are raging over whether the costs of the War in Iraq, sometimes estimated at $2–3 trillion (Stiglitz and Bilmes 2008), have prevented the United States from tackling a range of other problems, both domestic (health care, rebuilding infrastructure, Social Security, employment, budget deficits) and foreign (development aid, fighting disease, etc.), not to mention being able to react to the current financial crisis without triggering a 1970s-style fiscal or budgetary crisis (Cameron 2009). The maintenance or expansion of military and military-related capabilities is increasingly seen as having negative consequences for state, society, and economy. The implications of this shift are enormous, both in opening up the state to new international economic and institutional opportunities and constraints and in expanding the economic regulatory/domestic state. The Competition State, in particular, requires an agonizing reappraisal of the concept of "capabilities" in an increasingly economically competitive and interdependent world.

5. PLURALIZING THE STATE: "MULTIPLE GOVERNMENTALITIES" IN THE COMPETITION STATE

The second major organizational issue facing the state in the twenty-first century involves the internal coherence and hierarchical effectiveness of states in both domestic and foreign policy decision making. States that are internally divided, bureaucratically weak, torn asunder by civil conflict, and/or subject to the influence of special interests of various kinds may be ineffective or inefficient in pursuing so-called national interests. They may even themselves constitute the main cause of destabilization processes that undermine the very same state organization(s) and therefore limit or even destroy state capacity. But all states are facing analogous pressures, including the strongest. Competing domestic interests have often been at odds with the national interest in the modern era, and in the age of globalization, conflicts of interests are expanding rapidly.

This process involves, first, the competition of interests, previously analyzed primarily at domestic level but increasingly transnationalized and translocalized. Some critical analysts have identified the formation of a transnational capitalist class—or at least a transnational elite linked with multinational corporations, global financial markets, various transnational policy networks, epistemic communities, and the like, further associated with hegemonic opinion formers—especially in developed states. These groups are more than mere competing actors. Indeed, they are said to have a common interest in the spread of a neoliberal model of globalizing capitalism (Gill 2003). Not only do they have common goals across borders but also they have resource power and a set of institutional bases and linkages that go from the local to the global (glocalization)—not to mention the kind of personal connections traditionally associated in domestic-level political sociology with class, elite, and neopluralist analysis.

Even if such groups do not possess this kind of organizational coherence and instead are seen simply as a set of uneven, competing neopluralistic interests, their common concern with developing transnational power bases—cross-border sources of income and influence—gives them collectively a kind of political muscle that predominantly domestic groups cannot match, except during particular periods of crisis or electoral campaigns, where domestic groups might temporarily coalesce around emotive, usually protectionist issues such as illegal immigration or job outsourcing. Although the development (or imposition) of national identities has been crucial in the modern era in underpinning statehood, countervailing social and economic trends have become more salient in the global era.

The most powerful interest groups, as I have been arguing, are usually those that can mobilize resources transnationally and not just internally—especially multinational corporations, global financial market actors, social networks like ethnic and/or religious diasporas that cut across borders, some cause groups and social movements, and even consumers who don't care where particular goods are made, provided the price and quality are right. The "nation-state" represents sociological "nations" less and less and is characterized more and more by domestic fragmentation and cross-border linkages—what Rosenau calls "fragmegration," or transnational integration alongside domestic fragmentation (Rosenau 2003), despite the ideological glue of neoliberalism.

The second major organizational issue of the twenty-first century concerns whether the state itself is becoming increasingly splintered or disaggregated, both internally and, as suggested earlier, transgovernmentally. In studies of bureaucracy in the twentieth-century tradition of Max Weber, the key to effective rule was to have a hierarchically organized state in which officials knew their specific tasks, roles, and functions in the larger structure. Although a full command hierarchy in the authoritarian or Soviet planning modes was seen to be counterproductive, the state required a certain amount of centrally organized institutional coherence and administrative efficiency in order to develop and prosper. Today, that logic has been turned on its head. The most effective bureaucratic structures and processes are those that link officials in particular issue-areas with their counterparts in other countries, so that they might design and implement converging international standards, whether for global financial market regulation, trade rules, or accounting and auditing standards. Slaughter's expanding transgovernmental networks among regulators, legislators, and legal officials are effectively taking the lead in internationalizing such issue-areas, redlining them from domestic protectionist interests, dominating policy-making processes, and transnationalizing the most important component parts of the state in order to promote economic growth and other key policy goals in a globalizing world (Slaughter 2004).

A third level of internal organizational change concerns the Competition State in the narrow sense. In some ways, this is not new. Modern nation-states, in the pursuit of the public interest or the general welfare, have traditionally sought to decommodify key areas of public policy—to take them out of the market through some form of more or less authoritative state intervention—in order to protect strategic industries or financial institutions, bail out consumers or investors, build infrastructure, counteract business cycles, and integrate workers into cooperating with the capitalist process through unionization, corporatism, the welfare state, and the like. This process in the twentieth century was linked with the growing social and economic functions of the state, especially in terms of welfare and the promotion of industrialization, and tended to come about through the expansion of what have been called "one-size-fits-all" bureaucracies for the delivery of public and social services (Osborne and Gaebler 1992).

Today, governments are concerned not so much with decommodification of social and economic policy but rather with the endogenous *commodification of the state itself.* This has two goals. The first is to promote the international competitiveness of domestically based (although often transnationally organized) industries. Domestic sources of inputs and domestic markets for products are too small to be economically efficient; only competitiveness in the international marketplace will do. The second is to reduce the costs of the state—getting more for less (Osborne and Gaebler 1992). These two processes are aimed at both streamlining and marketizing state intervention in the economy and reorganizing the state itself according to organizational practices and procedures drawn from private business. The welfare state, for example, is increasingly under pressure in the developed world to adopt market principles, and developing states are often not able to provide meaningful welfare systems at all.

Indeed, perhaps most important, today economic growth itself is in general more the result of global economic trends and developments than of state policies or endogenous qualities of circumscribed national economies. To take a recent example, any future recovery of the United States from its self-inflicted financial crisis, triggered (but not solely caused) by the peculiarly American subprime mortgage crisis, will depend more on the evolution of the world political economy and internationally integrated financial markets than on any specifically U.S.-based regulatory or reregulatory policies—and is indeed linked with deepening crises in other regions.

Politics, politicians, and policies are required to tack to the requirements of global competition rather than pursue domestic autonomy and the common good of the citizens of a particular state. Both inflation and, increasingly, deflation, heavy-handed government intervention, trade protectionism, taxation seen as burdensome on businesses, and bureaucracy in general are likely to deter investment and reduce economic activity. The wider result is often a "democratic deficit," where government is seen to be "the problem, not the solution" (Ronald Reagan)—despite emergency Keynesian bailouts and fiscal stimulus packages. This combination of transnationalized interests, disaggregated states, and the Competition State itself, especially in times of economic crisis, is fundamentally transforming how states work—eroding, undermining, and making end runs around the "inside," traditional Weberian state.

Finally, different states have distinct institutional (or organizational) log-ics. Each is subject to a form of path dependency, in which historical devel-opments create both specific constraints and specific opportunities that become embedded in the way states work. The United States, for example, is characterized by a loose and fragmented form of federal organization that has been crucial in enabling individuals and capitalist actors to operate in a market-friendly fashion that has led to its becoming the leading economy or economic hegemon of the contemporary era—although certain characteris-tics of that system often also create blockages, turf conflicts, and gridlock, undermining policy effectiveness in a globalizing world (Cerny 1989). France, Germany, and Japan have been characterized by a much stronger role for the state in political, social, and economic development, although each model is quite different from the others in specific ways. China is a complex mixture of the centuries-old legacy of imperial China, the commu-nist period, and rapidly encroaching global capitalism. Latin American countries are still bound in many ways by the era of import substitution industrialization of the mid-twentieth century, mixed with anti-American-ism and the tradition of the caudillo, or military strongman, although this has been changing, albeit unevenly. And African states are still deeply scarred by the legacy of European colonial administration, which, when mixed with tribal and clan legacies, has made it very difficult to develop effective states at all. Nevertheless, all are increasingly subject to complex transnational interdependencies and wider global economic—and social and political—trends.

6. CONCLUSION: THE DISORIENTED STATE

In other words, the organization of the state is not a given, but a *probléma-tique* or analytical puzzle, the parameters of which are continually evolving, especially in the current era. Organizationally strong states are to some extent able to both internalize and resist the pressures of economic, social, and political globalization. Organizationally weak states are undermined by glo-balization, and crisis becomes endemic. Most states are between these two extremes, with state actors—still crucial players in the international "system of states," as well as the expanding globalization process—seeking to alter, reform, or completely restructure states in order to cope with the organiza-tional challenges of a globalizing world. National varieties of neoliberalism are certainly emerging, but this is not simply a process of convergence, but one of *diversity-in-convergence* (Soederberg, Menz, and Cerny 2005).

Nevertheless, the overall direction of change—whatever the divergences among states in terms of speed, direction, or depth—is clearly and overwhelmingly toward the Competition State. Smaller and vulnerable states are even more subject to the Competition State rule than big, economically powerful states. The only partial exception to the rule among the latter in 2009 is Russia, whose leaders, especially Vladimir Putin, are obsessed with restoring nineteenth-century *raison d'État* and state monopolistic practices at home and in their former regional sphere of influence, the "near abroad," rather than embedding neoliberal forms of economic competition. What is interesting here is the contrast between Russia and China. Russia has a comparatively quasi-democratic form of government, whereas China still has an undemocratic, quasi-Leninist form of party rule. Yet the former has put its eggs in the monopoly/military capabilities basket, whereas China is becoming a Competition State, albeit a nondemocratic one. The key difference lies in contrasting governmentalities. China has chosen the path of *raison du monde*.

In fact, neoliberal governmentality, as Foucault argues, is not a seamless web. Civil society—and the Competition State?—may be the "motors of history" (Foucault 2008: 305), but the ongoing tension (contradiction?) continues between totalization and individuation, competition and monopoly, liberalism and neoliberalism, and the nation-state and globalization. They embody an ongoing, pluralistic conflict among groups. Sanford Jacoby has recently chronicled the ongoing tension and conflict between processes of financialization and the role of financial elites in promoting that particular form of regulatory reform (financial elites being the main beneficiaries, he argues), on the one hand, and counterprocesses embodied in labor interest groups.

> Upswings in financial development are related to political pressure exerted by elite beneficiaries of financial development. Political objectives include policies that favor financial expansion—and finance-derived earnings—and the shunting of investment gains to top-income brackets. Against financial interests is arrayed a shifting coalition that has included middle-class consumers, farmers, small business, and organized labor.... When successful, these groups can cause a contraction in the economic and political significance of finance, which registers in the distribution of income and wealth. In other words, politics drives the swings in financial development and mediates the finance-labor relationship. (Jacoby 2008: 2)

More broadly speaking, this kind of political competition reflects a key characteristic of the Competition State itself. It is internally increasingly pluralistic, although all the groups competing increasingly must develop their transnational, cross-border connections to be viable and effective. Foucault goes perhaps too far in concluding:

> You can see that in the modern world, in the world we have known since the nineteenth century, a series of governmental rationalities overlap, lean on

each other, challenge each other, and struggle with each other: the art of governmentality according to the sovereign state, and the art of government
according to the rationality of economic agents, and more generally, according
to the rationality of the governed themselves. And it is all these different arts
of government, all these different ways of calculating, rationalizing, and regulating the art of government which, overlapping with each other, broadly
speaking constitute the object of political debate from the nineteenth century.
What is politics, in the end, if not both the interplay of these different arts of
government with their different reference points and the debate to which
these different arts of government give rise? It seems to me that it is here that
politics is born. (Foucault 2008: 313)

Foucault did not live to see the expansion and deepening of globalization in
the way we see it now in the twenty-first century. The "interplay of these different arts of government" is increasingly being circumscribed and fragmented in a globalizing world and often leads not to a unilinear process of
governmentalization but to growing bricolage and a global "governmentality
gap" (see the next chapter). Indeed, the result is often seen to be not a clearly
defined new form of governmentality, but what Arts, Lagendijk, and van
Houtum (2009) felicitously dub the "disoriented state." The disciplinarity of
the Competition State is certainly limiting, defining, and parameterizing
twenty-first-century politics even in comparison with the world he knew and
described in the late 1970s, but it is leading not to the kind of organizational
homogeneity one expected of the industrial welfare state, or even of *raison
d'État* in general, but increasingly to organizational disorientation and even
schizophrenia. *Raison du monde* does not lead to simple solutions.

As I stated in my earlier work on the Competition State, the key to understanding the *politics* of the Competition State is to see it as an ongoing struggle between those groups that are able to—or at least aim to—capture the
benefits of globalization by transnationalizing their activities, networks,
strategies, and tactics (or the "winners"), on the one hand, and those who
bear the brunt of the downside of globalization in terms of unemployment,
reduced incomes, limited opportunities, political repression, and civil strife
(or the "losers"), on the other. The Competition State is therefore an evolving
terrain of conflict between these groups and, in Foucault's terms, primarily—
and increasingly—between traditional liberalism and its decommodifying
role for the state, on the one hand, and neoliberalism with its commodifying, marketizing Competition State, on the other, all in the wider environment of complex interdependence, transnational neopluralism, and critical
events such as the current financial crisis. Nevertheless, overall, the advance
of globalization and the complex interdependencies it entails lead to the
increasing hegemony of *raison du monde*. Neopluralism and neoliberalism,
not laissez-faire and what Polanyi called the "self-regulating market,"
increasingly represent the "motor of history."

Chapter 9

Institutional Bricolage and Global Governmentality

From Infrastructure to Superstructure

1. INTRODUCTION: THE CHALLENGE OF GOVERNMENTALITY IN A GLOBALIZING WORLD

So far, this book has addressed a range of core issues involved in the process of globalization and the emergence of transnational neopluralism: emergence of three-level games, the changing character of spatiality and borders, the reconfiguration of power structures and relationships, the process of structuration, the transnationalization of the policy-making process, the evolution of a hegemonic neoliberal paradigm, and the transformation of the state. These issues have primarily focused on the transformation of what might be called the base, or *infrastructure*, of world politics and on why and how various dimensions of that infrastructure are changing.

In this chapter, the focus shifts upward, to the *superstructure* of world politics—those international institutions and regimes, state and nonstate networks and actors, and formal and informal processes of politicking and decision making that are sometimes said to constitute an emerging international architecture or mixed form of global governance. I argue that this architecture, while becoming denser and weightier, is also highly fragmented, disorganized, and tangled—an inextricably intertwined combination of fragmentation and integration (Rosenau 2003). For this reason, it is often ineffective, inefficient, riddled with gaps, and even counterproductive. Nevertheless, it is not only increasingly salient and significant but also indirectly guided by the new governmentality of *raison du monde*—that is, a form of governmental rationality that sees problems, interests, values, and potential solutions as having a critical and growing transnational or even global dimension. *Raison du monde* prioritizes a process of groping toward a new world political superstructure, however messy and incremental.

The core of the notion of governmentality, as described in the previous chapter, lies in the practices that have grown up over the past three

centuries for creatively shaping—and transcending—the underlying structural tension that permeates the modern world and the process of modernization. That tension centers on a recurring conflict in both theory and
practice between the two most fundamental structural trends of modern
society, economy, and polity—namely, between institutional hierarchy, on
the one hand, and the liberal primacy of the individual, on the other. Each
of these is fundamental to a different strand of Enlightenment thought,
but while antipodes in principle, they are inextricably intertwined in
modernity. The first involves what Foucault calls the "totalization" of modern bureaucratic institutions, both public and private, not to mention cultural and artistic symbols such as grand architecture—the legacy of the
early-nineteenth-century administrative theorist Henri de Saint-Simon.
The second involves the "individuation" of people through capitalist com-
merce and markets, liberal-minded freethinking, the primacy of the individual in liberal democracy, and the role of personal consciousness.

This essentially modern (but also postmodern) governmental rationality
is, however, not only an admixture of these competing traditions in and of
themselves but also an ongoing process of manipulation of the two into a
creative synthesis—the *art* of governmentality. Globalization involves an
extension of these practices to world politics. This wider process of governmentalization is instantiated in:

- the development of institutions or regimes of so-called global
  governance, both intergovernmental and supranational
- the crystallization of uneven pluralist (or neopluralist) processes of
  group politics across and below borders
- the marketization of the state and the spread of more complex
  processes of promarket regulation
- the privatization of governance across borders
- the spread of transnational norms such as human rights
- especially, the renewed incorporation of more and more people,
  cutting across class, into a paradoxically politically promoted and
  regulated culture of individualistic empowerment that embeds liberal
  capitalism at new levels, especially in individual consciousness and
  behavior (Rose and Miller 1992; Larner and Walters 2004; Rose,
  O'Malley, and Valverde 2006)

Thus world politics involves neither an embryonic global state nor an integrated world marketplace as such, but a complex, multilayered, fungible—yet
increasingly hegemonic—set of simultaneously globalizing and governmentalizing political *practices*. These include, in particular, the management of
processes of transnational convergence and divergence through the emergence of new varieties of neoliberalism in politics and public policy. But

governmentalization by its very nature is always incomplete, generally poorly organized except in circumscribed issue-areas, uncoordinated, and unwieldy. In this context, the traditional power politics of national interests, for example, the War in Iraq, constitutes a predictable but anachronistic backlash. However, these politics merely exacerbate the confusion, boost the search for alternatives, and ratchet up demands for yet more transnational governmentalization, thus accelerating the process of bricolage and piling ad hoc experiments on top of each other. This new world (dis)order leads to decidedly mixed results more akin to neomedievalism than to the development of any systematically organized, hierarchical form of governmental authority.

2. GOVERNMENTS AND GOVERNMENT IN INTERNATIONAL RELATIONS

The central conundrum of international relations as both academic discipline and political practice concerns the extent to which order, security, and public goods can be provided internationally without the existence of a state-like—sovereign or quasi-sovereign—international government that could exercise authority over the separate states within that system. Traditional approaches, as I argued in chapter 2, underplay the role of agency in shaping the dialectical element in processes of change and structuration and give too much weight to the increasingly anachronistic inside/outside distinction. The concept of governmentality, in contrast, captures a dynamic and ongoing element of the process of governing that, although originally developed primarily at the domestic level, is now at the heart of international political change.

Governmentality, in Foucault's sense, has come to characterize the dominant practices of liberal states and economies since the eighteenth century and has been essential to their success in providing both security, on the one hand, and market-based prosperity, on the other. It is thus the prevailing political practice of modern capitalist states. It is governmentality—rather than other diverse forms of statehood, such as what in the eighteenth century was called "police" in French (i.e., a hierarchically ordered state characterized by centralized policy making and the supremacy of *raison d'État*), the rule of the capitalist class, the ascendancy of Saint-Simonian bureaucracies in both public and private sectors (the "administration of things"), the invisible hand of the market, or the political forms of liberal democracy—that has enabled modern states to survive, adapt, and develop. Indeed, all these major modern forms of social organization fail when put into practice in isolation or where one is set hierarchically above the others. Rather, it is the art of weaving them together into a whole that is greater than the sum of the parts that enables and empowers the elements of modern society to work together.

In today's globalizing world, an expanded, transnational form of governmentality has become an ongoing and expanding process—being understood, learned, and practiced above, across, and beyond the level of the state. It is increasingly being redefined not only in terms of actors capacity to weave together elements of successful liberal practices at the level of national societies, regions, or cultures but also in the perceived necessity to *link together and actively manage* the various layers of contemporary globalizing liberal capitalist society and the relationships among them. It involves the ability to navigate not just between states, as diplomats have traditionally done, but among those uneven and multiple layers, through negotiation, policy innovation, power brokering, policy transfer, and the like. Nevertheless, in all of these processes, the art or practice is not so different when practiced *across* state borders as it has been throughout the modern period *within* national states. In this sense, globalization and governmentalization are inextricably intertwined. Globalization itself is being brought about above all through a process of the governmentalization of world politics—of the transfer of practices that are seen and thought to be those, pragmatically arrived at for the most part, instituted through the trial-and-error, issue-area-specific process of bricolage, analogous in principle at least to that which has enabled liberal states to be so successful domestically—to the international and transnational levels. What we are seeing is not so much a constitutionalization of the international sphere as an untidy but progressive expansion of the hegemony of those practices learned from the domestic sphere. At the same time, Foucault's version of neoliberalism is also intended to be liberating and self-empowering—emancipatory—rather than simply self-disciplining (Lemke 2006; Pogrebinschi 2008).

3. THE ROOTS OF GOVERNMENTALITY

Governmentality is not embodied in institutions as such. Rather, the *practices* of governmentality are what enable institutions to work in the first place. It is not merely norms or ideas that count, but actors' on-the-job experience in managing the contradictions and tensions inherent in governing, their ability to impart those practices to others through social learning, and the internalization of self-limiting and self-regulatory behaviors on the part of individuals and groups otherwise competing for power and influence. It is not simply that economic growth and prosperity emerge because of some spontaneous bottom-up, self-generating process. These factors are in turn dependent on two kinds of practices: (a) the way actors engage in political practices that enable markets to thrive, not only avoid market failure but also become more efficient and competitive, and (b) the way the system as a whole empowers individuals to become *Homo economicus* at one level while recognizing that pursuit of their self-interest is also at the same time part of a wider social process that is to the general good—what has been known since the eighteenth century as "enlightened self-interest." This process therefore involves an ongoing effort to reconcile *apparently* incompatible structural tendencies in circumstances where those incompatibilities continually reappear, get refashioned and reshaped in political processes, and are exacerbated by the conflicting interests and values of the actors in question.

The capacity for such a dynamic if disorderly developmental process—the balancing act at its heart—has been forged in the historical experience of liberal states. The category of "liberal" states, of course, includes both those societies that have been liberal (or liberal capitalist) throughout the modern era, on the one hand, and those that have become liberal capitalist only through a series of historical tests—only having become liberal more recently and/or having gone through periods of bureaucratic authoritarianism of one kind of another—and that have become more liberal for various reasons. These reasons include the demonstration effect and a desire to emulate prosperous, developed societies; popular demand for liberal democracy; the rise of newer, especially transnational, capitalist elites and other groups; and defeat in war.

The core of this balancing act lies in the practice of modernity, in particular the need to reconcile in proactive fashion the requirements of the antipodes of totalization and individualization described previously. The modern experience involves both. This dimension of governmentality is often neglected by Foucault's interpreters, who focus on the disciplinary (or self-disciplinary) dimension of the concept in entrenching and internalizing neoliberalism and the market society. However, Foucault is quite clear on this point, and his emphasis on the seminal role of the Scottish Enlightenment in pioneering this fundamental underpinning of modern thought and practice—especially the work of Adam Ferguson on civil society—comes through very strongly in his lectures (Burchell, Gordon, and Miller 1991; Foucault 2007 and 2008).

Nevertheless, images of modernity presented by both modernists and postmodernists often emphasize and privilege the former element, totalization, whether in terms of Le Corbusier's architecture and urbanist giantism; images of fascism and state communism—authoritarianism mixed with mass politics—and even the state Panoptikon presented by Foucault himself (Foucault 1980); the Second Industrial Revolution factory with its integrated mass production lines and economies of scale, with Henry Ford's

1913 factory at River Rouge and the Model T car achieving iconic status in this regard; or Hollywood's domination of world cultural production (Bohas 2006). Saint-Simon's idea of "the administration of things" as the wave of the future, also represented in Foucault's work by reference to the Cameralist school and the notion of "police" in social theory (with the state presented as knowing what is best for people), along with the rise and fall of political totalitarianism, represents this tendency. The capacity for governments to collect and use information about more and more people has expanded dramatically with the development of information and communications technology. Human lives today can potentially be micromanaged in ways that were easier to escape even in the authoritarian societies of old, and systems of economic production and exchange often resemble Weber's notion of capitalist organization rather than the diffuse and decentralizing fluidity of the market's invisible hand.

But merely to raise this point highlights an equal and opposite critical reaction. After all, modernism is also about the spread of notions of individual freedoms and human and civil rights, about markets where the efficient allocation of resources in theory depends on millions of micro-choices, about liberal democratic political systems where citizens and voters do actually have some say in the choice of their governors, and about plural-ist political processes in which a range of groups contest and engage in bargaining within the public policy process. Of course, some actors are more endowed with resources and power than others, as in the concept of neopluralism, as I have pointed out throughout this book. They predomi-nate, but they do not necessarily control. Even powerful actors are unlikely to agree with each other on a range of matters across the board, although they may have common priorities, such as the promotion of some version of capitalism. And other groups also have resources to mobilize and rules to appeal to. They can frequently exert leverage and punch above their weight in crucial situations. Thus even in a neopluralist political process, outcomes are determined not by simple coercion and/or structural power, but even more by how coalitions and networks are built in real-time conditions among a plurality of actors. This sort of modernism is more like modernism in literature, especially poetry, characterized by a stylized anarchy that is directed against precisely the kind of giantism implied by the totalizing modernism discussed previously.

Governmentality, then, involves the continuous—and uneven—confron-tation and management of the multiple incompatibilities of totalization and individualization at a variety of levels and nodal points. But it is much more than just that. Governmentality as an art does not merely juxtapose. It also involves taking advantage of a creative, *dynamic tension* between the two contrasting and conflicting, but inextricably intertwined, forms of action and structuration. Thus it requires at one and the same time the development, mainly by political actors, of the art not only of reconciling the two but also of ensuring that the creative disequilibria that result can be channeled into a dynamic process of social and economic growth and development. There is an analogy here with Austrian economics, which dispenses with the notion of equilibrium but sees economic development as the management of continually transmuting and dynamic disequilibria in innovative directions (Thompson, Frances, Levaçić and Mitchell 1991).

Even more, Foucault's approach to modernity in general, as well as to governmentality in particular, is set explicitly, as noted before, in the philosophical context of the Scottish Enlightenment—in the tradition of Adam Ferguson, Adam Smith, and David Hume, with their practical, humanist, and consequentialist emphasis—as well as in the later utilitarian tradition of Jeremy Bentham. (For a recent excellent intellectual and political history of the Scottish Enlightenment and its global repercussions, see Herman 2003.)

Without such navigational skills, disequilibria are likely to be set in stone. After all, it was the increasing dominance of one form of disequilibrium—that between workers who possessed only their own labor power and the bourgeoisie who owned capital—that Marx saw as leading to the collapse of capitalist society and that Lenin saw as becoming even more entrenched through liberal democracy, "the best shell for capitalism." Karl Polanyi described these developments as involving distinct (if overlapping) time periods—a "double movement" between periods when the abstract notion of self-regulating markets would hold sway and loosen social bonds, thereby creating a backlash that would lead to anomie, social unrest, and resistance, on the one hand, and periods when governments would try to reestablish those bonds and reembed markets in social values, on the other. The "Great Transformation" (Polanyi 1944) was seen as emblematic of lessons having been learned from Fascism and the Great Depression, thereby leading to more socially solidaristic public policy through the industrial welfare state. Of course, globalization is often seen as the double movement revived, as destabilizing forms of market liberalization return (Murphy 1994).

But in Foucault's account, history is both messier and more coherent. Not only does the double movement occur throughout at micro and meso levels, as well as the macro level, but its creative management is the crowning achievement of the modern liberal state. In this sense, Foucault's supposed radicalism, born in his postmodernist critiques of prisons and asylums with their emphasis on discipline, punishment, and control, seems to me to merge paradoxically into an almost triumphalist neoliberal pluralism. Foucault makes quite clear that he sees governmentality not as a method of exercising authority or top-down control but as a creative and constructive art of developing the positive human potential of modern liberal society. Indeed, his notion of governmentality is about the *self-limita-tion* of government and the state, and of social and political behavior, in the interests of achieving practical results. Governmentality is all about an ongo-ing process of dynamic, innovative, expansionary, and, on the whole, suc-cessfully learned practice of reconciliation and management of such supposedly contradictory tendencies—despite its unevenness and the smaller scale tyranny and yet emancipatory potential (Pogrebinschi 2008) of micro-"circuits of power." In this sense, governmentality is always a work in progress, never complete.

So what does governmentality involve in more concrete terms? Although Foucault is rather vague on this point, focusing as he does on the longer term history and general principles, it seems to me that there are several lines of development in a range of issue-areas that go well beyond Foucault's specific comments but that can be seen in relationship to each other as giv-ing rise to more generalizable "practices" of governmentality. These prac-tices or *ongoing balancing acts* could include, in particular:

- the capacity for the state administration to be both an efficient bureaucratic structure in the Weberian sense—rationally organized offices with clear functions and rules—and yet flexible enough to conciliate opposing interests, adapt to new economic and social developments, reflect and act on bottom-up as well as top-down inputs, allow bureaucrats to innovate, and the like
- the capacity for liberal democratic institutions to be both *expressive*, representing public opinion and pressure groups, yet also *effective*, that is, capable of providing leadership where necessary and working through administratively and managerially coherent processes of public policy formulation, adoption, and implementation
- the capacity for state intervention in the economy to promote economic and industrial development through central promotion and support, while internalizing norms of efficient market behavior, entrepreneurialism, innovation, investment, and genuine competition on the part of the private sector in both industry and finance, counteracting market failure but not featherbedding firms
- the capacity of a system of legal and quasi-legal regulation not to constrain positive, growth-oriented market behavior but actually to anchor those markets in an institutional framework that stabilizes them, prevents fraud, sanctions contracts but involves clear, legitimate, and agreed procedures for *ex ante* litigation, protects property rights, and basically enforces market rules of the game
- the capacity of the state in international affairs to promote the wider competitiveness of the national economy through trade, finance, and

production while avoiding the beggar-thy-neighbor temptations of old and new mercantilism and promoting various forms of embedded neoliberalism

- the capacity of governments to ensure the economic as well as the physical security of citizens, especially through the welfare state and liberal neocorporatist arrangements, while attempting to prevent the welfare state and corporatist arrangements from undermining the market economy, for example, by leading to inflationary government spending, producing "creeping socialism" or what Sir Keith Joseph called the "ratchet effect," rewarding dependency, entrenching rigid working practices, or otherwise raising costs to business
- managing macroeconomic—fiscal and monetary—policy in ways that can flexibly react to quite subtle indicators of overheating and cooling, inflation and deflation, boom and slump

Each of these balancing acts is partially open-ended. There are no clear prescriptions or instruction books that lay down hard-and-fast principles about what to do in particular historical circumstances. Each depends on actors gaining on-the-job experience in handling the delicate and challenging issues that are faced on a day-to-day basis. It is in this setting that we need to evaluate the late British Prime Minister Harold Wilson's famous (or notorious) saying: "A week is a long time in politics." There are issues of managing tensions between short-term problems, especially if there is a crisis or potential crisis in the offing, on the one hand, and often unpredictable but equally necessary medium- and long-term considerations, on the other. This kind of uneven, open-ended balancing act is patently obviously at the heart of political reactions at both national and international levels to the current financial crisis and recession, too.

There are issues of linking together various horizontal and vertical layers and divisions of government and society, from executive power, to the separation of powers, to complex ministries (and the relations between them), to layers of regional and local governance, to social groups, "interests" in Bentley's sense, classes, organized groups like trade unions, cause groups, and many others. Foucault extensively cites Adam Ferguson's concept of "civil society" as the key to understanding the process of governmentality (Ferguson 1767/1995). And there are questions of linking and weaving the different processes and policy issue-areas listed earlier into some sort of coherent overall social process of "governing" in Foucault's sense of the word. Clearly, these practices or aspects of the art of governing provide the key to the success of liberal or neoliberal capitalist states.

The overall key to understanding contemporary governmentality along all the dimensions listed here—and the intrinsic complex interaction among them—is found in the necessity for *self-limitation* on the part of the state, political actors, and even ordinary people. The limitations on government, as Foucault argues at length in several places, derive not so much from moral or ethical principles such as rights or liberties. Rather, they are rooted in a kind of systemic pragmatism. Governmental actors do not intervene (or choose not to intervene) in economic and social affairs out of moral principles per se but instead are constantly careful not to overstep their own practical boundaries, because in a complex world—especially a world of *Homo economicus*, where the everyday life of the population, the success of market society, and continued economic growth depend on the spontaneous action and interaction of individuals—the state is forever in danger not only of overreaching itself in terms of efficiency and effectiveness but also of stifling progress and human activity more broadly.

States and state actors therefore have to look at the practical and potentially counterproductive effects of trying to control people too closely, for fear of choking off individual initiative, disrupting group solidarity, and undermining the very enlightened self-interest on which society and the state depend for their existence and stability in the modern world. Today, it is often said that policy makers should pursue policy options according to the criterion of what works. This is also true for Foucault. But the discovery of what works is rooted precisely in the balancing act between Saint-Simonianism and individual or group initiative and continuous activity—Fergusonian civil society—described previously and in a particularly modern pragmatism.

4. GOVERNMENTALITY IN AN AGE OF GLOBALIZATION

Going further—extending the notion of governmentalization as an ongoing process to international relations and international political economy—this chapter argues that neopluralist governmentalization is the key independent variable in contemporary world politics that the standard approaches to international relations do not succeed in capturing. Foucault's own presentation of governmentality is confined to the governance of the domestic political systems of nation-states or of particular policy issue-areas and agencies (as is evident from most of the still embryonic literature on this subject). At this point—and especially in Foucault's rather broad-brush treatment of the topic—the concept does not yet take us much further along in specifying how it applies to our original quest to bridge the government or governance gap in international relations theory. Nevertheless, I will try to demonstrate through some illustrative examples analogous to the issue-areas listed previously that it is actually central to that quest.

In particular, I see governmentality as the key to understanding the process of globalization more generally. Globalization is primarily and fundamentally an extension of the same—not merely analogous, but fundamentally isomorphic—practices to world politics. The similarity of the balancing acts and governing practices that a wide range of actors engage in—especially those actors I stylize as "political" and "social" actors (see chapters 5 and 14)—suggests that rather than simply adapting their behavior to the structural imperatives of traditional anarchic international relations, as distinct from hierarchical domestic state politics, these actors are increasingly learning to adapt and apply domestic practices in ways that are transcending international relations as such. In this process, these actors are not merely adapting practices of governmentality to the dictates of traditional international relations; rather, they are transforming specific practices and using them to manage and shape the process of globalization, in turn transforming world politics more generally in fundamental ways.

What is perhaps most intriguing about this analysis is the suggestion that governmentality is not only an art or practice in Foucault's context of modern *raison d'État* but also an art or practice that can be exercised and applied in diverse political and institutional settings. In domestic politics, of course, we normally associate these practices with the main developed liberal capitalist states. However, at the domestic level they can not only be represented and embedded in a range of alternative developed "national models" or "varieties of capitalism" (Crouch and Streeck 1997; Hall and Soskice 2001; Soederberg, Menz, and Cerny 2005) but also found in mixed, quasi-capitalist authoritarian societies.

For example, some influential members of the ruling dynastic family in Saudi Arabia some time ago began debating the possibilities for transforming that country into a more participatory model yet at the same time shunning the idea of actual democratization. Their domestic situation (and location in the Middle Eastern geopolitical cauldron), their economic interdependence with Western oil-consuming countries, the assertive U.S. role in Iraq and elsewhere, their Western educations, and increasing strains on the alliance between the Saud dynasty and the fundamentalist Wahhabi sect, taken together, seemed at the time to be setting the ruling family on the road to attempting to develop some kind of governmentalization without moving toward formal liberal democracy. Other Middle Eastern states are attempting to chart analogous courses, without much success so far. Of course, such attempts in the past have often proved merely transitional in the longer term, empowering as they do the participation of competing and conflicting social, economic, and political forces, in turn leading them to demand further pluralization and/or democratization—while also creating further resistance (see chapter 11). Similar comments could be made about a number of other countries, for example, China, Iran, and Kazakhstan (Rustemova 2008). But that is part of the process of the social learning of the practices of governmentality, too.

In the international sphere, an increasing number of actors are involved in a wide range of processes, their successful navigation of which, I suggest, requires approaching and managing those processes according to the domestically learned liberal practices of governmentality. But in partial contrast to the development of governmentality at the domestic state level, these lessons and practices must, of course, be applied in a far more structurally heterogeneous institutional and processual context. When I say in "partial" contrast, of course, I am referring to the fact that political scientists and other social scientists in recent years have been discovering (or rediscovering) the structural and processual heterogeneity of domestic states and societies, too. The word that is increasingly applied in this context is not "governmentality" but "governance," seen as a process (Rhodes 1997). In contrast, however, the term "global governance" has often been applied not to political processes but rather to the heterogeneous *institutional* super-structure of world politics. In this context, analysts have written about the existence of a *governance gap* at the global level. This is true. But at the same time, the process I call "governmentalization"—the uneven but inexorable proliferation of the key practices of the art of "governmentality" and of *raison du monde* as a reference point or ideological talisman—has been spreading tentacle-like through both domestic and international politics.

Therefore, the key to bridging the governance gap in international relations is recognizing that governmentality, being essentially a pluralistic conception, *does not require the construction of a hierarchical domestic-type state order at an international level* to be practiced effectively. In some ways, indeed, the very heterogeneity of the globalizing international order makes governmentality particularly appropriate to managing, shaping, and internalizing the complex processes of transnational liberal capitalism without being in danger from a reawakening at an international level of totalizing alternatives, whether called fascism, bureaucratic authoritarianism, state socialism, or whatever. Indeed, the very fact that there is no international government to a large extent obviates the temptations of totalization. Even empire, in the guise of the recent George W. Bush administration's attempt to reassert American hegemony and national interests in the world, is based on a form of what William Appleman Williams (1959) called "informal empire" rather than formal colonial empire, and can—and increasingly has been—constrained and circumscribed by various forms of opposition and even resistance, as well as, more directly, by the need for coalition building and international institutional legitimacy. Therefore, the fact that the international system does still involve structural elements that, relatively speaking, can be seen as anarchic paradoxically opens up a range of heterogeneous spaces for the development of continually evolving governmentalizing practices.

This wider process of international and/or global governmentalization can thus be identified as being instantiated at a number of structurally quite diverse levels and in a range of partly complementary, partly competing arenas or structured fields of action, some of which are listed later. However, this process does not merely involve separate forms of governmentalization tailored to each level or arena. Rather, it involves a *dialectical process of convergence and divergence*, again both reconciling and creatively managing, through what Foucault calls the art or practice of governmentality, the dynamic processes of interaction among these levels and arenas, linking them and weaving them together in an evolving—and, of course, incomplete and often disorderly or "fragmegrating"—(neo)liberal capitalist world order.

In the first place, *governmentalization does not necessarily mean the strengthening or growth of existing institutions of global governance as such*. The challenges facing these institutions or regimes, both intergovernmental and supranational, constitute probably the most visible ostensible opportunity for governmentalization, but the results can be mixed and even perverse. Actors in these regimes must continually play off the demands of states, economic actors, social interest groups, and the like, attempting to parlay them into relatively effective outputs. This complex superstructure can be schematized as shown in table 9.1.

There are at least two fundamental problematics here. The first is to deal with the issue-area in question in a way that actually does the job. The second is to pursue and promote the continued institutional existence and further development of the regime in question itself. These imperatives can often conflict. For example, actors within or interacting with environmental regimes often see their first order or a priori goal to make sure the institution itself is not undermined by states (both developing and developed, in different ways) and by business interests seeking to avoid the costs of

Table 9.1 Transnational Governance Structures and Processes

	FORMAL	INFORMAL
PUBLIC	International institutions and intergovernmental regimes	Transgovernmental networks and policy communities
PRIVATE	Private regimes, self-regulatory bodies, law merchant, etc.	Transnational policy networks, NGOs, advocacy coalitions, transnational interest and value groups

pollution control and the like; only then can the real issues be tackled (Young 1994). At the same time, maintaining and expanding those regimes in such conditions often means that regulations and substantive policy outputs have to be watered down. The dispute between the United States and other signatories over the future of the Kyoto Protocol is a rather extreme case.

Another example was the role of the United Nations with regard to Resolution 1441 and the disarmament inspection regime in Iraq during the 1990s. When the George W. Bush administration wanted to go to war with Iraq in 2001–2003, what was likely to undermine UN legitimacy more: for the administration's proposals to be accepted by a reluctant Security Council under pressure from the "hegemon," or for those proposals to be vetoed or otherwise blocked in the Security Council itself, with the United States attacking Iraq with only a small "coalition of the willing"? The challenge, the balancing act, is ongoing, as is seen in today's attempt to circumscribe Iran's nuclear ambitions or deal with the humanitarian crisis in Darfur. In the post–cold war era, in fact, the United Nations saw its profile and effectiveness increase somewhat in the 1990s, but its present role and practices are increasingly seen as problematic.

A third example is the World Bank (and, to a lesser extent, the International Monetary Fund), which effectively shifted in the mid-1990s from imposing more radical market-oriented forms of restructuring represented by the structural adjustment policies of the 1980s and the Washington consensus of the early 1990s, to a post–Washington consensus, rhetorically, at least, focused on a new overriding goal—poverty reduction. One astute academic observer, Peter Willetts, has suggested that the World Bank has effectively adopted a "social democratic" approach to globalization (oral intervention at the British International Studies Association annual meeting, London School of Economics and Political Science, December 2002)—far from the laissez faire version of neoliberalism of Thatcher or Reagan. Nevertheless, this attempt to shift Foucauldian biopolitics to the international level has come under increasing strain as it conflicts with the domestic priorities of the governments of both developed and developing states, more concerned with domestic power games than with increasing the welfare of their citizens.

With regard to such continually expanding and institutionalizing arenas, while the social learning and on-the-job experience of actors—not only within those regimes themselves but also among political, economic, and social actors at all levels—are in the process of expanding and adapting forms of governmentality, however unevenly and incompletely, governmentalization is inevitably incomplete, paradoxical, and often counterproductive in terms of both regime durability and policy effectiveness. The balancing act is a complex and often ambiguous one, as critics of the World Bank's poverty reduction approach are keen to point out. Nevertheless, to the extent that the discourse of international regimes is increasingly being superseded by that of global governance, we can also see a reflection of the extent to which the art and practices of governmentality are altering people's *perceptions* of how the superstructure of the international system is evolving. With regard to these international institutions and regimes, then, there may be a growing governmentality gap, not merely a governance gap, between aspirations and capabilities—in particular, emphasizing the primacy of *process* over institutions.

The crystallization of uneven pluralist or neopluralist processes of group politics across and below borders, including the emergence of so-called global civil society, is also a crucial aspect of governmentalization. Actors in both national political systems and international regimes increasingly interact with a wider range of more and more assertive interests, pressure groups, cause groups, and the like. Although these categories are still primarily domestic, (a) more and more of those domestic groups have a growing transnational dimension and perceive their interests as embedded in the state of international relations and the international political economy, and (b) certain groups have become effectively multinational and/or transnational, as I have argued at length in this book. Even antiglobalization protestors have been changing their discourse over the past decade, looking toward more social democratic—or "social neoliberal"—approaches to globalization and opposing key aspects of the *form* of globalization rather than opposing globalization per se. Yet these groups are as yet only embryonic in their ability to shape superstructural processes and policy outcomes, which are more likely to be effectively influenced by resource-rich, materially oriented interest groups than by the sorts of value groups usually included in the category of global civil society.

At the same time, of course, these governmentalizing practices involve the acceptance at an international (transnational? global?) level of the opening of markets for trade, finance, and production; the liberalization of regulation both at the national level and across borders through transgovernmental linkages and networks; the prioritization of the promotion of international competitiveness as the hallmark of state intervention; and even the marketization of the state itself. State actors, both politicians and bureaucrats, have over the past three decades been on a steep learning curve about how to adapt government policies to globalization. This experience has been transforming *domestic* governmental practices in ways that were less viable before the globalization processes of the past three decades or so took shape, as was pointed out in chapter 8. Governmentalization in international relations therefore increasingly involves a process that cuts across and links domestic, regional, transnational, and intergovernmental levels in a range of multilevel and multinodal creative balancing acts.

So far, the institutions and superstructures we have mainly been talking about are public or quasi-public institutions that are to a large extent inherently *intergovernmental* rather than supranational or global. The question of whether they can develop a genuine institutional autonomy or quasi sovereignty is not only open but also unlikely. However, there is also the development of a phenomenon familiar enough with liberal capitalist states, that is, the emergence of quasi-corporatist transnational private regimes—what David Lake (1999) has called the "privatization of governance" across borders. Such private organizations in global politics fill crucial parts of the government gap, whether in expanding the effective scope and reach of international diplomacy, the organization of international financial markets, a range of transnationally organized industrial sectors, or the evolving process of administering and managing the Internet (Ronit and Schneider 2000).

These developments interact and overlap with the growing role in this book of interest groups, transnational cause networks, and epistemic communities. Indeed, as Lake argues, the very structure of the traditional international or interstate system, blocking as it does the capacity for more authoritative world governmental institutions to develop, actually encourages experimentation with private and quasi-private process development and institution building by both private-sector *and public*-sector actors frustrated by the institutional weaknesses of much of the international governmental superstructure. This form of institutional bricolage is represented not only by firms, sectors of national bureaucracies, and the like but also by both formal transnational trade associations—crucial but analytically and politically neglected actors in the economic and financial spheres, for example—and myriad informal networks. Governmentalization proceeds at different levels, and the growth of privatized international governance structures and processes have become a crucial part of filling those gaps.

Finally, the governmentalization of world politics, like the governmentalization of the modern state, involves the renewed incorporation and inclusion of more and more people, individuals as well as groups, cutting across class, into a paradoxically politically promoted and regulated culture of individualistic "empowerment" that embeds liberal or neoliberal capitalism at new levels. This last dimension is actually even more multidimensional than the first four dimensions discussed here, becoming an essential element of them all. Just as governmentality in the modern state has entailed the promotion and development of a market-oriented individualization of consciousness, mainly through discourse, so, too, the governmentalization of world politics involves the discursive assertion—and behavioral actualization—of individual empowerment in legitimizing globalization processes. For the World Bank, for example, the adoption of a poverty-reduction strategy does not merely involve aid to the poor; it adopts the rhetoric of enabling and empowering the poor to actively participate in capitalist development, incorporating them into market-friendly practices, and supposedly giving them a stake in the governmentalization process itself.

For the politics of transnational neopluralism and civil society, this new international governmentality involves encouraging such groups to develop crosscutting links with states, global governance institutions, private-sector economic organizations, and the like, making these "social actors" into proactive carriers and practitioners of governmentality themselves. For the Competition State and the reformed, marketized welfare state, rhetoric such as that of the Third Way (Giddens 1998) is based on a new contractual relationship between welfare recipients (and other ordinary citizens) and the state, with government support conditional on the willingness of welfare clients to learn how to involve themselves proactively in work (workfare, etc.) and market exchange (Jessop 2002). Furthermore, globalization rests on a new consumptionism that encourages workers, migrants, and others to perceive themselves as *Homo economicus*—essentially as consumers—rather than as merely sellers of labor power or as producers (see chapter 13). And finally, for the growing sector of private organizations in global politics, there is a new social partnership between business and global governance, a new self-regulatory field of action, which actively integrates international business into wider globalizing norms, including the social neoliberal Global Compact pursued by Kofi Annan when he was secretary general of the United Nations, or the concept of "corporate social responsibility" (Lipschutz 2005), although the effectiveness of this trend is debatable.

5. CONCLUSION: CAN THE GOVERNMENTALITY GAP BE CLOSED?

Closing the government gap in world politics and international relations theory involves neither an embryonic post-Weberian "global state" (Shaw 2000) nor a fully integrated, bottom-up world marketplace, but a complex, multilayered, fungible, and increasingly hegemonic set of simultaneously globalizing and governmentalizing political practices. Linking these practices together is not merely a new global elite but rather an increasing pluralization of actors, all learning the art of balancing and managing an expanding process of transnational governmentalization, using still-heterogeneous superstructures to experiment and innovate in policy and discourse—leading in turn to a further, if uneven, pluralization of transnational society, economy, and politics. In particular, such actors must creatively manage complex processes of convergence and divergence through bricolage, mainly rationalized through the emergence of varieties of neoliberalism.

In this context, attempts to revive the traditional power politics of national interests constitute a predictable but anachronistic backlash, especially when linked with the neoconservative concepts of empire and hegemony in the United States. However, I would suggest that the backlash is likely to be viewed in historical perspective as temporary—as one step back in a longer historical process of combined globalization and governmentalization, which in turn constitute two steps forward. The rhetoric of the Obama presidential campaign and administration, along with some policy initiatives such as the recent opening to the Islamic world, hold out this prospect, but it is too early to tell. The actors involved in the latter increasingly have a critical stake in the development and expansion of the governmentalization of world politics. Such a process is a logical—and historical—extension of the art of governmentality and the transnational spread of *raison du monde.*

Nevertheless, the inherently ambiguous process of governmentalization is much more likely to be realized only through a much looser, "fragmegrated" governmental superstructure that will inhibit not only most coherent policy making at the global level but also the consolidation of a truly authoritative, overarching, and hierarchical global institutional structure. In this context, the expansion of transnational neopluralism will create a more horizontally pluralistic world through ongoing, experimental institutional bricolage and multinodal politicking. This may not be democracy (see chapter 10), but it may enable the development of something resembling forms of limited, more pluralistic quasi democracy by proxy across a range of niches and circumscribed issue-areas, including greater influence for a wider range of bottom-up pressures and interests, such as labor, environmental groups, and other social as well as economic actors.

Part III

IMPLICATIONS OF CHANGE

Chapter 10

Some Pitfalls of Democratization in a Globalizing World

1. INTRODUCTION: THE ROCKY ROAD TO GLOBAL DEMOCRACY

One of the most important political issues in the twenty-first century, as it was in the twentieth, is the spread, stabilization, and institutionalization of democracy. Whether in the 2003 American invasion of Iraq, the future of authoritarian or quasi-authoritarian regimes in places like China and Russia, attempts to democratize unstable postcolonial developing countries, or proposals to create more quasi-democratic and accountable mechanisms at the international and global levels, democratization is increasingly on the political agenda in one form or another. Nevertheless, as with all such developments, obstacles are sticky, institutions problematic, goals too often vague or ill formed, and, in what is perhaps the most significant issue in terms of the argument in this book, key interests are often either opposed to democratization or seeking to control it for their own ends.

In this context, it is crucial to distinguish between two analytically distinct yet intertwined and overlapping concepts: democratization and pluralization. For a variety of reasons, from the legacies of history to the basic question of "What is democracy?" in the first place, I argue that although the world is undergoing a process of uneven pluralization—transnational neopluralism—any transformation to a more globalized form of democratization is unlikely, except in a few circumscribed structural niches and issue-areas where the configuration of interest groups is favorable. The road to democracy has in the past been rocky—involving predemocratic state building, revolutions, wars and civil wars, the development of capitalism, the mobilization of mass movements, the integration of antidemocratic and antisystem groups and parties, the repression and/or buying off of opposition, the development and/or imposition of "shared values" and a consensus on rules of the game, and the often painful and problematic institutionalization of constitutional mechanisms that qualify as democratic only in lowest-common-denominator terms.

In these circumstances, therefore, uneven pluralization is likely to continue to trump democratization as the predominant process of widening and deepening transnational political processes in a globalizing world, at least in the short and medium term. The relationship between pluralization and democratization is a complex one. On the one hand, liberal democracy cannot be stable and effective unless it is based on plural*ism*, not merely a plurality of groups or factions. Groups must accept common rules of the game; losers must be willing to tolerate electoral losses, policy reverses, and marginalization without revolting or opposing the system as such; and winners must be self-restrained, that is, not suppress or take revenge on opponents (Cerny 2006a). On the other hand, while pluralism may be a necessary precondition for stable and effective democratization, it is not a sufficient condition. Indeed, debates over what sort of pluralism might or might not lead to democratization, at what stage, and under what conditions are at the heart of democratic theory. Finally, however, a certain amount of pluralism may not be wholly inconsistent with political systems that are not fully democratic; once again, the lessons of history—and of twenty-first-century experience—are ambiguous and complex on this matter.

In terms of the possibilities of constructing more globalized democratic political processes, a number of issues crop up that further problematize the relationship of democracy and pluralism. In the first place, there is the historical dimension. It is all too easy to forget that democracy as a stable, institutionalized form of government is a very new phenomenon in historical terms. Although its roots go back to ancient Athens, only three major countries before the First World War had relatively democratic systems: Britain, France, and the United States. Even those countries were not fully democratic in the way we think about it today. All three had experienced a rocky road to democracy in the nineteenth century, including a range of restrictions on the franchise, limits on associational activity, revolutions (France), civil war and slavery (the United States), class struggle (Britain), deep inequalities, and power struggles over the fruits of capitalist industrialization. Indeed, between the two world wars in the first half of the twentieth century, democracy was not expanding but retreating in the world, under profound threat from fascism, Soviet communism, and both old and new antidemocratic social hierarchies (Stamps 1957; Newman 1970).

Furthermore, attempts to set up new international institutions that were supposed to, in Woodrow Wilson's words, "make the world safe for democracy" were undermined by their own core intergovernmental structures in a world where the foreign policies of both democratic and nondemocratic states were driven by the imperatives of national interest, territorial conflict, international sovereignty, and the Westphalian imperative of looking after their relative power positions vis-à-vis other states—namely, realism (Morgenthau 1949; Carr 1947). In turn, the spread of democracy after the Second World War, especially in Western Europe and Japan, did not simply emerge from the bottom up, but was enabled and driven by the dominant power position of the victorious (Western) Allies. Decolonization in the 1950s and 1960s was almost everywhere followed by the breakdown of fragile democratic constitutions and their replacement by one-party states, military dictatorships, clientelist regimes, and civil wars. And the cold war kept many nondemocratic regimes in power for decades on both sides of the divide.

Nevertheless, democracy came at the same time to be seen almost everywhere as the wave of the future and the right and proper outcome of historical evolution, the highest stage of political modernity. Nondemocratic regimes were increasingly viewed as fundamentally illegitimate. The only way regimes could claim genuine political authority was to include the vast majority of their populations in comprehensive democratic political processes. Eastern Europe, Latin America, most parts of Asia, and some parts of Africa have eventually adopted liberal democratic political systems, however unevenly at times. And democratization came to be seen as one of the ambitions of international institutions and organizations, too.

Today the spread of globalization—whether in economic, social, or political terms—has raised that ambition to the level of world politics (Burnell 2003). Several potential pathways have been canvassed and promoted, including:

- the establishment of new global democratic institutions such as a world parliament (Monbiot 2003)
- the spread of liberal democratic constitutional and legal norms (Held 1995)
- the democratization of international institutions such as the United Nations
- the example of quasi-democratic regional institutions such as the European Union
- the addition of more democratic states to the international system
- the spread of democratic capitalism and free market economic systems
- even the imposition of democratic systems from the outside, like the War in Iraq

Recent contributions to this debate reflect this new expectation that democratization no longer involves merely transplanting democratic institutions and practices from one area to another but has been raised to the level of a global ambition (Archibugi 2008).

Nevertheless, this attention to democracy and democratization has in many ways merely highlighted the pitfalls of such a level shift, in a world still profoundly divided into legally sovereign states. However strong cross-cutting transnational, international, and global ties may be becoming, and no matter how deep the growing complex interdependence of states may be, a range of both old and new issues in the analysis and understanding of democracy make the idea of global democratization highly problematic. The purpose of this chapter is to highlight some of these issues and pose the question of whether they make the prospect of global democracy illusory, on the one hand, or illuminate the path to that goal, on the other, in the context of the continuing uneven pluralization of world politics. I am not what is sometimes called a "globoskeptic," insofar as I see many of the political dimensions of globalization as highly promising in terms of inclusion, the spread of more pluralistic political processes, and the possibilities for creating wealth and prosperity. But I am skeptical whether the outcome will look like democracy as we have known it, or even whether democratization as such is becoming the kind of dominant global political process we would all like it to be. In setting out this argument, I outline five of what I see as the main problems and potential pitfalls of overegging the democratic pudding in today's world: historical trajectories, democratic stability/instability, the philosophical and normative substance of democracy itself, the question of "Who democratizes?" and the problem of institutionalization.

2. HISTORICAL TRAJECTORIES

As the Spanish American philosopher George Santayana once wrote: "Those who cannot remember the past are condemned to repeat it" (Santayana 1905). The history of real existing democracies is studded with paradoxes that reappear in manifold new versions in a globalizing world. In particular, it has rarely been the case in the modern world that such systems have arisen from the bottom up from endogenous popular national roots. To paraphrase General de Gaulle, modern democratic states have not been constructed on a tabula rasa. In early modern Europe, the centralization and embedding of an authoritative national state apparatus was the product of profound nondemocratic or even antidemocratic forces. Whether dominated by monarchies, aristocracies, nonaristocratic landed elites (the gentry), the urban bourgeoisie, military hierarchies, centralizing state bureaucracies, or international capitalist and colonizing elites, modern states as we know them are the product of elites seeking to entrench their political dominance and expand their resources and wealth while co-opting subaltern groups into supporting their power.

The painful secular process of democratic development has not therefore been one of linear, steady evolution over the centuries. It has been one of uneven, spiky, stochastic adaptation to circumstances. And the main process has been one of declining elites already in place trying to counteract the rising power of competing elites, and vice versa, including ongoing attempts to manage conflicts among elites, to incorporate new and rising elites into the power structure while buying off opposition, and to head off revolution and rebellion among excluded or underrepresented groups and classes. Elites need a power base. As modernization has progressed, as new groups have found alternative power bases in a changing economy and an international economic as well as political power balance, and as popular groups—the masses—have played a more and more important part in economic production processes and gained political resources of their own, the need to incorporate them into political processes has led elites to concede formal political power to "the people" through constitutions and other forms of *relative* democratization while simultaneously attempting to maintain or even extend their clout and influence within those institutions and processes.

Elite theorists, of course, argue that these concessions have usually been superficial, effectively maintaining existing power relationships and often preventing alternative groups from pursuing their goals (Mayer 1981). Nevertheless, a wider proportion of the population of industrializing countries has been drawn out of their previously "subsumed" status in feudalistic and prefeudalistic societies and become active participants—and resistants—in political as well as economic processes (Laslett 1965). At the same time, as this incorporation process has become increasingly complex and problematic, it has led to the emergence of class compromises in the form of liberal democracy. Liberal democracy, of course, protects private property relations and confines democracy to representative forms, while granting votes, civil rights, and parliamentary-type deliberative institutions to the populace as a whole.

This process has taken different forms in different countries and, as already noted, only led to a general democratization of nation-state politics in the mid-twentieth century. Indeed, it could be argued that democratization, even in the developed North, only prevailed in that the three main older democracies were more effective at war fighting than their authoritarian opponents. Despite the successes of late industrialization in Germany, Japan, and later Soviet Russia (Gerschenkron 1962) and the huge contribution of the Soviet Union to the victory in Europe in 1945, it was the democracies, especially the Anglo-Saxon allies, who won the two world wars. Indeed, Walter Russell Mead has recently argued that today's democratization has specifically been the product of an Anglo-American consortium in which the synergy of religion, capitalism, and military power eventually defeated other forms of social organization (Mead 2007).

After the obvious failure of democratization in Italy, Germany, Japan, and other countries in the interwar period and the success of fascist and corporatist dictatorships in constructing an alternative authoritarian model of national quasi capitalism—and, indeed, whether the Soviet Union itself constituted a form of socialism or communism, on the one hand, or a form of "state capitalism," on the other (Buick and Crump 1986)—only defeat in the Second World War and the occupation of those countries by the United States and Britain (and by France in the case of West Germany) ensured their democratization by imposing liberal democratic forms from the outside. Furthermore, as Sandra Halperin has suggested, it could even be argued that only the need for mass mobilization in modern warfare ensured the embedding of national democracy in Britain itself as the result of the two world wars (Halperin 2003 and 2008), an argument that could be extended to the American Civil War.

Indeed, the historical debate about the success of democratization in the nineteenth and twentieth centuries concerns just how various socioeconomic groups could increasingly demand and receive concessions. Among the classical explanations, alongside the emphasis on war and popular mobilization, are the growth of a capitalist bourgeoisie challenging entrenched aristocratic elites (Moore 1966), the growth of popular pressures from below such as peasant rebellions and trade unions, the spread of democratic ideologies of various kinds, and, in particular, wider dislocations and structural socioeconomic changes such as depressions, industrialization, and migration. Also, there is an inevitable feedback effect, as, for example, the development of education and communications systems spread the awareness of democratic possibilities and empowered new groups to claim what they saw as their rightful place in the political process. This feedback can be both endogenous, in altering domestic power and bargaining processes, and international-transnational, as with the impact of Western German television on East Germany in the 1950s through 1980s and the later spread of liberal ideas that led to the fall of the Berlin Wall in 1989 and the crumbling of Communist regimes in Eastern Europe.

These paradoxes of democratic transition are crucial today. In post-Soviet Russia, for example, the combination of democratic incompetence in the Yeltsin era of the 1990s and the impact of financial crises in 1998 and 2008 has undermined opposition to the kind of statist economic and political recentralization carried out by Vladimir Putin since the turn of the century. China's rapid and dramatic economic transformation has simultaneously reinforced the control of the Communist Party at the same time as it has sponsored economic neoliberalization, on the one hand, and threatened to undermine it as dissidents and previously subsumed groups in both rural and urban areas, emerging around economic, political, religious, and environmental issues, increasingly attempt to claim a place in the process, on the other.

In Latin America, the attempt by Venezuela's President Hugo Chavez to develop what he calls "Bolivarian socialism" has been democratically problematic, with the electorate sometimes approving, sometimes disapproving his initiatives; other examples abound in Bolivia, Nicaragua, Ecuador, and other countries. Africa is probably the most problematic region, where ostensible moves toward democratization have often foundered on the resistance of dominant elites, the persistence of ethnic conflict, and the role of corruption and clientelism. Indeed, the impact in academic circles today of postcolonial theory, especially among sociologists and anthropologists, suggests that Western-style liberal democratization might prove highly counterproductive. Much sociology and anthropology has focused on the role of nondemocratic hierarchies in clans and tribes—as well as practices that are today considered highly corrupt or immoral, for example, with regard to the role of women—as having played a deeply historically rooted *stabilizing* role in such societies, although that analysis can be disputed in specific cases like Saudi Arabia, which as a state is of relatively recent historical origin.

Whether good or bad, the disruption of such practices, especially today as democratic experiments and market capitalism spread, can lead to socioeconomic crisis and deep destabilization rather than to democracy as it is perceived in the West, actually undermining the crucial social supports that democracy needs to succeed. This is particularly true where nondemocratic systems have been imposed from the outside through various forms of imperialism (Comaroff and Comaroff 2006). These contradictions are nowhere more obvious than in today's Zimbabwe, with the breakdown not only of democracy but also of any semblance of socioeconomic order. They can be seen in a rather different guise in transition countries, where the reestablishment of autocratic rule, along with the deceptive pretense of democratic practice, is becoming more frequent. This is not the end of predemocratic history, nor its mere repetition, but its ratcheting up in the context of globalization, with economic liberalization combining with infantile democratization to create disorder rather than stable democracy. In a world in flux, pluralization can therefore have contradictory effects. Where it leads to a classical pluralism based on the mutual tolerance of groups and the sharing of power, on the one hand, it can engender democratization. However, where it leads to conflict, especially violent conflict between groups and the breakdown of social order, on the other hand, it can undermine or prevent democratization.

3. THE PROBLEM OF STABLE DEMOCRACY

The embedding of democracy is problematic not only in past history, therefore, but also in context of current political conflicts and developments.

Political culture, economic change, forms of bureaucratization, and the like can often entrench structures and processes that inhibit or even counteract democratization. This reflects one of the thorniest issues in the study of democracy and democratic theory—democratic stability. Opponents of democracy have always traditionally claimed that democracy is inherently unstable, as it opens the way for irreducible socioeconomic and cultural conflicts to be displaced into political and bureaucratic institutions themselves, leading to state decomposition or even failure—or to the violent or institutionalized dominance over the others by one group that feels that if it is not totally in control, it will lose its own internal rationale. The alternative to authoritarianism in these circumstances is often seen to be chronic instability, crisis, and even civil war. Therefore, premature attempts to democratize can themselves entail future failure, unless democracy can come to represent a new form of compromise and shared values, as Michael Allen argues (Allen 2008). This is very much the dilemma the United States faces in Iraq at the moment.

Can such problems be avoided in global democratization? The history of globalization has been that, however deep and complex transnational interdependencies might be, ultimately the key stabilizing factor is cooperation, pooled sovereignty among relatively autonomous states, and bargaining among neopluralist interests—not transnational democracy per se. Attempts to globalize democracy therefore might well lead to increased state failure and international conflict. Nevertheless, the secular march of democratic values, continuing growth of the global economy (with the obvious caveat that the current financial crisis needs to be overcome in a democratic manner), the political and economic clout of the more globalized democratic economies, and the support of international organizations are sometimes seen to open the way to the emergence of a more cosmopolitan democracy. But that is highly dependent on events and seems unlikely in the foreseeable future.

Several key scholars of democracy in the past, looking at the sort of historical trajectories discussed here, have argued that what makes democracies stable is not how *"democratic"* they are, but paradoxically *how they integrate de facto, nondemocratic procedures and socioeconomic hierarchies* into some sort of ostensibly democratic order. Probably the most influential author developing this argument has been Samuel Huntington, especially in his book *Political Order in Changing Societies* (Huntington 1969). Arguments about the significance of quasi-authoritarian elements in enabling and sustaining democracy have been around for a long time. In Britain, the nineteenth-century writer Walter Bagehot distinguished between the customary or "dignified" elements in the British Constitution, on the one hand, and what he called its "effective" elements, arguing that it was precisely the incorporation of nondemocratic elements—especially the monarchy—that created a space of stability, shared acceptance, and internalization of the rules of the game, *within which* relatively democratic debate and policy making could take place.

The core of this argument is twofold. The first part is that if democracies are to be stable, there needs to be a sphere of shared values that enables groups with conflicting goals to agree to disagree and, in particular, to accept short-term defeat in elections or policy-making processes, provided they can remain in the game and continue to vie for influence over time. The basic condition is that no significant group should perceive itself as a permanent loser—that is, each group can perceive what game theorists call the "shadow of the future" and continue to participate. Often this sort of minimal, lowest-common-denominator form of consensus is transferred from first attempting to achieve the value or material goals of the group as such, to later simple maintenance of the democratic rules of the game. The second part of the argument is that alternative or *uneven, interacting pathways* must always exist for loser groups, either to influence or control certain outcomes of the policy-making process in their favor or to resist outcomes in ways that do not undermine the democratic system itself, for example, through the courts.

There are essentially five sorts of endogenous, nondemocratic alternative pathways of this kind. The first is that any dominant combination of groups—the "majority," however composed—must, in order to get into power and maintain that power, build a broad coalition that itself involves making concessions to nondominant groups. This usually involves the competition of political parties and is the least controversial of these pathways—in principle, at least. Nevertheless, it is strewn with obstacles. The existence of what have been called "anti-system parties" like the Fascists, Nazis, and Communists of the 1930s is only the tip of the iceberg. Religious and ethnic groups often form parties that are really factions and that are designed not to lead to shared norms and rules of the game, but to conquering power from within unstable democratic processes and to excluding their opponents from any meaningful sharing of the spoils (Sartori 1976; Wong 2007). These parties often mirror one another in rejecting the others' legitimacy, leading to a vicious spiral of instability—or the return of authoritarianism.

The second pathway is the development of bureaucratic structures that manage and administer social and economic policies in such a way that a wider range of interests are listened to. This, too, is relatively uncontroversial in theory. However, it is no less problematic. On the one hand, relatively autonomous and efficient Weberian bureaucracies can be characteristic of *both* authoritarian and democratic forms of government. Indeed, it is often claimed that they actually work better within an authoritarian framework, where the kind of hierarchical command structures they represent can be relatively free of competing claims, destabilizing conflicts, and special interests—although the lack of such competition may involve other forms of counterproductive monopolistic rent-seeking and bureaucratic inefficiencies. This is the crux of the main critique of bureaucratic theories since Saint-Simon and the totalizing trend of modernity.

On the other hand, those competing claimants can often capture parts of the administrative structure, leading to sometimes extreme forms of clientelism, family or clan dominance, personal favoritism, and, of course, corruption (Clapham 1982). It has taken centuries for the older democracies to deal with such practices; indeed, they are often still at the forefront of political debates today, with "reform" perennially on the agenda. Italy since the Second World War has been the highest profile case in point. In newly democratizing countries, moreover, the predominance of such practices has often been a key element in *both* stabilizing the state—where democracy is subordinated to patron-client relationships, as is usually the case—*and* destabilizing it, where competition for spoils undermines the bureaucracy itself.

The third pathway is more controversial and assumes a more elitist background structure. This is where existing socioeconomic hierarchies (and, in some cases, institutional hierarchies) have sufficient resources, connections, control of key information, and ability to define debates and issues in the first place to control bureaucratic processes and policy implementation and, probably most crucially, evoke sufficient *status deference* among other groups to ensure that their goals and methods are given disproportionate weight. This is similar to classic elite theory in political sociology and is usually seen in a critical light (Mills 1956).

Political parties and bureaucracies that appear to be relatively effective are epiphenomenal in this context, with little or no relative autonomy. Authoritarianism, rather than the messier phenomenon of clientelism, means the dominance of social, economic, and/or bureaucratic monopolies and little else. This is the case in today's Russia, where the *siloviki* control both the bureaucratic state and the political state—and increasingly the "commanding heights" of the resource-cursed economy. It is, however, also the goal of most groups in more divided countries, who seek dominance and control rather than shared power—although such dominance is prevented by the plurality of groups, leading to factional conflict, stagnant clientelism, or state failure rather than effective governance, democratic or otherwise.

The fourth pathway is more complex and involves various forms of "corporatism" and "neocorporatism" (Schmitter 1974). Corporatism in this context means that key interest groups, especially business and trade unions, are incorporated into sometimes informal, sometimes formal, bargaining structures, usually sponsored by and sometimes including parts of the state apparatus, that regularly negotiate agreements *outside the scope of formally democratic institutions* on crucial economic policy issues. These issues include wages, working conditions, levels of employment, and—most controversially—social and economic policies more generally, including macroeconomic demand management, welfare policy, pensions, and active employment policy.

The resulting solidarity is seen as a crucial bulwark against potentially destabilizing elements arising from deep socioeconomic conflict and from a fear that the combination of democracy and free markets will undermine social cooperation and shared values. And because it draws a range of otherwise competing groups into cooperative but fluid—continuously bargained—arrangements, a certain element of pseudodemocratization can be seen to be at work, at least behind the scenes. The stability of a range of postwar European democracies, especially Germany, Austria, and Sweden, has been attributed to their neocorporatist systems of "organized" or "coordinated" capitalism, usually linked with the strength of quasi-solidaristic social democratic and Christian Democratic political parties and ideologies. In another version, business-government collaboration in countries like France and Japan, with their relatively weak trade unions, can lead to a kind of "corporatism without labor" (Schain 1980). Newly democratizing countries, however, given the constraints described previously, are rarely capable of institutionalizing effective corporatist arrangements, which tend to degenerate into either oligopolistic clientelism or monopolistic authoritarianism.

The fifth pathway is more cultural and invokes patriotism and national identity, along with symbolic and dignified elements of the system, to inculcate shared values and national solidarity. Calls to patriotism may be a fine thing in inspiring people to higher ideals for their countries, to counteract forces of instability, and to defend the national territory against attack. However, patriotism is also well known to have a serious downside: that such calls to patriotism and national belonging can be used to mask authoritarianism, excuse corruption, entrench the dominance of one particular group over another, foment violence against opponents, and the like. In Samuel Johnson's comment alluded to earlier in this book: "Patriotism is the last refuge of a scoundrel."

All five of these pathways are deeply problematic in terms of stable democratization at a national level. But they are far more complex and problematic at a global level. There are no dignified, authoritative, hierarchical infrastructural arrangements to underpin a global democracy. Political parties, bureaucracies, clientelism, elitism, neocorporatism, and patriotism have been seen as parts of a very uneven and very frequently unsuccessful set of solutions at the national level, but in many places—especially those parts of the world where democracy has not yet reached—*they are part of the problem, not part of the solution.* Transnational neopluralism, in a world with no overarching political superstructure, may lead, in the best case scenario, to a world of greater competition rather than conflict and to Pareto-optimal bargaining rather than zero-sum or negative-sum games, but whether it will lead to democratization as such is another question. Only perhaps the highly circumscribed and relatively ineffective, bricolage-built quasi bureaucracies of intergovernmental regimes and the problematic constellation of so-called global civil society groups and transnational interest groups—many of which are not only marginal to the exogenous bargaining of outcomes but endogenously elitist and/or clientelist, not to mention focused on specific issue-areas rather than concerned with the overarching pursuit of the public good—can be seen to have any "global" presence. And international summits, like the recent 2008 G20 meeting in Washington on the financial crisis, always end up by handing the baton back to national governments, however great the convergence on substance.

Given the history of democracy as inextricably intertwined with the development of national state systems, then, there is likely to be a tendency for loser groups to exit the system if they lose, reigniting destabilizing socioeconomic—and political—conflicts. Furthermore, transnational elites and capitalist classes are, of course, usually seen as inherently undemocratic (Gill 2003; van der Pijl 1998; Sklair 2000). Transnational neocorporatism may eventually develop to some extent if more regularized relationships between civil society groups, transnational firms, financial markets, and international institutions reach a critical mass. However, conflicts of interest and the fluidity of developing forms of governmentality may not be enough to produce a stable corporatist-type bargaining process. In particular, up until now, labor and popular elements have not developed extensive cross-border cooperation mechanisms, and transnational businesses have, if anything, provoked opposition and resistance rather than representing social consensus. Furthermore, such a development might well be seen as undemocratic rather than democratic and as imposing elite bargains on the people. And of course, there is as yet no global patriotic identity to compete with national forms of identity.

Nevertheless, many observers concerned about global democratization see transnational neopluralism as the best we can hope for. Therefore, the sort of nondemocratic stabilizing mechanisms that have been so important in previous waves of democratization are not available to global democratic institutions and processes, and their potential for instability and failure may be huge.

4. PLURAL DEMOCRATISMS?

The third pitfall of democratization concerns the concept of democracy itself. The differences—even incompatibilities—between fundamental conceptions of democracy have been with us since the Greek philosophers invented the term, especially between participatory democracy and representative democracy, between the rule of the mob and the role of elites, between institutions and processes, between equality and inequality, and between all of these and the *outcomes* of political processes. Is a procedurally democratic system that entrenches the rule of elites and dominant classes truly democratic if it creates classes of losers in the process? What is the relationship between procedure and substance? This issue has been addressed, in particular, by Milja Kurki and Chantal Mouffe (Kurki 2008; Mouffe 2008). It has particular resonance for the question of transnational neopluralism. On the one hand, neopluralist processes are sometimes seen as merely a weak form of elitism, entrenching the power of those groups with the greatest resources, despite whatever disagreements and conflicts may exist among them. On the other hand, such bargaining and horse-trading can sometimes get results that are superior to more diffuse political processes with mass participation. Such was the justification in the twentieth century for neocorporatism, for example.

It is in this context that consolidation of "democratic" political systems at the level of the nation-state has historically involved a shift toward a very specific type of democracy—*procedural* liberal democracy. In this type, democracy is measured by the presence of several key criteria, including:

- a broad electoral franchise, especially universal suffrage, which became the norm in the twentieth century although generally not before that
- the existence of representative institutions, whether presidential or parliamentary
- the supremacy of a guaranteed legal/constitutional order
- basic civil rights, including both sociopolitical rights such as freedom of speech, personal security, and religious toleration, on the one hand, and economic rights such as the protection of private property, on the other

The significance of procedural liberal democracy is fourfold. In the first place, it emphasizes that the core human unit of a democratic system is the individual, not the group, class, or society as a whole. Second, nevertheless, it sees the active participation of those individuals in the political system as limited to either voting or holding an elected or appointed office in the institutional superstructure. In particular, ordinary people's role in the act of voting is seen as choosing between competing elites who will make governmental decisions for them, rather than making such decisions themselves through wider forms of participation (Schumpeter 1954). Third, it envisages the system as being more about protecting the individual from repression by government or by other private individuals or groups than about coming to collective decisions about the public good—which is itself seen to be embedded in procedure rather than substance. In other words, procedural democracy is seen a minimalist form of government in which the best achievable outcome is more akin to Adam Smith's invisible hand of the market than to a system aimed at improving socioeconomic equality, social justice, the quality of life per se, or other social, solidaristic values on a collective, authoritative basis.

Procedural democracy is therefore seen by its critics as drained of substance. It neglects the qualitative and normative aspects that make democracy attractive to subaltern groups and to those who would associate democracy with a range of far-reaching normative goals, in particular, according to Kurki:

- participatory democracy, concerned with expanding bottom-up input into decision-making processes
- delegative democracy,[1] in which representatives have to follow more closely the wishes of the people who elect them, rather than being autonomous Burkean representatives
- social welfarist democracy, concerned primarily with the well-being of the people
- feminist democracy, concerned with breaking down the unequal power relations between men and women
- green democracy, concerned with the ecological health of the planet
- radical models of democracy, primarily concerned with promoting social and economic equality, especially by transforming property relations
- cosmopolitan democracy, looking to spread democratic values globally through legal and constitutional norms

1. "In delegative democracy, delegates are selected and expected to act on the wishes of the constituency. In this form of democracy the constituency may recall the delegate at any time. Representatives are expected only to transmit the decisions of electors, advance their views, and if they fail to do so they are subject to immediate representative recall with only minimal process" (*Webster's Online Dictionary*, http://www.websters-online-dictionary.org/de/democracy.html). Guillermo O'Donnell has developed a definition of delegative democracy that is quite different, virtually the contrary of the traditional definition and rooted in personalist presidentialism and patrimonialism (O'Donnell 1994).

Indeed, Kurki argues, procedural democracy does not even concern itself with other values underpinning liberal democracy itself, such as the emancipation of individuals from arbitrary socioeconomic constraints, open discourse, a belief in socioeconomic progress and social justice, or toleration (Kurki 2008).

Nevertheless, procedural democracy has become the hegemonic model in the twentieth and twenty-first centuries, for, I would argue, three main reasons. In the first place, it has happened for historical reasons. The various experiments with different forms of democracy characteristic of the eighteenth through the twentieth centuries winnowed down real existing democracies to procedural liberal democracies by undermining other alternatives, including more communitarian, socialist, anarchist, and local solidarist forms. Procedural democracy is therefore the outcome of a process of evolutionary artificial selection. Second, it has occurred for structural reasons. The emergence and hegemony of the nation-state as a political form, especially in the context of the international competition of capitalist states, ensured that state hierarchies were more concerned to protect private property and markets than to pursue social justice for its own sake—unless the lack of the latter endangered the former, as in the wake of various depressions, when the welfare state was born. These hierarchies could resolve collective action problems from within while resisting complex *political* interdependencies from without. The third reason is that procedural democracy is the easiest form to achieve—the lowest common denominator. It does not require complex mechanisms of social intervention, can keep redistribution to a minimum, and yet call on collective norms of national defense and patriotism.

Paradoxically, then, the success of democratization may indeed stem from the very fact that it has been drained of substance, socially, economically, and politically. This fact, of course, ironically makes procedural democracy weak as well as strong. In a world where qualitative issues are increasingly salient, democracy has little to say. It does not address the huge inequalities in the world—inequalities generally far greater in parts of the developing and postcolonial world that is the target of the democratization thrust than in the developed world, where capitalism has produced a high secular rate of economic growth for three centuries. It does not address the substantive religious claims of groups that either see themselves as threatened by economic development and first world hegemony or wish to convert the rest of the world to their views—not to mention other cultural issues that are surfacing in the wake of the departure of traditional empires. And it does not address a range of substantive policy issues such as the ecological imperative, the regulation of transnational firms and global financial markets, or the management of global conflict. These questions are increasingly addressed not by formal democratization, but through transnational neo-pluralist political processes.

Nevertheless, it is one thing to call for a more theoretically pluralistic and locally or regionally contextualized form of democracy, as Kurki and Mouffe do, in order to reinject substance into the concept. It is quite another thing to see how this could be practically achieved without multi-plying overlapping and crosscutting *oppositions* to democracy at various levels, too. Pluralism and liberal democracy work when there is accep-tance of the rules of the game and shared values—as well as elites who want to broaden the base of their power. If this means narrowing the sub-stance, then that may be the price to pay. Democracy cannot be all things to all people, particularly in terms of the complexities of extending it into new areas—democratization.

Therefore, although the ideal of moving from procedure to substance may be normatively desirable and may respond to the values and world-views of many people in different parts of the world, such a shift also intro-duces the same kind of destabilizing elements that were seen in Europe between the two world wars and in the first wave of failed postcolonial con-stitutions. Democratization, as a process in a globalizing world, can be cir-cumscribed, eroded, and undermined from both sides, from too much as well as too little substance. Despite the substantive shortcomings of the Western form and without the sort of shared values, institutional super-structure, and interstate pressures that made democracy—a relatively sim-ple form of liberal representative democracy—viable within modern nation-states after centuries of socioeconomic change and political struggle, the central problematic of world politics today is not democratization but uneven pluralization and the development of transnational neopluralism.

5. DEMOCRATIZATION, TOO, IS WHAT ACTORS MAKE OF IT

The idea of democracy, in all its forms as analyzed here, is of course an immensely attractive one, and when taken as a whole, it, along with capital-ism, represents the Zeitgeist of the past hundred years. But ideas, however they spread in terms of culture and communication, need real people to put them into practice. And human agents face numerous complex constraints, personal, ideational, and structural, as well as economic, social, and politi-cal. So who will take the global democratization project forward? The par-ticular shape democratization is likely to take in a globalizing world will be determined primarily by which sets of actors are most effectively situated and motivated to take the project forward. As with the embedding of democ-racy at nation-state level, this is not a linear process, nor is it dominated by democratic idealists. It is messy and uneven, and it reflects the complex, ever-widening configuration of forces unleashed by globalization.

Most of the literature on globalization asserts that the key category of actors in terms of developing transnational linkages with transformational structural potential is economic actors, mainly because globalization is most often seen as primarily an economic process. Nevertheless, such groups are constrained by their traditional sectional character—their primary concern with material economic objectives rather than politics. The labor movement, for example, could grow and succeed in the twentieth century only because of the permissive conditions embodied in the consolidation of the nation-state and the mass politics of the Second Industrial Revolution. Today, given the increasing significance of flexible manufacturing processes and transnational management practices, the potential collective power of labor has been greatly diminished. Although these groups may call for wider democratization, their impact is generally limited to particular niches and issue-areas (Macdonald 2008; Evans 2007). In other words, what really matters is not democracy as such but the potential of such groups to participate in and have more than a marginal impact on transnational neopluralist political processes.

Another set of strategically situated economic actors includes owners, managers, and shareholders of multinational corporations. Nevertheless, these actors generally still depend on states and the states system for providing the basic public goods, by enforcing property rights and the like, necessary for their businesses to survive over time. These limits are reinforced by "enduring national differences" in corporate organizational forms (Pauly and Reich 1997) and "state-societal arrangements" (Hart 1992). And these actors are, of course, primarily concerned with the profitability and management of their firms. They do not expect or want to have to provide public goods themselves, as public goods are costly, returns may be undermined by free riding, and the managerial problems of doing so are immense in addition to producing the private goods their businesses were set up to produce and sell. They therefore expect public goods to be provided by governments and international institutions—and are often extremely suspicious of demands that could be mobilized by democratization, if not outright hostile.

Financial market actors are more accustomed to operating instinctively on a transnational playing field. However, the links between the kinds of institutionalization that would be supported by financial market actors, on the one hand, and democratization, on the other, is extremely tenuous, if not virtually nonexistent. Furthermore, the recent meltdown of global financial markets in the wake of various crises since the mid-1990s has done much to undermine their influence, in the short term at least, and handed the policy-making initiative back to governments.

Nevertheless, economic globalization has had a wide-ranging impact on *other* categories of agent—in particular, on political actors attempting to reconfigure forms of political authority to meet the potential challenge of transnationally rooted market failures and the demands of popular constituencies for the reassertion of political values such as the public interest. Democratization, if it spreads, may be more a reaction against current forms of neoliberal globalization, rather than stemming from the action of economic actors themselves, especially in terms of the mobilization of groups pursuing transnational interest and value goals. However, this may be an obstacle rather than a help in a world of states. Political actors, especially state actors, are tightly bound by existing structural constraints, as noted in chapter 5, and they also suffer from a growing disillusionment with governments, politicians, and bureaucrats generally. Traditional domestic pressure and interest groups have little interest in undermining their own influence, sustained through their existing state-bound networks. And although transnationally linked interest groups may, in theory, have the potential for new and complex cross-border patterns of political bargaining and influence and for coordinating their influence at a number of different domestic and transnational levels at the same time, they are, in reality, poor democratizers. They are more likely to seek quasi-corporatist roles in transnational decision-making processes than to pursue broader forms of democratization. Furthermore, political actors—state actors, in particular—are not about to try to deconstruct the state itself and design overtly transnational democratic processes to replace it, thereby undermining the most significant single source of their own power.

Social actors are in a complex position with regard to their capacity to pursue global or transnational democratization. The depth of politically imposed national identities in the developed world enabled nation-states and the states system during most of the twentieth century to spawn two world wars and the cold war, as well as dominate processes of political development in the postcolonial era. Nevertheless, the uncertain and destabilizing processes of democratic transition at a domestic level and the rapid formation of new collective identities have created tremendous social, as well as political, volatility and inspired popular pressure both for new kinds of control and accountability and for specific policy remedies, as noted earlier in comments on postcolonial theory. Nevertheless, the proliferation of social actors on the international and transnational levels has been widely observed, especially in the literature on global civil society. The numbers and activities of such groups have grown in range, scale, and scope. They can bring together a range of coalition partners who would not normally be prepared to work closely in a national setting. Furthermore, transnational cause groups can strategically whipsaw policy makers at local, national, and international levels. More important, however, as with the economic and political actors discussed before, it is unclear whether democratization per se is really at the heart of their objectives—which are usually narrower and more policy oriented—or whether they are merely paying lip service to it in the pursuit of their own more limited values and interests.

Nevertheless, the development of a limited form of pluralism or neo-pluralism at the transnational level could be seen as creating new forms of feedback, path dependency, and the ratcheting up of global politics in such a way as to lead to a certain amount of de facto quasi democratization. We may be seeing the emergence of what Diane Stone has called a "global *agora*"—"a growing global public space of fluid, dynamic, and intermeshed relations of politics, markets, culture and society... [characterized by] multiple publics and plural institutions... a social and political space—generated by globalization—rather than a physical place" (Stone 2008). But will it be truly *democratic*? Indeed, most critical theorists see the level shift supposedly taking place as involving something more like what Allen calls a "transnational authority network (TAN) of International Financial Institutions, banks, firms and states that governs global market reproduction. These are the citizens of the global polity and their right to participation in deliberation derives from elite roles in finance, security, production and knowledge networks. This polity is eerily reminiscent of property based citizenship in pre-emancipation American and British territories!" (Allen 2008).

6. INSTITUTIONAL BRICOLAGE AND THE AD HOC PROLIFERATION OF PSEUDOGOVERNANCE

The final pitfall faced by processes of democratization in a globalizing world is the existing superstructure of so-called global governance and the role it has played and is likely to continue to play in hindering the spread of *either* procedural *or* substantive democracy. As I argued in chapter 9, this superstructure exhibits a range of patchy, even erratic characteristics that seem, on close inspection, almost designed to make democratization improbable or impossible. In the first place, rather than constituting a structured field of action friendly to or even susceptible of democratization, this superstructure actually further entrenches and reinforces the political and policy-making power of *both* state *and* nonstate components of Allen's transnational authority networks. Their authority may not confer legitimacy, except insofar as neoliberalism has become a hegemonic ideology in today's world, but it does prevent the emergence and consolidation of *other* either workable or legitimate democratic institutions.

On the one hand, this situation reflects the profound intergovernmental nature of international regimes and global governance. Although it has been suggested that practices of multilateralism have given these institutions a certain degree of relative autonomy from their member states in limited issue-areas (Ruggie 1993a), in fact, these institutions are dependent on national states for their funding, staffing, and ways of working. Their missions are decided by interstate treaties and negotiations, their key decision makers are appointed by leading governments, their funding depends primarily on the largesse of the richest and most powerful states, and they have few effective sanctions on state behavior—with the partial and very limited exception of the dispute-settlement mechanism of the World Trade Organization, which itself depends on politically negotiated bargains among parties to effect compliance and enforcement by individual aggrieved states upon other states (Wolfe 2005). In other words, insofar as global governance is institutionalized, rather than just being instantiated in evolving practices of governmentality, it continues to rest on a Westphalian bargain and not on an authoritative, effectively supranational superstructure. Any genuine institutionalization of democracy at a transnational or global level, I believe, requires at least *some* semblance of an appropriate institutionalized superstructure, whether preexisting or systematically constructed, in order to emerge and develop.

On the other hand, as numerous commentators on international institutions and global governance have noted, these multilateral regimes are almost always and everywhere concerned first and foremost with their own *institutional survival*. Sociologists of the firm since Max Weber have noted that capitalist businesses must continually balance and juggle two structural imperatives: making profits and institutional survival. International institutions do not, of course, need to make profits, but they do need to satisfy their patrons—not only governments of nation-states but also their main *clients*, namely, the firms and markets they regulate. Although they are perhaps not as prone to regulatory capture by specific clients or special interests as in smaller jurisdictions, such regimes do have to cater to the needs and health of the industries and markets it is their very mission to sustain. And the institutional survival imperative can be very damaging to the substantive mission of such an institution, for example, diverting environmental regimes from taking effective action because their member governments and the economic sectors they have to deal with would resist and undermine them if they did so in a way that endangered those governments and/ or sectors (Young 1994). The history of the Kyoto Protocol, abandoned by the United States, resisted by rapidly growing developing countries, and hamstrung by its huge intergovernmental, summit-based structure, is a key case in point.

Any push for genuine democratization is therefore inconceivable in the context of real existing international regimes and institutions, despite the well-intentioned hope that the clientelist bargaining processes they entail might transmute itself into a pseudodemocratic pluralism or agora. However, far more important than the internal structure of such regimes— intergovernmentalism, survivalism, clientelism, and the like—is the super-structure of regimes in general. Rather than constituting a coherent, interlinked cosmos of interlinked institutionalized processes that increases the rationality of the international system, as Robert O. Keohane (1984) has so cogently argued, they comprise a messy, overlapping, competing, and generally toothless universe, at least as far as genuinely democratic institutional change is concerned. The whole is far less than the sum of the parts.

The existing system of international regimes has been the product not of coherent evolution, but of ad hoc trial and error, setting up divided, competing, overlapping, inconsistent processes of governance that more often lead either to impotent ratification of outcomes bargained within Allen's transnational authority network or, crucially, to gridlock rather than to genuine collective action. This process of institutional bricolage and the spread of *raison du monde* may eventually lead to some sort of evolutionary convergence, but the obstacles to such a development are currently greater than the opportunities. The result so far has too often been not coherent decision making, but frantic venue shopping. Within this context, any possibility for genuine democratization looks more like checks and balances gone wild— lots of checks, few balances—than like real governance. Pseudogovernance may be better than no governance at all, of course, but it is unlikely to lead to even procedural democracy, much less any of the substantive varieties discussed by Kurki and Mouffe.

7. CONCLUSION: KEEP PUSHING TOWARD THE LIGHT, BUT DON'T HOPE FOR TOO MUCH

Nevertheless, as Ian Clark has observed, there does appear to be some sort of halting and fragile process of democratization taking place *within* more and more nation-states—hopefully two steps forward, one step back (Clark 2008). However, this fact merely highlights the gap between *internationalization* and *globalization*. The notion of a global democracy, even in the very limited multilevel form proposed by Macdonald, will, in my opinion, require a fundamental a priori transformation of the very international system itself. Not only is that unlikely in current circumstances but also, in the words of Benjamin Franklin's *Poor Richard's Almanack*, "there's many a slip twixt cup and lip."

Will the international system remain relatively stable and coherent—as despite the cold war, decolonization, small wars, financial crises, and the like, it has mainly been since 1945? Or will it move toward something like neomedievalism? Given recent trends in Russia and a number of failed states and unstable democracies, along with the rise of ethnic and religious strife, it could even be argued that a perfect storm involving the pitfalls set out in this chapter—perhaps triggered by the failure of states to cope with global economic collapse—could actually lead to more Westphalianism and less scope for global democracy.

I would not go that far. There are numerous trends that could conceivably converge if the pitfalls are avoided or counteracted in evolutionary fashion. Niches of quasi democratization, more akin to pluralism, will develop in narrow sectors and issue-areas and may spread in very limited ways through emulation and the transfer of ideas and practices, as Macdonald has argued with reference to the rise of trade union activism in parts of the developing world (Macdonald 2008). Nevertheless, political will, constructive thinking, idealism, and institution building will not be enough. In my opinion, however, there is a process of transnational neopluralism emerging in which a coherent cross-border political bargaining process is developing. Furthermore, in the context of globalization, there is a growing *demand* for democratic regulation in key issue-areas, even if the *supply* is limited by the structure of the system and the relative impotence of supranational actors. But whether this can lead to anything that resembles even procedural, much less substantive, democratization is a very problematic proposition indeed. The road to global democracy is far rockier than the nation-state road has been in the past, and that was rocky enough.

Chapter 11

The New Security Dilemma

1. INTRODUCTION: BEYOND THE TRADITIONAL SECURITY DILEMMA

International security specialists have generally resisted attempts to trans-late into the international arena the kind of relations and structures of power, interest group politics, democratic (or authoritarian) principles, notions of social justice, and the like that are traditionally characteristic of the domestic political sphere and increasingly taken on board in fields like international political economy and sociology. They have overwhelmingly believed that national-level self-interest and self-help imperatives remain dominant in a world of states, especially given the absence of an authorita-tive supranational world governmental structure. The overriding incentives built into the structure would cause those states to defect from cooperative agreements at key times when national interests were seen to be threatened or inadequately served, thus causing the system to revert to a default-like, anarchic state of nature, if not a state of outright war. In this context, the primary—and, in many cases, the only—overarching stabilizing and ordering mechanism in the international system would be rooted in the way balances of power among states operate to permit basic stability in a highly fragile environment.

That environment itself, however, is seen to contain the seeds of its own breakdown. The most important factor at the center of this process is the so-called security dilemma, probably the most crucial dynamic of international relations as a whole and one that must be monitored and managed vigorously if the international system is to be protected from instability and war (Herz 1950). This is a complex issue in itself. Managing uncertainty, developing cooperation and trust among states, and constructing a society of states or a community of nations is a long-standing practical and normative problematic in international relations (Booth and Wheeler 2008). In contrast, I argue that a predominant focus on the state and the states system for understanding the problem of security in today's world increasingly misses the point. This is not only about political economy or social change but also the causes, manage-ment, and prevention of violent conflict. State and interstate imperatives, especially the security dilemma and the balance of power—while still highly significant—are being transformed into *second-order imperatives*.

Traditional ways of pursuing international security, especially through military force, are proving less effective and more counterproductive *in and of themselves* in a world of complex interdependence. Thus they are taking a back seat to norms, practices, institutional experiments, and political processes that privilege pluralistic interest group and value group politics, crosscutting linkages and bargaining processes, global economic growth, and organizational forms that look more and more like those traditionally characteristic of domestic politics. A New Security Dilemma (NSD) is evolving in the world that is less about how states as unit actors interact through traditional forms of diplomacy and military power, and more about how increasingly disaggregated state actors and nonstate actors interact, compete, haggle, fight, police themselves and each other, and attempt to build coalitions around particular issue-areas. Of course, states are still, and will be for a very long time, concerned with national interests, defense, power, and hegemony. But those concerns are of less utility in the twenty-first century, and new ways to handle security issues, threats of violence, and fundamental sociopolitical upheavals are increasingly on the agenda.

The Traditional Security Dilemma (TSD) is the notion that *in a context of uncertainty and bounded rationality*, (a) perceived external threats (real or imagined) generate feelings of insecurity in those states that believe themselves to be the targets of such threats, thereby (b) leading those states to adopt measures to increase their power and capability to counteract those threats (alliance creation, arms buildups, etc.). The very attempts of individual states to strengthen their own security in an anarchic world lead *other* states to try to ratchet up their own power, thus in turn making the first state to have kicked off the process feel even *less* secure, not more so, for its efforts. These countermeasures in turn are (c) perceived (or misperceived) as threatening by yet other states, leading to further counter-countermeasures—potentially undermining existing power balances and creating a vicious and potentially tragic spiral or negative feedback loop of ever-increasing overall insecurity (Herz 1950; Jervis 1976; Buzan 1983; Booth and Wheeler 2008) and the tendency to defect and even go to war. Events leading up to the First World War are usually the main case study alluded to in this perspective.

In such a system, it is only by creating, maintaining, and re-creating balances of power internationally—whether through war, manipulation of power resources, interstate diplomatic mediation, or politically effective foreign policy—that this underlying tendency to conflict and potential system breakdown can be counteracted. In game-theoretic terms, the payoff matrices built into the international system create incentives for states to defect rather than cooperate, unless restrained by the operation of the balance of power and its institutionalized instances (Niou, Ordeshook, and Rose 1989; Little 2007). Such an analysis has been at the heart of both classical realism and neorealism (Waltz 1979; Buzan, Jones, and Little 1993). Furthermore, paradoxically, at the domestic level, too, without an exogenous balance of power—that is, without a quasi-Hobbesian stabilization mechanism with neither a sovereign nor even a proper social contract (Merle 1982)—the capacity of societies to maintain stable domestic political systems would be fatally undermined as well.

The central question today is whether this mechanism retains both its internal logic and its wider stabilizing capacity in a changing structural context. In a globalizing world, how do such changes affect the nation-state itself and, in turn, the structural coherence of the states system? I argue in this chapter that, indeed, such a process of reconfiguring security is going on; that it is inextricably intertwined with globalization; that it involves different sources of insecurity, both new ones and reconfigured old ones; and that it is making traditional balances of power, along with the Traditional Security Dilemma, increasingly redundant. The key to this transformation is that balances of power are subject to crosscutting pluralistic or neopluralistic pressures that undermine the ability of states themselves, separately or together, to exert control at a systemic level. A new dynamic of third-level games is emerging, games that are more and more important in ensuring people's security in a globalizing world.

These changes therefore bring into question the very raison d'être of the states system itself, along two dimensions. The first concerns the nature of the benefits confronting the states system itself in the security area, that is, whether benefits such as (or especially) security can be provided separately by states or centrally by collective security organizations as an indivisible public good, or whether they involve a greater degree of *divisibility*—that is, whether security can be provided more efficiently by more decentralized, bottom-up processes. In the latter case, security might be more effectively provided through more multinodal forms of cooperation, such as multilevel law-and-order mechanisms, whether by states or by nonstate actors. Indeed, if so, there might not even be a need to provide or make available an overarching command-type security apparatus in the international arena, just as there is no need for a heavy, authoritarian, command-type state apparatus in well-functioning pluralistic political and economic systems. The presence of extensive "divisible benefits" may make possible the emergence of a process of what has been called the "civilianization" of world politics.

The second dimension concerns the nature of the states system per se. The history of the states system was not only about providing international order but also about ensuring favorable exogenous conditions for domestic collective action. In other words, it was also necessary to ensure that other substate and transstate actors—originally the feudal nobility, the church, bandits, potential political and economic rebels in both town and country, and the urban bourgeoisie—were integrated into the domestic state and thus subordinated to the overarching discipline of the states system as such. *Therefore, the security dilemma has always been challenged not only by the threat of defection by particular states ("defection from above") but also by the threat of defection by a range of social forces, whether ideological, economic, cultural, ethnic, or purely political ("defection from below").*

In this chapter, I argue that fundamental changes along both dimensions are undermining the Traditional Security Dilemma by subsuming it in a wider and more complex NSD, in which the roles of a more pluralistic universe of social, economic, and political forces are challenging the capacity of states as such to provide security. Indeed, in the presence of more divisible benefits, security may be provided in the future by processes analogous to civilian police forces and court systems, as well as more informal mechanisms at local (or glocal) and intermediate levels, where world politics becomes less and less a zero-sum, essentially militaristic power game among states and more a competition among interest and value groups. In this context, as with the other developments addressed in this book, the key to understanding how the New Security Dilemma works is the growing role of transnationally organized and linked groups in dealing with the causes and manifestations of conflict and insecurity.

The New Security Dilemma, however, like the old one, also involves a potentially damaging logic of vicious spiraling—a logic rooted in the complexity and uncertainty of the postmodern world and the uneven and multilayered nature of globalization itself. Defection *by social forces* can potentially undermine the kind of civilianized processes suggested previously, as is the case with terrorism, failed states, international criminal gangs, financial fraudsters, and the like. But these sorts of actors are not likely to be effectively counteracted by traditional military means. Therefore, one of the consequences of globalization is the need not only to move to a system of "civilian states" (Sheehan 2008) but also to develop a more effective transnationalized or supranationalized *civilian superstructure,* much as states did on the domestic level in the modern era. Transnational political forces, social movements, and transgovernmental networks, of the kind inherent in transnational neopluralism, will be drawn to attempt to develop, in an ad hoc, bricolage fashion, a more civilian, "police"-oriented superstructure (in both Foucault's and today's commonsense meaning of the term "police") as the twenty-first century proceeds.

2. DIVISIBILITY, DEFECTION, AND THE DYNAMICS
OF SECURITY ORDERS

Divisibility and defection are common concepts in the international cooperation literature on a wide range of issues. The interaction of the two can
provide the analyst with a hypothetical set of alternative pathways for patterns of change and institutionalization (Simmons 1996). On the one hand,
when benefits are highly divisible in an ideal-type collective action problem,
a wide range of actors acting autonomously can gain those benefits through
spontaneous action or with some sort of minimal, even informal agreement
on the rules of the game, as in an ideal-type neoclassical market. They need
not depend on the existence of command-type hierarchical governance
institutions to reap those benefits. Other players do not need to be brought
on board a formal, binding collective structure. This is analogous to the
notion of private goods or nonspecific assets in the collective action and new
institutional economics literature, in particular, the notion of "recurrent
contracting" or developing flexible responses to new conditions as you go
along. Indeed, it may be that attempting to negotiate more complex cooperation agreements with additional participants—analogous to "long-term contracting" in new institutional economics—will actually *raise* the costs of
negotiating and enforcing agreements ("transactions costs") and make the
structure more inefficient and unwieldy, as with overheavy and bloated
bureaucracies, thus ironically making it more possible for actors to avoid
compliance with the rules in the absence of effective sanctions.

   Therefore, where benefits are *highly divisible*, the system could be either
stably pluralistic and self-regulating, on the one hand, or relatively unstable
and centrifugal, on the other—but it is unlikely to be efficiently hierarchical
and unified, as in an authoritative governance superstructure characterized
by effective long-term contracting. The coherence of such a relatively decentralized system will be determined by whether there exist widespread temptations to defect. Because benefits are divisible, and some are more divisible
than others, it may be more possible to obtain those benefits by remaining
outside the structure or by manipulating and whipsawing it from inside,
rather than by following the rules. Nevertheless, where such temptations to
defect are low, for example, where the trickle-down benefits of economic
growth are sufficiently widespread to make defection economically unattract-
ive, we might expect some sort of relatively self-regulating pluralism to
develop; in contrast, where temptations to defect are high and rewards for
staying within the system low, we might expect instability and possible breakdown of the system itself, or at least of parts of it. The issue of piracy off the
East African coast, along with the continued anarchy in the failed state of
Somalia, is a particularly salient example of the latter at the time of writing.

On the other hand, where benefits are *highly nondivisible*, one would expect the same sorts of criteria to come into play as with public goods and specific assets. Benefits can be gained only if a wide range of actors can be brought on board, long-term commitments made to the rules of the game, and the primacy of authoritative, institutionalized decision-making processes kept strong. High transactions and related costs would then be justified to benefit from cooperation and avoid the potential dangers of noncooperation—especially, in the security issue-area, the destructiveness of war. Local or limited agreements will, on the contrary, be ineffective and may even be extremely costly if they lead to conflicts between participants and outsiders. In terms of security, limited agreements might antagonize certain actors, make them feel insecure and threatened, and thereby cause them to take preventive action. Thus where benefits are highly nondivisible and where temptations to defect are high, the system could be chaotic and negative-sum, requiring top-down authoritative imposition to prevent free-riding on any agreements. But where temptations to defect are low, the result would be more likely to involve a form of leadership or command-type bureaucratic hierarchy in which "major players at the center of the issue agree to central rules to which peripheral players tacitly or explicitly sign on with minimal political pressure" (Simmons 1996: 7).

Given that the states system is seen as fundamentally anarchic and the main issue is the threat or danger of defection and war, the main benefits involve not the kind of public goals that are normally attributed to the domestic politics of states, but more bottom-line goals of preventing war and maintaining a certain relative, if uneasy, stability in the international system. In this context, it is possible to distinguish among several different ideal types of security orders. We can identify four kinds of dynamics at work in different security orders. Two of the types, those with low temptations to defect, can be characterized as "centripetal"; the others, with high temptations to defect, can be characterized as "centrifugal." These basic tendencies vary in their outcome, depending on whether the perceived benefits of agreement (or the perceived dangers of disagreement) are high or low. Of course, all these hypothesized outcomes are subject to caveats of uncertainty and bounded rationality that cannot effectively be controlled for but institutionalized mechanisms are intended to minimize. Such institutionalized mechanisms can, of course, be the product either of deductive design or of inductive trial-and-error (iterative game or even bricolage) processes.

The first category consists of the case where nondivisible benefits are high and the temptation to defect is low (Centripetal I). In this case, a set (or subset) of great powers or superpowers provides proactive *leadership* in institutionalizing cooperative security arrangements and institutionalizing a form of top-down control, whether by one state or a group of allied states. Perhaps the most obvious form this category can take involves the hegemony or empire of one dominant power, but there are other forms, too, familiar enough from the history of international relations. This type can also be seen, for example, in (a) a "concert" system, such as the Concert of Europe in the nineteenth century (reacting *ex post* to the Napoleonic Wars), in (b) a stable balance of power system in which relatively evenly balanced antagonists act in condominium (and peripheral actors perceive gains from defection to be low also), or (c) within particular alliances where both the external danger and the potential benefits from internal cooperation on other levels (e.g., economic or political stability) are perceived to be high. Nonstate actors such as business firms, trade unions, and/or ethnic groups may also be kept on board if the benefits of cooperation and dangers of noncooperation are seen to be high (e.g., through anticommunism or anti-imperialism in the cold war).

The second category is where nondivisible benefits are high but temptations to defect are also high (Centrifugal I). This can be the case where higher potential benefits are perceived as potentially accruable *outside* the arrangement, in particular, where peripheral actors—whether state or nonstate actors—perceive larger benefits from nonalignment, revolution, delinked development, or the like. In such cases, if either the danger from a widening of the conflict (say, a domino effect) and/or the benefits of keeping everyone on board (capitalist prosperity or socialist planning) are seen to be high, then the central actors will be tempted to coercively impose the norms of the order on potential defectors, mainly through military intervention or other forms of forceful pressure. The process is therefore likely to be one of attempted or real *central coercion*, that is, the actual exercise of force, rather than bottom-up acquiescence to hegemonic control.

The third alternative pathway is where benefits are divisible and temptations to defect low (Centripetal II). This is often the case where economic prosperity and/or the so-called democratic peace reduce the aggressive drive of actors and potential opponents alike by diminishing the perceived benefits of traditional international power politics, that is, where a nonviolent positive-sum game is perceived to arise out of the autonomous actions of the various actors at different levels, for example, through the benefits of economic cooperation and growth. In such a more perfect world, cooperation agreements per se might not be seen to be necessary to the establishment and maintenance of a stable security order. However, where agreements do arise, they would do so in a relatively bottom-up fashion, where arrangements on a local, regional, or specific issue-based level may emerge, gaining and/or losing adherents, depending on shifting perceptions of benefit. The process here is one of *shifting centripetal pluralism*, a quasi-self-regulating system in which dangers are low and benefits incremental.

The final pathway occurs where benefits are divisible and temptations to defect are high (Centrifugal II). This is the case when defectors can carve out private or public fiefdoms that can increase their private benefits in a situation because potential dangers resulting from defection are perceived to be low and control mechanisms seem weak. Indeed, there is an assumption here on the part of certain actors that those private benefits can be gained *only* by defection; that is, despite high ostensible divisibility, they are still essentially involved in a zero-sum game. This might be states engaging in trade wars, monopolistic or oligopolistic multinational firms allying with local warlords, regional revolts against central control, or the whole gamut of civil and cross-border wars, including tribal and ethnic wars but also economic backlashes among globally deprived groups. The main process here is one of *uneven disorder*, characterized by multilayered and asymmetric conflict and coalition building, whether under the aegis of the state or outside it, leading to piecemeal and potentially unstable agreements. We can schematize these four pathways in this fashion as show in table 11.1.

In this context, the strength of the Westphalian order can be seen to have been rooted in the increasing nondivisibility of benefits in the international political, economic, and social system in the transition from feudalism—within which benefits were by definition highly divisible—to *the modern state, the very rationale of which was to manage and control the increasing indivisibility of benefits*, that is, developing cohesive systems of collective action at the domestic level, and the capacity to make credible commitments at the international level. Indeed, as nondivisible benefits increased, so did nondivisible costs, leading to the emergence and consolidation of state bureaucratic hierarchies for purposes of taxation, war, industrial development, and other public goods. Furthermore, as the number of core states declined

Table 11.1 Divisibility, Defection, and Security Dilemmas

	Traditional Security Dilemma	New Security Dilemma
Divisibility Defection	*Nondivisible*	*Divisible*
Low Temptation	Centripetal I: Leadership	Centripetal II: Shifting Centripetal Pluralism
High Temptation	Centrifugal I: Central Coercion	Centrifugal II: Uneven Disorder

from many real and potential units in the seventeenth century, to a few great powers in the nineteenth and early twentieth centuries, to only two superpowers in the cold war, and as the absolute and relative military power and industrial strength of those core units increased with industrialization, imperialism, and the Second Industrial Revolution, so the potential dangers of defection also increased dramatically, as evidenced by two world wars, the cold war, and the threat of big-power interventionism (e.g., Hungary 1956 and Czechoslovakia 1968)—not to mention nuclear annihilation, a nondivisible cost that would have an impact on all states.

This nondivisibility of costs and benefits, and increasingly of political and economic institutions and processes in order to cope with them, led to two linked developments in the control mechanisms of the international system. At one level was a two-step move away from unstable and shifting patterns of interstate conflict—initially to a more stable European balance of power system between the Napoleonic Wars and the First World War, and later to a more centralized alliance system in the cold war (a version of Centripetal I). At a second level was a three-step move involving the external extension of those control mechanisms to the rest of the world—starting with European imperialism, continuing with the incorporation of other great powers such as the United States and Japan, and culminating in the superpowers' attempt after the Second World War to co-opt not only small powers in the core but also the decolonized third world into the competing cold war alliance systems (a version of Centrifugal I).

In the cold war, two types of temptation to defect existed. In the first place, certain states within the two alliance systems periodically attempted to gain greater autonomy and sometimes form a rapprochement with states in the other alliance. France was the main maverick in the North Atlantic Alliance, whereas the Soviet-led "communist" alliance was continually faced with defections, whether from China or from the USSR's European satellites. The Western alliance was maintained by the carrot of capitalist prosperity and the ideological stick of the communist threat. But the Eastern alliance was shored up more and more uneasily by force, as in Hungary and Czechoslovakia. Where defection became too big a problem to be managed within an alliance, as with the Sino-Soviet split, the alliance system itself was seriously destabilized.

Second, however, the third world constituted a double defection threat. On the one hand, the rise of the Nonaligned Movement from the 1950s onward, along with potential alliance switching linked to frequent domestic regime changes and development crises, undercut the ability of the core alliances to integrate third world states; on the other hand, domestic instability, revolutionary movements, tribal and ethnic loyalties, and other endogenous and cross-border sources of conflict challenged the states system itself as an effective control mechanism. Ultimately, both superpowers came to grief in this way, as exemplified by the American defeat in Vietnam and the Soviet defeat in Afghanistan, which played a crucial role in the breakup of the Soviet Union itself. Nevertheless, the Western alliance, with its core of capitalist prosperity, was better able to employ carrots, while the Soviet alliance system, in economic decline from the 1970s onward and only able to employ less-and-less effective sticks, found its relative power both in core and periphery declining rapidly.

In this context, the post–cold war era has seen several crucial developments that have changed the nature of the international game, although many of these changes began earlier. In the first place, I would argue that *globalization*, whether economic, social, or political, actually represents a much wider evolution toward an *increasing divisibility of benefits* in the international system. Participation in a more open world trading system or more integrated international financial markets, to name but two dimensions of this complex process, involves the growing provision of public goods in non-security issue-areas through forms of private or mixed public/private governance organized around and through transnational and transgovernmental networks and processes, rather than just through the states system as such. Second, states and other actors are far less dependent on the centralized structure of the states system as such to be the sole provider of international security per se as an indivisible public good, as in Weber's famous "monopoly of legitimate violence" (Centripetal II). The road is open for more pluralistic political processes and third-level games to develop, even in the once predominantly realist, state-dominated security issue-area.

When security is provided today by states as such, it is increasingly through shifting alliances such as the twenty-nine-member ad hoc alliance that confronted Iraq in the 1991 Gulf War, multilateral mechanisms such as the United Nations, or a plurality of overlapping organizations—the North Atlantic Treaty Organization, the European Union, the Western European Union, and the Organization for Security and Cooperation in Europe (Cerny 1990b). These shifting alliances can be unreliable, as has been shown in Iraq and other recent hot spots. Perhaps most important, however, the control mechanisms the core exercises with regard to the periphery have changed. Neither imperialism nor interventionism works any longer as an integrative mechanism. Except for limited and often failed attempts, usually by directionless international institutions or shaky ad hoc alliances around former imperial powers, the costs of such intervention are now seen as prohibitive and the benefits of control few (Centrifugal II).

Consequently, resort to different forms of *exit* from the predominant security order, especially the temptation to defect from the states system itself—rather than participation, that is, voice or loyalty (Hirschman

1970)—becomes attractive to an increasing number of actors, whether private and quasi-private governance structures in the more prosperous capitalist world, new mafias in Russia, or private armies, tribal militias, and "archipelago states" in Africa. In seeking to exit the constraints of the states system, actors—whether state actors or nonstate actors, and whether seeking economic gain, power, or justice, as well as security—can further undermine and erode the capacity of the states in the system, individually or collectively, to provide *either* external or internal security, or both, in a vicious circle. Such a vicious circle in turn increases the element of uncertainty and aggravates the boundedness of rationality, increasing the dangers of misperception.

Thus actors are *rationally induced to resort to nonstate forms of power*, decision making, and/or institutional mechanisms to provide security (and other goals and values that security is thought to make possible). On the one hand, this process can lead to the emergence and development of a range of newly embedded, but originally ad hoc, private or quasi-private regimes and circuits of power, both formal and informal, surrounding and crosscutting the state in a new web of complex relationships. Thus the New Security Dilemma is inextricably intertwined with the processes of internationalization and transnationalization that comprise our wider notion of globalization and would reflect any synergies stemming from their intersection. On the other hand, given uncertainty and bounded rationality, the same process can lead to the breakdown of existing bulwarks of order *without* replacing them with effective new institutionalized mechanisms, leading to a self-feeding expansion of endemic, low-level conflict and spreading violence. In this sense, therefore, the reconfiguring of power in a globalizing world, the security dimension of twenty-first-century world politics, may lead not to a new world order but to a new world *disorder*, a vicious circle that potentially might not be easily or effectively counteracted by states (and the states system) at home or abroad. Therefore, the challenge of the New Security Dilemma is to develop a sufficiently stable, civilianized, transnational political process to maximize divisible benefits while minimizing temptations to defect and thereby to prevent more unstable forms of neomedievalism and potential centrifugal system breakdown from developing.

3. DIVISIBILITY AND DEFECTION IN THE TWO SECURITY DILEMMAS

In this context, therefore, the emergence of the New Security Dilemma represents a fundamental change in the working of the international system. The way the Traditional Security Dilemma worked depended on the presence of two fundamental preconditions. In the first place, it required that states, in their relations with each other, were able to function as effective unit actors. The foreign policies of states and their respective stances toward each other had to minimally mimic the thought processes of reified individual decision makers making quasi-rational choices on the basis of imperatives derived from the structured relations among the wider constellation of states acting in analogous fashion in the international systemic context, not that of domestic politics.

Of course, such rationality was bounded in several crucial ways: (a) by imperfect information, leading to misperception; (b) by a highly mistrustful set of preconceptions about the nature of the international, based on the assumption that power was the bottom line of international relations and that altruistic forms of cooperation were therefore inherently counterproductive (see chapter 4); (c) by the exogenous and endogenous realities of economic, ideological, and cultural interdependence and crosscutting linkages throughout the modern era (*not* just in the current era of globalization); and (d) by the realities of domestic political conflict and coalition building. Nevertheless, it was not only in the minds of realist academics that these other realities were assumed away. These assumptions were embedded in the traditions of Realpolitik, diplomatic practice, and military preparedness throughout the Westphalian era. The TSD reflected real social practices, whatever the deeper structural realities.

The second precondition was that domestic state structures had to be hierarchical and self-enclosed enough in their internal sovereignty, their political institutions (at least in the foreign policy issue-area generally), and, in particular, their capacity to act coherently in times of crisis, when elites in the security issue-area assumed an even more reified holistic role. The external Leviathan had to be underpinned by a sufficiently developed *internal* Leviathan, involving political culture, especially a cosmopolitan elite culture in the foreign policy and security issue-areas (Rosenau 1961), cross-class social solidarity, effective political institutions and processes, and a relatively developed and self-sufficient national economy, to be able to mobilize national resources successfully to counter perceived external threats.

In effect, then, the TSD depended crucially on *the perception by states*— that is, by state actors who saw themselves as mere agents in a principal-agent relationship with the reified state as the imagined principal—*that benefits in the international system were deeply, inherently, structurally nondivisible.* This perception has reflected both a particular historical/cultural memory, and a particular commonly held interpretation of the accepted "continuing realities" or "perennial problematics" of international politics per se. The historical-cultural memory more or less began with the Middle Ages and the disintegration of the feudal system from the disastrous fourteenth century (Tuchman 1978) through the wars of religion, which of course led to the Peace of Westphalia itself. In other words, *cosmopolitan elites believed that a breakdown of the states system would threaten a breakdown of civilization itself* and a reversion of world politics to endemic, uncontrollable local conflicts.

Furthermore, their interpretation of the perennial problems of international relations was that war, as a means to establish, maintain, and enforce balances of power, was a predominant and essential regulatory mechanism in the international system—that is, that stable periods rooted in a particular interstate balance of power were inevitably followed by the undermining of that stability as the power capabilities and intentions *of states* changed over time, whether in an evolutionary or revolutionary manner. The dangers of the breakdown of the international system were seen as potentially disastrous, with any hoped-for benefits from its erosion as being ephemeral and counterproductive. Thus consensual cooperation was desirable, but, failing that, *coercion of potential defectors was necessary for survival itself* in such an uncertain environment.

That is not to say that incentives to defect were low in the TSD; indeed, quite the opposite. In elite as well as popular understanding, international defectors such as Napoleon's France, Hitler's Germany, and the Soviet Union have provided a template for the dangers of defection among states (*defection from above*), while Marxist revolution, international capitalism (often represented through anti-Semitism), and third world fragmentation have provided an analogous template for the dangers of defection among substate and/or transstate social, economic, ideological, and political forces (*defection from below*). This possibility of defection has haunted politicians, diplomats, military leaders, and professors of history and later international relations throughout the modern era. Indeed, it has led some of the last of these to reify the international states system to the virtual exclusion of all other international politics (e.g., Waltz 1979). In this context, the traditional "security dilemma"—both as a technical term used by mid-twentieth-century authors and in its virtual sense of an embedded practice of the states system throughout modern history—has played a particularly strong normative role.

In the course of the twentieth century, the TSD was at the core of historical understanding. Study of the causes of the First World War in mainstream international relations has always focused on the classic TSD problem of arms racing and the vicious spiral of state defection. Studies of the Second World War have emphasized the dangers of psychologically or ideologically pathological leaders not only defecting but also seeking to develop more holistic coercive empires. And the mainstream understanding of the cold war was rightly obsessed, despite some exceptions among Goldwaterites in the 1960s and war-fighting theorists in the 1980s, with a fear of the nondivisible "unthinkability" and ultimately unwinnable character of nuclear warfare.

The contrast between the TSD model and the actor mind-set that accompanied and reinforced it, on the one hand, and the New Security Dilemma, on the other, could therefore not be starker. The NSD instead depends crucially on the double perception that (a) costs and benefits in the contemporary world are much more divisible, perhaps even predominantly so (if not wholly so, even in terms of nuclear proliferation), thereby altering the payoffs for defection, and (b) temptations to defect have also evolved in such a way that, rather than being primarily applicable to states as such, they increasingly involve transnational and subnational actors, whether ethnic and/or religious groups, warlords, losers in the global economy, criminal gangs, or terrorists—as well as, of course, value groups, nongovernmental organizations (NGOs), antiwar factions and pressure groups among mass publics, and others. Of course, some sources of the temptation to defect may not have changed much in terms of motivations and material sources—for example, international oil cartels and pseudorevolutionary states like Ayatollah Khomeini's Iran or Saddam Hussein's Iraq from above and ethnic warfare, mafias, and socioeconomic deprivation from below. Others may, however, be newer or involve an intensification of the old (as discussed later). Whether from above or below, however—although especially from below—the very divisibility of benefits is widely seen to loosen and undermine centralized control of the international cooperation process and, in turn, further raising the potential payoffs for defection. These developments potentially further shift the parameters of uncertainty and bounded rationality and thus make outcomes harder to predict in quite different ways.

4. DIMENSIONS OF DIVISIBILITY AND THE NEW SECURITY DILEMMA

This increasing divisibility of benefits, plus linked changes in the temptation to defect, comprises at least four dimensions. Each involves the diminishing capacity of states to provide security and the growing role of transnational pluralist political processes in the security issue-area. The first is *economic globalization*, which implies the possibility of positive-sum material gains (in terms of both private and public goods) as a much less costly and less potentially counterproductive alternative type of benefits to war and to wasteful, spiraling defense expenditures. The second is the *death of ideology* in the sense of the predominance of conflict between macroideological, state-promoted worldviews as experienced through most of the twentieth century, first proclaimed by Daniel Bell in the 1960s (Bell 1960) and then revived by Francis Fukuyama in the early 1990s (Fukuyama 1992). The third involves both *social multiculturalism* and *cultural postmodernism*, in which one of the core conditions for the underpinning of the TSD, the widespread imagination from below—or, more accurately, the state-led construction from above—of a common national-state identity and consciousness, is increasingly eroded by demands for cultural or other forms of autonomy, by the rejection of grand narratives, and by the crosscutting media linkages of the global village. And the fourth is the emergence of new forms of *transnational governance*—public, private, and mixed—and of forms of politicking that cut across states and national territories.

A. Economic Globalization

In the period of the "high" modern nation-state, the TSD took on an ever more inexorable character because of the linkage between state building, nation building, and the Second Industrial Revolution. In contrast to the British model, which eventually succeeded in reconciling a seventeenth-century liberal state with the more decentralized First Industrial Revolution (Hobsbawm 1968), the Second Industrial Revolution imposed far greater centralizing institutional and policy-making imperatives on states, particularly with regard to government-economy relations. Competition for relative power capabilities in the international system required the achievement of national economic self-sufficiency through "late industrialization" (Gerschenkron 1962), which in turn required huge Chandleresque investments in large-scale mass production processes, mass marketing of products, and an expanded "scientifically" organized bureaucratic management superstructure (Chandler 1990; cf. Galbraith 1967/2007).

These organizational developments in turn not only depended on the development of centralized and government-backed finance capital (Lenin 1917) but also generated the growth of matching Weberian state bureaucracies for the pursuit of a range of public objectives, including the public promotion and even management of core multiplier sectors of the economy, infrastructure projects (railways and roads), the coordination of industrial development by sponsoring cartels and corporate expansion (while also co-opting trade unions), and acting as a monopsony or oligopsony purchaser of, for example, military and infrastructural goods—effectively promoting the chemicals, textiles, communications, shipbuilding, automobile, and steel industries, as well as, and often driven by, the production of finished armaments.

At the same time, in order to embed the newly legitimated and often fragile authority of the state in the social base and the political superstructure, nation-state authorities increasingly co-opted nationalist ideology—originally a form of defection from below from absolutist monarchies—and spread it by means of the ideological apparatuses of the state. Such developments reinforced and extrapolated the TSD. The very collective existence of the social body, the economic and social nation, became inextricably intertwined with the *nondivisible survival of the state* in the international system.

Economic globalization, however, fundamentally challenges the parameters of this fused national security culture by disaggregating the economic benefits of industrial and financial development, thereby dramatically increasing the divisibility of benefits. This shift has been taking place at several levels, which increasingly interact with each other. The organizational requirements of mass production can be bypassed, leading to more decentralized structural patterns more reminiscent of the First Industrial Revolution. So-called post-Fordist production processes based on flexible manufacturing systems reduce the optimal economies of scale of production, so that factories and workshops can be not only physically disaggregated but also rapidly adapted to changing production techniques and patterns of consumer demand. Locational incentives increasingly respond to cross-border market pressures and signals. Although technological innovations may primarily be generated within national architectures of supply, technological diffusion is extremely rapid, so that gains from technological advances spread quickly across international-transnational spaces. Changes in information and communications technology are revolutionizing management, facilitating strategic and operational decision making (with regard to both production and marketing), and intensifying supervision and monitoring of performance (including more exacting application of financial criteria). "Lean management" is the transnational fashion.

Markets can be extensively disaggregated, too, with flexible production enabling firms to switch rapidly to meet increasingly segmented consumer demands across wider spaces. Furthermore, globalization of financial markets has disaggregated investment, widened the sources of even quite small investments across borders, and generated further financial innovation in the process—leading to a more unstable cycle of growth and crisis (see chapter 12). Labor processes are being flexibilized as well, feeding into job insecurity and undermining solidaristic identification with the national-political economy. The growth of the service sector, although usually said to be more closely responsive to domestic economic conditions (involving "nontradable" assets), has nevertheless been a global phenomenon. And the state's role has changed from protecting business activities and promoting self-sufficiency to promoting competitiveness in the international marketplace (see chapter 8). Even weapons production and procurement increasingly conform to the norms of "military post-Fordism" (Latham and Hooper 1995).

This increased divisibility of benefits in the contemporary international political economy has had two sorts of effects on the security environment. In the first place, it has attenuated (though not entirely severed) the link

between the state and industrial development that was at the heart of the
late-nineteenth- and twentieth-century intensification of the TSD. On the
one hand, war can no longer be waged profitably by industrial states, and
mass publics know this, too. Not only can it not be waged profitably but also
social as well as economic losses are more evident, too. Political actors, economic elites, and military leaderships are often less convinced that war plays
an effective regulatory role, as evidenced by the role of the Vietnam Syndrome
in the United States and American awareness of failures in Lebanon,
Somalia, Iraq, and Afghanistan. On the other hand, too, the dependence of
industry on military and government contracts, while still great for some
sectors, is crucial for far fewer industries than previously.

Although the development of information technology and communications industries was originally closely linked with government promotion,
including defense sponsorship of the development of the Internet from its
earliest phases, private transnational markets and production processes are
increasingly taking over (Ronit and Schneider 2000). And in a world in
which anti-inflationary policy, embedded financial orthodoxy, and the New
Public Management have become touchstones of public policy across a
widening spectrum of issue-areas, the built-in structural inflation traditionally characteristic of cutting-edge defense industries, the tendency of military bureaucracies to spend what is seen to be desirable rather than what
can be afforded, and the maintenance of a large defense bureaucracy allied
with specific domestic constituencies, manifested in political opposition to
base closures or the continuance of outdated weapons programs and the
like, are all coming to be seen as luxuries rather than necessities. The military pork barrel is shrinking and will shrink further despite the buildup of
the Bush-Cheney-Rumsfeld years. Defense spending is also increasingly
inefficient in terms of civilian spin-off and domestic pump priming, and it
is likely to be replaced more and more, in the name of both domestic welfare
and international competitiveness, by domestic infrastructure projects and
other forms of stimulus, as was briefly the case in the mid-1950s and is now
at the core of President Obama's recovery program.

In the second place, of course, economic globalization has created alternative possibilities for divisible benefits to arise through trading relationships, boundary-crossing production structures, and the like. As a result of
experience with Germany and Japan after the end of the Second World
War—a new kind of cultural memory—it is taken for granted nowadays that
the best way to ensure security (whether international, national, or personal
security; Buzan 1983) is to integrate past and potential enemies into a prosperous and interdependent capitalist global economy. Potential enemies are
not only bought off directly but also, more important, brought into the very
web of the new structure of complex interdependence, redistributing *political*

resources at both domestic and international levels away from actors seeking the violent expropriation of others' assets toward those who are (relatively) successful at accumulating those assets through economic exchange. Thus the increasing range and scope of alternative, *substitutable* benefits available in a global economy come to dominate not only the economic issue-area but also the security domain. So long as the economic globalization game remains positive-sum—clearly a major issue in the current economic crisis, however—temptations to defect are likely to remain low.

B. The "Death of Ideology"

Macroideological conflict played a crucial role in generating nondivisible benefits in the TSD, especially during the twentieth century. Universalistic ideologies invested state actions in both domestic and international arenas with an identification with a higher mission, fusing national solidarity with moral righteousness. The benefits of ideological cooperation and the dangers of defection were internalized by both elites and mass publics, first through the fight against Nazism and fascism and later in the conflict between communism and anticommunism. The prize was confirmation of the immanent superiority of one's own social system. The danger was the defeat of the public interest and of civilization itself in the perceived barbarism of either totalitarian communism or exploitative, oppressive capitalism. In an anarchical world, it was seen as potentially disastrous to fall behind the ideological opponent. Both sides presented their stances in this Manichaean fashion. Furthermore, ideology was often the main linkage between central players and peripheral players in the states system itself, generating strong internalized bonds between central players and potential defectors, although as the cold war dragged on, this was truer for one side than for the other, as capitalism proved more successful in generating economic growth and development than Soviet-style communism.

At the periphery of the cold war system, however, such ideological stances tended increasingly either to be mere add-ons for potential defectors playing the two sides against each other or else were compounded with local cultural elements to give them indigenous legitimacy and coherence. For example, the particular blend of communism, nationalism, a localized version of Confucianism, and village values that constituted the ideology of Ho Chi Minh and the Vietnamese revolution was one such hybrid, as were Uhuru socialism in Tanzania and the attempt of the Czechoslovak leadership under Alexander Dubček in 1968 to embody "Communism with a human face." Such deviations in the anticommunist sphere tended, in contrast, to involve authoritarian variations, such as military regimes in Latin America and Asia. On both sides, however, the aim of elites was to further imbricate the prevailing ideology with national solidarity, reinforcing and embedding the nondivisible character of the stakes in the wider conflict—a key characteristic in both American patriotism and Stalinist "socialism in one country" aligned with antifascism. As suggested by our model, ideological defection threats—usually generated by challenges from below—led to increasingly coercive attempts to impose ideological hegemony. However, it was the dwindling success of such attempts as the cold war dragged on that critically exposed the weaknesses of the TSD in coping with East-West conflict, leading to the breakdown of cold war itself in the late 1980s.

In the meantime, the ideological division of the world into communist and anticommunist camps was caught in a pincer movement that undermined its credibility and legitimacy both domestically and internationally. In the first place, the range of ideological alternatives widely perceived to be on offer proliferated, with partly successful defections in the third world and quasi defections in Western and Eastern Europe. The effect of the various events of the mid to late 1960s in diverse parts of the world was to validate alternative models of both capitalism and socialism, even bringing to the fore long-simmering ideological disputes within and among the purer brands of Western Marxism, not to mention African socialism, welfare and corporate capitalism, antiracist and national liberation movements, extreme right-wing movements, and more.

Ideology swiftly became more divisible, undermining willingness to serve in a limited war where ideological lines were blurred (the Vietnam syndrome) or to die in a nuclear war for one's beliefs—later catalyzed by the widespread movement in Europe in the 1980s against the deployment of American Cruise and Pershing missiles. Increasing ideological divisibility loosened the link between national solidarity and international alliances, too. The denouement came when the arch-neoconservative ideologist, President Ronald Reagan, and the arch-pragmatist, Mikhail Gorbachev, ironically broke the vicious TSD arms race spiral with the Intermediate Nuclear Forces Treaty (1987) and other subsequent agreements.

In the New Security Dilemma, this divisibility has manifested itself at several levels. The most benign outcome has been the crystallization of a trend in several parts of the world toward democratization and pluralization, at least at the national if not the transnational level (see chapter 10). Democratization necessarily involves as a bottom line some considerable defusing of both internal and external ideological conflicts—conflicts once deeply embedded in the social formation of newly independent African countries, for instance. In such cases, temptations to defect have declined because of the very perception that a positive-sum game was possible, especially in a world in which the divisibility of economic benefits made democratization (especially democratic capitalism) potentially a more profitable option. However, the main temptation to defection has come not from political ideology but from religious fundamentalism. Nevertheless, even the most intense of these defections, whether Shiite Islam in Khomeini's Iran after 1979 or the "clash of civilizations" (Huntington 1997), foundered not on the rock of Western ideology, but on the sands of splits and internecine wars within and between Islamic nations, sects, and factions. Temptations to defect have faltered because of the ideological divisibility of the defection itself.

Ideological defection, where it has occurred, has been very much the product of local conditions. In an NSD world, however, where threats as well as benefits are increasingly seen as divisible, and despite (or because of) the American invasion of Iraq, the tendency of central actors has been to reduce their intervention—with the exception of limited multilateral peacekeeping and as yet embryonic forms of so-called humanitarian intervention—and merely tinker around the edges of the more serious defection threats. This ad hoc approach generally has effectively isolated many of those threats, which are unlikely to ripple out beyond their core local or regional areas except through sporadic outbreaks of terrorism in some more serious cases.

Al Qaeda's attack on the World Trade Center in New York on September 11, 2001, despite its dramatic impact, has not been repeated; terrorism, while growing in Iraq since the American invasion, has effectively been confined to its core geographical areas, and even the terrorist attack on Mumbai in December 2008 represented a regional issue rather than a global threat. Nevertheless, the uncertainty created by those temptations to defect seems to be ensuring their continuation and expansion, in some cases (Congo-Rwanda, Somalia) spiraling out of control. Despite the Bush administration's declaration of a "global war on terror," the possibility of a widely destructive *interstate* world war analogous to the two world wars of the twentieth century or even to the threat of the cold war turning hot has receded to near impossibility. Twenty-first-century ideologies are far too fissiparous, dispersed, and fungible to continue to prop up the interstate system and the Traditional Security Dilemma. They do, however, embody key aspects of the New Security Dilemma, especially in terms of whether they can be contained in pluralist fashion, on the one hand, or instead constitute sufficiently strong temptations to defect to destabilize world politics more generally, on the other. The development of political processes of transnational neopluralism is more likely to incorporate and co-opt such groups through economic growth and coalition building in the long term.

C. Multiculturalism and Postmodernism

It should be clear from what has already been said that one of the main preconditions of the Traditional Security Dilemma was the development not

only of an ideological commitment to nationalism (and later to the ideological division of the cold war) but also of solidaristic, collective cultural orientations *within* national societies. This Gemeinschaft function, so to speak,
has been one of the most problematic aspects of nation building and the
states system. The history of class conflict, separatist movements of various
types, transnational identities, and tribal, ethnic, and local conflicts shows
just how far "national culture societies," as Znaniecki (1952/1973) called
them, or "imagined communities," as Benedict Anderson called them
(Anderson 1991), have been not established facts but precarious political
projects.

They have, however, left a nonetheless powerful residual legacy at both
mass and elite levels. Without people having a holistic sense of naturally
belonging to the territorial nation-state in which they live—their perception
of proximate space—and to which they are attached as citizens, it is argu-
able that modern society might have been as rootless and internally fragmented as the late feudal order. Replicating or approximating extended
kinship identity at the much wider level of national "society" is one of the
most deeply embedded products of the modern era and will be one of the
last to erode—although this is mainly true of longer established states that
are no longer split by fundamental zero-sum social conflicts. Without
national cultural solidarity, the temptation to defect *internally*, as well as a
greater temptation to see state boundaries as permeable and amorphous
(and therefore, in effect, to defect externally even while remaining in geographically the same location), would clearly undermine the nondivisibility
of benefits and threats so essential to the TSD.

Nevertheless, cultural nationalism is being eroded from both above and
below, and that erosion is, predictably, the result of the increasing *divisibility
of cultural benefits* in the contemporary world. From above, the emergence of
a cultural "global village" (McLuhan 1964) might seem to imply convergence
and therefore greater nondivisibility at the global level at least. However, as
Roland Robertson has pointed out, the very constitution of cultural globalization embodies complex diversity—"the universalization of the particular
and the particularization of the universal" (Robertson 1992: 102).
Furthermore, postmodernism has declared the death of the great narratives
of modern society, with a focus on microlevel and mesolevel circuits of
power, on the necessity for resistance to the oppression embedded in these
circuits, and on the possibility of using evolving circuits of power for emancipation (Foucault 1980; Pogrebinschi 2008). In this context, the demand
among a range of groups for greater autonomy within a broader multicultural space draws from both of these sources.

The desire of religious and ethnic groups for autonomy is not merely the
result of their desire for local self-government but is also inextricably

intertwined with (a) their transnational identities, whether in history or in space, and (b) their understanding that to effectively fuse their endogenous autonomy with their global identities, they will have to accept that *they cannot be territorially exclusive*. They cannot make a claim to domination or homogeneity within one particular territorial space, except perhaps a supra-national regional space—for example, the former territories of the Ottoman Empire (the Caliphate) for Al Qaeda or the dispute over whether some reference to Christianity should be included in the European Union's constitutional treaty. Instead, they must accept operating within a complex, overlapping, multinodal set of spaces characterized by a transnationally crosscutting plurality of groups claiming analogous autonomous status. Multiculturalism and postmodernism, then, while promoting greater *endogenous* homogeneity at one level—the religious group, following, greater church, the "faithful," or whatever—simultaneously put such groups in a position where *to achieve their internal goals, they must accept greater exogenous heterogeneity* at another. Cultural benefits, rather than being confined to the territorial cage of the nation-state, are necessarily both particularistic and global at the same time. More holism paradoxically leads to a greater divisibility of cultural benefits.

In this context, multiculturalism acts as a serious constraint to the rather different holism of the state in the states system and the TSD. In the NSD, in contrast, the greater divisibility of benefits means that "cultural security" is increasingly divorced from the imperatives of the nation-state and the states system. Indeed, the state must be kept at arm's length. The bottom line of sovereignty, as Hobbes noted, was the willingness of individuals to die for the state in battle, that is, to subordinate their individual survival, through the social contract, to the survival of the state. But where first loyalty is to religion, sect, or ethnic group, survival of the state takes second or even a lower place. Indeed, at this level, temptations to defect are particularly high in the NSD, especially in the periphery, where Somalia is an extreme case of cultural conflict and fragmentation.

It is therefore in the cultural issue-area where the main manifestations of the centrifugal form of the NSD, where the greatest tendencies to endemic violence and civil wars, and where the greatest vulnerability to cross-border mobilization of power rooted in cultural bonds will arise. Indeed, this has already been the case in many parts of the world, especially on the periphery where local and regional, tribal, and ethnic cultures in earlier periods have been *least* transformed by, eroded through, or integrated into the national culture societies of the modern states system. This is where the greatest challenge of the New Security Dilemma occurs: whether to ignore or tolerate ethnic, civil, and transnational violence and conflict on the periphery, or attempt to revive the use of force and interventionism for humanitarian purposes—the dilemma currently faced in Congo and Darfur. Huge resources and problematic long-term commitments are necessary for effective intervention, and experience in recent decades indicates that such conflicts are often intractable in the face of external pressures and can easily be exacerbated rather than stabilized—and therefore that such endeavors are likely to be unsuccessful and even counterproductive in terms of wider global and cultural security.

D. Transnational Governance

The entire logic of the Traditional Security Dilemma, as argued here, is rooted in the international system of states. Although organized around the self-help imperatives of individual states, its normative significance and its tragic potential lie in the prospective success, or not, of attempts to resist or *break* its vicious circle. The abilities of states to generate balances of power, engage in diplomatic negotiations, and, as de Gaulle said of Bismarck, "know when to stop" are crucial in resolving the TSD, however ephemerally. Indeed, as states developed greater and greater absolute power capabilities in the Second Industrial Revolution era, the imperatives of marshaling and deploying such capabilities in order to achieve or retain relative gains inhibited the development of transnational governance structures and international regimes. The story of the failure of the League of Nations as the result of the defection of key states is well known.

In contemporary terms, only the capacity of a hegemonic power to provide international public goods (and to pay for them) has sometimes been seen as sufficient to counteract the temptation to defect, although that sort of hegemony and empire has been discredited by the American invasion of Iraq, among other things (Cerny 2006b). Although the United States set up a range of international regimes in the post–Second World War era to try to transcend this limitation and base the TSD on a more benign form of hegemonic leadership rather than central coercion, these regimes generally succeeded only insofar as they were limited to the sphere of influence of the American superpower. For much of the world, central coercion, whether by the United States in the periphery or the Soviet Union in both core and periphery, was required to resist defection. International regimes in this context were also essentially *interstate* regimes, not "transnational" regimes (Krasner 1982). Although such regimes went beyond simple interstate interaction of a self-help kind by saving on transaction costs in terms of cooperation among states, thereby softening the edges of the TSD, they still reinforced the states system by buying off potential defectors.

Nevertheless, interstate regimes constituted a key precursor of the sort of transnational governance structures and processes discussed earlier in this

book and are still an entrenched part of this wider universe (Booth and
Wheeler 2008). Today, there has been a proliferation of such structures and
processes, from the public to the private and from the formal to the informal, as set out in the schema presented in table 9.1 (page 187). Of course,
that table does not begin to portray the immense and exploding universe of
transnational governance processes. It merely identifies some of the polar
types, whereas the main area of growth is in institutional forms that link or
cut across these types. Indeed, the recurring terms "network" and "process"
imply that formal and informal linkages intersect and interact with each
other in mixed public-private and formal-informal configurations. The proliferation of such structures and processes engenders an expanding division
of benefits, even where state actors are intimately involved.

Of course, most transnational governance structures and processes
operate in much more mundane ways and involve intense elite networking. In many issue-areas, defection is still the rule rather than the
exception—especially where local conditions and coalitions resist both participating in the processes and implementing the outcomes. Nevertheless,
the dynamic density of this trend indicates not only that transnational governance structures and processes are significant carriers of increasing
divisibility of benefits in the contemporary world—including growing
niches within the security issue-area—but also that they constitute a fundamental mechanism for co-opting and/or disciplining potential defectors.
Furthermore, the *private* dimension of such structures and processes (even
supposedly spontaneous market processes per se) is often crucial to their
operation in issue-areas where the role of governments is constrained for
other reasons. They constitute an essential mechanism in the process of
internalizing the logic of the NSD.

5. CONCLUSION: UNCERTAINTY IN THE NEW SECURITY DILEMMA

As we have seen, the New Security Dilemma involves a logic that is new in
comparison with the Traditional Security Dilemma, although not new in
the *longue durée*. The feudal era also involved a high divisibility of benefits,
but growing temptations to defect led to two centuries of crisis and to the
birth of the Westphalian system. The main question today is whether the
divisibility of benefits in the twenty-first century will lead to a more stable,
pluralistic system in which defection is low or to a more unstable and even
crisis-ridden system in which defection is high. In the latter case, the erosion of the traditional constraints of the states system may lead a vicious
spiral of defection, as different substate and transstate social, cultural, and
economic actors protect their newly autonomous niches in the wider

system—what has been called neomedievalism. Terrorism is often seen to constitute an extreme version of this potential (Cerny 2005a). These back-lashes do not develop in a vacuum. They interact with economic and social processes of complex globalization to create overlapping and competing cross-border networks of power, shifting loyalties and identities, and new sources of endemic low-level conflict—a "durable disorder" analogous to some of the key characteristics of the medieval world (Minc 1993).

Nevertheless, in this environment of increased uncertainty concerning potential defection, especially from below, the states system will not, of course, evaporate. The United States, for example, still attempts to play the role of hegemon but is challenged on wider fronts and may be stretched thinner and thinner in the future (Cerny 2006b). Whether a layer of supra-national institutionalized power will crystallize and converge to provide effective collective security at a global level is highly problematic. New con-straints are also being created by expanding intergovernmental and multi-lateral cooperation, whether UN peacekeeping or NATO expansion. However, these essentially involve a process of catch-up and are also vulner-able to microlevel and mesolevel defection, as in the Balkans or Congo. The state, as we have already seen, is in the process of disarticulation or disag-gregation. Complex globalization may thus exacerbate the existing gover-nance gap in which uncertainty and bounded rationality—the inability to predict the future actions of potential defectors—can again lead to tragic consequences.

In this hypothetical environment, the international system could be char-acterized once again by a number of attributes usually associated with the medieval era (Cerny 1998): (a) competing institutions with overlapping jurisdictions (states, regimes, transgovernmental networks, private interest governments, etc.); (b) more fluid, nebulous and permeable territorial boundaries (both within and across states); (c) a growing alienation between global innovation, communication, and resource nodes (global cities), on the one hand, and disfavored, fragmented hinterlands, on the other; (d) increased inequalities and isolation of permanent subcastes (the under-class); (e) multiple and/or fragmented loyalties and identities (ethnic con-flict and unstable multiculturalism); (f) contested property rights and legal boundaries (e.g., disregard for rules and dispute-resolution procedures, attempts to extend extraterritorial jurisdiction, etc.); and (g) the spread of what Minc has called "zones grises," or geographical areas and social contexts where the rule of law does not run, including both localized ghettos and international criminal activities (Minc 1993).

Today we live in an era of increasing speed, global scale, and extremely rapid diffusion of information and technological innovation, characteristics, too, that seem to be outgrowing the political capacities of the existing state-based order, multiplying the effects of uncertainty and bounded rationality. An extended phase of low-level disorder, punctuated by episodic structural mutations and the uneven maintenance of pockets of pluralism and elements of sectoral hegemony by, for example, international financial markets and multinational corporations, seems the most likely scenario. The result could well be the crystallization of increasingly suboptimal forms of governance at both the state and transnational-international levels and the threat of growing institutional entropy in world politics generally. The "hollowing out" of the state may not be matched by any equivalent "filling in" by multilateral, transnational, regional, supranational, or whatever governance structures—thereby creating not only a "democratic deficit" but also a wider and deeper governance gap as we move through the twenty-first century.

The main structural fault lines—political, social, and economic—in this complex world reflect not clear territorial boundaries enclosing hierarchical authority structures, but new distinctions between different levels of socioeconomic cleavage, urban-rural splits, and the like. Sociological and geographical literature on global cities, for example, reflects the notion that a range of "virtual spaces" in the global political economy will increasingly overlap with and possibly even replace the "hard" space of traditional geographical and topological territories. These new spaces are embodied—and increasingly embedded—in transaction flows, infrastructural nodes of communications and information technology, corporate headquarters, "edge city" living complexes for "symbolic analysts" (Reich 1991), increasingly "dematerialized" financial markets, and cultural and media centers of activity (and identity). Control of new ideas and innovations will be increasingly concentrated in such areas, protected and secured by a growing panoply of international and transnational intellectual property rights.

On the one hand, therefore, specific spaces that people perceive and identify with are likely to become increasingly localized and/or microlevel and mesolevel in structure; on the other hand, the very perception of space being partitioned vertically, whether among nation-states or at the level of other "spatio-temporal fixes" (see chapter 13), will be eroded. People will have to learn over time to navigate between different overlapping, asymmetric layers of spatial perception and organization. The poorer residents of such areas will find themselves increasingly excluded from decision-making processes. And in those areas where this kind of navigation is more difficult—for example, where such nodes, infrastructure, activities, and the like do not exist within easy physical or perceptual distance—many will simply be out of the loop, country bumpkins, or even roaming, deprived bands, like Hobsbawm's primitive rebels (consider contemporary Somalia or Bulgaria), forced once again to become predators or supplicants on the cities, as in the Middle Ages (Hobsbawm 1969).

Changes in institutions, the fluidity of territorial boundaries, and the increasing hegemony of global cities will interact with new forms of flexible labor processes and economic organization to increase inequalities and turn downwardly mobile workers (especially the less skilled, the ghetto dwellers, etc.) into a new lumpen proletariat, underclass, or subcaste—a process well under way in the first world and already dominant in large parts of the third world. In this context, it will not be merely ethnic loyalties and tribal enmities that will undermine the ersatz Gemeinschaft of the nation-state. It will be the development of complex new inequalities of both material class and virtual geography. Such inequalities will be far more difficult to counterbalance and neutralize without effective or legitimate state institutions and are likely to become an increasing source of civil and cross-border violence, especially when they are allied to other cleavages. Such a situation will not merely be one of fragmentation, but one of crosscutting and overlapping *multiple loyalties and identities*—of social and political schizophrenia—with shifting patchwork boundaries and postmodern cultural images. Any truly global cultural identity structure would have to be not so much homogeneous or unifying as intrinsically multilayered and flexible, able to adapt chameleon-like to a wide range of differentiated contexts.

In such a reconfigured world, there will be not only niches for the maintenance of pluralist autonomy for individuals and groups but also more escape routes, organizational opportunities, and technical advantages for those operating more or less outside the law. Exit from political society is likely to become a more viable option for a wider range of actors and activities. At one level, these phenomena involve more than just international (and domestic) criminal activities such as the drug trade, the (semitransnational) Russian mafia, or the control of blood diamonds or minerals by "rebel" groups in Sierra Leone or Congo. They also involve the areas where excluded people live—especially urban ghettos, at one geographical extreme, and enclaves in inaccessible areas (jungle, mountains, etc.), at another. Indeed, these new cleavages may crystallize into diverging "zones of peace" and "zones of turmoil" in the wider world order, further institutionalizing the contrast between center and periphery and reinforcing centrifugal tendencies in a more salient way in the latter than in the former (Singer and Wildavsky 1993).

Finally, all these factors are further exacerbated by changing economies of scale in warfare, a critical issue that unfortunately there has not been space to address here. The nature of weaponry in particular is being transformed from nondivisible nuclear standoff and big-ticket cold war weapons like aircraft carriers, tanks, long-range bombers, fighter planes designed for aerial dogfights, and the like (Kaldor 1981), to highly divisible improvised explosive devices, suicide bombings, robots, and fragmented guerrilla warfare. It is today far more economic for small groups to be the main agents of violence, something statelike command bureaucracies have not yet learned to counter (Singer 2009). "New wars" are, indeed, structurally transformative (Kaldor 1999).

Challenges thrown up in the twenty-first century in the form of the New Security Dilemma are therefore likely to significantly reduce the effectiveness of traditional state-based and state-systemic approaches in the stabilization of international politics even further. Where it is not primarily states that defect from interstate balances of power, but rather a range of transnational and subnational actors and structures, then interstate alliances and other traditional means of reequilibrating the balance will be insufficient to control those defections. The world of the NSD, like the Middle Ages, may be one of chronic but durable disorder, riddled with uncertainties, limiting the possibilities of genuine collective action and constraining the ability of actors and institutions to make credible commitments. Consequently, if the international order is eventually to be transformed into a more horizontally bordered, interdependent, yet stable global system, then *the sources of that transformation must come from within its newer, essentially transnational structures.*

The main source of security in the twenty-first century, therefore, is most likely to come neither from states nor from intergovernmental superstructures. Rather, it will come from the capacities of transnational actors to develop relatively stable patterns of bargaining and coalition building across borders, to compete relatively peacefully over the kind of divisible benefits discussed previously, and to counteract the potentially disruptive temptations of defection characteristic of today's (and tomorrow's) world politics through global economic prosperity, the nonviolent pursuit of non-exclusive ideologies, the coexistence of multiple cultures, the development of multinodal political processes, and socialization into a governmentality rooted in *raison du monde*, that is, a positive-sum form of transnational—neopluralist—politics rather than the obsolete power games of nation-states, the idealistic hopes for global democracy, or the durable disorder of neomedievalism.

Chapter 12

Financial Globalization, Crisis, and the Reorganization of Global Capital

1. INTRODUCTION: FINANCE AND WORLD POLITICS

In the traditional understanding of the nature of international relations, the bottom line or default situation was immanent (though not necessarily imminent) war and a balance of power among states in a system dominated by the interactions of sovereign states. In the twenty-first century, not only have there been an expansion of crosscutting interdependencies, the emergence of transnational interest and value groups, the destatization of violence, as examined in the previous chapter, and the fragmented and uneven development of a quasi-"governmental" superstructure but also a fundamental shift in the infrastructure of world politics. As has been the case within modern state societies, too, economics and finance have increasingly replaced war and force as the focus of political, as well as purely economic, interaction across borders. This is nothing new. Indeed, war itself in the past has often—some might say almost always—been about economics.

However, the tension between war, on the one hand, and economic growth and development, on the other, is increasingly obvious in a globalizing world. War as the progenitor of new world orders, including economic orders, as at the end of the Second World War, has always been in profound conflict with war the destroyer, and this conflict has escalated dramatically since the advent of the industrial age. Complex interdependence has amplified this tension in profound ways, such that states today rarely see the advantage in waging war—and when they try to do so, it proves increasingly counterproductive in terms of economic, social, and political development (Gallarotti 2009). The profound shift in European priorities, in particular, illustrates this transformation (Sheehan 2008), but all states are grappling with this issue in more and more salient, everyday ways.

At the same time, economic globalization has developed rapidly at many levels in recent decades, especially across three sectors: production, trade, and finance. Until recently, the power of multinational corporations and the issue of free trade have dominated the headlines. But finance has a particularly significant and central role in driving the globalization process, a role that recently burst into public view in the financial crisis and recession that gathered speed in 2008 while I was writing this book. For finance is not just another economic sector or issue-area. Finance is the *infrastructure of the infrastructure*—the brain and nervous system of any economy. What makes finance special, and what gives it its particular significance in the globalization process, is its *universality*, its *fungibility*, and its *immateriality* (see Cerny 1993 and 1994a).

Finance is, first of all, universal. Before the advent of money, which in its more primitive forms probably arrived very early in human history, exchange had to be carried out through barter. A specific good had to be exchanged for another specific good, which made production, distribution, and consumption extremely complex and problematic beyond (and even within) limited and static village societies. But with money, any item could be bought and sold. This leads to the second characteristic of finance, fungibility. It can be substituted for any good or asset and can be transformed into financial instruments that themselves can be traded. Money takes whatever shape is required by widely varying circumstances. And third, money is immaterial. Although for millennia money took specific commodity forms such as shells or, in the modern world, gold and silver, today money and finance are mere bits of information held not even on paper but in computer memories. With contemporary information technology, in particular, money is the only purely global asset, instantly traded, measured, recorded, stored, and reallocated from one use to another, in electronic form.

The traditional way of analyzing money is that it has three functions or roles. In the first place, it is a *means of exchange*, as just described. It allows exchange of other goods and assets to be expanded and universalized. Second, it is a *unit of account*, making different goods and assets *commensurable* and immediately recordable. That way, people can confer relative values on those goods and assets (what economists call "utilities"), make decisions about their preferences, and decide what they think is relatively cheap or expensive. Third, it is a *store of value*. In other words, you can build up monetary reserves to use in different ways in the future. It permits both commensurability and strategic deployment over time. Various writers have suggested further functions of money. However, I will stress one particular function here that has been at the heart of economic development in modern capitalist economies and is perhaps the most important function of all in the present day—*the provision of credit*.

In other words, we are not simply talking here about money as such, but about *finance*, or how economic growth is enabled, promoted, and managed, both stabilized and made dynamic. Modern economies are built on credit and the multiplier effect of shifting funds from relatively static or unproductive uses to more dynamic, productive uses with higher added value. Without banks, stock and bond markets, insurance companies, providers of mortgage finance and consumer credit, and, increasingly, derivatives markets—for all their problems today—there would be little productive investment, technological innovation, transportation and communications infrastructure, employment, marketing, education, mass consumption, social or geographical mobility, or, for that matter, government itself, which is dependent on the taxation of growing economic surpluses to oversee and stabilize the system. Consumers, too, have increasingly relied on credit since the invention of time payments or hire purchase, originally for consumer durables but increasingly for all purchases.

What these financial institutions and markets do is to *create money* that can be redeployed to new (as well as old) uses and to manage it, once created. Economic growth, especially of the dramatic kind experienced by modern capitalist economies over the past three centuries or so, can take place only where there are abundant and relatively safe sources of credit to fuel the process, oil the wheels, and enable the products to be produced, exchanged, distributed, and used in the first place. Money may be the root of all evil, but it is also at the root of the very development of human societies.

The globalization of finance is the main driver of complex economic interdependence today. However, finance is not some sort of spontaneous or automatic material phenomenon, if such a thing exists, but a profoundly political process. In terms of the analytical framework developed in this book, the political character of finance can be illustrated by looking at the three interacting categories of actors that are central to the concept of neopluralism. In the first place, the characteristics of money, as just outlined, involve the interaction of a range of sectional interest groups. These include, at the most basic level, both investors and/or lenders, on the one hand—that is, those who have capital to deposit or redeploy—and borrowers, those who need or wish to use money, whether as entrepreneurs or consumers, employers or traders, industrialists or workers.

Within different sectors of the private financial system itself, both formally organized or informally networked groups are often in conflict or competition, but are also inextricably interlinked, representing banks, stock markets, bond markets, and the like. In other words, there is a universe of sectional groups that have an interest in how much money there is to fuel the economy and to pursue their own perceived needs, wants, or undertakings; how that money is distributed; and how stable the system is—what is called "safety and soundness"—if they are to protect their investments and realize their projects. Of course, within these categories, as in any group, there are those motivated by greed and personal power, too. Because of the

universality, fungibility, and immateriality of money, along with the centrality of finance and credit to the whole economy—now global—the scope for
their schemes can be enormous, as we have seen in the past few years leading up to today's financial crisis and recession.

State actors, the second category, have crucial roles to play. As has been
pointed out by numerous critics of the theory of pure or efficient markets
over many decades, the financial system is not self-regulating. (For the classic critique, see Polanyi 1944; more recently, cf. Nesvetailova 2007; Soros
2008; Morris 2008; Cooper 2008; Ariely 2008; and Fox 2009.) The *Ordoliberal*
and neoliberal founding fathers believed that the state was the indispensable guarantor of competitive markets, as noted in chapter 8 (see Hayek
1944/2007). Thus financial markets neither operate in a vacuum, nor work
spontaneously, nor find a stable equilibrium level if left to their own devices.
In other words, the financial system does not act like Adam Smith's invisible hand, but requires management, regulation, stabilization, and, in crisis
periods, bailouts and state-supervised restructuring. I have already looked at
the way such functions have been seen through the lens of the Competition
State. But the reality is even more complex.

Within government bureaucracies, regulators, central banks, treasuries,
and other parts of the state often have different perspectives and objectives
on how the financial system should be organized and supervised; each of
these also operates in conjunction with the transgovernmental networks
described earlier in this book; all of them have links, often very close ones,
with politicians and elected officials; there are usually competing regulators
even within the same or closely connected sectors; and each of these sets of
state actors, whether bureaucratic fiefdoms, political parties and factions,
international networks, or whatever, will be interacting on a regular basis
with private-sector interest groups, financial institutions and market organizations, different economic sectors, and the like.

Finally, as pointed out before, everyone has an interest in how the financial sector works and will try to gain access to it and exert influence at
numerous levels. Therefore, it is important not to forget the third category,
value groups and social movements. These can range from traditional critics of the "money interest," whether anticapitalist or not, to proponents of
corporate social responsibility and socially responsible investment, cam-
paigners for lending to particular sectors—for example, expanding financial resources for inner cities—or to innovative projects aimed at allowing
disadvantaged groups to benefit from financial support such as venture
capital, advocates of international aid for poverty reduction (not to mention
their opponents; see Moyo 2009), those who would educate people to be
more financially responsible, and innovators in such areas as microfinance.
Such groups often punch above their weight by using political and media

campaigns to put forward their objectives, especially where public opinion is sympathetic. They may have less clout than entrenched sectional groups or public officials, but given the development of information and communications technology, they can develop a high public profile. They can also be very well connected transnationally.

2. FINANCE AND CAPITALIST DEVELOPMENT

The politics of financial governance in the contemporary world are the product of a complex, ongoing process of historical evolution. In this process, the role of the nation-state in financial governance is both a historical given and profoundly problematic in an era of financial globalization. These intertwined processes of change have derived from the need to construct *political* mechanisms to cope with the potential (and often very real) volatility and uneven distributive consequences of financial market expansion. This quest for an institutional framework—not only to tame capitalism but also to capture its benefits by making it work more effectively and efficiently—first led to the emergence and consolidation of the modern nation-state and the international states system themselves, as medieval and early postfeudal institution building proved inadequate to the task, but there has always been a massive transnational and international dimension to this process (Kindleberger 1984). Today, however, that process is developing more institutionally intricate and structurally dense, if still somewhat fragmented, cross-border linkages.

In the eighteenth and nineteenth centuries, European—mainly competing British and French—capitalism spread around the globe. This process was characterized not only by military imperialism and colonization but also by the development of new international and transnational mechanisms to finance trade, commodity production, and industrialization. International mechanisms developed to finance that expansion, especially the gold standard, backed up by the powerful alliance of London's financial markets and the British state (Ingham 1984; Eichengreen 1996). But at the same time, late-developing industrial states and new actors such as national corporate interests, trade unions, and political parties of both right and left sought to consolidate capitalism at a national level, reinforced by the Second Industrial Revolution and the large-scale mass-production industries that all "modern" industrial societies had to possess. This required massive investments that in most rapidly industrializing countries (after Britain) necessitated extensive government coordination and intervention, except to some degree in the United States (Cerny 2000b).

The growth of large private investment banks such as J. P. Morgan and Co., which nevertheless had a special relationship with government, raised more than enough capital, much of it from abroad (especially Britain), to finance American Second Industrial Revolution expansion (Chernow 1990), as well as to bail out the financial system, playing the role of lender of last resort in times of financial panic—later to be seen as a "public" function, leading to the establishment of the American central bank, the Federal Reserve, to play this role (Bruner 2009). The automobile industry was archetypal. In the United States, with its growing automobile market, long distances, and synergies with other sectors—steel, rubber, glass, electrics, and more, not to mention the huge road-building programs from the 1920s to the 1950s subsidized by local, state, and eventually federal government—it was possible for Second Industrial Revolution firms to raise this sort of capital from private sources. General Motors, Chrysler, and others competed with Ford on this basis. Similar synergies developed in a range of other Second Industrial Revolution sectors (Chandler 1990; Reich 1983).

In other countries, however, it was not such an easy task, and governments had to step in to help. The electricity industry was another crucial sector (Hughes 1983). Britain, again, was a partial exception, as its head start in industrialization, foreign investment, and imperialism meant that it never really experienced a full-blown Second Industrial Revolution, even after the Second World War. The competitive drive of elites and masses alike toward rapid, domestically led industrialization led from the late nineteenth to the mid-twentieth centuries to a breakdown of relatively open international financial governance and to a protectionist, nationalist response—including increasing state regulation of and support for domestic sources of investment—that intensified through the 1930s and contributed to the causes of both world wars. By the middle of the twentieth century, what Ruggie has called the "regime of embedded liberalism" blended the freeing of trade with the maintenance of capital controls to insulate the welfare state from "hot money"—destabilizing speculative cross-border capital flows (Ruggie 1982; Helleiner 1994; Block 1977). Thus until recently, history seemed to be a process of centralizing key aspects of financial governance in the nation-state. Paradoxically, it was this very centralization of financial governance at the national level that enabled an "inter-national" financial system to develop (for a more detailed historical survey, see Cerny 2005d).

There were several ways such capital could be raised, separately or in some combination. In the first place, firms could sell stock to the public or to other firms. Crucial to this development was an organizational innovation called the "limited liability company," developed during the nineteenth century and first legalized in New York State. Stockholders, officially the owners of the company, could stand to lose only as much as the value of their stock was worth. If a company went bankrupt with huge debts, stockholders would therefore not stand to lose their livelihoods, houses, and everything else to pay off the creditors. The limited liability company, once attacked by Adam Smith for potentially taking the entrepreneurial dynamism out of capitalism, proved to be its most important driving force in the modern world. It could attract whole classes of new, mainly small and medium investors—the new and rapidly growing middle classes of modern capitalism—who would otherwise be deterred by the risks of unlimited liability, namely, the threat of losing not only their particular investments but all their savings and even their possessions, too. The British and American economies have relied on stock markets for far more of their capital-raising activities than have other major economies, permitting the kind of separation of ownership from control that is seen as the basis of the modern corporate system (Zysman 1983; Berle and Means 1932; Ingham 1984; Germain 1997).

However, outside Britain and the United States, two other methods of raising these large amounts of capital were generally preferred—long-term bank finance and state investment financed through taxation and/or government borrowing. The countries in which these firms were located did not have access to broad and liquid stock markets and therefore to mass-based sources of investment; they did not have an existing industrial base and retained earnings to draw upon and, moreover, faced stultifying cheap import competition, especially from Britain; and their internal consumer and intermediate goods markets were too small for the kind of mass sales that would make such firms profitable by themselves. In political terms, dominant social and political groups in those countries wanted to accelerate and promote development in the national interest while retaining the power to control that process for themselves, and at the same time, workers wanted to protect their jobs from international competition. An unholy alliance of business, labor, and the state—often called "corporatism," with its mid-twentieth-century variant called "neocorporatism"—generally supported state- and bank-led industrialization behind protectionist barriers. National industrialization came to be seen as an urgent priority for governments, as well as for the private sector. International finance lost much its domestic political and economic constituency.

The first of these methods involved expanding debt finance rather than market finance, borrowing rather than selling shares—that is, setting up or supporting large banks that would take a leading role in supplying big loans. In return, the banks usually retained some element of strategic influence or even control over the development and management of the firms in order to boost the industrialization process. The second involved government subsidization and often direct or indirect control, including setting up new parastatal and/or nationalized industries in the public sector. Usually there was some combination of the two, with a state-bank-industry nexus promoting heavy industry. This frequently, but not always, involved some sort of cartelization, in other words, price fixing and/or agreed carving up of markets among different firms, as in Germany and Japan. At the same time, industry and the state were themselves each becoming increasingly bureaucratized, as well as more closely intertwined (Galbraith 1967/2007).

In the twentieth century, this approach was sometimes also linked with different versions of state planning, from Soviet-style command planning to postwar French "indicative planning." But usually such interventionism was more ad hoc, undertaken in response to democratic demands for economic growth, trade union integration, public service provision, and the like, coming both left and right, feeding into a "postwar consensus." This sort of intertwining of state and capital has been at the core of a whole range of scholarly debates about the nature of the modern capitalist state, usually seen as starting with Andrew Shonfield's masterpiece *Modern Capitalism* (Shonfield 1965) and since the 1980s, the "new institutionalism" in political science, sociology, history, and economics (Hall and Taylor 1996). Indeed, some neo-Marxists have argued that the state is the "ideal collective capitalist" (Hirsch 1978), as it is concerned with maintaining the capitalist system as a whole and not just the profitability or survival of particular firms.

In the literature on finance and the state, the distinction between financial market systems and bank- or institution-based financial systems is seen as a pivotal reflection of the divergence between different forms or "national varieties" of capitalism, embedded and locked in at the national level (Zysman 1983). On the one hand, there is the internationalist, globalizing, liberal, financial market–based Anglo-American (or "Anglo-Saxon") model. It is often asserted, however, that such a development is politically and socially destabilizing, undermining nationally rooted forms of labor organization, political culture, and social values. Germany, Austria, and Scandinavia, on the other hand, are usually seen as the paradigmatic examples of "organized" or "concerted" capitalism (Crouch and Streeck 1997; Hall and Soskice 2001); some writers also include a more statist version based on Japan and/or France (Zysman 1983; Schmidt 2002; Johnson 1982). Whether firm-led or state-led, however, concerted capitalism is the product of systematic and mutually reinforcing organizational linkages between the two at national level. Such writers argue that the Anglo-Saxon model can be poor at nurturing a whole range of industries that either retain Second Industrial Revolution characteristics or benefit from close proximity ("economies of agglomeration") and develop network effects (synergies) under the supportive aegis of the state—and, in some cases, of social democratic values.

On the other hand, a different range of scholars, usually those who give explanatory priority to globalization in their analyses, emphasize convergence rather than divergence—and usually see financial globalization as the key independent variable driving such convergence, up to a point. Less sophisticated versions of this perspective simply suggest the "end of geography" (O'Brien 1992) or the coming of a "borderless world" (Ohmae 1990). More sophisticated versions focus on three interconnected developmental trends. The first of these is financial globalization. The second is the argument that industrial structures are changing fundamentally, becoming more fragmented and flexible again, primarily because of technological change—so-called post-Fordism. And the third is that liberal and neoliberal values and market norms are superseding the kinds of national political solidarity that characterized Second Industrial Revolution state interventionism (Soederberg, Menz, and Cerny 2005).

The key to understanding the situation as it existed in the 1930s is to look at the role of the United States in the international financial system. The interwar period was basically a time, as I have said, of monetary and financial nationalization. Kindleberger (1973) has called this period one of "hegemonic interregnum," a gap between British leadership in stabilizing and running the international monetary system and the emergence with the Second World War of what the Americans saw as their own "reluctant leadership"—a new hegemonic phase with the United States playing the financial stabilizer. Nevertheless, the seeds were sown in the 1930s for that reluctant leadership or new American hegemony, especially after the passing of the Reciprocal Trade Agreements Act and the banning of domestic private gold trading and the statutory linking of the dollar to a gold value that would last until the late 1960s—$35 an ounce. Thus the dollar succeeded sterling as the anchor of a revamped gold exchange standard in a system of expanding trade, setting the stage for the 1944 Bretton Woods Agreement and the dollar standard of the postwar world (Gardner 1980). The Roosevelt administration went down this internationalizing road because of the experience of the first two years of the New Deal. Domestic reflation, industrial promotion, and the welfare state were not enough to cure the Depression, and the balance shifted in 1934 to those groups within the administration who came to believe that only a new wave of internationalization and an end to zero-sum, so-called beggar-thy-neighbor policies in international trade and monetary policy could "solve" the problems causing the Depression by promoting exports and foreign investment that would boost profits at home (Gardner 1964).

In the postwar period, the combination of a larger interventionist role for the state at home, plus the promotion of a more open international economy, what Ruggie (1982) would later call "embedded liberalism," had its roots in this transformation of the New Deal. This did not mean merely promoting economic growth through expanding international trade, although that was perhaps the highest profile element of the change. It also meant putting the dollar at the heart of a postwar system that would not only stabilize the value of international money, as the gold standard was supposed to have done, but also provide sufficient liquidity to the international economy to promote a virtuous circle of growth—and to avoid the deflationary effects and sociopolitical disadvantages of the gold standard. The complex negotiations and agreements that constituted the Bretton Woods system attempted to reconcile those goals (Gardner 1980).

Of course, those goals were reconcilable only up to a point. As other countries became more prosperous, there was plenty of liquidity around, especially in the form of dollars exported through American overseas defense expenditures (from the Korean War boom, to the expansion of U.S. multinational corporations, to inflationary spending on the Vietnam War) and through the chronic U.S. balance of payments deficit after 1958 (Block 1977; Odell 1982). Those dollars were increasingly recycled through the budding Eurodollar market in London and came to be seen by Europeans as swelling the world money supply—the United States "exporting inflation" to other countries through an overly strong dollar protected by the maintenance of its gold value. For a decade from the late 1950s to the late 1960s, successive U.S. administrations rejected the possibility of devaluing the dollar, which they felt would destabilize the system by restricting liquidity for trade and economic expansion, while European governments increasingly called for dollar devaluation. This dollar glut or dollar overhang eventually led the Nixon administration to withdraw the dollar from the Bretton Woods exchange rate system in 1971—"closing the gold window" (Gowa 1983).

3. OPENING THE INTERNATIONAL FINANCIAL SYSTEM: DEREGULATION AND REREGULATION

The result was to prove revolutionary for the international financial system. Although the dollar has remained the "top currency" (Strange 1986; Cohen 2004), exchange rates among the major financial powers had, by 1973, shifted from a semifixed or managed system—the "adjustable peg," as represented by Bretton Woods—to a floating exchange rate system. Despite interventions and attempts to set up target zones by various governments (especially the French in the early 1980s) and the fixing of their currencies to the dollar by various developing countries, the major players became the various financial firms and traders in the currency markets themselves. In the 1950s only a small fraction of international capital movements were private-sector flows; the overwhelming majority were public-sector flows. However, by the mid-1990s, public-sector flows constituted only a small fraction of the total, and international financial flows were overwhelmingly in the private sector. Dominant flows of political influence and policy clout between public and private sectors were thus reversed, too.

Since the move to floating exchange rates, governments' attempts to fix or manipulate the values of currencies have increasingly led to damages and transformations of whole economies, from various third world crises and the failure of the "snake," a basket of European semifixed currencies in the 1970s and 1980s, to the forced withdrawal of the sterling from the European Exchange Rate Mechanism (the precursor of the euro) in September 1992, to the Mexican crisis of 1994, the Asian and Russian crises of 1997–1998, the Argentine and Turkish crises of 2001–2002, and ultimately to the American and global crisis and recession of 2008 (*Review of International Political Economy*, August 2009). The main beneficiary of volatility in currency markets in recent years has been the new euro, which weakened against the dollar when it was first introduced but then rose well above its first issue level. Ironically, however, the current financial crisis, which began in the United States with the subprime mortgage meltdown, has hit the dollar harder than the euro, but this process is highly volatile, and the dollar still retains much of its strength as a "refuge" currency. A key reason for this is the openness of the American economic system generally. Thus the evolution of the American financial system since the 1960s—despite the austere regulatory and general financial environment of the 1930s, 1940s, and 1950s, when U.S. securities markets were generally stagnant, and despite the current meltdown—has significantly reinforced and expanded its financial market–based character.

Despite the need both American political parties recognize today for large-scale bailouts and economic stimulus packages in the short term, over the longer term, promarket regulations are increasingly thought to be the only way to create financial systems where hyperinflation and financial crises can be controlled and economies stabilized. In spite of attempts to moderate and tinker with financial marketization by key member states of the European Union, for example, the European Commission has increasingly taken the stance that completion of the single market for capital flows and financial services requires significant moves toward American- and British-style market regulations, corporate governance norms, state withdrawal from industrial subsidies, a more open takeover code, greater disclosure and transparency practices, and investor protection. In Southeast Asia, Korea, Japan, Argentina, Mexico, and other areas of the world bypassed or disadvantaged by financial globalization, neoliberal domestic financial regulatory reform is steadily if unevenly gaining ground. International organizations have been helping to consolidate this trend (Abdelal 2007). Financial scandals, too, have been spurring calls for more international regulation and the development of a "new financial architecture" (Armijo 2002; Soederberg 2004 and 2009).

Perhaps the most significant aspect of this change is a move *not* toward increasingly unsupervised markets or deregulation, what some economists call "competition in laxity," but, if anything, toward an increasingly complex *promarket* reregulation of American and other systems that is compatible with the neoliberal approach discussed in chapters 7 and 8. To the extent that the American model is actually a model, its lessons are somewhat different from the ones usually associated with financial globalization, liberalization, and deregulation. The United States is strengthening and expanding its statutory regulations after a period of laxity, becoming increasingly what Michael Moran, writing mainly about Britain, calls a "regulatory state" (Moran 2002). This trend is being massively reinforced by the current financial crisis (Acharya and Richardson 2009).

Some years ago, University of California political scientist David Vogel, writing about environmental regulation, made a distinction between the "Delaware Effect" and the "California Effect" (Vogel 1997). The U.S. state of Delaware, in a number of issue-areas including finance, has developed a track record for creating a highly permissive regulatory environment, seeking to attract firms and economic activities to the state through deregulation and competition in laxity. California, by way of contrast, has developed a highly complex and weighty superstructure of environmental and other regulations. Vogel argues that firms and economic actors do not only seek permissive regulatory environments but also want to ensure both stability and high standards of market behavior among their counterparties and competitors, as well as a strong legal system to provide *ex post* sanctions for opportunistic or fraudulent behavior. Thus it is not the presence or absence of regulations per se that counts, but what *kind* of regulations they are. These actors, like international traders in the nineteenth century looking to the City of London for financial services, want a stable, predictable but expansionary, promarket system for price discovery, contracts, bargaining, and the like.

In today's multilevel governance, however, it is not merely the governments of states that provide the increasingly critical public good of promarket, California Effect regulation. Cities and city-regions are also crucial (Sassen 2003; Brenner 2004). And probably the most salient level involves international regimes. The World Bank and the International Monetary Fund shifted in the 1990s from simply promoting the liberalization of capital controls and domestic economies to giving priority to getting effective financial regulatory systems up and running *before* opening up vulnerable domestic economies to global capital flows (for a controversial take on this, see Stiglitz 2002). This is what is often called the move from the Washington

Consensus of the late 1980s (Williamson 1990) to a post–Washington Consensus today. Finally, the core of the attraction of the World Trade Organization today is not simple pressure to reduce trade barriers and open up domestic economies to international competition, but rather the Dispute Settlement Mechanism, which increasingly provides a quasi-legal forum for negotiating reciprocal forms of liberalization—and using sanctions to enforce them.

As mentioned earlier, these changes also mirror changes in the United States itself, where a series of critical events has put the ball back in the court of the reregulators. Arthur Levitt, chairman of the Securities and Exchange Commission (SEC) from 1992 to 2001, has chronicled his efforts to improve transparency, corporate governance, and investor protection in the complex world of Washington lobbies, bureaucracies, and congressional politics (Levitt 2002). The legacy of those efforts was significantly eroded when President George W. Bush appointed an accountancy industry lawyer, Harvey Pitt, to succeed Levitt in 2001. But as so often happens, Pitt became locked into pursuing certain not too dissimilar structural changes himself, especially when the huge fraud and accounting scandals involving major firms like Enron, WorldCom, and Arthur Andersen broke in 2001. Pitt was forced by the Sarbanes-Oxley Act of 2002 to set up another statutory body under the aegis of the SEC, the Public Company Accounting Oversight Board, to supervise the previously self-regulating accountants. Furthermore, the campaign by New York State Attorney General (now ex-Governor) Eliot Spitzer to penalize the biggest financial services firms for falsely touting stocks in return for nonauditing services further highlighted the way the bull market of the 1980s and 1990s created huge opportunities for market abuse. Pitt was forced to resign because of his various stumbles and was replaced in 2003 by William Donaldson, who sought to streamline the overly complex regulatory system and reassert the SEC's authority before he was replaced in turn by Christopher Cox, whose tenure was criticized, once again, for laxity.

The reaction to volatility and crisis, then, is not deregulation as such, but more and more promarket reregulation. Pressures for further reregulation are predictably mushrooming as the result of the 2008 financial crisis. These trends are not confined to national financial services markets, nor are they limited to statutory regulation. Self-regulation and mixed, public-private forms of regulation are being reshaped, too. One of the most important developments in recent years has involved negotiations between the U.S. private-sector-based Financial Accounting Standards Board (FASB) and the mainly British-based International Accounting Standards Board (IASB) to come up with harmonized, convergent norms and, indeed, organizational templates not just for accounting standards per se but for corporate governance more widely. Despite some fundamental differences in approach, the negotiations are proceeding and look likely to eventually succeed. National regulatory agencies, international agencies like the International Organization of Securities Commissions, and transgovernmental and epistemic networks and policy communities have been converging for some time on accounting and auditing standards, among other things.

At the same time, the expansion of financial markets themselves, even within the banking sector (and the state) has led to a complex and controversial process that has been called *securitization*. Securitization actually has two meanings in the world of finance. In the broad sense, it means that the allocation of capital increasingly follows financial market techniques for the trading of securities rather than bank loans: the investor is supposed to make the basic decision as to where to invest, while the broker merely follows instructions. In other words, the investor is the principal, and the broker merely his or her agent. Of course, it doesn't quite work this way in practice, especially for smaller investors. Securitization, broadly speaking, is usually guided by a set of theoretical principles or practical guidelines that has become dominant in financial markets, primarily based on the concept of portfolio diversification. In other words, investors, unlike banks and states, should protect themselves against catastrophic losses by holding a number of different and contrasting kinds of securities, balancing different kinds of risks and potential returns. They must hedge as well as speculate. Efficient portfolio diversification is, however, important not only to individual investors but also to how financial market systems themselves work. Like limited liability, it attracts much wider and more diverse classes of investors into the system.

Nevertheless, the finance needed to fuel securitization in the broad sense since the 1990s has increasingly come—ironically—not from stock markets but from...bank loans and other forms of borrowing and debt, what is known as "leverage." Leverage mushroomed further after regulatory limits were lifted by the SEC in 2004. Indeed, the current financial crisis is seen as primarily one of the overleveraging or excessive indebtedness of key sectors of the economy. As leverage increases, so does the pressure to make riskier and riskier loans, until risk outruns the ability of one or two key sectors to repay those loans, as with poor mortgage holders in the U.S. subprime housing market, leading to a cascade of illiquidity throughout the entire financial system. At the core of this failure was the process of "securitization" in a second, more specific sense.

In this second, narrower sense, securitization has come to mean the repackaging of various securities, as well as forms of debt obligation such as housing mortgages and car loans, into tradable securities that are then sold to financial institutions who seek to expand their portfolio diversification in the belief that such securities are relatively safe. For example, until recently, it was generally believed that in the medium to long term, housing prices would continue to rise, and therefore packaged mortgages were as "safe as houses," as the British saying goes (Ferguson 2008: chapter 5). These particular derivatives were sold in tranches, that is, different packages, ranging from what were considered to be the most secure to the riskiest.

They were snapped up and were also given the imprimatur of the prestigious credit-rating agencies, whose role has been greatly criticized recently because while they were originally paid by investors, they have increasingly come to be paid by the institutions issuing the derivative securities themselves, creating a huge conflict of interest. Buyers thought they were purchasing safe income streams. However, as any even superficial reading of the financial press as the current financial crisis has exploded will tell you, these sorts of securities, for example, derivatives based on subprime mortgages (loans to house buyers who would be unable to pay back the loans as interest rates rose), have been at the heart of the cascade of illiquidity and bankruptcy that has characterized recent events. The dogma of portfolio diversification led to a misplaced faith in the process of securitization that has undermined trust in free markets today, as exemplified by former Federal Reserve Board Chairman Alan Greenspan's mea culpa to the U.S. Congress in October 2008. (In my view, the best book on this topic published by the time of writing is Tett 2009.)

The successes of financial markets in recent decades stemmed from their flexibility and their ability to create new credit and new forms of securities trading, as well as the higher returns associated with increased risk. In contrast, banks in many countries, and state bureaucracies all over the world, are limited by their deposit and tax bases, respectively. When asked why he robbed banks, the mid-twentieth-century American bank robber Willie Sutton said: "Because that's where the money is." But in a world of relatively disintermediated and securitized financial markets, with the possibility of reallocating capital anywhere in the world, financial markets are, or were until recently at least, where the money is—not in traditional banks and especially not states. Nevertheless, as banks have had to adjust to a securitized world, their role is no longer that of traditional intermediary but increasingly that of market players in their own right, adapting to and reinforcing the securitization process, especially in providing leverage.

But states, in contrast, quickly bump up against the limits of their tax bases and, especially (but not exclusively) in poorer and developing countries, have all too often resorted to printing money as a way of creating new investment—leading to hyperinflation and the repeated bailing out of underinvested failing industries. Such an outcome penalizes the poor more than the rich, as low wages are sticky and welfare systems underfunded in such circumstances. Lower-middle-class households are relatively penalized the most, as they lose the value of any investments they have and become rapidly downwardly mobile.

In this context, then, political actors of all kinds have increasingly espoused neoliberal financial restructuring, the marketization of financial systems, and adjustment to the demands of global capital as a crucial public good, in the long term at least. Nevertheless, while neoliberalism involves acceptance of financial market liberalization, regulatory convergence, privatization, and the like, political demands for social protection, equity, and welfare are still strong and growing stronger as the result of a range of critiques of globalization—and in the context of financial crisis. Democratic accountability, although still almost exclusively organized through national jurisdictions, requires political actors to play both sides of the street—to accept the disciplines or constraints of financial globalization while increasingly seeking ways to reinject the social into an otherwise predominantly neoliberal world, as was pointed out in chapter 7. This means operating on a number of different playing fields at the same time, attempting to manipulate the specific patterns of opportunities and constraints on each while reconciling the outcomes with both financial globalization and domestic demands—the essence of transnational neopluralism.

4. FINANCIAL CRISIS, REGULATORY INADEQUACY, AND THE REORGANIZATION OF GLOBAL CAPITAL

Existing international political economy accounts of the globalization of finance, including my own, have focused primarily on the process of transnational marketization. Scale shift of financial transactions from the national to the transnational has widely been said to derive from a combination of the greater competitive "efficiency" of market forces in finance (to some extent in contrast to, for example, multinational corporations) because of reduced transactions costs and the increasing competitiveness of marketized finance linked with disintermediation and securitization, on the one hand, and the ability of financial markets (actors and structures) to escape the regulatory hand of the state, on the other. The rapid expansion and structural hegemony of endogenously and exogenously competitive financial *markets*—not finance or money in and of themselves—are therefore often seen as a driving force for wider economic globalization, as well as for *both* the "retreat of the state" (Strange 1996) *and* the lack of effective international or supranational political institutionalization in the financial services issue-area (with the partial exception of the EU).

Nevertheless, there remains a fundamental conundrum underlying financial globalization—the ongoing tension, characteristic of capitalism in general, between relatively efficient competitive markets on the one hand and monopolistic or oligopolistic behavior on the other. As neoliberal theorists since the 1930s have argued, the core of efficient markets is not only establishing relative values of things exchanged but also creating conditions that support and promote competition and counteract monopolistic behavior. This has historically been as true of finance as of other sectors. Scale by itself does not guarantee an increase in competitive behavior on the part of market actors and institutions; indeed, it can create conditions for an increase in opportunism and monopoly, as many critics have asserted (Cooper 2008). And given that economically efficient competitive behavior is not a predominant trend in human nature and society (see chapter 8) and that markets cannot be self-regulating in and of themselves (Polanyi 1944), only *procompetitive* government intervention—especially arm's-length regulation and so-called prudential regulation—can establish the conditions for, stabilize, and promote capitalism in general and financial markets and institutions in particular. Nevertheless, although financial innovators may be effectively controlled for a period of time, the search for loopholes and for new ways of avoiding existing constraints and making end runs around regulations always reappears and grows. Regulatory systems decline into senescence, unable to deal with new challenges.

The significance of the contemporary crisis is therefore not simply its severity. Although various bottom bounces and bear market rallies have not resolved the crisis of the financial institutions and markets themselves, and the world is now in recession, the world economy and the financial system have proved remarkably resilient. However, a further question is a more qualitative one. Will the current crisis, like Crash of 1929 and the subsequent Great Depression, lead to a substantive reorganization of the character of regulation and/or capitalism itself? This becomes particularly significant when considering the issues of regulating international capital flows and the institutional characteristics of the global financial sector, that is, whether the marketization characteristic of the sector since the 1970s and 1980s will be superseded by a process of institutional concentration.

Will this process—moving away from the kind of competitive globalizing financial markets we all thought represented the future, and toward increasing government-sponsored concentration and even oligopolization—lead to a mixed, transnationalized public-private sector version of Lenin's "finance capital" emerging? In current conditions, the capacity of national governments to provide *either* procompetitive *or* more traditional decommodifying forms of regulation is problematic. It is, of course, problematic simply because the writ of national governments is increasingly being undermined by globalization, especially financial globalization. Despite talk of an emerging international financial architecture, the result so far has been extremely disappointing, with institutional and regulatory bricolage frequently merely leading to a form of regulatory gridlock that throws the regulatory burden right back at states (Kahler and Lake 2008). Effective supranational regulation itself has become more and more unlikely in this context, as the apparent failure of the G20 meeting in London in April 2009 demonstrates. This reregulatory process brings together a number of specific issues, each complex and problematic in its own right, that will be the focus of both policy debate and intense interest group, legislative, executive, and judicial politicking over the next few years (Acharya and Richardson 2009).

The first of these is that the kind of promarket, arm's-length regulation (transparency, antifraud, market design, *ex post* supervision, etc.) that has been the ideological and policy-making order of the day since the 1980s may not only not address the real problem but also may actually make things worse. As Bookstaber (2007) has argued, the problem lying behind recent attempts to regulate or cope with financial innovation is that they do not deal with the real issue—the lack of liquidity. In fact, especially because it is by its very nature *ex post* in its implementation and enforcement, the bailout culture may exacerbate procyclical tendencies while proving capable *neither* of providing enough liquidity for bailout purposes *nor* of creating the kind of structural conditions in which liquidity problems can be smoothed out and crises prevented *in advance*. Crisis prevention and promotion of efficient competition require *ex ante* modes of intervention and regulation—that is, must be able to predict when excess leverage and risk may cause cascading failures—and existing arrangements have little policy capacity in this regard.

Second, existing regulatory institutions are not capable of providing effective regulation, not only because they are embedded in the *ex post* mode but also because they are often divided, especially in the United States. Whether a more unified institutional model like that of Britain's Financial Services Authority would perform better is also problematic, given that merging regulatory institutions can simply lead to duplication and endogenous turf conflict (William W. Gruver in the *New York Times*, 13 September 2008), as demonstrated by the failure of the British bank Northern Rock, where conflicts between the United Kingdom Treasury (and the government more widely) and the Bank of England complicated and delayed the bailout. In the United States, pressure from financial sector lobby groups to prevent such a restructuring as of mid-2009 is apparently making it less likely that Congress will go down this road, for example, probably blocking even the merger of the Securities and Exchange Commission and the Commodities and Futures Trading Commission. Attempts at regulatory reform in Japan have not led to a more efficient, market-led financial sector either (*Financial Times*, Special Report, 12 September 2008). And so-called deregulation has often led to more spending on attempts to implement increasingly inefficient regulation (Tyler Cowen, the *New York Times*, 14 September 2008).

Third, of course, "moral hazard ye shall always have with you." Moral hazard is a somewhat broader principle similar to the notion that if financial market actors know they are going to be bailed out, they will take chancier and chancier risks. Ultimately, effective, comprehensive, "joined-up" (as the British would say) regulatory reform can end up being undermined in the response to crises. Priority number one is to bail out systemically significant institutions, but as the U.S. Treasury decision to let Lehman Brothers go bankrupt demonstrates, how far can governments go—especially in the context of preexisting huge government budget deficits in the United States? Fannie Mae and Freddie Mac, the heirs of New Deal institutions that guarantee mortgages ostensibly to expand home ownership to the working classes, may prove to constitute the limits of acceptable action, mainly because they are "government-sponsored enterprises" (GSEs) with a populist New Deal and Great Society legacy that united 2008 presidential candidates John McCain and Barack Obama in support.

But bank bailouts and, now, industrial bailouts, such as that being implemented with regard to the American automobile industry, are a whole different kettle of fish. With regard to bailouts and moral hazard, furthermore, will there be an increasing need to provide such a backup service at a *transnational* level if twenty-first-century crises are to be confronted? And, if so, who will do it? The summit of the Group of 20 in mid-November 2008 handed the ball back to the states. The capacity doesn't exist now at the international level. And as one of the results of the current crisis is likely to mean more, not less, international capital mobility and capital flow once recovery is under way, national governments will be less and less capable of providing what James Grant (1992) called "socialism for the banks," further exacerbating the regulatory deficit with regard to liquidity.

Studies of "organized" or "coordinated" capitalism, as noted earlier, have emphasized the role of the state as the key variable in guaranteeing stability and promoting investment and growth. However, organized, concerted, and coordinated capitalism are themselves contested categories. I would suggest a distinction between the self-organization of capital and the social or political organization of capital. Martin Höpner (2007) has convincingly argued that there is a distinction—the terminology is slightly different here—between "coordinated" and "organized" capital. The former, the equivalent of what I would call "self-organized capital," concerns the role of firms—in this case, of financial market actors of various kinds—organizing among themselves in their basic role of making profits and appropriating surplus value. There is an element of monopoly or oligopoly here, but this is not a power-based or opportunism-based version—more a particular manifestation of what Williamson (1975 and 1985) called "hierarchy," that is, that certain forms of economic governance in particular circumstances are more efficient *not* through competitive markets (nonspecific assets and recurrent contracting) but rather through relationship-specific, *ex ante* contracting and management decision making by fiat (specific assets and long-term contracting). Indeed, in finance, the traditional role of banks has been as intermediary institutions—not as financial marketplaces. The resulting transaction cost savings have been at the core of much of capitalist financial development—the state- and bank-led model discussed earlier—especially in late industrialization and the Second Industrial Revolution.

But is organized *financial* capital itself going global, or are we merely seeing still-national banks, sovereign wealth funds, and other institutions shift to operating on a transnational playing field? This question raises, in turn, the question of what sort of role *public* institutions have played, should play, or will play in the organization of capital. As others have argued, for example, Kahler and Lake (2008), international or supranational regimes in the field of finance are extremely circumscribed. They are partly circumscribed because *regulation*, both in the sense of particular financial regulatory policies and in the wider sense of French regulation theory (i.e., the Polanyian need to stabilize a fundamentally unstable, crisis-prone mode of production and exchange), is deeply institutionalized at the level of the state, through national currencies, embedded systems of financial regulation, powerful national institutions like central banks, and the perceived primacy—on the part of politicians, practitioners, and the general public, too—of national priorities in counteracting market failure and preventing systemic risk.

The International Monetary Fund doesn't really do much in this area despite attempts to strengthen it at the recent G20 meeting, the Bank for International Settlements is more important but limited in scope, the Organization for Economic Cooperation and Development has no real clout (despite some very useful reports, etc.), the World Bank is focused on other issues such as development, and the International Organization of Securities Commissions (IOSCO) is pretty much captured by the sector. As Abdelal has pointed out, these international institutions' attempts to draw up and implement clear capital rules at the international level appeared to play an important role in the expansion of capital mobility in the 1990s and early 2000s, but there has been a "rebirth of doubt" (Abdelal 2007: chapter 8) in recent years, as markets have become more volatile and rules have been challenged by the behavior of actors in the recent bubble.

The closest we get to transnational regulation is therefore by osmosis or convergence through bricolage and informal networking, as with Slaughter's transgovernmental networks. Private networks and institutions are important here, too, like stock exchanges, bond and derivatives markets, various clearing houses, the International Swaps and Derivatives Association (ISDA), and the other trade associations that have developed around accounting and audit standards. Tett, for example, chronicles the role of the ISDA in particular in "dancing around the regulators" in the 1990s and early 2000s in the successful quest to prevent the regulation of the mushrooming derivatives sector (Tett 2009: chapter 2). But self-regulation is, as always, limited and problematic in the Polanyian sense (Polanyi 1944). A bit of institutional bricolage, like the Financial Stability Board (successor to the Financial Stability Forum) and the Group of 20, can help around the edges. But the venerable proto-"realist" fact is that there is no authoritative supranational state, which in turn means that there is unlikely to be any real development of an international financial architecture or organized capital in Höpner's subsidiary, more political, sense of Durkeheimian, social-values-oriented organization, or what I have called "social neoliberalism."

Nevertheless, I would suggest that "self-organized"—or Höpner's "coordinated"—capitalism is increasingly alive and well in global finance. Credit and leverage are increasingly the way to create new sources of capital, in spite of the current crisis with regard to particularly fragile and vulnerable forms of leverage caused by the overexpansion of the use of highly structured derivatives. Self-organized transnational capital is represented in particular by institutional investors and private equity, but increasingly by hedge funds, too, despite their current troubles. Furthermore, "organized capital" in Höpner's stricter sense may be making a reentrance as well in the guise of sovereign wealth funds, although it is much too early to evaluate their impact on the broader structural trends identified here. In the current financial crisis, however, the interaction of these various forms of concerted capitalism (both self-organized and politically organized) is turning into a volatile but intriguing process. At the same time, national regulators are increasingly unable to regulate effectively. Every suggested new regulation has a serious downside, especially for liquidity, in a complex global financial system (Bookstaber 2007), and political processes seem to seize up as soon as "glimmers of light" or "green shoots of recovery" appear. Nevertheless, the state must still take on the vital and growing backup role of bailing out institutions in trouble and stimulating the real economy if it is to recover. Like the poor, we will always have moral hazard with us when the system is frozen by such factors as the drying up of liquidity. This problem has yet to be properly addressed by policy makers at the time I write, despite awareness of the problem, good intentions by the Obama administration and other governments, and the policy formulation skills of actors like American Secretary of the Treasury Timothy Geithner.

There are three questions here. In the first place, are we moving from a market-driven world to a newly institutionalized and oligopolized global finance, where the role of states and fragmented international regimes will be mainly just to prop up the financial sector? In the second place, is this evolution being driven by economic efficiency criteria—saving transactions costs, economies of scale, and the like—or by old-fashioned opportunistic (monopolistic/oligopolistic) behavior? How big are the "rents" or unearned benefits, who is seeking them, and will this trend lead to upward development and expansion—the increased availability and flexibility of investment capital for development, greater liquidity, more dynamism, and ultimately sustained economic growth—or to endemic crises and the kind of negative consequences radical critiques of financial globalization have always posited? And third, what are the implications of this change for the real economy and for politics and society—for what Foucault calls "biopolitics"? Does financial globalization lead to economic progress or to incipient stagnation and/or decline? And will there emerge—in the sense of a global-level Polanyian "double movement"—a transnational public or quasi-public regulatory system of some sort that will effectively cope with and proactively shape systemic development in the way the state did in the national Keynesian era?

Discussions of possible changes regarding the regulation of investment banks and other subsectors of the shadow financial system such as structured investment vehicles are at the forefront of the policy debate right now, but to a large extent, regulators are still fighting the last war. Bailouts and moral hazard are far more important in the midst of meltdown, what Anna Gelpern calls "containment" (Gelpern 2009). National regulators are caught between taking immediate action—which only they have the authority to do—and formally or informally coordinating longer term transnational responses. In this environment, those transnational responses may be becoming harder and harder to negotiate, at least in the near future. At the same time, as noted previously, interest group lobbying, especially in the United States, with its institutional system of checks and balances (Cerny 1989), to block significant regulatory reform is already gaining steam. The likelihood of either effective transnational regulation or systematic domestic-level reregulation is fading as the economy begins to recover. The haste with which American banks are currently repaying TARP funds (the Treasury's Troubled Assets Relief Program) in order to escape the regulatory imperatives of high levels of government shareholding clearly exemplifies the lack of potential movement on regulatory reform.

The solution advocated by some—to democratize decision making and to strengthen the national state itself (e.g., Pettifor 2006)—is a red herring. The national state, except for mopping up after the fact, is increasingly surrounded and outmaneuvered by *both* market forces *and*, increasingly, transnationally organized/coordinated capital. Issues such as accounting standards (see especially the current debate on "mark-to-market" or "fair value" accounting), transparency versus liquidity-oriented regulations (for a useful survey, see Fuchita and Litan 2007; cf. Bookstaber 2007), expanding capital adequacy requirements to the shadow banking world, restructuring regulatory institutions, directly regulating derivatives and other structured products (mortgage-backed securities, collateralized debt obligations, credit default swaps, and the like), and ensuring that more categories of assets are routed through regulated exchanges and clearinghouses are a long way from consensus, both within states and transnationally. State actors in different countries have different policy proposals and goals, too, not only the French and Germans coming up with different policy responses from the United States but also the actions of individual European governments effectively stymieing attempts to develop Europe-wide reregulatory responses via the European Union. The content of rules is equally contentious. Can decision makers come up with detailed regulations that will not simply create further complications, or should they try to draw up what Bookstaber calls "coarse decision rules" that move away from quantifiable models? And in the broadest sense, does this mean a thoroughgoing transition in terms of quantitative analysis away from a Gaussian to a Mandelbrotian mind-set (Taleb 2007; Cooper 2008)?

At the moment, however, the key question is how these trends will play out in the aftermath of the current financial crisis. It seems to me that there are fundamentally three possibilities. The first is that there will once again be increasing Minskyian instability (Nesvetailova 2007) and a growing, if episodic, global financial crisis. In such an environment, I would expect some version of self-organized and/or coordinated financial capital to come further to the fore, operating on a more monopolistic or oligopolistic basis and creating an overarching, hierarchical-plus-network-based form of transnational *self*-regulation or sectoral hegemony, a possibility that is already in evidence in the reactions of various private-sector trade associations and self-regulatory bodies, both domestic and transnational. The second is that the current crisis will constitute a learning experience for both financial market actors and policy makers, leading to a new, more stable boom (see, in particular, Gross 2007 for a fascinating historical take on why bubbles are good for the economy; on hedge funds, see Andrew Hill in the *Financial Times*, 17 December 2008).

There may conceivably be a rosy scenario in which what is good about, for example, derivatives, structured products, hedge funds, and private equity is increasingly understood analytically and can come to be used more wisely—in the ways they were originally supposed to be used: creating value, restructuring inefficient firms, spreading risk, diversifying portfolios, and creating greater liquidity for a new round of investment and growth. Indeed, American regulators, especially the Federal Deposit Insurance Corporation, have recently been reported to be "drawing up new rules to facilitate private equity acquisitions of troubled banks in an effort to unlock tens of billions of dollars that could be deployed to recapitalize ailing lenders" (*Financial Times*, 13 June 2009). This initiative could not only put private equity—a particularly important sector of contemporary organized capital, both domestically and internationally—into the driving seat in significant sectors of the banking system but also touch off new conflicts between trade associations linked with different financial sectors and also between regulators, including the Treasury and the Federal Reserve. Such conflicts will also play out in diverse ways in different countries. Might this lead to a healthier balance between market capitalism and hierarchical, self-organized, coordinated capitalism that will have less need for public intervention—although requiring supportive, more sophisticated neoliberal promarket regulation at various levels—or is it likely to just reinforce the control of private capital, both domestic and transnational, over the state itself? This question is at the core of the ongoing problematic of transnational neopluralism.

And third, there is the possibility—especially given the lack of an effective transnational public sphere or architecture in the financial issue-area—that policy makers, interest groups, and market actors will simply engage in continuing policy and institutional bricolage, use trial and error rather than clear agendas and policies, and respond in an ad hoc manner to events. In this final case, too, the key institutional actors are likely to be some interactive but fluid set of changing coalitions between self-organized capital and policy makers at various levels, creating new nodes of decision making and coordination. This final scenario is likely to be intermittently unstable in the short term, always fighting the last war, based on changing (im-)balances of power, and crisis-prone, but it is also likely to be fairly durable and increasingly global over the medium to long term—a durable disorder. The way actors navigate through this complex political process, from state actors like President Barack Obama to investors and borrowers, managers and workers, international funds and institutions and local entrepreneurs, will shape whatever outcomes emerge in an ongoing bargaining and decision-making process, another dimension of what I have called transnational neopluralism.

5. CONCLUSION: FINANCIAL GLOBALIZATION AS A POLITICAL PROCESS

The national state in developed capitalist countries has had and continues to have a privileged strategic position, stemming from its long institutionalization and embeddedness, as lead regulator of financial institutions and markets. However, this position does not stem from the essence or property of "sovereignty" or "autonomy" as such, that is, from some sort of elemental independence from other actors, institutions, and processes. Rather, it stems from the very *inter*dependence of those actors and institutions themselves. It results from the state's crossroads position in a complex *network* of actors, institutions, and processes—nodes of power and authority—from the local to the global. However, the state today is increasingly stuck at the crossroads, faced with a much larger and more complex road network to deal with, a growing traffic jam, and a vehicle that is breaking down. It must share and coordinate more and more of its regulatory power with those other nodes. The state becomes less a sovereign unit actor and more an enforcer of rules that must dovetail with the wider trends of financial globalization and the proliferation of transnational interests—not so much a strategic controller as a traffic cop.

Nevertheless, social, political, and economic actors are increasingly learning to live with financial globalization and trying to develop strategies and tactics for shaping it in the future. Finance for investment can be obtained from a wider range of sources and in a greater range of types potentially suited to different uses than in the past, and globalization has been the main driving force in enabling that development to occur. Although there may be no "ideal collective capitalist" in such a world, transnational neopluralism and multilevel governance provide a greater range of points of access to complex political and economic processes, new possibilities for expanding the public good of financial stability and liquidity across the world—despite the frequently painful financial crises that mark this transition—and new opportunities to capture the benefits of globalization for a wider range of constituencies. In this context, the multilevel governance of global finance does not merely produce constraints in terms of complexity, messiness, and a lack of broad accountability but may also generate significant new potential opportunities for political action, competition, and coalition building—not to mention a new awareness of the need for the reconceptualization of the underlying logic of governmentality itself around *raison du monde*, whether operationalized at international, transnational, or domestic levels.

Chapter 13

Rescaling the State and the Pluralization of Marxism

1. INTRODUCTION: CLASS FRACTIONS, HEGEMONY, AND THE RESCALING OF THE STATE

One of the dominant themes in contemporary political economy is how capitalism shapes the future of the state, statehood, and world politics. Are states being hollowed out? Are they retaining their autonomy (if they ever had it) or becoming increasingly a tool of global capital? Are they converging, or are they evolving into distinct varieties of capitalist state, old and/or new? And are they fragmenting, or are they morphing into a new sort of capitalist global governance? Recent critical scholarship has taken a number of different directions in addressing these questions. Poststructuralism and postmodernism argue that the modern grand narratives of politics and society have broken down; they claim that they are not intending to develop alternative narratives analogous to those of totalization and individuation or capitalism versus socialism, but rather simply intend to identify the myriad manifestations and fragmented power relations of those representations of modernity as they decay.

Marxism, in particular, has had to contend with the poisoned legacy of Soviet communism. The Communist Party of the Soviet Union and the Soviet state after the Russian Revolution were organized according to Lenin's concept of democratic centralism, in which pluralistic forces were strictly controlled, and Stalin imposed a brutal form of totalitarianism on the party and country. Since the mid-twentieth century, however, Marxist political parties and movements, neo-Marxist theorists, and communist states before and since the end of the cold war have been grappling with the implications of internalizing pluralistic trends from both outside and within the Marxist political and intellectual universe. This was never more obvious than in the events of May 1968 in France and its aftermath, which have shaped the subsequent theoretical agenda. Of course, neo-Marxists, including the 1970s and 1980s version represented by Nicos Poulantzas and others (Poulantzas 1974 and 1976; Miliband 1969; Holloway and Picciotto

1978), as well as the neo-Gramscianism of the 1990s and early 2000s (Cox 1987; Gill 2003), continue to prioritize the relations of production and the labor theory of value as the key wellsprings of modern political economy. However, the translation of those fundamental concepts into paradigmatic understandings of how politics works in a globalizing world has evolved dramatically.

Poulantzas and the German neo-Marxists of the 1970s put more emphasis on the structural role of the state in intermediating between the main classes of capitalist society, leading to an analytical focus on the state that in the 1970s and 1980s partially merged with Weberian state theory to compete in paradigmatic terms with American-style pluralism. These theorists saw the dynamics of the political process as less holistic and class as less cohesive than in traditional Marxism, as populated by "fractions of capital" and a wider range of middle- and lower-middle-class "class fractions" caught between the bourgeoisie and the proletariat in "contradictory class locations," and most important for the contemporary analysis of global capitalism as well as "state capitalism," diverse elements of the state bourgeoisie and petty bourgeoisie. These include different kinds of bureaucrats, functionaries, career politicians, and the like, including clerks, schoolteachers, local notables, and other groups such as the media, parts of the "ideological state apparatus," as well as police, courts, and the military, parts of the "repressive state apparatus."

The livelihood and identity of such groups were said to be formed not only by their objective class position but also by the role of the state as the key organizational structure or apparatus. This apparatus is charged, in its self-identification and organizational rationale, with the stabilization of the society and economy as a whole, the development of cross-class coalitions, and the embedding of capitalism *as a system*, rather than merely representing the instrumental objectives of "capitalists" as such. These groups become more numerous and significant as modern society expands. In their contradictory class locations, their class position paradoxically results in their internalizing a false consciousness, supporting the state, and engaging in ostensibly pluralist, liberal democratic, or other forms of modern democratic politics that merely further entrench capitalism structurally through the state. As a result, they tend to identify with subclass or cross-class interest groups, compete with each other, ignore the underlying class struggle of capitalism, and reinforce the pluralist myth that underpins the capitalist state and the continuity of state monopoly capitalism (Jessop 1982). Nevertheless, these theorists argue that the core of the sorts of changes we have been discussing in this book are still to be found in the structural character of capitalism itself and the nature of the relations of production. The underlying contradictions of capitalism will be determining "in the last analysis" as the ultimate crisis of capitalism approaches (Poulantzas 1974).

Neo-Gramscian theory takes this process of pluralization two steps further. In the first place, class power is not simply a form of "domination" by the bourgeoisie, whether instrumental or structural, but rests on an even deeper quasi–false consciousness, called "hegemony" (quite different from the notion of hegemony in realist international relations). Hegemony is instilled in the people at large not simply through exploitation or repression, but rather through the internalization of bourgeois values by all classes, who are socialized to perceive capitalist society as beneficial to all and in the common interest. In addition to processes like democratization, the rhetoric of rights, universalistic political rhetoric, and workers' co-optation into corporatist cooperation, the roles of "civil society" and "organic intellectuals" are crucial in defining an ideology of voluntary acquiescence, turning it into a "common sense," and carrying the banner for notions like modernity, individual freedom, capitalist prosperity, and social justice, perceived as counteracting the underlying exploitative conditions of capitalism (Cox 1987).

In a second step, class power is said to be exercised not through a unified ruling class or even a "committee for managing the common affairs of the whole bourgeoisie" (Marx and Engels 1848/2005), but through a durable coalition of apparently pluralistic but actually hegemonic social forces—a "historic bloc" that makes society safe for capitalism. Nevertheless, historic blocs are not monolithic, unlike a ruling class. Rather, they are prone to internal conflict among fractions of capital, include various working- and middle-class fractions, and change with historical circumstances. These characteristics give capitalist political systems, in both democratic and non-democratic forms, a more nuanced and fluid appearance, reinforcing the impression of pluralism while maintaining the hegemony and social discipline of capitalism per se.

More recently, a further dimension of pluralization has appeared in neo-Marxist theory—the "rescaling of the state" itself. In other words, capitalism is not only characterized by fractionated classes maintained by ideological hegemony and historic blocs but also pluralized by the growing multilayering of the state apparatus itself in a globalizing world. Capitalism, this approach asserts, does not simply exist in a vague ether of the relations of production. It needs to be organizationally anchored in space and time, to include a "spatiotemporal fix" (Jessop 2002). The state is what anchors capitalism in this way, and as the world changes, the state has to change with it. In a globalizing era, therefore, where politics, economics, and society—or capitalism in general—are being fundamentally transformed by the changing scale of capitalism and the requirements of relations of production, the state itself, in its symbiotic relation with capital, embodies the requirements of finding not just one spatiotemporal fix, as in the nation-state, but multiple and shifting spatiotemporal fixes, reflecting the complexity of multidimensional, multilevel globalization.

I will focus here on two contemporary theorists of rescaling, Bob Jessop and Neil Brenner. Jessop places this reconceptualization of space within a broad analysis of the changing "capitalist type of state" (Jessop 2002); Brenner develops a more circumscribed study of urban governance but places it clearly in the larger context of capitalism and globalization (Brenner 2004). In addition to these sources, both authors also contributed to an edited volume that expands on these themes through a range of both classic readings and new scholarship (Brenner, Jessop, Jones, and MacLeod 2003). These analyses argue that a capitalist globalization per se entails a fundamental process of rescaling the state—or, for Brenner, rescaling the more abstract concept of "*statehood*"—on multilevel, multinodal playing fields, from the local to the global (see also Arts, Lagendijk, and van Houtum 2009). Both Jessop and Brenner emphasize the structural shift from concentrated political processes, policy making, socialization, economic regulation, and the like that have tended to converge at the quasi-holistic spatial or territorial scale of the nation-state, to a more structurally differentiated, messy process of multilevel restructuring. Jessop calls this process the "relativization of scale."

In this chapter, I examine these authors' depictions of the shape of structural change and argue that despite the rigor of these analyses and the many insights they provide, the authors are nevertheless hampered by the elements of classical Marxist analysis they retain, especially their focus on "accumulation strategies" and Marxist theories of value. Marx saw capitalism as an inherently international (or global) phenomenon but did not anticipate and therefore did not address the question of what sort of *capitalist* institutional superstructure might succeed the capitalist nation-state. The latter was to have already been overthrown by an international workers' movement and succeeded by socialism and eventually communism, but the mechanism of this transformation would involve revolutions either developing spontaneously at an international level and/or spreading from nation-state to nation-state.

Marxist analysis today, therefore, must grapple with the transformation of capitalism through globalization in ways that were not envisaged in nineteenth-century—or even most twentieth-century—Marxist theorizing, despite the emergence of Poulantzian and neo-Gramscian interpretations since the 1970s. Finally, I ask where rescaling is leading and suggest some alternative theoretical considerations. The search for an alternative "spatiotemporal fix" to replace the nation-state and the interstate system in the study of world politics is ongoing, and I argue that the more specifically political variables represented in transnational neopluralism provide both a fuller and a better explanation of globalization than a focus on capitalism, especially Marxist interpretations of capitalism, as such.

2. MARKETS, VALUE, AND EXTRAECONOMIC SUPPORTS

The various analytical pathways explored by Jessop, Brenner, and other scholars who analyze the relationship between spatiality and globalization generally start from the interaction of three sets of potential independent variables and attempt to assess the relative contribution of each to the changing morphology of the contemporary state—the *economic*, the *extraeconomic* or sociopolitical, and the *geographical/territorial*. Most Marxist analyses leave out this last category, so these authors' attempt to assess its importance and reintegrate it is extremely important in terms of potentially bringing Marxism back into the contemporary analysis of world politics.

Much of Jessop's work involves the clarification of an approach that has been at the heart of so-called neo-Marxist and post-Marxist state theory (vague and fungible categories actually rejected by Jessop himself) since the 1970s and has been traditionally derived from Marx's thoughts on the French state in his *The Eighteenth Brumaire of Louis Bonaparte* (1852/1987) through the concept of the "relative autonomy of the state" (and politics). Indeed, Jessop has been one of the leading authors on this subject for a number of years, and he systematically identifies the elements of classical Marxist analysis he retains and those he rejects (Jessop 2002: table 1.3, 35). This kind of state theory has formed part of a wider body of work and set of debates—including debates with neo-Weberians and other theorists who see the state as analytically primordial and organizationally superior to capital—that in earlier decades have interpreted the existence and development of the modern state, especially the industrial state and later the welfare state and the democratic state, as not merely an instrument of capital but as a necessary precondition and essential support or shell for the development of capitalism itself.

Jessop's innovatory contribution to Marxist theorizing today has been to argue that the kind of extraeconomic institutional supports that the industrial welfare state (which he calls the Keynesian Welfare National State, or KWNS) provided during the Second Industrial Revolution or the Fordist phase of capitalist development are no longer sufficient to support capitalist accumulation in its globalizing, post-Fordist phase. Therefore, attempts to revive the modern national-territorial state—whether in the name of social justice, or in order to prevent capitalism from collapsing from the weight of its own internal contradictions, or indeed as the basis for a future transition to socialism—are doomed to fail. Methodological nationalism, like political nationalism (of left or right), is, under conditions of globalization, an inherently unsatisfactory and counterproductive approach to an increasingly unstable set of conditions. Nevertheless, in my interpretation, Jessop ultimately still derives these changes from the material requirements of capital accumulation and of the extraction of surplus value, as in classical Marxist theory, although he rejects the notion that any single explanatory independent variable can be identified. He distinguishes among complex processes of "economic determination," "economic domination," "economic hegemony," and "ecological dominance." These categories reflect the characteristic conundrum at the heart of Marxist theory that is most often criticized by non-Marxists—economic determinism.

On the one hand, Jessop writes that "it is precisely because capitalism cannot secure through market forces alone all the conditions needed for its own reproduction that it cannot exercise *any sort of economic determination in the last instance* over the rest of the social formation" (2002: 11, emphasis added). Jessop argues essentially that *neither* market forces *nor* nonmarket social relations (extraeconomic supports) can be determining in the last instance. Rather, the process is one of the coconstitution of accumulation. On the other hand, however, it is this very coconstituted process of capital accumulation that in turn actually determines the form that real-world capitalism will take, and this process in turn creates structural requirements that determine the parameters of the political. The requirements of capital accumulation still determine the limits and constitution of politics.

Jessop is at his most classical in his derivation of the imperatives of capital accumulation: "What distinguishes capitalism from other forms of producing goods and services for sale is the generalization of the commodity form to labor-power" (2002: 12). The key to the relationship between the economic and noneconomic is therefore grounded in the assertion that labor in particular (in the form of labor-power)—but also land, money, and knowledge—are "fictitious commodities" à la Polanyi (1944). They are not themselves "created in a profit-oriented labor process subject to the typical competitive pressures of market forces to rationalize production and reduce the turnover time of invested capital." Fictitious commodities require cooperation and trust for their reproduction, and therefore their "use value" in traditional Marxist terms (both material and symbolic) can never be fully converted into "exchange value"—the hard core of Jessop's analysis, too. This means that their exchange value (mainly but not entirely represented in their price) is related only in highly problematic ways to their intrinsic worth to the people involved in processes of production and reproduction.

The commodification of their labor-power alienates people from their work and from other elements of social reproduction, thereby creating permissive conditions for their exploitation by the owners of capital—unless they are effectively able to engage in class struggle or other forms of resistance. However, exploitation (apparently) *only* concerns fictitious commodities; it would seem that nonfictitious commodities, namely, those that *are* created in the sort of labor process just specified, may be produced and exchanged quite efficiently through capitalist mechanisms. The commodification of fictitious commodities—especially labor—is the bottom line. It is so fundamental to capitalism that the exploitation derived from this process forms the overriding necessary condition for the stabilization and growth of capital itself. Of course, the commodification of fictitious commodities is not in itself a sufficient condition for capitalist development; politics and extraeconomic institutions are an essential part of the process. Nevertheless, the extraction of surplus value is the key. Markets are merely mechanisms for the translation or reallocation of surplus value into various uses. The key sentence is: "For while markets mediate the search for added value and modify its distribution within and across classes, *they cannot themselves procure it*" (2002: 19, emphasis in original).

For non-Marxists, of course, these distinctions are problematic. First, I would argue that what distinguishes market capitalism from other modes of production is not the simple transfer of surplus value to other uses, but actually the *creation* of value through complex, decentralized market mechanisms, including the so-called multiplier effect of technological innovation in production, distribution, and exchange. At the same time, labor, land, and so forth can be seen in turn to be no less "real" commodities than supposedly nonfictitious ones; therefore, the emphasis on their representing an irreducible core of intrinsic worth is itself a fiction. In particular, the very concept of "use value" is itself problematic in this context. People have idiosyncratic notions of use value—notions that in precapitalist, primitive capitalist, and noncapitalist societies have notably been exploited by religious, kinship, tribal, feudal, absolutist, and other hierarchies, often in authoritarian fashion, in order to impose mystical notions of value that kept people subsumed and immobile in traditional economic activities, especially subsistence, sharecropping, or feudal agriculture. Thus it can even be argued that labor and land are not in and of themselves "fictitious" commodities and instead can be seen as *unrealized* commodities in a precapitalist or noncapitalist system. Their role depends as much or more on exogenous social, political, and economic conditions than on any intrinsic, nonmarket use value—except insofar as this feeds into the process of generating exchange value, as does capitalism itself.

In turn, exchange value may be seen as nonfictitious or "real" value inso-far as it involves a social process of comparing what economists call "utili-ties," which are themselves no more than the subjective values people place on particular goods, assets, activities, relationships, and the like. As people find out what other people are willing to pay for the things they own or pro-duce, and compare this with their own subjective estimates, that crucial process—called *commensuration*—creates a genuinely common or mutually acceptable value, a value all the more significant because it can be indepen-dently activated and operationalized through relatively decentralized market processes, mainly through the price mechanism (so long as it is not overly distorted by monopoly rents or negative feedback loops). One of the classic critiques of the Marxist concept of surplus value is that it remains highly abstract, opaque to measurement, and therefore virtually impossible to operationalize.

Of course, exchange value is not "objective" in the philosophical sense, but it does constitute a genuinely *intersubjective* criterion for valorization. Furthermore, it provides a new incentive not only to exchange supposedly nonfictitious commodities in the first place but also to offer your land or labor-power on the market in an ongoing process—to transcend traditional restrictions or limits of custom, superstition, hierarchy, entailment, and the like—and to realize a newly generated value (or a revaluation) that otherwise would be dormant, mystical, or status-bound. Most important, exchange value generates incentives and mechanisms for redeploying that value into alternative uses that can create further added value through investment, technological progress, new products and processes, expanded consump-tion, and prosperity.

Exploitation nevertheless frequently occurs in the course of this process. However, exploitation is confined neither to capitalism nor to the expropria-tion of surplus value. Indeed, exploitation in its monopoly or oligopoly forms is usually seen in mainstream capitalist economic theory itself as counterproductive in the medium and long term precisely because it *limits* and constrains the creation of added value through competitive market pro-cesses. Therefore, markets, far from being nonproductive and non-value-creating, in fact constitute necessary (if not sufficient) conditions and essential facilitating mechanisms for the creation and realization of value—and perhaps even for the liberation of people from static, exploitative, extra-economic sociopolitical conditions. Furthermore, markets, while not self-regulating in the Polanyian sense—only the most obtuse free market fundamentalists still argue that extraeconomic supports are unnecessary for markets to operate in a reasonably competitive and efficient manner—do represent a face of capitalism that is not fully included in the concept of accumulation, with its assumptions of built-in tendencies toward market failure. Accumulation, as seen by Marx, is a complex process characterized by tendencies and countertendencies, but it is also one that in the long run leads to the accumulation of more and more capital in fewer and fewer hands, making it less and less effective and efficient in productive terms, until it can be stopped only by crisis, systemic breakdown, and revolution.

The extraction of surplus value from the labor of workers by the owners of the means of production—not merely making a profit, but expropriating the amount of labor that the worker produces for the capitalist over and above that which is required to produce an item—allows the capitalist to redeploy that surplus value into further profit-making activities and to buy more of the means of production, leading inevitably to cartelization, oligopoly, and monopoly. Indeed, the competitive dynamism of capitalism itself is ultimately undermined by the drive for ever-expanding accumulation for its own sake—monopolistic behavior—causing increased rent seeking, overpricing, underconsumption, growing inefficiencies, unemployment, and the long-term tendency of the rate of profit to fall. Capitalism, for Marx, thereby undermines itself, because accumulation simply begets more accumulation, generating *neither* use value *nor* exchange value. In the long run, capitalism destroys *all* value and destroys itself through a generic crisis of capitalism.

Non-Marxist theorists, especially neoliberal market theorists, by way of contrast, would argue that the core of successful capitalism is precisely *not* anticompetitive accumulation, where capital is essentially built up and hoarded for its own sake, but rather competitive market behavior. Marxists assert that competitive market behavior is just one part of the complex story of long-run market failure—undermining value and causing the long-run tendency of the rate of profit to fall—whereas in virtually all non-Marxist market theory, effective competition (whether spontaneous or induced by regulation) is the touchstone of efficient market behavior. Except for doctrinaire free marketers, markets for most theorists are not self-regulating in an ideal-type way, as I have argued in the earlier discussion of neoliberalism. Property rights, a legal system that sanctifies and enforces contracts and protects those without market power at least to some extent, antitrust laws, transparency regulations, a system of financial and commercial regulations, and the like are all required to prevent excessive rent seeking and market destabilization. Efficient and competitive market behavior is a human construction, not a structural imperative or metaphysical law. Accumulation is not the first cause, but rather the by-product, of a trial-and-error process of seeking prosperity and economic growth.

In this process, opportunistic actors are forced to be competitive if they are faced with some combination of (a) new entrants, (b) competitive market behavior by others in a "large numbers condition" where many buyers and sellers compete over price (and therefore exchange value), and (c) regulation and other extraeconomic supports. When larger markets become institutionalized and growth results, actors in other geographical settings emulate market behavior—the demonstration effect—and experiment with their own versions of extraeconomic supports and promarket regulation, creating a variety of competitive advantages and disadvantages that are increasingly locked into relations of interdependence. Under certain conditions, this interaction can be manifested in a vicious circle of conflict, oppression, exploitation, zero-sum outcomes, and the like. But when properly politically promoted, managed, and regulated, it can result in a virtuous circle of growth, positive-sum outcomes, and increased choice and welfare. In other words, I am arguing that the kinds of trends and developments that Jessop focuses on can be just as easily, and in my view more precisely, identified using non-Marxist theories that privilege sociopolitical variables, especially politically instituted market mechanisms, rather than through Marxist-style capital accumulation as such. Although Jessop's analysis is a very valuable and sophisticated contribution to the Marxist canon, its most important arguments are quite familiar outside that canon, where they are interpreted in a very different light.

3. THE SHAPE OF STRUCTURAL CHANGE

Brenner follows Jessop fairly closely in privileging the requirements of capital accumulation, although his main theoretical focus is at a rather different level, that of rescaling. Indeed, he seems to have a much broader conception of capitalism, more like a label for modernity than a paradigmatic mode of production (correspondence with the author, 2005). The contributions to the *State/Space* reader (Brenner, Jessop, Jones, and MacLeod 2003) are far more eclectic, including theoretically minded authors, such as Michael Mann, who come from a Weberian perspective, or Henri Lefebvre, who is often perceived to be the main guru of state/space theorizing—not to mention a range of more historical and empirical studies that do not fall neatly into a Marxist or non-Marxist categorization. However, although Jessop and Brenner ground their analyses in the perceived structural requirements (however coconstituted) of capitalist accumulation, this does not prevent them from deriving a range of highly insightful hypotheses about the character of state restructuring and rescaling in the context of globalization. Indeed, most of Jessop's book does not extensively address the finer theoretical points of capitalist accumulation strategies as critiqued previously, but focuses on the significance of the extraeconomic dimension of state restructuring. Like Gramsci, Poulantzas, and Offe (1984), Jessop is more concerned with distancing himself from the more economic determinist versions of Marxism than he is with arguing the case for accumulation and against market theory. He is most convincing when he is apparently least Marxist. As well as the ways the "ecological dominance" and "economic dominance" of capitalist accumulation feed into political struggles (2002: 32, table 1.2), he points to five particular caveats to the notion of the structural dominance of capital itself (2002: 34):

1. "Institutions matter."
2. Structural and institutional forms "are always constituted in and through action, always tendential and always in need of stabilization."
3. "Structural forms and institutions never wholly constrain actions."
4. Actors' strategies are not "purely products of contradictions."
5. Struggles always take place on "strategically selective terrains" that both constrain and enable actors.

However, the main direction of change in the context of globalization is still determined by the changing form of capital accumulation—not merely the transition from Fordism to post-Fordism (a central theme for both authors nonetheless) but also the shift from an economy based on industrial production to what Jessop calls a "knowledge-based economy" (KBE): "the changing forms of competitiveness associated with globalizing, knowledge-based economies lead to a major rearticulation of the economic and the extra-economic." This shift is analyzed at three levels: the changing forms of state intervention (economic policy), the changing conditions of the social reproduction of capitalism (social policy), and a "broader restructuring, rescaling and retemporalizing of market-state-society relations" through both changing scalar organization and the shift of the primary mode of statehood from government to network-based, self-organizing "governance" (2002: 36 and 53). The main theoretical focus here, however, is less on particular "macropolicies, mesopolicies and micropolicies"—although these do get their due in Jessop's more empirically supported surveys of the crisis of the KWNS and "Atlantic Fordism" and the ascendancy of its successor, the Schumpeterian competition state or Schumpeterian workfare postnational regime (SWPR) (2002: chapters 3, 4, and 7)—and more on such concepts as "metapolicies," "metasteering," and, most important, "metagovernance" (2002: chapter 6).

These metalevel concepts, however, are merely a restatement of the long-standing adage in political philosophy that the main task of the state is to provide the general conditions for the stabilization and continued existence of the endogenous society itself—what Marxists would call the conditions for social reproduction and what Oakeshott called a "civil association"

(Oakeshott 1976). The stories Jessop tells are not very different from those told by non-Marxist analysts of globalization since the 1950s. Flexibilization, the knowledge-based economy, intellectual property issues, financialization and other "abstract flows in space and concrete valorization in space," the role of "soft variables" ("audits, ... local untraded interdependencies, institutional thickness, knowledge assets, regional competencies, social capital, trust, capacities for collective learning, and local amenities and culture"), and the like are familiar themes. It is hard to see where the Marxist added value lies. Nevertheless, he argues: "As yet there is no obvious predominant post-Fordist *mode of societalization* directly analogous to the urban, industrial mass society aspiring to the American dream in Atlantic Fordism" (2002: 101, italics in original). In contrast, non-Marxist analysts increasingly point to *consumerism*. Many mainstream economic theorists argue that capitalism is, in the last analysis, consumer-driven rather than producer-driven, as it is consumers who ultimately must confer exchange value on the final product by agreeing to purchase it.

The most novel aspect of Jessop's argument, however—and one that Brenner treats at much greater length and depth—is that of state rescaling. In contrast to much looser empires, multilayered feudal orders, kinship-based village or tribal societies (especially nomadic ones), extended ethnic societies such as the centuries-old networks of overseas Chinese or Jews, or transnational religion-based political organizations like the Roman Catholic Church—with absolutist monarchies constituting a transitional category—nation-states lay claim to exclusive territorial sovereignty, that is, internal hierarchical control and citizenship, on the one hand, and external unithood or territorial integrity, combining the inviolability of territorial borders and freedom from external interference in domestic affairs, on the other. Territorial nation-states have been a crucial carrier of modernity and, of course, of the development of capitalism as a mode of production.

The heart of the issue of rescaling, then, is to ask whether this holistic, quasi-exclusive territorial dimension is an inherent, intrinsic, and indispensable feature of modern society, without which the gains associated with the modern nation-state—creating the conditions for economic growth, industrialization, welfare, and so on—are in jeopardy by definition, or whether, in Lefebvre's words, the contemporary (as opposed to the merely modern) world is characterized by a creative, innovative, potentially progressive—but also potentially destabilizing—"explosion of spaces" (Lefebvre 2003). Brenner asserts: "The postwar project of national territorial equalization and sociospatial redistribution has thus been superseded by *qualitatively new* national, regional, and local state strategies to position major urban economies optimally within global and supranational circuits of capital" (2004: 3, emphasis added).

This theme is also widely canvassed in the non-Marxist literature. Many writers have spoken of "multilevel governance," "reinventing government," and the enmeshing of the state in transnational webs of governance. But the core of Jessop's and Brenner's approaches continues to lie in capital accumulation per se—the driving force of both national "statehood" in earlier eras and the transformations involved with globalization in the present day. It is the adoption of particular *accumulation strategies* that determines the direction of structural development and institutional change in an interactive process.

Brenner situates state rescaling in a broad overall perspective, including wider debates on globalization, multilevel governance, and the like. He argues that his focus is not on rescaling the state as such, but at identifying more abstract, statelike structural forms and processes that he refers to as "statehood." Globalization for Brenner is not about the crystallization of a particular global-level space as fixed and/or pregiven within a unilinear Parsonian process of structural differentiation—thus his critique of Roland Robertson's work (2004: 49)—nor about a neat crystallization of "nested" scales (although he is rather more ambivalent about this conceptualization; 2004: 8–9). Rather, it is "the aggregate consequence of a variety of interrelated tendencies" (2004: 31) involving *temporarily stabilized "scalar fixes"* that are "successively secured, destabilized, junked and remade." These are the result of an ongoing tension between "strategies of dispersion" and "strategies of concentration," with no single privileged scale, characterized by uneven development, negative externalities, coordination problems, and legitimation deficits, involving the "polarizing, disrupting, and politically volatile effects of uneven geographical development at any spatial scale" (2004: 10–17).

Actors are therefore continually and increasingly faced with the challenges of "reterritorialization" and the "production of space" (Harvey 1989), wherein "each sociospatial configuration is merely temporary, a chronically unstable 'dynamic equilibrium' within a chaotic see-saw of perpetual sociospatial change." A crucial part of this process is the "creative destruction of sociospatial configurations" (2004: 31–34). "Jumping scales," the continual "reinvention of space," and a dialectical process of deterritorialization and reterritorialization are ongoing (2004: 54–60). Brenner's analysis, however, is in fact not as chaotic or messy as it would seem from these quotations. He sees the search for a sociospatial fix as a necessary structural imperative of capitalism itself. For Brenner, *capitalism is thus not spaceless, but indeed fundamentally depends on* spatial fixes. At the same time, state policies have "indirect spatial effects," whether or not they explicitly address the spatial dimension (2004: 54). Similarly, old state layers persist, new layers may have unintended consequences, and so forth, feeding into an ongoing process of *contestation over space* (2004: 110). In the last analysis, however, this process does not represent either geographical or political determinism, but the requirements of capital accumulation; "it is no longer capital that is to be molded into the (territorially integrated) geography of state space [as was the case with the 'modern' nation-state and, especially, Atlantic Fordism and 'spatial Keynesianism'], but state space that is to be molded into the (territorially differentiated) geography of capital" (2004: 16).

The key imperative that shapes various actors' conflicting accumulation strategies is competitiveness, and for Brenner the conditions for competitiveness in contemporary capitalism are increasingly determined by international, transnational, and translocal imperatives. In recent decades, therefore, the main ostensible scalar winners, however temporarily, in this search for a new spatiotemporal fix are urban regions. These possess a range of uniquely appropriate and significant structural competitive advantages with regard to coordinating strategies of dispersion and strategies of concentration (2004: chapter 5; for a fuller outline of relevant strategic options, see pp. 214–219). "[M]etropolitan city cores…[are] being delinked from their immediate hinterlands and connected instead to a transnational inter-urban network," characterized as an "archipelago" structure. Furthermore, the restructuring of such urban regions provides a range of political mechanisms for pursuing structural competitiveness strategies.

Whereas in the Keynesian Fordist era, urban and regional policy, especially of the social democratic type, sought to equalize conditions among cities and regions in order to reduce social inequalities and integrate their inhabitants and local economies into the nation-state, today urban policy revolves around the search for differences and the *exploitation of those differences* for the maximization of competitive advantages globally. These competitive advantages are not merely economic, however, despite the fact that urban regions are crucial for state policy makers for such objectives as supporting provision of the skills of "symbolic analysts" in the KBE or favoring "mobile factors of capital" (against immobile factors) in order to maximize value added (Reich 1991). Urban regions are also the main loci of the coming together of political actors with an interest in prioritizing rescaling to the urban regional level. This process involves "preservationist alliances," coalitions around "fire-brigade crash programmes," managing deindustrialization while removing barriers to investment elsewhere, fiscal restructuring, "diverse restructuring oriented political alliances," appealing to new suburban classes of voters and interest groups, new social democratic forms of localized welfare provision in the face of the hollowing out of the national welfare state, "cross-class, sectoral and place-based alliances," and attempts at radical reform.

This is not necessarily a progressive development, however. Social democratic forms of urban governance will inevitably conflict with some of the requirements of competitiveness, especially cost containment. Deregulation or promarket reregulation may also create relative disincentives for business location. High inequalities within urban regions can exacerbate tensions where welfare and/or fiscal austerity is required, especially where local antitax alliances are strong. The delegation of decision making to a range of government agencies and appointed bodies often leads to "quangoization" at local level, that is, the institutionalized hegemony of special interest groups, undermining democratic accountability. Private competition and public-private partnerships may not lead to fiscal savings but to growing inefficiency and waste if not strongly regulated—again, a potential disincentive to investment. There is an inevitable tendency toward short-termism, as competitive advantages secured by first movers are often rapidly eroded by other urban regions copycatting or improving on their own competitive advantages. "Global enclavization" may occur, wherein a locked-in focus on endogenous competitive advantages may actually make it more difficult to adapt to evolving exogenous conditions.

Limited spillover effects, especially where national policies spread public funds ever more thinly among diverse local initiatives, may lead to macroeconomic instability and divisive political conflicts. A regulatory race to the bottom may ensue, making change a lose-lose situation for all. Uneven development can strengthen the strong but weaken the weak. Interscalar coordination problems may lead to zero-sum competition with other urban regions, even within the same nation-state. And the potentially dysfunctional side effects of all of these can further exacerbate democratic accountability and legitimation problems, creating new zero-sum political conflicts (2004: 242–248 and 262–266). "Metropolitan institutional reforms may enhance intergovernmental synergies, policy coordination and metagovernance capacities within individual urban regions" in the broader context of state rescaling, but "intense struggles between opposed class fractions, political coalitions and territorial alliances regarding issues such as jurisdictional boundaries, institutional capacities, democratic accountability, fiscal relays and intergovernmental linkages" may also result. These parallel the potential flaw in the core strategy of "reinventing government"—what Osborne and Gaebler (1992) called "getting more for less."

4. WHITHER THE RESCALING OF THE STATE? SOME ALTERNATIVE CONSIDERATIONS

The rescaling of the state, therefore, for both Jessop and Brenner, derives from changing conditions of economic competitiveness in a globalizing world. The competition state for Jessop and Brenner is not merely a state that shifts its economic policies toward promoting competitiveness, nor is it one that simply attempts to build the goal of competitiveness into processes of social reproduction (for example, through "workfare"), but rather one that transforms the morphology of its very self-organization in response to the interplay of various actors' accumulation strategies. Jessop's focus is, of course, on the wider theoretical implications of rescaling, while Brenner, in addition to considering the theoretical aspects of changing forms of urban governance at much greater length, also surveys a range of case studies of the restructuring of urban governance in Europe (2004: chapter 5). This is all fine as far as it goes, but I have some reservations.

On the empirical side, both authors focus almost entirely on developed industrial states, particularly Western Europe. One wonders how much state rescaling is actually taking place in developing countries, and whether it is in response to the same sorts of variables; indeed, states in the developing world do not seem to be devolving or rescaling, but are often still attempting to centralize further in the face of centrifugal forces and threats of violent conflict and potential state collapse. The situation is thus far messier and more politically complex in parts of the world where the nation-state has always itself been a more problematic project in the making, and where the requirements of competitiveness are far more demanding. Furthermore, the emergence and consolidation of the urban state space—with the exception of world cities and the archipelago relations among them—often constitute an ad hoc and uneven process. Just how far these can be identified as comparable, converging, and—to repeat Brenner's crucial phrase—constituting a "qualitatively new" spatiotemporal fix is murky at best outside the core territories surveyed, as well as inside those regions. More important, perhaps, if capital accumulation ultimately derives its capacity to determine structural outcomes from the ability of capitalists to extract surplus value from workers through the commodification of the fictitious commodity of labor-power in the process of production, and if markets do not create value but merely redistribute it, then the theoretical explanations provided by Jessop and Brenner—however much they may be an advance on earlier, more economic deterministic forms of Marxist theory because of their increased focus on extraeconomic support mechanisms—seem to be stretched beyond breaking point.

The core of this new neo-Marxist analytical school consequently lies in the assertion that the transition from Fordist to post-Fordist forms of production and to the knowledge-based economy is the main driving force in the transformation of the state, state rescaling, and the crystallization of new forms of statehood. However, three different sorts of alternative theoretical claims could equally be made. The first is that the transition to post-Fordism and the KBE is *itself a dependent variable*, derived from the expansion of markets (not necessarily of production, but including production as well as, for example, financial markets) to a transnational and global scale, that is, globalization. The ability to trade globally and, later, the ability to move financial capital around the world more freely, provided tremendous incentives for producers to reorient their competitive strategies. Post-Fordism is today more viable than the national industrialization and national development processes that dominated the period from the late nineteenth to the mid-twentieth century. Such market expansion has also required geometrically more extensive knowledge and information simply to generate effective market signals—the basis for calculating exchange value and developing an efficient price mechanism.

The second sort of claim is that these changes did not result spontaneously from processes of production but from *political* decisions—the construction of the Bretton Woods system in particular (Helleiner 1994). Embedded liberalism was originally a Fordist project that turned into a post-Fordist one because of the expansion of the scale of markets, especially financial markets. This process of market expansion did not take place by itself, but was the result of a now well-researched political process of trade and financial market opening. The extraeconomic supports for increased marketization can be seen to have preceded and generated the process of value creation itself, in ways analogous to the political creation of private property rights at the beginning of the capitalist era. One feature of this transformation is the transfer of certain labor-intensive production processes from the first world to developing areas, but that, it could be argued, is but one subsidiary dimension. In this context, it is not clear what added value a Marxist approach brings to the issue of state restructuring and rescaling.

A third sort of alternative theoretical claim brings into question the authors' assertion that capitalism in general *requires* a spatiotemporal fix of whatever sort for it to be stable and efficient. Institutional economics has long held that there are certain kinds of goods and assets that are specific and others that are nonspecific (Williamson 1985), that is, some that are limited to specific uses and others that are more fungible, substitutable, tradable, and marketable. High on the list of specific assets are those characterized by "economies of agglomeration" or location, those that require being located in specific, fixed geographical circumscriptions to be efficiently exploited. Fordism is a system characterized by high levels of economies of agglomeration; Fordism requires a clear spatiotemporal fix, and the organizational scale and scope of the nation-state—the product of secular political developmental processes that long preceded the emergence of Fordism—provided a reasonable (if problematic, nonetheless) fit.

But does a world characterized by an increasing proportion of nonspecific assets, especially those associated with financialization, global market scales, virtual economies and information and communications technologies (ICTs), mobile firms, flexible small businesses, and craft synergies, require a particular spatiotemporal fix as such? Rescaling the state is primarily a political trial-and-error process—an attempt to see "what works," as the saying goes. What is in question here is not whether globalizing capitalism requires a specific—if fluid and ever-changing—spatiotemporal fix, but indeed whether the changing balance in a wider world market economy toward a higher proportion of nonspecific assets and mobile factors of capital is increasingly relegating the need for a spatiotemporal fix per se to secondary status. Perhaps what we are seeing is not merely a reinvention of geography but rather a demotion of the relative importance of geography itself—although not, of course, "the end of geography" (O'Brien 1992).

In this context, it might be preferable simply to downgrade the structural imperative of Marxist-style capital accumulation and its relationship with spatiotemporal fixes in general, and to upgrade the other variables Jessop and Brenner continually discuss but insufficiently privilege in theoretical terms. These involve the real activities of social, economic, and political actors engaged in a neopluralist political process, not so much of state restructuring and rescaling per se, but increasingly operating simultaneously on multiple political playing fields or, in other words, transnational neopluralism and multinodal politics. As these actors reshape economic intervention and regulation, attempt to provide the general conditions for social reproduction or civil association in a globalizing world, and experiment with restructuring and rescaling administrative, political, and territorial structures across borders, capitalists and capitalism will adjust to those preconditions. The coconstitution of state restructuring owes more to political projects that reshape market scale and market structure—altering the conditions for the creation of value and even creating value from market processes themselves—than to the extraction of surplus value from the commodification of labor-power in the process of production.

5. CONCLUSION: NEOPLURALISM AND THE EROSION OF SPATIOTEMPORAL FIXES

Jessop, Brenner, and the spatial-capitalism school in general provide a fascinating and challenging analysis of the restructuring and rescaling of the state or statehood, and in terms of Marxist analysis, their work is cutting-edge. The critique developed here is not intended to detract from these achievements. Nevertheless, it seems to me that at one key level, a Marxist analysis is redundant. The processes and outcomes surveyed by Jessop and Brenner can be as easily, and perhaps better, explained by other approaches.

The search for a new spatiotemporal fix for capitalism, if it is such, is a more complex and politically driven process than even Jessop and Brenner can depict. Will hierarchies become ever more tangled, to use their term, or will a new spatiotemporal fix emerge analogous to, but fundamentally different in scalar terms from, the nation-state in the Fordist era? Just how important is urban governance as a particular manifestation of the rescaling of state-hood? Will it become institutionally and territorially hegemonic, or is it just one of a number of competing possibilities? How important is territory any-way in an age of globalization, marketization, financialization, virtual econ-omies, networks, "spaces of flows" (Castells 1996), and the like?

My view is that there is a world order emerging of competing institu-tions, overlapping jurisdictions, multiple identities, territorial flux, and the reduced capacities of states to provide order and security—linked and cross-cut by transnational neopluralist political processes and the governmental-ity of *raison du monde*. In the last analysis (to echo Poulantzas), the outcome will be determined not by the structural imperatives of capital accumulation rooted in the expropriation of the surplus value produced by the fictitious commodity of labor-power—however coconstituted and realized through extraeconomic supports and class-type exploitation. It will be the product of old-fashioned, more structurally open and politically fluid processes of con-flict, competition, and coalition building carried on by a range of relevant actors seeking to create and capture the benefits of globalization for some combination of self-interest, on the one hand, and notions of the public good, on the other, through unevenly pluralized political processes expand-ing on various global, international, transnational, and translocal scales. But the future shape of those mixed processes is still far from clear and will depend on political conflicts yet to be fought, coalitions yet to be built, and choices yet to be formulated, much less made. Globalization is what actors make of it, and that goes for capitalism, too.

Chapter 14

Conclusion

Globalization Is What Actors Make of It

1. CONSTRUCTING A NEW WORLD ORDER?

Karl Marx wrote in *The Eighteenth Brumaire of Louis Bonaparte*: "Men make their own history, but they do not make it as they please; they do not make it under self-selected circumstances, but under circumstances existing already, given and transmitted from the past." However, those circumstances, I argue, permit a far wider range of history-making choices than the quotation might suggest. From a structurational perspective, they do not consist of straightforward, predetermined pathways, but sets of complex multilevel and multinodal constraints and opportunities—including realistic opportunities to significantly alter and transform those circumstances themselves in permissive conditions, in pursuit of credible goals, using smart strategies and tactics, and informed by *raison du monde*. Therefore, I have tried in this book to set out a range of situations where actors can not only navigate within a pregiven set of alternatives but also actually shape those alternatives to a greater or lesser degree (see also Cerny 1990a: especially chapter 1). The theory of transnational neopluralism derives from and depends on the hypothesis that a fairly diverse range of key actors, in the process of competing, politicking, and coalition building, are able to make significant choices that—in the context of an ongoing, evolving process of change, and in the presence of potential multiple equilibria—may make it possible to effectively bring about fundamental structural change in world politics. Indeed, they may be doing so already—whether they know it or not.

Thus the main problematic of this approach is to identify and describe what kind of choices actors *might* actually be able to make in complex, changing circumstances that in turn could have the potential to shape future processes of change in world politics and to determine under what conditions they may be likely to make and implement those choices effectively. On the one hand, the development of a range of transnational opportunity structures, for example, provides vital, if unevenly malleable, structural spaces for key actors to act in potentially transformational ways in shaping processes such as globalization. On the other hand, in an environment characterized by multiple equilibria, those spaces merely constitute necessary but not sufficient conditions for future structural change. Action—human agency—is the crucial independent variable.

The particular shape a transformed world politics might take will be determined primarily by which sets of actors are best placed to most effectively exploit the manifest and latent structural resources or political opportunity structures available to them in a period of flux, how those actors perceive the possibilities for their actions to lead to transformational outcomes, and how they perform their strategic and tactical roles in practice— all in a context where they are competing with other groups over values and resources. A key variable in explaining actor-led change is thus the presence of strategically situated actors in flawed and/or fluid structural circumstances. These circumstances must be mediated through the goals and strategies adopted in such circumstances, along with elements like strength of preferences, determination, self-control, strength of character, and the like. Actors' structural location, along with their perceptions of the possible and their actual decisions about what actions to take, will in turn set their goals and shape their practices and actions. However, where what is perceived to be a highly constraining organizational or behavioral pattern has been deeply embedded over a long period of time, most actors, even strategically situated ones, are likely to take that pattern for granted and work within it, rather than trying to change it. There is thus a strong tendency toward inertia and adaptive behavior built into most social structures most of the time. Nevertheless, there are two main ways in which strategically situated actors are more likely to effect change.

On the one hand, they *believe* (as in constructivist analyses) that the combination of their preferences and objectives, along with a perceptive understanding of the fault lines and gaps in the existing structure, can bring about change. Therefore, they systematically and consciously act in a strategically rational fashion to pursue their preferred structural outcomes, manipulating structural constraints and opportunities effectively in the process. On the other hand, they simply interact with others on a relatively spontaneous, day-to-day basis in such a way that the pursuit of their self-interested and/or value-driven preferences puts strain on the structure itself in contingent fashion, leading to unanticipated or even unintended consequences. This strain or pressure can further open up existing gaps and in turn create new de facto opportunities for forms of innovative coalition building and power seeking that alter existing resource distributions and ultimately lead indirectly to structurally significant changes in fundamental, system-sustaining rules and/or resource distributions. In other words, actors can be prompted to act in system-altering fashion not only because of their conscious intention to act that way but also because they are faced with challenges that various features of the embedded system cannot cope with. Judging the state of that balance of possibilities is a risky business, both intellectually and practically. But in either case, the durability, the fungibility, and ultimately the evolving morphology of the system are, in the last analysis, the product of actors' actions and not directly the product of purely material or metaphysical structural preconditions per se. The fact that we live on a particular planet in an evolving material universe is one thing; how we organize the way we live on that planet is another. That is at the core of human consciousness itself.

Within this context, for example, key sets of actors who in the past have been closely bound up with the territorial nation-state may increasingly experiment with new forms of transnationalization of their activities—an issue touched on frequently in earlier chapters. For example, businesses and business pressure groups are more and more divided between those seeking old-fashioned government protection, but whose economic base is often declining, and those more active in transnational markets, generally seeking deregulation and liberalization—although this equation is complicated by the current financial crisis and recession. Furthermore, the securitization and transnational integration of financial markets have undermined traditional state-bank-industry relationships of finance capital, despite current (temporary) bailouts. Labor movements, which were such a crucial element in the consolidation of the welfare state, although their positions are being eroded from both above and below as their relationships with state actors and agencies are becoming increasingly ineffectual in achieving their collective demands, are nevertheless starting to adapt to change in ways that may well involve reinventing themselves transnationally and taking more entrepreneurial stances (Cerny 2002).

State actors, too, once said to be "captured" by large, well-organized domestic constituencies, are increasingly at least partly captured instead by transnationally linked sectors. The latter paradoxically both set state agencies against each other in the desire to level the playing field for their domestic clients in the wider world—a process called "regulatory arbitrage"—and yet at the same time promote the development of transgovernmental networks and convergence. And social movements and value groups are increasingly oriented toward transnational or global problems such as climate change, poverty reduction, global inequality, human rights, the prevention of violence, and genocide.

Although specific changes may take place in these circumstances, whether change overall is fundamental and far-reaching enough to constitute genuinely transformational change will ultimately depend on the *balance of forces between those sets of actors whose actions continue to reinforce existing structural forms and practices and those whose actions generate and rein-force new forms and practices.* Fundamental systemic transformation, there-fore, depends on the way potentially transformative actors actually act in practice, organize their operations, especially across borders, and compete with groups that represent either the status quo or domestic backlashes and special interests. There is a new balance of power emerging in world poli-tics, but it is not a balance of power among states. It is a transnational bal-ance of power among groups—sectional interest groups, value groups and social movements, and transgovernmental networks of state actors—pursu-ing their objectives across unevenly globalizing playing fields. Therefore, those groups that can network, coordinate, and organize their action across borders possess significant advantages in shaping and even potentially transforming that balance of power.

At the same time, however, although potentially transformative groups might be expected to act in ways that challenge existing structural forms and practices, they may also, for various reasons—including cultural and ideo-logical reasons, as well as calculations of short-term gains—not be able, or even *not choose*, to act in such ways. In the first place, existing structures may be characterized by what in chapter 5 was called "tight structural coher-ence" (table 5.1). In such cases, transformational behavior may be especially difficult to conceive, operationalize, and steer. In traditional realist interna-tional relations theory, especially in its neorealist version, the states system constitutes such a structural context. However, this book has argued that this is no longer the case in the twenty-first century. Furthermore, adaptive behavior, consciously or unconsciously attempting to maintain the essen-tials of the status quo, may in the end be the *preferred* course of action, even for many strategically situated actors, if the status quo is perceived to be potentially more effective in pursuing their goals. Finally, those alternative structural forms—the potential but contingent outcomes (multiple equilib-ria) that may in theory be possible—may prove either too ambitious, on the one hand, or too amorphous and fragmented, on the other, to form an effec-tive foundation for those actors' strategic or tactical calculations and for building effective coalitions for change. Thus alternative equilibria may also be too flawed and/or fluid to be a ground for effective action. The continu-ous interaction of choice and context is highly contingent.

In attempting to interpret the longer range implications of this situation today, I will expand on my three stylized sets of actors—economic, political, and social—and attempt to generate some broad hypotheses about when and under what circumstances each set is likely to act as transformative agents or institutional entrepreneurs, when as adaptive or routine agents, and whether—and how—the interaction between the two modes of action is likely to lead, directly or indirectly, to transformational outcomes.

2. ECONOMIC ACTORS: WORKERS, MANAGERS, FINANCIERS

Because globalization is most often seen as primarily an economic process, most of the literature on globalization asserts that the key category of actors in terms of developing transnational linkages that have structurally transformational potential are economic actors. The modern division of the international economy into relatively or partially insulated national economies is widely seen to be flawed, although the opposite notion of a "borderless" or "flat" world has been widely debunked too (Aronica and Ramdoo 2006; Florida 2005). In this context, economic actors are identified as potentially the main drivers of change, although there is a hierarchy of mainly sectional groups, with some having more autonomous influence and being more caught up in transnational developments than others.

Of the main groups of economic actors, the least likely to take on the role of institutional entrepreneur thus far is the labor movement. The labor movement could grow and succeed in the twentieth century only because of the permissive conditions embodied in the consolidation of the nation-state as the hegemonic structural arena of both political and economic action. This arena was structurally suited to the large-scale mass politics of the Second Industrial Revolution and created the conditions for a de facto alliance between trade unions, national-reformist or social democratic political parties, and national capital. Today, given the increasing significance of flexible manufacturing processes for large firms and the growing resort to flexible contracting and subcontracting among both large and small firms, including transnational strategic alliances, as well as other management practices, the potential collective power of labor has been greatly diminished. Nevertheless, the possibility of labor movements shifting their focus from collective industrial action of a Second Industrial Revolution type to more widespread (if more fragmented) forms of social action in alliance with transnational social movements may provide more potential for labor to participate in a transformative fashion in transnational structural change (Macdonald 2008; Evans 2007). Furthermore, labor movements cut across the categories of economic actors and social actors (as discussed later), increasing their potential clout if they can get their transnational act together.

Another set of strategically situated economic actors includes owners and managers of multinational corporations. Whether at a localized, regionalized, or genuinely transnational level, for example, owners and managers of high-technology firms large and small are often seen as taking on a collectively transformative role—but only the major executives of the larger firms, such as Bill Gates of Microsoft, are seen as credible potential institutional entrepreneurs. Nevertheless, such actors are generally still dependent on states and the states system for providing basic public goods, enforcing property rights, and similar matters. In other words, the capacity of even the most cutting-edge multinational corporations, widely seen as the main carriers of transnational capitalism since the 1970s, to live up to their structural potential is probably fairly limited at a strategic level. These limits are reinforced by "enduring national differences" in corporate organizational forms (Pauly and Reich 1997) and "state-societal arrangements" (Hart 1992). Of course, economic actors are nevertheless being drawn into transnational opportunity structures in extensive, if tactical, ways on an ever-increasing scale. One of those ways involves the increasing participation of both large and small firms in transnational financial markets, which could well give leading-edge firms in high-tech fields a strong competitive advantage in those markets themselves. Recent moves by U.S. financial regulators, especially the Federal Deposit Insurance Corporation, to facilitate acquisitions of troubled banks by private equity firms provide another example of potential developments along these lines (*Financial Times*, 13 June 2009).

Therefore, probably the main group of economic actors most often seen as having the potential to become institutional entrepreneurs on a wider scale are participants in global financial markets. Their (mainly indirect) ability to constrain macroeconomic and microeconomic policy and their close links with certain government agencies that play an enforcement role, such as central banks (Pauly 1997; Maxfield 1997), mean that the immediate transnational impact of their actions is evident both to them and to other groups, including mass publics. Indeed, recent turmoil on various financial markets, from Asia in 1997 to the financial crisis in the United States eleven years later, not to mention the destabilizing impact this is having not only on developed countries but also on the ability of middle-income developing countries to expand their role and influence in international markets and for poor countries to get up off the floor, has highlighted both the centrality and the limitations of international finance. In terms of economic actors, then, despite their central and widespread interaction with the latent and manifest transnational opportunity structures existing in both political and economic terms, it is unlikely that the more powerful among them will seek to promote a fundamental shift in the broader transnational structuration process. As neo-Marxist commentators argued in the 1970s, their concerns are essentially microeconomic or at most mesoeconomic; that is, they are concerned with the profitability and stability of their particular firms and sectors, not with the health of the world economy—or world politics—as a whole. Nevertheless, they may inadvertently drive *other* actors to attempt to effect more far-reaching structural change to counteract the perceived negative political, economic, and social consequences of economic transnationalization.

This is particularly critical at the time I am writing, as various political and institutional responses to the current financial crisis and recession take center stage. To be successful, such broader strategic action, until recently blocked for the most part at the domestic level, will need to be played out on the international and transnational fields, as well as through national-level bailouts and stimulus packages. Economic actors themselves, however, are most likely to continue adaptive forms of behavior in structurational terms, such as promoting a dialectic of regulatory competition and cooperation in the financial market sector and supporting the continuing reduction of trade barriers and the consolidation of international regimes such as the World Trade Organization and fora like the G7, rather than taking the lead as institutional entrepreneurs in a transnationalizing world. Even financial market actors, especially investment bankers, are increasingly dependent on national governments for bailouts, recapitalization, and economic stimulus packages to promote recovery not only for national economies but also for the global economy. This process is paradoxically reinforcing the perception that markets are increasingly tightly coupled transnationally and globally, and that in the medium term, policy responses must at least lead to convergence of national policies—and perhaps even to the kind of global regulation called for by British Prime Minister Gordon Brown and, in a rather different form, by French President Nicolas Sarkozy.

The main direct influence of economic transnationalization in terms of agent behavior will nevertheless be felt in two ways. First, we can identify the spread of an ideology of market globalization through the mass media, the teaching of management in business schools, popular business literature (the "airport bookshop" approach to globalization), and the like. Policy proposals around themes such as global financial regulation, in particular, are increasingly reinforcing this ideational trend in the current context of financial and economic crisis. Second, economic transnationalization has had a wide-ranging indirect impact on *other* categories of agent. This is obvious in the case of political actors as they attempt to reconfigure forms of political authority to meet the challenge of transnationally rooted market failures and the demands of popular constituencies for the reassertion of political values such as the public interest in the face of the economic, social, and indirect political power of economic actors.

3. POLITICAL ACTORS: POLITICIANS AND BUREAUCRATS

In this context, pressures on political actors, mainly state actors, to act as transnationalizing institutional entrepreneurs are likely to grow. Nevertheless, their actual capacity to act is more problematic—likely to increase in some ways and decline in others. Such patterns of opportunity and constraint are distinct in several ways from the patterns described for economic actors, however. In the first place, politicians and bureaucrats are to a great extent *expected* to act as institutional entrepreneurs in the modern world, their very raison d'être—a role they previously attempted to fulfill in the world of the nation-state and states system. Their authority and legitimacy depend on their role as upholders—and, to some extent, designers—of constitutions and institutional systems, as well as their capacity to use "non-economic coercion" (Holloway and Picciotto 1978; Jessop 2002) to protect and further the national interest. Political actors are expected to combine carrots and sticks in the pursuit of, ideally, collective goals (or at least the goals of dominant groups), to blend voice and loyalty (in different combinations), while minimizing threats of exit or free riding. At the same time, that very authority and legitimacy are inextricably intertwined with the multifunctionality of their authority—that is, their capacity to act simultaneously on several different levels *within* the state, as well as to engage in Janus-like two-level games linking inside and outside. However, that multifunctionality was generally only made possible through the institutional structure of the state itself.

The capacity of state actors to act as institutional entrepreneurs is therefore extremely uneven. At one level, of course, they can engage in institutional bricolage. Most of the time, however, such actors are relatively bound by existing structural constraints, especially given the embeddedness of state institutions, which remain the main sources of legitimate political power despite trends of disaggregation and transnational policy innovation. At the same time, however, they suffer from a growing disillusionment with governments, politicians, and bureaucrats generally. Traditional domestic pressure and interest groups, especially sectional pressure groups, are perceived less and less as parts of a positive-sum, pluralistic process of negotiating satisfactory compromises within the national political arena, and more and more as special interests, acting against the public interest, or free riding on the collective actions of others.

With the splintering or disaggregation of the state, the crystallization of more complex transnational opportunity structures, and the development of transgovernmental networks, primarily domestically oriented interest and pressure groups are increasingly out of the loop, condemned to pursue politically problematic goals such as protectionism, and open to marginalization as obsolete representatives of the old left or the populist right. Transnationally linked interest groups, by contrast, are better able to use their influence at a number of different domestic and transnational levels at the same time, even playing state actors off against each other in their desire to level the playing field in a politically as well as economically competitive world. It is at this level where political actors can play a key entrepreneurial role by acting as intermediaries between (a) transnational pressures and interests and domestic pressures and interest, (b) a complex transnational public sector and transnational private sector, and (c) producer groups and social movements. A more limited "power triad" of this type has been identified as the core of contemporary neopluralist political processes in the United States (McFarland 2004: 48 and later), and its extrapolation to the transnational arena creates the potential for new and complex cross-border, three-level-game patterns, including what in chapter 6 I called "flexible pentangles."

However, with political actors no longer having the capacity to systematically privilege the domestic over the transnational, the new political consensus that enables them to become institutional entrepreneurs is one that identifies international competitiveness and other broader goals as the main criterion for policy success. Therefore, in terms of both discourse and coalition behavior, this state of affairs privileges those actors who are systematically linked to other transnationally connected actors, who are able to mobilize resources across borders, and who have consciously or subconsciously internalized *raison du monde* as an explicit or implicit framework of governmental rationality and action. Political actors, especially state actors, by identifying international competitiveness and *raison du monde*–type governmentality as the chief totem of political discourse and intuitive action, put themselves in a position where they may require of themselves—and evoke expectations in others, whether businesspeople or mass publics, domestic or foreign—that they must attack not only domestic protectionism but also the state-enforced decommodification of socially deleterious economic activities and practices in the name of leveling the international playing field—and, indeed, that they must provide domestic economic actors with greater competitive advantages in a more open world.

However, it is not at this obvious level but in the day-to-day transformation of state intervention by politicians and bureaucrats in their interaction with transnationalizing pressures and interests that the state itself becomes a major collective agent in the structuration process, in turn creating, through ongoing bricolage, a complex new set of transnational opportunity structures. Paradoxically, political actors are potentially among the main institutional entrepreneurs of the transnationalization process, simply because they must attempt to manage key developments in that process through participating in and attempting to manipulate transgovernmental networks and transnational policy communities—in other words, as the key practitioners of new forms of governmentality. Nevertheless, at the same time, the capacity of political actors to act is still inextricably intertwined with the maintenance of state institutions and national discourses. Political actors are not about to try to deconstruct the state itself and design overtly transnational constitutional processes to replace it.

On the one hand, the very organizational strength and embeddedness of state institutions and political processes inhibit the development of effective, autonomous institutions and processes via international regimes, global governance, international financial architectures, and the like. On the other hand, in paradoxical fashion, the overall weight of state interventionism in general tends to *increase*—often significantly—as states undertake enforcement functions on behalf of (especially) transnationally linked economic actors, functions that transnational institutions are structurally incapable of undertaking or politically unwilling to undertake. The state may be becoming the main terrain of political conflict and coalition building between forces favoring globalization and those seeking to resist it, but political actors will not be willing to undermine the state itself as the central institutionalized political arena and thereby undermine the most significant single source of their own power. This fact is powerfully underpinned by the traditional role of the democratic state, wherein political actors have to be seen to be acting first and foremost on behalf of their domestic constituents if their actions are to be perceived as legitimate. When governmental leaders go home from major international conferences like the G20, they are immediately faced with such domestic pressures, making the transnationalization of policy something that often has to be pursued surreptitiously and legitimated indirectly—or depoliticized— especially when the light of crisis or disruptive change is shone on particular domestic sectors and interests. Thus although the state may be dramatically altered through a wide range of *adaptive* behaviors on the part of political actors, it will not itself be fundamentally left behind.

4. SOCIAL ACTORS: SOCIAL MOVEMENTS, INTEREST GROUPS, ORDINARY PEOPLE

Social actors are in a complex but potentially crucial position with regard to their capacity to reinforce and generate transnational structural change. The depth of politically imposed national identities in the developed world enabled nation-states and the states system during most of the twentieth century to spawn two world wars and the cold war, as well as to dominate processes of political development in the postcolonial era. Nevertheless, especially in the last two decades of the century, increasing tensions over the distribution of economic and political goods and a proliferating set of demands by diverse social actors cutting across both global and domestic arenas throughout the world have fueled endemic dissatisfaction with existing institutions and processes of governance. Uncertain and destabilizing processes of democratic transition, globalization, and the rapid formation of new collective identities have created tremendous social, as well as political, volatility and inspired popular pressure both for new kinds of control and accountability and for specific policy remedies. As with the other two categories of actors discussed earlier, there are three aspects to consider: the population of agents, the changing structured action field in which they operate, and the potential for their action to direct or shape structural change.

In the first place, there is emerging a new range of pressures from below. The proliferation of social actors on the international and transnational levels has been widely noted. The numbers and activities of such groups have grown in range, scale, and scope. Some are more like traditional pressure or interest groups (Willetts 1982), adjusting the scale of their organization to conform to the scale of problems facing particular categories of people in a global setting. Probably the least represented at this level have been what the traditional pressure group literature called "sectional groups." However, more emphasis is placed today on the recent growth of what the traditional group literature called "cause groups" (Key 1953) or "value groups" or what at the global level are now called "transnational advocacy coalitions [or networks]" (Keck and Sikkink 1998). They include social movements in issue-areas like environmental activism, women's rights, population policy, socioeconomic development, and even military policy, as in, for example, the campaign for an international treaty banning the use of land mines. Such advocacy groups do not merely mimic domestic cause groups for three reasons.

In the first place, they specifically and intentionally target issues that are international and/or transnational in scope. In particular, they pursue objectives that either are not being responded to or *cannot* be effectively responded to at a national level because of the structural linkages among different levels and spaces (both territorial and virtual) *and* the constraints of domestic politics. Another reason is that they can bring together and coordinate the actions of a range of coalition partners who would not normally be prepared to work closely with each other in a national setting for a variety of structural and historical reasons. For example, rainforest campaigns in Latin America can bring together displaced workers and peasants, women, quasi-elite groups concerned with environmental degradation per se, and indigenous groups and organizations concerned with third world economic development—and that is just *within* the developing state or states involved in the action. Furthermore, each of these indigenous groups will have links with external, often first world–based organizations (nongovernmental organizations or NGOs) concerned with directing campaigns in the international and national media in the developed world, not to mention links with other kinds of elite and mass networks, including various scientists and experts ("epistemic communities"), in developed countries.

These broad (but shifting) coalitions usually either have established relationships, through transnational policy networks and policy communities, with international (intergovernmental) regimes and with state actors in particular agencies in the richer countries, too, or else they are in the process of developing those links through new activities. Finally, the Internet and other new communications and information technologies give these coalitions great reach and flexibility in the ways they can target different actors in states, international institutions, academics, the media, and the like. In this sense, the narrower pressure group model overlaps more and more with the NGO model, which in turn overlaps considerably with broader egalitarian New Social Movements (NSMs; Murphy 1998), creating a potential virtuous circle of action. Of course, the very diversity of such a process also can lead to overcomplexity and uncertainty. There is always a potential for quasi-neomedieval disorder and vicious spiraling, too. Therefore, how those actors operate in practice and how they are able to develop coordinated goals, strategies, and tactics are crucial to their capacity to act as transformative agents.

Second, these groups of social actors also benefit from the changing structured field of action, or the crystallization of Krieger and Murphy's "transnational opportunity structure" (TOS; 1998). The TOS refers to what in the traditional public policy and pressure group literature were called "points of access"—that is, structural openings in political and bureaucratic institutions where pressure groups can exert influence on particular interlocutors within the state apparatus, whether individual state actors and specific agencies or iron triangles and policy networks. Whereas the traditional group and social movement literature has focused on the more embedded institutional points of access of the state, commentators on NSMs and NGOs are increasingly pointing to broader opportunities at the international and transnational levels.

These points of access include:

- international regimes, particularly the United Nations, which has always been open to such groups in both formal and informal ways (Willetts 1982)
- particular state agencies with jurisdictional scope in the very issue-areas these coalitions (environmental agencies, etc.) focus on
- wider epistemic communities of experts, think tanks, scientists, and the like
- the proliferation of new fora such as UN-sponsored conferences on social development, population, human settlements, women's health, climate change, and the like (Betsill 1999; Clark, Friedman, and Hochstetler 1999; Dodgson 1999)
- private organizations in other spheres, such as international business trade associations

Indeed, transnational cause groups can strategically whipsaw policy makers and sectional groups, too, at local, national, and international levels, going back and forth between applying traditional pressure group tactics to government officials, organizing local resistance, and pursuing international or transnational media and other campaigns, as shown by a well-known case study of the Clayoquot and Great Bear rainforest campaigns in Canada (Krajnc 1999).

In this context, then, social actors involved in the processes just described are increasingly strategically situated in a changing global order. Their influence is still heavily constrained by the regularized allocation of resources and the public goods decisions faced on a routine basis by states and state actors. Nevertheless, it can also be argued that transnational opportunity structures, unlike national ones, are not configured primarily by hierarchical state structures, but by multilayered, quasi-anarchical, overlapping and crosscutting—transnational—political processes, including not only states-in-flux but also transnational economic linkages and transgovernmental linkages. In such conditions, it is at least conceivable that the standard wisdom may be stood on its head and transnational social movements may nurture the growing influence of sets of social actors who themselves will impose new structural forms on the transnational field. At one level, then, social actors, mainly in the form of NGOs and NSMs, may be the most strategically situated actors of all and have the greatest potential leeway to imagine and construct new forms of transnational structuration.

Nevertheless, there are still significant limitations to their scope and scale of action. At one level, the embeddedness of existing state and governmental institutions continues to constitute a major constraint. Interest and value groups must orient their pressure and influence toward key decision makers, who are still primarily state actors. At a second level, any kind of pluralist pressure group will have to focus on promoting its specific values and interests, often along the lines of what in the traditional interest and pressure group literature have been called "single-issue pressure groups," rather than taking an overarching normative posture on the nature of the international system. Broad strategies based on the notion of a "general (or public) interest" may actually dilute their activities and blunt their capacity to achieve their goals. And at a third level, they have limited and diverse bases of support. On the one hand, they may not carry their members with them if they attempt to pursue broad public interest strategies; on the other hand, their specific areas of involvement and expertise might well be inappropriate for the pursuit of wider goals. Therefore, there is unlikely to emerge a broad-based, public-interest-oriented global civil society that would permit social actors to develop an overall structural impact of a kind that could transform the international system itself.

As with economic and political actors, however, the key will not be the action of social actors taken in isolation. Rather, it will lie in the ways social actors can alter the shape of crosscutting networks linking all three categories of agent in a globalizing world. The three categories of actors discussed in this chapter are therefore pulled and pushed between adaptive and transformational forms of behavior. In the final analysis, however, *both kinds of behavior are likely to reinforce and entrench the globalization process*, although in quite uneven and often contingent ways. Outcomes are likely to take different forms in different circumstances. The result is a transnational political process that resembles even more complex sets of political opportunities, potential strategies, and forms of political action and interaction across multiple levels than the domestic neopluralism theorized by McFarland and others in the "research sequence" he describes (McFarland 2004: 2ff.).

Like this neopluralist process, transnational multinodal politics can be seen as creating new forms of feedback, path dependency, and the ratcheting up of global politics and of globalization itself. Indeed, we may be seeing, as noted earlier in this book, the emergence of Stone's global agora—"a growing global public space of fluid, dynamic, and intermeshed relations of politics, markets, culture and society...[characterized by] multiple publics and plural institutions...a social and political space—generated by globalization—rather than a physical place" (Stone 2008: 21). Nevertheless, the result will not be a coherent form of institutional selection, but rather an uneven process of politicking, bargaining, influence seeking, and the pursuit of self-interests in a classic neopluralist analytical context, veering between convergence and divergence, between a widening process of relatively stable horse-trading and bargaining, on the one hand, and a neomedieval durable disorder, on the other. Nevertheless, in the last analysis, it will be those networks that cut across the crude economic-political-social group boundaries examined here, and are therefore most likely to be characterized by a *raison du monde* mind-set, that will determine the shape of change.

5. CONCLUSION: SCENARIOS OF CHANGE

This chapter has focused on the role of different sets of actors in the global structuration process. What kind of outcomes might be hypothesized with regard to the ongoing process of transnational structuration, given the increasing openness of the system, will depend on the way strategically situated actors of all kinds consciously or unwittingly shape that process. Broadly speaking, however, it is possible to sketch four possible alternative scenarios of change: an incremental process shaped primarily by political actors reacting to specific challenges in historical time, in other words, through bricolage and the evolution of more transnational forms of de facto governmentality; the development of a more systematically coherent form of pluralist process with quasi-democratic features, what I call the "rosy scenario"; a more top-down form of domination by capitalist elites, what I call "sectoral hegemony"; and a more disordered, volatile, and uneven process more akin to neomedievalism.

The first scenario might suggest that the structural developments outlined here do *not* entail a fundamental shift in the international system. From this perspective, globalizing pressures merely trigger a range of adaptive behaviors on the part of strategically situated actors in each of these categories—actors who are still significantly constrained in their capacity to form effective transformative networks cutting across those categories. In such circumstances, it is likely that the key to understanding structural change (however limited) is most likely to rest with traditional political actors. Political actors, deeply enmeshed in the embedded nation-states system, would react to pressures for change by increasing the adaptive capacity of, for example, traditional forms of international cooperation, especially intergovernmental regimes, along with pressure on domestic actors to adapt, as well as continuing to depend on the nation-state as the main source of policy making, regulation, distribution, and redistribution (Hirst and Thompson 1999). Nevertheless, this kind of incremental, evolutionary developmental pathway would still be likely over time to privilege the kind of transnational neopluralist interest and value groups I have been discussing simply because policy challenges are becoming ever more transnational in scale. Crucial to longer term development will therefore be whether such groups, in the process of multinodal politicking, will be capable of adjusting gradually, if unevenly, to a *raison du monde* type of governmentality and move beyond this first scenario.

A second scenario is based on the predominance of transnational social movements and their ability to shape the agendas of other actors both within and cutting across states. Two linked hypotheses can be raised again here: on the one hand, the development of a "global civil society," based on common transnational norms and values; and on the other, the emergence of a self-regulating, crosscutting pluralism, with a growing consensus on international rules of the game and cosmopolitan legal-constitutional practices. Both of these changes imply a rather quicker shift to a *raison du monde* mindset and would support a more far-reaching transformation. Held (1995), for example, has suggested that some mixture of analogous developments might well lead, especially through the spread of transnational legal norms, to the emergence of a kind of "cosmopolitan democracy." Furthermore, should transnational social movements prove to be the predominant institutional entrepreneurs of the transnational structuration process, then a more complex, supranational process of mainstreaming might well provide the glue for some form of de facto democratization-without-the-state. However, this remains a rosy scenario, an idealized state of affairs that it might be unwise to expect, especially given the sorts of pitfalls identified in chapter 10.

Nevertheless, the dominant image of transnationalization and globalization today, as suggested earlier, is still that of economic and business globalization, which forms the core of the third scenario. Economic actors, through the transnational expansion of both markets and hierarchical (firm) structures and institutions, increasingly shape a range of key outcomes in terms of the allocation of both resources and values. Neoliberal ideology presents such developments as inevitable; in Prime Minister Thatcher's words: "There is no alternative" (TINA). Should transnational social movements prove more peripheral to the structuration process than a Polanyian double movement might suggest, and should political actors and the state continue to act as promoters of globalization and enforcement—that is, the state as a globalizing change agent—then the governance structures of the twenty-first-century international system will be likely to reflect in a more direct and instrumental way the priorities of global capital. Without a world government or a set of effective international (cooperative/interstate) governance mechanisms, private economic regimes such as internationalized financial markets and associations of transnationally active firms, large and small, are likely to shape the international system through their ability to channel investment flows and set cross-border prices for both capital and physical assets (see chapter 13). The shape of the governance structures of such a system would essentially mimic the structures of capital itself, rather than leading to a broader, more sociopolitical form of governmentalization.

This raises a number of issues. In the first place, it has been suggested that capital cannot directly control society. Capitalists are concerned first and foremost with competing with each other, not with policing the system (which can eat up profits), and there is no collective mechanism, no "ideal collective capitalist" to regulate the system in the interests of capital *as a whole*, other than the state (Holloway and Picciotto 1978). Nevertheless, indirect forms of control, for example, through Gramscian cultural hegemony, may become more important than the state per se, especially in its limited guise as a nation-state. Gill, for example, sees the Trilateral Commission, the World Economic Forum (Davos), and other formal and informal networks among transnationally linked businesspeople and their social and political allies as bearers of such hegemony—what he calls the "new constitutionalism" and "disciplinary neoliberalism" (Gill 1990 and 2003). At the same time, the possibilities for more repressive versions of this scenario are credible, too.

However, capital is rarely unified in this way in terms of political influence and policy making. The crystallization of other forms of international capital can also be envisaged, reflecting an unequal distribution of power or representation, for example, among different economic sectors. For example, in the 1970s, many on both sides of the political divide thought that what essentially were cartels of multinational corporations would be the form that international capital would take in the future. But in the world of dramatic international capital movements in the 1990s, it was more often the financial markets that could be seen as exercising a sectoral hegemony over the international system. In either case, however, any significant transfer of power or system control from political agents (via states) to economic actors would represent a fundamental change, representing what I have called the "governmentality gap" and the deficiencies of relying on bricolage rather than coherent, overarching institutional or superstructural selection.

A final scenario is, of course, that exogenous pressures on the nation-state and states system, interacting with and exacerbating the tensions within that system, will cause that system to erode and weaken in key ways, but *without providing enough structural resources to any particular category of actors (or combination of categories) to effectively shape the transnational structuration process.* In other words, no group or group of groups will be at the steering wheel of change in the international system, and competition between different groups will, in turn, undermine the capacity of any one of them to exercise such control. This is the outcome that has been called "neomedievalism": a fluid, multilayered structure of overlapping and competing institutions, cultural flux, and multiple and shifting identities and loyalties, with different niches at different levels for groups to focus their energies on. The medieval world was not a world of chaos; it was a world of durable disorder.

Unless some coherent group of institutional entrepreneurs emerges to control and direct the process of transnational structuration, the medieval analogy may provide a better guide to understanding the international system in the twenty-first century than previous models involving states and the states system, both domestically and internationally. There is no reason in principle, after all, that governance in this broad sense has to be tidy and logically coherent. The nation-state as such, and in particular the national industrial welfare state of the Second Industrial Revolution, may well be caught up in such wider, more complex webs, leading to increased uncertainty and possible disorder. At the same time, however, crosscutting networks of economic, political, and social actors might eventually lead to an increase in the influence and power wielded by transnationally linked institutional entrepreneurs, some of whom will certainly attempt to transcend the limits of adaptive behavior and develop new institutional strategies for transforming and reconstructing the political in this fluid, globalizing world. The concept of leadership, as increasingly examined and taught in business schools and departments of public administration and policy, suggests that training such potential internationally oriented institutional entrepreneurs and inculcating *raison du monde* is a conscious endeavor today (Raffel, Leisink, and Middlebrooks 2009).

In each of these scenarios, nevertheless, we can see either an incremental or a much more rapid feedback process, based on actors' evolving strategies, behaviors, and discourses, leading to a ratcheting up of the globalization process itself. Nevertheless, the shape that process takes will differ depending on which actors—and coalitions of actors—develop the most influence and power to manipulate and mold particular outcomes within and across a range of critical issue-areas. Therefore, the kind of analytical methodology most appropriate to defining, unraveling, explaining, and understanding the emergence and increasing paradigmatic predominance of multinodal politics is qualitative, discursive, historically informed process tracing, focusing on the competition among alternative paradigms suggested by Wolin (1968). Quantitative methods may permit testing certain hypotheses where clear and unambiguous data are available, and formal methods may assist in the development of logical connections, but both need to be clearly framed and operationalized within wider and more complex theoretical and historical parameters.

The continuing development of something called World Politics as an academic discipline is essential to our understanding of what is happening in the world today. We are faced with significant structural changes, but their import is uncertain. Such changes by themselves do not emerge full-blown from earlier processes of structuration, but are ambiguous and amorphous in their ramifications for short-term events, as well as for long-term transformation, generating multiple equilibria and leading to a range of alternative outcomes.

The transformation of the world in the twenty-first century revolves around the contingent interaction and interdependence of a range of actors, whether individuals or groups, who can simultaneously coordinate their actions in multinodal fashion across a globalizing world. They must be able to creatively interpret structural changes, alternative pathways, and opportunities through the evolving governmental rationality of *raison du monde*; change and refine their strategies; negotiate, bargain, build coalitions, and mobilize their power resources in ongoing interactions with other actors; and—both in winning and losing—affect and shape medium-term and long-term outcomes. By restoring political action and process to center stage, a focus on transnational neopluralism provides a way to begin to rethink the very way we conceive of world politics in this rapidly evolving century.

Bibliography

Abdelal, Rawi (2007). *Capital Rules: The Construction of Global Finance* (Cambridge, Mass.: Harvard University Press).

Acharya, Viral, and Matthew Richardson (eds.) (2009). *Restoring Financial Stability: How to Repair a Failed System* (Hoboken, N.J.: John Wiley and Sons).

Allen, Michael (2008). "The Global Mode of Production and Changing Forms of Democracy: Contradictions and Challenges," paper presented at the *Millennium: Journal of International Studies* conference, "Interrogating Democracy in International Relations," London School of Economics and Political Science (25–26 October).

Anderson, Benedict (1991). *Imagined Communities* (London: Verso).

Anderson, Eugene N., and Pauline R. Anderson (1968). *Political Institutions and Social Change in Continental Europe in the Nineteenth Century* (Berkeley: University of California Press).

Anderson, Perry (1974). *Lineages of the Absolutist State* (London: New Left).

Anderson, Perry (1975). *Passages from Antiquity to Feudalism* (London: New Left).

Archibugi, Daniele (2008). *The Global Commonwealth of Citizens: Toward Cosmopolitan Democracy* (Princeton, N.J.: Princeton University Press).

Ariely, Dan (2008). *Predictably Irrational: The Hidden Forces That Shape Our Decisions* (New York: HarperCollins).

Armijo, Leslie Elliott (ed.) (2002). *Debating the Global Financial Architecture* (Albany: State University of New York Press).

Aronica, Ronald, and Mtetwa Randoo (2006). *The World Is Flat? A Critical Analysis of Thomas L. Friedman's* New York Times *Bestseller* (Tampa, Fla.: Meghan-Kiffer).

Arts, Bas, Arnoud Lagendijk, and Henk van Houtum (eds.) (2009). *The Disoriented State: Shifts in Governmentality, Territoriality and Governance* (Berlin: Springer).

Baker, Andrew, Alan Hudson, and Richard Woodward (eds.) (2005). *Governing Financial Globalization* (London: Routledge).

Baldwin, David A. (ed.) (1993). *Neorealism and Neoliberalism: The Contemporary Debate* (New York: Columbia University Press).

Baumol, William J., Robert E. Litan, and Carl J. Schramm (2007). *Good Capitalism, Bad Capitalism, and the Economics of Growth and Prosperity* (New Haven, Conn.: Yale University Press).

Bell, Daniel (1960). *The End of Ideology and the Exhaustion of Ideas in the Fifties* (Glencoe, Ill.: Free Press).

Bendix, Reinhard (1964). *Nation-Building and Citizenship* (Garden City, N.Y.: Anchor).

Bentley, Arthur F. (1908). *The Process of Government: A Study of Social Pressures* (Chicago: University of Chicago Press).

Berger, Peter L., and Thomas Luckmann (1966). *The Social Construction of Reality: A Treatise in the Sociology of Knowledge* (Garden City, N.Y.: Doubleday).

Berle, Adolph A., and Gardiner C. Means (1932). *The Modern Corporation and Private Property* (New York: Macmillan).

Betsill, Michele M. (1999). "Changing the Climate: NGOs, Norms and the Politics of Global Climate Change," paper delivered at the annual convention of the International Studies Association, Washington, D.C. (16–20 February).

Block, Fred L. (1977). *The Origins of International Economic Disorder: A Study of United States Monetary Policy from World War II to the Present* (Berkeley: University of California Press).

Bohas, Alexandre (2006). "The Paradox of Anti-Americanism: Reflection on the Shallow Concept of Soft Power," *Global Society*, vol. 20, no. 4 (October), pp. 395–414.

Bookstaber, Richard (2007). *A Demon of Our Own Design: Markets, Hedge Funds, and the Perils of Financial Innovation* (Hoboken, N.J.: John Wiley and Sons).

Booth, Ken, and Nicholas Wheeler (2008). *The Security Dilemma: Fear, Cooperation, and Trust in World Politics* (New York: Palgrave Macmillan).

Brenner, Neil (2004). *New State Spaces: Urban Governance and the Rescaling of Statehood* (New York: Oxford University Press).

Brenner, Neil, Bob Jessop, Martin Jones, and Gordon MacLeod (eds.) (2003). *State/Space: A Reader* (Oxford: Blackwell).

Bruner, Robert F. (2009). *The Panic of 1907: Lessons Learned from the Market's Perfect Storm* (Hoboken, N.J.: John Wiley and Sons).

Bryan, Dick, and Michael Rafferty (2006). *Capitalism with Derivatives: A Political Economy of Financial Derivatives, Capital and Class* (London: Palgrave Macmillan).

Buchanan, Patrick J. (2006). *State of Emergency: The Third World Invasion and Conquest of America* (New York: Thomas Dunne).

Buick, Adam, and John Crump (1986). *State Capitalism: The Wages System under New Management* (London: Palgrave Macmillan).

Burchell, Graham, Colin Gordon, and Peter Miller (eds.) (1991). *The Foucault Effect: Studies in Governmentality* (Chicago: University of Chicago Press).

Burnell, Peter (ed.) (2003). *Democracy through the Looking Glass: Democracy and Democratization in the 21st Century* (Manchester, U.K.: Manchester University Press).

Buzan, Barry (1983). *People, States and Fear: The National Security Problem in International Relations* (Chapel Hill: University of North Carolina Press).

Buzan, Barry (2004). *From International to World Society? English School Theory and the Social Structure of Globalisation* (Cambridge: Cambridge University Press).

Buzan, Barry, Charles Jones, and Richard Little (1993). *The Logic of Anarchy: Neorealism to Structural Realism* (New York: Columbia University Press).

Cameron, Angus (2009). "Globalization and the Construction of a Global Political Economy," paper presented to the annual convention of the International Studies Association, New York (15–18 February).

Cammack, Paul (2004). "What the World Bank Means by Poverty Reduction, and Why It Matters," *New Political Economy*, vol. 9, no. 2 (June), pp. 189–212.

Campbell, Angus, Philip E. Converse, Warren E. Miller, and Donald E. Stokes (1960). *The American Voter* (New York: John Wiley and Sons).

Cardoso, Fernando Henrique (2001). *Charting a New Course: The Politics of Globalization and Social Transformation*, ed. Mauricio A. Font (Lanham, Md.: Rowman and Littlefield).

Carr, E. H. (1947). *International Relations between the Two World Wars (1919–1939)* (London: Macmillan).

Castells, Manuel (1996). *The Rise of the Network Society* (Oxford: Blackwell).

Castells, Manuel (ed.) (2004). *The Network Society: A Cross-Cultural Perspective* (Cheltenham, U.K.: Edward Elgar).

Cerny, Philip G. (1980). *The Politics of Grandeur: Ideological Aspects of de Gaulle's Foreign Policy* (Cambridge: Cambridge University Press).

Cerny, Philip G. (1982). "Gaullism, Advanced Capitalism and the Fifth Republic," in David S. Bell, ed., *Contemporary French Political Parties* (London and New York: Croom Helm and St. Martin's Press), pp. 24–51.

Cerny, Philip G. (1989). "Political Entropy and American Decline," *Millennium: Journal of International Studies*, vol. 18, no. 1 (Spring), pp. 47–63.

Cerny, Philip G. (1990a). *The Changing Architecture of Politics: Structure, Agency and the Future of the State* (London: Sage).

Cerny, Philip G. (1990b). "European Defence and the New Détente," *West European Politics*, vol. 13, no. 4 (October), pp. 139–152.

Cerny, Philip G. (1991). "The Limits of Deregulation: Transnational Interpenetration and Policy Change," *European Journal of Political Research*, vol. 19, nos. 2 and 3 (March-April), pp. 173–196.

Cerny, Philip G., ed. (1993). *Finance and World Politics: Markets, Regimes and States in the Post-Hegemonic Era* (Aldershot, England: Edward Elgar).

Cerny, Philip G. (1994a). "The Infrastructure of the Infrastructure? Toward 'Embedded Financial Orthodoxy' in the International Political Economy," in Barry Gills and Ronen Palan, eds., *Transcending the State-Global Divide: The Neostructuralist Agenda in International Relations* (Boulder, Colo.: Lynne Reinner), pp. 223–249.

Cerny, Philip G. (1994b). "The Dynamics of Financial Globalization: Technology, Market Structure and Policy Response," *Policy Sciences*, vol. 27, no. 4 (November), pp. 319–342.

Cerny, Philip G. (1995). "Globalization and the Changing Logic of Collective Action," *International Organization*, 49 (Autumn), pp. 595–625.

Cerny, Philip G. (1997). "Paradoxes of the Competition State: The Dynamics of Political Globalization," *Government and Opposition*, vol. 32, no. 2 (Spring), pp. 251–274.

Cerny, Philip G. (1998). "Neomedievalism, Civil Wars and the New Security Dilemma: Globalization as Durable Disorder," *Civil Wars*, vol. 1, no. 1 (Spring), pp. 36–64.

Cerny, Philip G. (1999a). "Globalization, Governance and Complexity," in Aseem Prakash and Jeffrey A. Hart, eds., *Globalization and Governance* (London: Routledge), pp. 188–212.

Cerny, Philip G. (1999b). "Globalisation and the Erosion of Democracy," *European Journal of Political Research*, vol. 36, no. 1 (August), pp. 1–26.

Cerny, Philip G. (2000a). "Restructuring the Political Arena: Globalization and the Paradoxes of the Competition State," in Randall D. Germain, ed., *Globalization and Its Critics: Perspectives from Political Economy* (London: Macmillan), pp. 117–138.

Cerny, Philip G. (2000b). "Money and Power: The American Financial System from Free Banking to Global Competition," in Grahame Thompson, ed., *Markets*, vol. 2 of *The United States in the Twentieth Century*, 2nd ed. (London: Hodder and Stoughton), 169–207.

Cerny, Philip G. (2002). "Labour Movement Faces Global Challenge," *Firefighter* (U.K. Fire Brigades Union), vol. 30, no. 1 (January-February), pp. 16–17.

Cerny, Philip G. (2005a). "Terrorism and the New Security Dilemma," *Naval War College Review*, vol. 58, no. 1 (Winter), pp. 11–33.

Cerny, Philip G. (2005b). "Governance, Globalization and the Japanese Financial System: Resistance or Restructuring?" in Glenn D. Hook, ed., *Contested Governance in Japan* (London: Routledge), pp. 90–110.

Cerny, Philip G. (2005c). "Political Globalization and the Competition State," in Richard Stubbs and Geoffrey R. D. Underhill, eds., *The Political Economy of the Changing Global Order*, 3rd ed. (Oxford: Oxford University Press), pp. 376–386.

Cerny, Philip G. (2005d). "Power, Markets and Accountability: The Development of Multi-Level Governance in International Finance," in Andrew Baker, Alan Hudson, and Richard Woodward, eds., *Governing Financial Globalization* (London: Routledge), pp. 24–48.

Cerny, Philip G. (2006a). "Plurality, Pluralism, and Power: Elements of Pluralist Analysis in an Age of Globalization," in Rainer Eisfeld, ed., *Pluralism: Developments in the Theory and Practice of Democracy* (Opladen, Germany: Barbara Budrich on behalf of International Political Science Association, Research Committee No. 16 [Socio-Political Pluralism]), pp. 81–111.

Cerny, Philip G. (2006b). "Dilemmas of Operationalizing Hegemony," in Mark Haugaard and Howard H. Lentner, eds., *Hegemony and Power: Force and Consent in Contemporary Politics* (Lanham, Md.: Lexington), pp. 67–87.

Cerny, Philip G. (2008). "Thinking outside the Bicycle: Shifting Gears on Global Trade Talks" (New York: Carnegie Council for Ethics in International Affairs, Policy Innovations, 10 December), http://www.policyinnovations.org/ideas/commentary/data/000097.

Cerny, Philip G., and Mark G. Evans (2004). "Globalisation and Public Policy under New Labour," *Policy Studies*, vol. 25, no. 1 (March), pp. 51–65.

Cerny, Philip G., and Martin A. Schain (eds.) (1984). *Socialism, the State and Public Policy in France* (London and New York: Frances Pinter and Methuen).

Chandler, Alfred D., Jr. (1990). *Scale and Scope: The Dynamics of Industrial Capitalism* (Cambridge, Mass.: Harvard University Press).

Chang, Ha-Joon, and Ilene Grabel (2004). *Reclaiming Development: An Economic Policy Handbook for Activists and Policymakers* (London: Zed).

Chernow, Ron (1990). *The House of Morgan: An American Banking Dynasty and the Rise of Modern Finance* (New York: Atlantic Monthly Press).

Clapham, Christopher (1982). *Private Patronage and Public Power: Political Clientelism in the Modern State* (London: Macmillan).

Clark, Anne Marie, Elisabeth J. Friedman, and Kathryn Hochstetler (1999). "Sovereignty, Global Civil Society, and the Social Conferences: NGOs and States at the U.N. Conferences on Population, Social Development, and Human Settlements," paper presented at the annual convention of the International Studies Association, Washington, D.C. (16–20 February).

Clark, Ian (2008). "Democracy and International Society," keynote address to the *Millennium: Journal of International Studies* conference, "Interrogating Democracy in International Relations," London School of Economics and Political Science (25–26 October).

Clausewitz, Carl von (1832/1989). *On War*, trans. and ed. Michael Howard and Peter Paret (Princeton, N.J.: Princeton University Press).

Clayton, Richard, and Jonas Pontusson (1998). "Welfare State Retrenchment Revisited: Entitlement Cuts, Public Sector Restructuring, and Inegalitarian Trends in Advanced Capitalist Societies," *World Politics*, vol. 51, no. 1 (October), pp. 67–98.

Cohen, Benjamin J. (2004). *The Future of Money* (Princeton, N.J.: Princeton University Press).

Comaroff, Jean, and John Comaroff (eds.) (2006). *Law and Disorder in the Postcolony* (Chicago: University of Chicago Press).

Cooper, George (2008). *The Origin of Financial Crises: Central Banks, Credit Bubbles and the Efficient Market Fallacy* (New York: Vintage).

Coser, Lewis A. (1956). *The Functions of Social Conflict* (London: Routledge and Kegan Paul).

Cowen, Tyler (2007). "To Know Contractors, Know Government," *New York Times* (28 October).

Cox, Robert W. (1987). *Production, Power, and World Order* (New York: Columbia University Press).

Cox, Robert W. (1993). "Structural Issues of Global Governance: Implications for Europe," in Stephen Gill, ed., *Gramsci, Historical Materialism and International Relations* (Cambridge: Cambridge University Press), pp. 259–289.

Coyle, Diane (2002). *Paradoxes of Prosperity: Why the New Capitalism Benefits All* (New York: Thompson/Texere).

Cronin, Bruce, and Joseph Lepgold (1995). "A New Medievalism? Conflicting International Authorities and Competing Loyalties in the Twenty-First Century," paper presented to the annual meeting of the International Studies Association, Chicago (23–27 February).

Crouch, Colin, and Wolfgang Streeck (eds.) (1997). *The Political Economy of Modern Capitalism: Mapping Convergence and Diversity* (London: Sage).

Crozier, Michel, and Erhard Friedberg (1977). *L'Acteur et le système: les contraintes de l'action collective* (Paris: Éditions du Seuil).

Curtius, Ernst Robert (1932/1962). *The Civilization of France: An Introduction* (New York: Vintage; originally Macmillan).

Cutler, A. Claire, Virginia Haufler, and Tony Porter (eds.) (1999). *Private Authority and International Affairs* (Albany: State University of New York Press).

Dahl, Robert A. (1989). *Democracy and Its Critics* (New Haven, Conn.: Yale University Press).

Datz, Giselle (2009). "Governments as Market Players: State Innovation in the Global Economy," *Journal of International Affairs* (forthcoming).

Deibert, Ronald J. (1997). *Parchment, Printing, and Hypermedia* (New York: Columbia University Press).

Deporte, Anton W. (1979). *Europe between the Superpowers* (New Haven, Conn.: Yale University Press).

Diehl, Paul F. (2005). *The Politics of Global Governance: International Organizations in an Interdependent World*, 3rd ed. (Boulder, Colo.: Lynne Rienner).

Dodgson, Richard (1999). "Contesting Neoliberal Globalization at U.N. Global Conferences: The Women's Health Movement and the International Conference on Population and Development," paper presented at the annual convention of the International Studies Association, Washington, D.C. (16–20 February).

Douglas, Ian Robert (1999). "Globalization as Governance: Toward an Archaeology of Contemporary Political Reason," in Aseem Prakash and Jeffrey A. Hart, eds., *Globalization and Governance* (London: Routledge), pp. 134–160.

Dunleavy, Patrick J. (1994). "The Globalisation of Public Services Production: Can Government Be 'Best in World'?" *Public Policy and Administration*, vol. 9, no. 2 (Summer), pp. 36–64.

Durkheim, Émile (1893/1933). *The Division of Labor in Society*, trans. George Simpson (New York: Free Press).

Easton, David (1953). *The Political System* (New York: Knopf).

Edwards, Michael (2004). *Civil Society* (Cambridge: Polity).

Eichengreen, B. (1996). *Globalizing Capital: A History of the International Monetary System* (Princeton, N.J.: Princeton University Press).

Eichengreen, Barry (2006). *The European Economy since 1945: Coordinated Capitalism and Beyond* (Princeton, N.J.: Princeton University Press).

Evans, Mark G. (2005). *Policy Transfer in Global Perspective* (London: Ashgate).

Evans, Mark G., and Philip G. Cerny (2003). "Globalisation and Social Policy," in Nick Ellison and Chris Pierson, eds., *New Developments in British Social Policy* (London: Palgrave Macmillan), pp. 19–40.

Evans, Peter (2007). "Is It Labor's Turn to Globalize? 21st Century Challenges and Opportunities," paper presented to the Democracy and Development Seminar, Princeton Institute for International and Regional Studies (24 October).

Ferguson, Adam (1767/1995). *An Essay on the History of Civil Society* (Cambridge: Cambridge University Press).

Ferguson, Niall (2008). *The Ascent of Money: A Financial History of the World* (London: Penguin).

Finnemore, Martha (1996). *National Interests and International Society* (Ithaca, N.Y.: Cornell University Press).

Florida, Richard (2005). "The World is Spiky," *Atlantic Monthly*, vol. 296, no. 3, pp. 48–51.

Foucault, Michel (1980). *Power/Knowledge: Selected Interviews and Other Writings, 1972–1977*, ed. Colin Gordon (New York: Longman).

Foucault, Michel (2007). *Security, Territory, Population: Lectures at the Collège de France, 1977–1978*, trans. Graham Burchell (London: Palgrave Macmillan; French edition 2004).

Foucault, Michel (2008). *The Birth of Biopolitics: Lectures at the Collège de France, 1978–1979*, trans. Graham Burchell (London: Palgrave Macmillan; French edition 2004).

Fox, Justin (2009). *The Myth of the Rational Market: A History of Risk, Reward, and Delusion on Wall Street* (New York: HarperBusiness).

Frank, Thomas (2004). *What's the Matter with Kansas? How Conservatives Won the Heart of America* (New York: Henry Holt).

Frieden, Jeffry A., and Ronald Rogowski (1996). "The Impact of the International Economy on National Policies: An Overview," in Robert O. Keohane and Helen V. Milner, eds., *Internationalization and Domestic Politics* (Cambridge: Cambridge University Press), pp. 25–47.

Friedman, Thomas L. (1997). "Dear Dr. Greenspan," *New York Times* (9 February).

Fuchita, Yasuyuki, and Robert E. Litan (eds.) (2007). *New Financial Instruments and Institutions: Opportunities and Policy Challenges* (Tokyo and Washington, D.C.: Nomura Institute of Capital Markets Research and Brookings Institutions Press).

Fukuyama, Francis (1992). *The End of History and the Last Man* (Glencoe, Ill.: Free Press).

Galbraith, John Kenneth (1967/2007). *The New Industrial State* (Princeton, N.J.: Princeton University Press).

Gallarotti, Giulio M. (2000). "The Advent of the Prosperous Society: The Rise of the Guardian State and Structural Change in the World Economy," *Review of International Political Economy*, vol. 7, no. 1 (January), pp. 1–52.

Gallarotti, Giulio M. (2009). *The Power Curse: Influence and Illusion in World Politics* (Boulder, Colo.: Lynne Rienner).

Galtung, Johan (1973). *The European Community: A Superpower in the Making* (London: HarperCollins).

Gardner, Lloyd C. (1964). *Economic Aspects of New Deal Diplomacy* (Boston: Beacon).

Gardner, Lloyd C. (1976). *Imperial America: American Foreign Policy since 1898* (New York: Harcourt Brace Jovanovich).

Gardner, Richard N. (1980). *Sterling-Dollar Diplomacy in Historical Perspective*, rev. ed. (New York: Columbia University Press).

Gellman, Barton (2008). *Angler: The Cheney Vice Presidency* (New York: Penguin).

Gelpern, Anna (2009). "Financial Crisis Containment," unpublished working paper, Rutgers School of Law, Newark (April).

Germain, Randall D. (1997). *The International Organization of Credit* (Cambridge: Cambridge University Press).

Germain, Randall D. (2001). "Global Financial Governance and the Problem of Inclusion," *Global Governance*, vol. 7, no. 4 (November), pp. 411–426.

Gerschenkron, Alexander (1962). *Economic Backwardness in Historical Perspective* (Cambridge, Mass.: Harvard University Press).

Giddens, Anthony (1979). *Central Problems of Social Theory: Action, Structure and Contradiction in Social Analysis* (London: Macmillan).

Giddens, Anthony (1998). *The Third Way: Renewal of Social Democracy* (Cambridge: Polity).

Gill, Stephen (1990). *American Hegemony and the Trilateral Commission* (Cambridge: Cambridge University Press).

Gill, Stephen (2003). *Power and Resistance in the New World Order* (London: Palgrave Macmillan).

Gills, Barry K. (ed.) (2000). *Globalization and the Politics of Resistance* (London: Palgrave Macmillan).

Gladwell, Malcolm (2000). *The Tipping Point: How Little Things Can Make a Big Difference* (Boston: Little, Brown).

Goldthorpe, John H. (1985). *Order and Conflict in Contemporary Capitalism* (Oxford: Oxford University Press).

Gourevitch, Peter A., and James Shinn (eds.) (2005). *Political Power and Corporate Control: The New Global Politics of Corporate Governance* (Princeton, N.J.: Princeton University Press).

Gowa, Joanne (1983). *Closing the Gold Window: Domestic Politics and the End of Bretton Woods* (Ithaca, N.Y.: Cornell University Press).

Granovetter, Mark (1985). "Economic Action and Social Structure: The Problem of Embeddedness," *American Journal of Sociology*, vol. 91, no. 4 (November), pp. 481–510.

Granovetter, Mark (1992). "Economic Institutions as Social Constructions: A Framework for Analysis," *Acta Sociologica*, no. 35, pp. 3–11.

Grant, James (1992). *Money of the Mind: Borrowing and Lending in America from the Civil War to Michael Milken* (New York: Farrar, Straus and Giroux).

Gross, Daniel (2007). *Pop! Why Bubbles Are Great for the Economy* (New York: Collins).

Guha, Krishna (2007). "IMF Plans Currency Crackdown: Global Stability Will Be the Watchword," *Financial Times* (19 June), p. 12.

Haas, Peter (ed.) (1992). *Knowledge, Power, and International Policy Coordination*, special issue of *International Organization*, vol. 46, no. 1 (Winter).

Haggard, Stephan (1990). *Pathways from the Periphery: The Politics of Growth in the Newly Industrializing Countries* (Ithaca, N.Y.: Cornell University Press).

Hall, Peter A., and David Soskice (eds.) (2001). *Varieties of Capitalism: The Institutional Foundations of Comparative Advantage* (Oxford: Oxford University Press).

Hall, Peter A., and Rosemary C. M. Taylor (1996). "Political Science and the Three New Institutionalisms," *Political Studies*, vol. 44, no. 4 (December), 936–957.

Hall, Rodney Bruce, and Thomas J. Biersteker (eds.) (2003). *The Emergence of Private Authority in Global Governance* (Cambridge: Cambridge University Press).

Halperin, Sandra (2003). *War and Social Change in Modern Europe: The Great Transformation Revisited* (Cambridge: Cambridge University Press).

Halperin, Sandra (2008). "Socio-Economic Requisites of Democracy: A Reconsideration," paper presented at the *Millennium: Journal of International Studies* conference, "Interrogating Democracy in International Relations," London School of Economics and Political Science (25–26 October).

Hardt, Michael, and Antonio Negri (2000). *Empire* (Cambridge, Mass.: Harvard University Press).

Harnisch, Sebastian, and Hanns W. Maull (eds.) (2001). *Germany as a Civilian Power? The Foreign Policy of the Berlin Republic* (Manchester, England: Manchester University Press).

Harris, Nigel (1986). *The End of the Third World* (Harmondsworth, England: Penguin).

Hart, Jeffrey (1992). *Rival Capitalists: International Competitiveness in the United States, Japan and Western Europe* (Ithaca, N.Y.: Cornell University Press).

Hartz, Louis (1955). *The Liberal Tradition in America* (New York: Harcourt, Brace and World).

Harvey, David (1989). *The Condition of Postmodernity* (Oxford: Blackwell).

Harvey, David (2005). *A Brief History of Neoliberalism* (Oxford: Oxford University Press).

Hayek, Friedrich A. (1944/2007). *The Road to Serfdom: Text and Documents—The Definitive Edition*, ed. Bruce Caldwell (Chicago: Chicago University Press).

Heclo, Hugh (1978). "Issue Networks and the Executive Establishment: Government Growth in an Age of Improvement," in Anthony King, ed., *The New American Political System* (Washington, D.C.: American Enterprise Institute), pp. 87–124.

Helbling, Thomas, and Robert Wescott (1995). "The Global Real Interest Rate," in *Staff Studies for the World Economic Outlook* (Washington, D.C.: International Monetary Fund).

Held, David (1995). *Democracy and the Global Order: From the Modern State to Cosmopolitan Governance* (Cambridge: Polity).

Helleiner, Eric N. (1994). *States and the Re-emergence of Global Finance* (Ithaca, N.Y.: Cornell University Press).

Henderson, Jeffrey, Peter Dicken, Martin Hess, Neil Coe, and Henry Wai-Chung Yeung (2002). "Global Production Networks and the Analysis of Economic Development," *Review of International Political Economy*, vol. 9, no. 3 (August), pp. 436–464.

Herman, Arthur (2003). *The Scottish Enlightenment: The Scots' Invention of the Modern World* (London: Fourth Estate).

Herz, John H. (1950). "Idealist Internationalism and the Security Dilemma," *World Politics*, vol. 3, no. 2 (January), pp. 157–180.

Higgott, Richard A. (1993). "Economic Cooperation: Theoretical Opportunities and Practical Constraints," *Pacific Review* 6 (Spring), pp. 103–107.

Higgott, Richard, Geoffrey R. D. Underhill, and Andreas Bieler (eds.) (1999). *Non-State Actors and Authority in the Global System* (London: Routledge).

Hinsley, F. H. (1966). *Sovereignty* (London: Watts).

Hirsch, Joachim C. (1978). "The State Apparatus and Social Reproduction: Elements of a Theory of the Bourgeois State," in J. Holloway and S. Picciotto, eds., *State and Capital: A Marxist Analysis* (London: Edward Arnold), pp. 54–107.

Hirschman, Albert O. (1970). *Exit, Voice, and Loyalty: Responses to Decline in Firms, Organizations, and States* (Cambridge, Mass.: Harvard University Press).

Hirst, Paul, and Grahame Thompson (1999). *Globalization in Question: The International Political Economy and the Possibilities of Governance*, 2nd ed. (Cambridge: Polity).

Hobsbawm, Eric J. (1968). *Industry and Empire* (London: Weidenfeld and Nicolson).

Hobsbawm, Eric J. (1969). *Bandits* (London: Weidenfeld and Nicolson).

Hobson, John M., and Leonard Seabrooke (eds.) (2007). *Everyday Politics of the World Economy* (Cambridge: Cambridge University Press).

Hollis, Martin, and Steve Smith (1990). *Explaining and Understanding International Relations* (Oxford: Clarendon).

Holloway, John, and Sol Picciotto (eds.) (1978). *State and Capital: A Marxist Debate* (London: Edward Arnold).

Holton, R. J. (1985). *The Transition from Feudalism to Capitalism* (London: Macmillan).

Hook, Glenn D., ed. (2005). *Contested Governance in Japan: Sites and Issues* (London: Routledge).

Höpner, Martin (2007). "Coordination and Organization: The Two Dimensions of Neoliberal Capitalism," paper presented to the annual meeting of the American Political Science Association, Chicago (August 30–September 2).

Hughes, Thomas P. (1983). *Networks of Power: Electrification in Western Society, 1880–1930* (Baltimore: Johns Hopkins University Press).

Hülsemeyer, Axel (ed.) (2003). *Globalization in the 21st Century: Convergence and Divergence* (London: Palgrave Macmillan).

Huntington, Samuel P. (1969). *Political Order in Changing Societies* (New Haven, Conn.: Yale University Press).

Huntington, Samuel P. (1997). *The Clash of Civilizations and the Remaking of World Order* (New York: Simon & Schuster).

Hurrell, Andrew (2007). *On Global Order: Power, Values and the Constitution of International Society* (Oxford: Oxford University Press).

Ingham, Geoffrey (1984). *Capitalism Divided? The City and Industry in British Social History* (London: Macmillan).

Jacoby, Sanford M. (2008). "Finance and Labor: Perspectives on Risk, Equality, and Democracy," Robert Heilbroner Memorial Lecture, Schwarz Center for Economic Policy Analysis, New School for Social Research (New York, September 10).

Jayasuriya, Kanishka (2005). *Reconstituting the Global Liberal Order: Legitimacy and Regulation* (London: Routledge).

Jervis, Robert (1976). *Perception and Misperception in International Politics* (Princeton, N.J.: Princeton University Press).

Jessop, Bob (1982). *The Capitalist State* (New York: New York University Press).

Jessop, Bob (1997). "The Future of the National State: Erosion or Reorganization? Reflections on the West European Case," paper presented at the conference "Globalization: Critical Perspectives," University of Birmingham (14–16 March).

Jessop, Bob (2002). *The Future of the Capitalist State* (Cambridge: Polity).

Johnson, Chalmers (1982). *M.I.T.I. and the Japanese Miracle: The Growth of Industrial Policy, 1925–1975* (Stanford, Calif.: Stanford University Press).

Johnson, Chalmers (2004). *Blowback: The Costs and Consequences of American Empire* (New York: Metropolitan Books).

Jordana, Jacint, and David Levi-Faur (eds.) (2004). *The Politics of Regulation: Institutions and Regulatory Reform for the Age of Governance* (Cheltenham, England: Edward Elgar).

Joseph, Keith (1974). "Britain: A Decadent New Utopia," speech, Birmingham, England (19 October), reprinted in the *Guardian* (21 October).

Kagan, Robert (2003). *Of Paradise and Power: America and Europe in the New World Order* (New York: Alfred A. Knopf).

Kahler, Miles, and David A. Lake (eds.) (2003). *Governance in a Global Economy: Political Authority in Transition* (Princeton, N.J.: Princeton University Press).

Kahler, Miles, and David A. Lake (2008). "Economic Integration and Global Governance: Why So Little Supranationalism?" paper presented at the annual convention of the International Studies Association, San Francisco (26–29 March).

Kaldor, Mary (1981). *The Baroque Arsenal* (London: Hill and Wang).

Kaldor, Mary (1999). *New and Old Wars: Organized Violence in a Global Era* (Stanford, Calif.: Stanford University Press).

Kaldor, Mary, Gerard Holden, and Richard Falk (eds.) (1989). *The New Détente: Rethinking East-West Relations* (London, New York, and Tokyo: Verso and the United Nations University Press).

Kanter, Rosabeth Moss (1985). *The Change Masters: Innovation and Entrepreneurship in the American Corporation* (Glencoe, Ill.: Free Press).

Kaplan, Robert D. (1994). "The Coming Anarchy," *Atlantic Monthly* (February), pp. 44–76.

Kapstein, Ethan B. (2006). *Economic Justice in an Unfair World: Toward a Level Playing Field* (Princeton, N.J.: Princeton University Press).

Keck, Margaret E., and Kathryn Sikkink (1998). *Activists beyond Borders: Advocacy Networks in International Politics* (Ithaca, N.Y.: Cornell University Press).

Kemp, Tom (1969). *Industrialization in Nineteenth Century Europe* (London: Longman).

Kemp, Tom (1983). *Industrialization in the Nonwestern World* (London: Longman).

Kennedy, Paul (1987). *The Rise and Fall of the Great Powers: Economic Change and Military Conflict from 1500 to 2000* (New York: Random House).

Keohane, Robert O. (1984). *After Hegemony: Cooperation and Discord in the World Political Economy* (Princeton, N.J.: Princeton University Press).

Keohane, Robert O., ed. (1986). *Neorealism and Its Critics* (New York: Columbia University Press).

Keohane, Robert O. (1989). *International Institutions and State Power* (Boulder, Colo.: Westview).

Keohane, Robert O., and Helen V. Milner (eds.) (1996). *Internationalization and Domestic Politics* (Cambridge: Cambridge University Press).

Keohane, Robert O., and Joseph S. Nye Jr. (1977/2000). *Power and Interdependence*, 3rd ed. (New York: Longman).

Kerr, Clark (1983). *The Future of Industrial Societies: Convergence or Continuing Diversity?* (Cambridge, Mass.: Harvard University Press).

Key, V. O., Jr. (1953). *Politics, Parties, and Pressure Groups* (New York: Thomas Y. Crowell).

Kindleberger, Charles P. (1973). *The World in Depression, 1929–1939* (Berkeley: University of California Press).

Kindleberger, Charles P. (1984). *A Financial History of Western Europe* (Oxford: Oxford University Press).

King, Anthony (ed.) (1978). *The New American Political System* (Washington, D.C.: American Enterprise Institute).

Kitching, Gavin (2001). *Seeking Social Justice through Globalization: Escaping a Nationalist Perspective* (State College: Pennsylvania State University Press).

Klein, Naomi (2000). *No Logo: Taking Aim at the Brand Bullies* (New York: Picador).

Klein, Naomi (2007). *The Shock Doctrine: The Rise of Disaster Capitalism* (New York: Metropolitan).

Kobrin, Stephen J. (1998). "Back to the Future: Neomedievalism and the Post-Modern World Economy," *Journal of International Affairs*, vol. 51, no. 2 (Spring), pp. 361–386.

Kofman, Elinore, and Gillian Youngs (eds.) (2008). *Globalization: Theory and Practice*, 3rd ed. (London: Continuum).

Kotkin, Joel (1992). *Tribes: How Race, Religion and Identity Determine Success in the New Global Economy* (New York: Random House).

Krajnc, Anita (1999). "Learning in British Columbia's Clayoquot and Great Bear Rainforest Campaigns: From Public Pressure to Global Civic Politics," paper presented at the annual convention of the International Studies Association, Washington, D.C. (16–20 February).

Krasner, Stephen (ed.) (1982). *International Regimes* (Ithaca, N.Y.: Cornell University Press).

Krieger, Joel, and Craig N. Murphy (1998). "Transnational Opportunity Structures and the Evolving Roles of Movements for Women, Human Rights, Labor, Development, and the Environment: A Proposal for Research," Department of Political Science, Wellesley College.

Kuhn, Thomas (1962). *The Structure of Scientific Revolutions* (Chicago: Chicago University Press).

Kurki, Milja (2008). "Democracy and Conceptual Contestability: Towards Pluralisation and Contextualisation of Conceptions of Democracy in Democracy Promotion," paper presented at the *Millennium: Journal of International Studies* conference, "Interrogating Democracy in International Relations," London School of Economics and Political Science (25–26 October).

Kütting, Gabriela (2004). *Globalization and the Environment: Greening Global Political Economy* (Albany: State University of New York Press).

Lake, David A. (1999). "Global Governance: A Relational Contracting Approach," in Aseem Prakash and Jeffrey A. Hart, eds., *Globalization and Governance* (London: Routledge), pp. 31–53.

Larner, Wendy, and William Walters (eds.) (2004). *Global Governmentality: Governing International Spaces* (London: Routledge).

Laslett, Peter (1965). *The World We Have Lost* (London: Methuen).

Latham, Andrew, and Nicholas Hooper (1995). *The Future of the Defence Firm: New Challenges, New Directions* (Dordrecht, Netherlands: Kluwer Academic).

Leander, Anna (2007). "Regulating the Role of PMCs in Shaping Security and Politics," in Simon Chesterman and Chia Lehnardt, eds., *From Mercenaries to Markets: The Rise and Regulation of Private Military Companies* (Oxford: Oxford University Press), pp. 49–64.

Lefebvre, Henri (2003). "Space and the State," in Neil Brenner, Bob Jessop, Martin Jones, and Gordon MacLeod, eds. *State/Space: A Reader* (Oxford: Blackwell), pp. 84–100.

Lehmbruch, Gerhard, and Philippe C. Schmitter (1982). *Patterns of Corporatist Policy-Making* (London: Sage).

Lemke, Thomas (2006). "Governance and Governmentality," in Austin Harrington, Barbara L. Marshall, and Hans-Peter Müller, eds., *Encyclopedia of Social Theory* (London: Routledge), pp. 232–234.

Lenin, Vladimir Ilich (1917). *Imperialism: The Highest Stage of Capitalism* (London: Lawrence and Wishart).

Levitt, Arthur (2002). *Take on the Street: What Wall Street and Corporate America Don't Want You to Know, What You Can Do to Fight Back* (New York: Pantheon).

Lewis, Flora (2001). "The Anti-Globalization Spoilers Are Going Global," *International Herald Tribune* (6 July).

Lindblom, Charles E. (1977). *Politics and Markets: The World's Political Economic Systems* (New York: Basic Books).

Lippmann, Walter (1982). *The Essential Lippmann: A Political Philosophy for Liberal Democracy*, ed. Clinton Rossiter and James Lare (Cambridge, Mass.: Harvard University Press).

Lipschutz, Ronnie D., with James K. Rowe (2005). *Globalization, Governmentality and Global Politics: Regulation for the Rest of Us?* (London: Routledge).

Litan, Robert E., and Jonathan Rauch (1998). *American Finance for the 21st Century* (Washington, D.C.: Brookings Institution Press).

Little, Richard (2007). *The Balance of Power in International Relations: Metaphors, Myths and Models* (Cambridge: Cambridge University Press).

Lowi, Theodore J. (1964). "American Business, Public Policy, Case Studies, and Political Theory," *World Politics*, vol. 16, no. 4 (July), pp. 677–715.

Macdonald, Kate (2008). "Global Democracy for a Partially Joined-Up World: Toward a Multi-Level System of Power, Allegiance and Democratic Governance?" unpublished paper (London School of Economics and Political Science).

Machin, Howard, and Vincent Wright (eds.) (1985). *Economic Policy and Policy-Making under the Mitterrand Presidency, 1981–84* (London: Pinter).

Majone, Giandomenico (1996). *Regulating Europe* (London: Routledge).

Malcolm, James D. (2001). *Financial Globalization and the Opening of the Japanese Economy* (London: Curzon).

Mann, James (2004). *Rise of the Vulcans: A History of Bush's War Cabinet* (New York: Penguin).

Marks, Gary, Lisbet Hooghe, and Kermit Blank (1996). *European Integration and the State* (Florence, Italy: European University Institute).

Marx, Karl (1852/1987). *The Eighteenth Brumaire of Louis Bonaparte* (London: Lawrence and Wishart).

Marx, Karl, and Friedrich Engels (1848/2005). *The Communist Manifesto* (London and New York: Penguin and Longman).

Maxfield, Sylvia (1997). *Gatekeepers of Growth: The Politics of Central Banking in Developing Countries* (Princeton, N.J.: Princeton University Press).

Mayer, Arno J. (1981). *The Persistence of the Old Regime: Europe to the Great War* (London: Croom Helm).

Mazower, Mark (2004). *Salonica, City of Ghosts: Christians, Muslims and Jews, 1430–1950* (New York: Knopf).

McFarland, Andrew S. (2004). *Neopluralism: The Evolution of Political Process Theory* (Lawrence: University of Kansas Press).

McGann, James (2009). "The Think Tank Index," *Foreign Policy* (January–February), http://www.foreignpolicy.com/story/cms.php?story_id=4598.

McLean, Iain (1987). *Public Choice: An Introduction* (Oxford: Blackwell).

McLuhan, Marshall (1964). *Understanding Media: The Extensions of Man* (New York: McGraw Hill).

McNamara, Kathleen R. (1998). *The Currency of Ideas: Monetary Politics in the European Union* (Ithaca, N.Y.: Cornell University Press).

Mead, Walter Russell (2007). *God and Gold: Britain, America, and the Making of the Modern World* (New York: Random House).

Merle, Marcel (1982). *Sociologie des relations internationales*, 3rd ed. (Paris: Dalloz).

Middlemas, Keith (1979). *Politics in an Industrial Society: The Experience of the British System since 1911* (London: Andre Deutsch).

Miliband, Ralph (1969). *The State in Capitalist Society* (New York: Basic Books).

Mills, C. Wright (1956). *The Power Elite* (New York: Oxford University Press).

Minc, Alain (1993). *Le nouveau Moyen Âge* (Paris: Gallimard).

Monbiot, George (2003). *The Age of Consent: A Manifesto for a New World Order* (London: Flamingo).

Moore, Barringon, Jr. (1966). *Social Origins of Dictatorship and Democracy: Lord and Peasant in the Making of the Modern World* (Boston: Beacon).

Moran, Michael (2002). "Understanding the Regulatory State," *British Journal of Political Science*, vol. 32, no. 2 (April), pp. 391–413.

Moran, Michael (2003). *The British Regulatory State: High Modernism and Hyper-Innovation* (Oxford: Oxford University Press).

Moravcsik, Andrew (1997). "A Liberal Theory of International Politics," *International Organization*, vol. 51, no. 4 (Autumn), pp. 513–553.

Moravcsik, Andrew (2007). "Make Way for the Quiet Superpower: The Year Ahead Offers the Perfect Chance to Remake Transatlantic Relations," *Newsweek* (international ed.), 31 December.

Morgenthau, Hans J. (1949). *Politics among Nations: The Struggle for Power and Peace* (New York: Alfred A. Knopf).

Morris, Charles R. (2008). *The Trillion Dollar Meltdown: Easy Money, High Rollers, and the Great Credit Crash* (New York: Public Affairs).

Mostov, Julie (2008). *Soft Borders: Rethinking Sovereignty and Democracy* (London: Palgrave Macmillan).

Mouffe, Chantal (2008). "Interrogating Democracy," keynote address to the *Millennium: Journal of International Studies* conference, "Interrogating Democracy in International Relations," London School of Economics and Political Science (25–26 October).

Moyo, Dambisa (2009). *Dead Aid: Why Aid Is Not Working and How There Is a Better Way for Africa* (New York: Farrar, Straus and Giroux).

Mügge, Daniel (2006). "Private-Public Puzzles: Inter-firm Competition and Transnational Private Regulation," *New Political Economy*, vol. 11, no. 2 (June), pp. 177–200.

Murphy, Craig (1994). *International Organization and Industrial Change: Global Governance since 1850* (Cambridge: Polity).

Murphy, Craig (1998). "Egalitarian Social Movements and New World Orders," paper presented at the annual conference of the British International Studies Association, University of Sussex (14–16 December).

Nesvetailova, Anastasia (2007). *Fragile Finance: Debt, Speculation and Crisis in the Age of Global Credit* (Basingstoke, England: Palgrave Macmillan).

Nettl, J. Peter (1967). *Political Mobilization: Sociological Analysis of Method and Concepts* (London: Faber and Faber).

Newman, Karl J. (1970) *European Democracies between the Wars* (London: George Allen & Unwin).

Niou, Emerson M. S., Peter C. Ordeshook, and Gregory F. Rose (1989). *The Balance of Power: Stability in International Systems* (Cambridge: Cambridge University Press).

Nordlinger, Eric J. (1981). *On the Autonomy of the Democratic State* (Cambridge, Mass.: Harvard University Press).

Nye, Joseph S., Jr. (2004). *Soft Power: The Means to Success in World Politics* (New York: Public Affairs).

Oakeshott, Michael (1976). "On Misunderstanding Human Conduct: A Reply to My Critics," *Political Theory*, vol. 4, no. 2 (August), pp. 353–367.

O'Brien, Richard (1992). *Global Financial Integration: The End of Geography* (London: Pinter).

O'Connor, James (1973/2001). *The Fiscal Crisis of the State* (Piscataway, N.J.: Transaction).

Odell, John S. (1982). *U.S. International Monetary Policy* (Princeton, N.J.: Princeton University Press).

O'Donnell, Guillermo (1994). "Delegative Democracy," *Journal of Democracy*, vol. 5, no. 1 (January), pp. 55–79.

Offe, Claus (1984). *Contradictions of the Welfare State* (Cambridge, Mass.: MIT Press).

Ohmae, Kenichi (1990). *The Borderless World: Power and Strategy in the Interlinked Economy* (Pensacola, Fla. Ballinger).

Olson, Mancur (1965). *The Logic of Collective Action* (Cambridge, Mass.: Harvard University Press).

Osborne, David, and Ted Gaebler (1992). *Reinventing Government: How the Entrepreneurial Spirit Is Transforming the Public Sector, from Schoolhouse to Statehouse, City Hall to the Pentagon* (Reading, Mass.: Addison-Wesley).

Ostrom, Vincent, Charles M. Tiebout, and Robert Warren (1961). "The Organization of Government in Metropolitan Areas: A Theoretical Inquiry," *American Political Science Review*, vol. 55, no. 3 (September), pp. 831–842.

Parsons, Talcott (1964). "A Functional Theory of Change," in Amitai Etzioni and Eva Etzioni, eds., *Social Change: Sources, Patterns and Consequences* (New York: Basic Books).

Pauly, Louis W. (1997). *Who Elected the Bankers? Surveillance and Control in the World Economy* (Ithaca, N.Y.: Cornell University Press).

Pauly, Louis W., and Simon Reich (1997). "National Structures and Multinational Corporate Behavior: Enduring Differences in the Age of Globalization," *International Organization*, vol. 51, no. 1 (Winter), pp. 1–30.

Pettifor, Ann (2006). *The Coming First World Debt Crisis* (Basingstoke, England: Palgrave Macmillan).

Pierson, Paul (1994). *Dismantling the Welfare State? Reagan, Thatcher, and the Politics of Retrenchment* (Cambridge: Cambridge University Press).

Pijl, Kees van der (1994). "The Cadre Class and Public Multilateralism," in Y. Sakamoto, ed., *Global Transformation: Challenges to the State System* (Tokyo: United Nations University Press), pp. 200–227.

Pijl, Kees van der (1995). *Transnational Historical Materialism: An Outline* (unpublished manuscript, Research Center for International Political Economy, University of Amsterdam).

Pijl, Kees van der (1998). *Transnational Classes and International Relations* (London: Routledge).

Pin-Fat, Véronique (2005). "The Metaphysics of the National Interest and the 'Mysticism' of the Nation State: Reading Hans J. Morgenthau," *Review of International Studies*, vol. 31, no. 2 (Summer), pp. 217–236.

Plehwe, Dieter, Bernhard Walpen, and Gisela Neunhöffer (eds.) (2006). *Neoliberal Hegemony: A Global Critique* (London: Routledge).

Plender, John (2008). "The Return of the State: How Government Is Back at the Heart of Economic Life," *Financial Times* (August 22).

Poggi, Gianfranco (1978). *The Development of the Modern State* (Stanford, Calif.: Stanford University Press).

Pogrebinschi, Thamy (2008). "Power as Emancipation," paper presented at the annual meeting of the American Political Science Association, Chicago (27–31 August).

Polanyi, Karl (1944). *The Great Transformation: The Political and Economic Origins of Our Time* (Boston: Beacon).

Poulantzas, Nicos (1974). *Political Power and Social Classes* (London: New Left).

Poulantzas, Nicos (1976). *Classes in Contemporary Capitalism* (London: New Left).

Prakash, Aseem, and Jeffrey A. Hart (eds.) (1999). *Globalization and Governance* (London: Routledge).

Preston, P. W. (2000). *Understanding Modern Japan: A Political Economy of Development, Culture and Global Power* (London: Sage).

Pursell, Carroll W. (1994). *White Heat: People and Technology* (Berkeley: University of California Press).

Putnam, Robert D. (1988). "Diplomacy and Domestic Policy: The Logic of Two-Level Games," *International Organization*, vol. 42, no. 3 (Summer), pp. 427–460.

Radice, Hugo (1996). "The Question of Globalization: A Review of Hirst and Thompson," prepared for the annual meeting of the Conference of Socialist Economists, Newcastle-upon-Tyne (12–14 July).

Raffel, Jeffrey A., Peter Leisink, and Anthony E. Middlebrooks (2009). *Public Sector Leadership: International Challenges and Perspectives* (Cheltenham, U.K.: Edward Elgar).

Reich, Robert B. (1983). *The Next American Frontier* (New York: Times).

Reich, Robert B. (1991). *The Work of Nations: Preparing Ourselves for Twenty-First Century Capitalism* (New York: Knopf).

Review of International Political Economy (RIPE) (2009). *Financial Crisis and Renewal? Diversity and Convergence in Emerging Markets*, special issue edited by Philip G. Cerny, vol. 16, no. 4 (August).

Rhodes, Martin (2007). *Globalization and the Welfare State* (Oxford: Blackwell).

Rhodes, R. A. W. (1996). "The New Governance: Governing without Government," *Political Studies*, vol. 44, no. 4 (September), pp. 652–667.

Rhodes, R. A. W. (1997). *Understanding Governance: Policy Networks, Governance, Reflexivity and Accountability* (Milton Keynes, England: Open University Press).

Riggs, Fred W. (1964). *Administration in Developing Countries: The Theory of Prismatic Society* (Boston: Houghton Mifflin).

Robertson, Roland (1992). *Globalization: Social Theory and Global Culture* (London: Sage).

Robinson, Neil (1999). "The Global Economy, Reform and Crisis in Russia," *Review of International Political Economy*, vol. 6, no. 4 (November), pp. 531–564.

Rodrik, Dani (1997). *Has Globalization Gone Too Far?* (Washington, D.C.: Peterson Institute for International Economics).

Rogers, Paul (2000). *Losing Control: Global Security in the Twenty-First Century* (London: Zed).

Ronit, Karsten, and Volker Schneider (eds.) (2000). *Private Organisations in Global Politics* (London: Routledge).

Rose, Nikolas, and Peter Miller (1992). "Political Power beyond the State: Problematics of Government," *British Journal of Sociology*, vol. 43, no. 2 (June), pp. 172–205.

Rose, Nikolas, Pat O'Malley, and Mariana Valverde (2006). "Governmentality," *Annual Review of Law and Social Science*, vol. 2, pp. 83–104.

Rose, Richard (ed.) 1980. *Challenge to Governance: Studies in Overloaded Politics* (London: Sage).

Rosenau, James N. (1961). *Public Opinion and Foreign Policy: An Operational Formulation* (New York: Random House).

Rosenau, James N. (2003). *Distant Proximities: Dynamics beyond Globalization* (Princeton, N.J.: Princeton University Press).

Roy, Ravi, Arthur T. Denzau, and Thomas D. Willett (eds.) (2007). *Neoliberalism: National and Regional Experiments with Global Ideas* (London: Routledge).

Ruggie, John G. (1982). "International Regimes, Transactions, and Change: Embedded Liberalism in the Postwar Economic Order," in Stephen D. Krasner, ed., *International Regimes* (Ithaca, N.Y.: Cornell University Press), pp. 195–231.

Ruggie, John Gerard (ed.) (1993a). *Multilateralism Matters: The Theory and Praxis of an Institutional Form* (New York: Columbia University Press).

Ruggie, John Gerard (1993b). "Territoriality and Beyond: Problematizing Modernity in International Relations," *International Organization*, vol. 47, no. 1 (Winter), pp. 139–174.

Ruggiero, Guido de (1927). *The History of European Liberalism* (Oxford: Oxford University Press).

Rustemova, Assel (2008). "Economics of National Ideas in Kazakhstan and Uzbekistan," working paper, Research Center for East European Studies, University of Bremen (July).

Rutland, Peter (2000). *Business and the State in Contemporary Russia* (Boulder, Colo.: Westview).

Santayana, George (1905). *Reason in Common Sense: The Life of Reason or the Phases of Human Progress* (New York: Charles Scribner's Sons).

Sartori, Giovanni (1976). *Parties and Party Systems: Volume I, A Framework for Analysis* (Cambridge: Cambridge University Press).

Sassen, Saskia (2003). "Globalization or Denationalization?" *Review of International Political Economy*, vol. 10, no. 1 (February), 1–22.

Sassen, Saskia (ed.) (2007). *Deciphering the Global: Its Scales, Spaces and Subjects* (London: Routledge).

Savage, Charlie (2007). *Takeover: The Return of the Imperial Presidency and the Subversion of American Democracy* (New York: Little, Brown).

Schain, Martin A. (1980). "Corporatism and Industrial Relations in France," in Philip G. Cerny and Martin A. Schain, eds., *French Politics and Public Policy* (New York: Methuen), pp. 191–217.

Schain, Martin A. (2009). *The Politics of Immigration in France, Britain, and the United States: A Comparative Study* (New York: Palgrave Macmillan).

Schmidt, Vivien A. (2002). *The Futures of European Capitalism* (Oxford: Oxford University Press).

Schmitter, Philippe C. (1974). "Still the Century of Corporatism?" in F. Pike and T. Stritch, eds., *The New Corporatism* (Notre Dame, Ind.: Notre Dame University Press), pp. 85–131.

Scholte, Jan Aart (2000). *Globalization: A Critical Introduction* (London: Macmillan).

Schumpeter, Joseph A. (1918/1991). "The Crisis of the Tax State," in Richard Swedberg, ed., *Joseph A. Schumpeter: The Economics and Sociology of Capitalism* (Princeton, N.J.: Princeton University Press), pp. 99–140.

Schumpeter, Joseph A. (1954). *Capitalism, Socialism and Democracy* (London: George Allen & Unwin).

Seagrave, Sterling (1995). *Lords of the Rim: The Invisible Empire of the Overseas Chinese* (London: Bantam).

Shaw, Martin (2000). *Theory of the Global State: Globality as an Unfinished Revolution* (Cambridge: Cambridge University Press).

Sheehan, James J. (2008). *Where Have All the Soldiers Gone? The Transformation of Modern Europe* (Boston: Houghton Mifflin).

Shonfield, Andrew (1965). *Modern Capitalism: The Changing Balance of Public and Private Power* (London: Oxford University Press).

Simmel, Georg (1922/1955). *Conflict and the Web of Group Affiliations* (New York: Free Press).

Simmons, Beth A. (1996). "Divisibility, Defection and the Emerging Regulatory Framework for International Capital Markets," paper presented at the annual meeting of the American Political Science Association, San Francisco, 31 August.

Singer, Max, and Aaron Wildavsky (1993). *The Real World Order: Zones of Peace/Zones of Turmoil* (Chatham, N.J.: Chatham House).

Singer, P. W. (2009). *Wired for War: The Robotics Revolution and Conflict in the 21st Century* (New York: Penguin).

Sklair, Leslie (2000). *The Transnational Capitalist Class* (Oxford: Blackwell).

Skocpol, Theda (1979). *States and Social Revolutions: A Comparative Analysis of France, Russia and China* (Cambridge: Cambridge University Press).

Slaughter, Anne-Marie (2004). *A New World Order* (Princeton, N.J.: Princeton University Press).

Soederberg, Susanne (2004). *The Politics of the New International Financial Architecture: Reimposing Neoliberal Domination in the Global South* (London: Zed).

Soederberg, Susanne (2009). "The Politics of Smoke and Mirrors: The G20 London Summit and the Restoration of Neoliberal Development," in Martijn Konings, ed., *Beyond the Subprime Headlines: Critical Perspectives on the Financial Crisis* (London: Verso).

Soederberg, Susanne, George Menz, and Philip G. Cerny (eds.) (2005). *Internalizing Globalization: The Rise of Neoliberalism and the Erosion of National Varieties of Capitalism* (London: Palgrave Macmillan).

Soros, George (2008). *The New Paradigm for Financial Markets: The Credit Crisis of 2008 and What It Means* (New York: Public Affairs).

Spruyt, Hendrik (1994). *The Sovereign State and Its Competitors: An Analysis of Systems Change* (Princeton, N.J.: Princeton University Press).

Stamps, Norman L. (1957) *Why Democracies Fail: A Critical Evaluation of the Causes for Modern Dictatorship* (South Bend, Ind.: University of Notre Dame Press).

Starr, Amory (2000). *Naming the Enemy: Anti-Corporate Movements Confront Globalization* (London: Zed).

Stiglitz, Joseph E. (2002). *Globalization and Its Discontents* (London: Penguin).

Stiglitz, Joseph E., and Linda J. Bilmes (2008). *The Three Trillion Dollar War: The True Cost of the Iraq Conflict* (New York: W. W. Norton).

Stone, Diane (1996). *Capturing the Political Imagination: Think-Tanks and the Policy Process* (London: Frank Cass).

Stone, Diane (2008). "Global Public Policy, Transnational Policy Communities, and Their Networks," *Policy Studies Journal*, vol. 36, no. 1 (February), pp. 19–38.

Stopford, John, and Susan Strange (1991). *Rival States, Rival Firms: Competition for World Market Shares* (Cambridge: Cambridge University Press).

Storing, Herbert J. (ed.) (1962). *Essays on the Scientific Study of Politics* (New York: Holt, Rinehart and Winston).

Strange, Susan (1986). *Casino Capitalism* (Oxford: Basil Blackwell).

Strange, Susan (1990). "The Name of the Game," in N. X. Rizopoulos, ed., *Sea Changes: American Foreign Policy in a World Transformed* (New York: Council on Foreign Relations), pp. 238–273.

Strange, Susan (1996). *The Retreat of the State: The Diffusion of Power in the World Economy* (Cambridge: Cambridge University Press).

Subrahmanyam, Gita (2003). "Bringing the Empire Back In: Patterns of Growth in the British Imperial State, 1890–1960," unpublished PhD thesis, London School of Economics and Political Science.

Subrahmanyam, Gita (2006). "Ruling Continuities: Colonial Rule, Social Forces and Path Dependence in British India and Africa," *Journal of Commonwealth and Comparative Politics*, vol. 44, no. 1 (March), pp. 84–117.

Taleb, Nassim Nicholas (2007). *The Black Swan: The Impact of the Highly Improbable* (New York: Random House).

Tarrow, Sidney (2005). *The New Transnational Activism* (Cambridge: Cambridge University Press).

Taylor, Peter J. (1996). *The Way the Modern World Works* (London: Wiley).

Tett, Gillian (2009). *Fool's Gold: How the Bold Dream of a Small Tribe at J. P. Morgan Was Corrupted by Wall Street Greed and Unleashed a Catastrophe* (New York: Free Press).

Thompson, G., Jennifer Frances, Rosalind Levačić and Jeremy C. Mitchell, eds. (1991). *Markets, Hierarchies and Networks: The Coordination of Social Life* (London: Sage).

Tilly, Charles (ed.) (1975). *The Formation of National States in Western Europe* (Princeton, N.J.: Princeton University Press).

Tönnies, Ferdinand (1887/2003). *Community and Society [Gemeinschaft und Gesellschaft]* (Mineola, N.Y.: Dover).

Truman, David B. (1951). *The Governmental Process* (New York: Alfred A. Knopf).

Tuchman, Barbara (1978). *A Distant Mirror: The Calamitous 14th Century* (New York: Alfred A. Knopf).

Vogel, David (1997). *Trading Up: Consumer and Environmental Regulation in a Global Economy* (Cambridge, Mass.: Harvard University Press).

Wallerstein, Immanuel (1974). *The Modern World System* (New York: Academic Press).

Waltz, Kenneth (1979). *Theory of International Politics* (Reading, Mass.: Addison-Wesley).

Weinert, Matthew S. (2007). *Democratic Sovereignty: Authority, Legitimacy, and State in a Globalizing Age* (New York: University College London Press).

Wendt, Alexander (1992). "Anarchy Is What States Make of It: The Social Construction of Power Politics," *International Organization*, vol. 46, no. 2 (Spring), pp. 391–425.

Willetts, Peter (ed.) (1982). *Pressure Groups in the Global System: The Transnational Relations of Issue-Orientated Non-Governmental Organizations* (New York: St. Martin's Press).

Williams, William Appleman (1959). *The Tragedy of American Diplomacy* (New York: Norton).

Williamson, John (1990). "What Washington Means by Policy Reform," in John Williamson, ed., *Latin American Adjustment: How Much Has Happened* (Washington, D.C.: Institute of International Economics), pp. 5–20.

Williamson, Oliver E. (1975). *Markets and Hierarchies* (New York: Free Press).

Williamson, Oliver E. (1985). *The Economic Institutions of Capitalism* (New York: Free Press).

Wolfe, Robert (2005). "See You in Geneva? Legal (Mis)Representations of the Trading System," *European Journal of International Relations*, vol. 11, no. 3 (September), 339–365.

Wolin, Sheldon S. (1968). "Paradigms and Political Theories," in Preston King and B. C. Parekh, eds., *Politics and Experience: Essays Presented to Professor Michael Oakeshott on the Occasion of His Retirement* (Cambridge: Cambridge University Press), pp. 125–152.

Wong, Edward (2007). "Iraq's Curse: A Thirst for Final, Crushing Victory," *New York Times* (3 June).

World Commission on the Social Dimension of Globalization (2004). *A Fair Globalization: Creating Opportunities for All* (Geneva: International Labour Office).

Yamamura, Kozo, and Wolfgang Streeck (eds.) (2003). *The End of Diversity? Prospects for German and Japanese Capitalism* (Ithaca, N.Y.: Cornell University Press).

Young, Oran R. (1994). *International Governance* (Ithaca, N.Y.: Cornell University Press).

Znaniecki, Florian (1952/1973). *Modern Nationalities: A Sociological Study* (Westport, Conn.: Greenwood).

Zysman, John (1977). *Political Strategies for Industrial Order: State, Market, and Industry in France* (Berkeley: University of California Press).

Zysman, John (1983). *Governments, Markets and Growth: Financial Systems and the Politics of Industrial Change* (Ithaca, N.Y.: Cornell University Press).

Zysman, John, and Laura d'Andrea Tyson (eds.) (1983). *American Industry in International Competition* (Ithaca, N.Y.: Cornell University Press).

Index

Abdelal, Rawi, 264
accounting standards, 257–258
actor sets
    change questions, 7
    in flexible pentangles, 116–117
    in globalization hypothesis, 7–8, 11–17
    in globalization meanings, 25–26
    as institutional entrepreneurs, 17,
        289–292
    in iron triangle concept, 114–116
    and issue-area boundaries, 61–62
    in neo-Marxism, 270–273, 275–279,
        282–283
    in political paradigm alternatives,
        3–4, 8–11, 24–25
    and power dynamics
        dimensions, 68–69, 76–77
    role in democratization, 203,
        210–213
    role in neoliberalism consensus,
        3–4, 8, 148–156
    and security defection
        pathways, 226–227
    and state power organization, 68–69
    transnational linkage evolution, 4–5
    See also governmentality; public
        policy processes; structuration
        processes
Allen, Michael, 213
Anderson, Benedict, 237
Annan, Kofi, 155, 191
Argentina, 124–125
Aristotle, 6, 64, 164
arm's-length regulatory model,
    145–147, 148, 155, 262
articulated restructuring typology,
    structuration processes, 89–90

Arts, Bas, 174
asset structures, in boundary forms, 57
Austria, 205
authority distinction, domestic vs.
    international power, 66–67, 71–72,
    73–76
automobile industry, 124, 250

Bagehot, Walter, 202–203
balanced budget tenet, 143–144
banking. See financial market actors
base level strategies, in transnational
    effectiveness, 106–110
Bentley, Arthur F., 3, 8–9, 14–15
Berger, Peter L., 88
biopolitics, 42
Bookstaber, Richard, 262
border forms
    overview, 18–19, 40–41, 62–63
    enclosure process requirements,
        46–51
    functional boundary
        development, 51–57
    horizontal dimension, 7–8
    issue-based, 57–62, 79
    and nation-state development,
        41–46, 48–51
Brazil, 155
Brenner, Neil, 42, 273, 279, 281–283,
    284–285
Bretton Woods system, 52, 132, 137,
    253
Britain, 45–46, 138, 147, 196, 202–203,
    262
Brittan, Samuel, 24
budget deficits, financial orthodoxy,
    143–144

bureaucratic structure pathway, stable
    democracy, 203–204, 205–206
bureaucrats, in iron triangle
    concept, 114–116
Bush, George W. (and administration)
    economic policy, 125, 143–144, 257
    international regime resistance, 75
    Iraq War and United Nations, 188
    as traditional power approach, 81, 186
    unified action capacity, 70
business actors. *See* economic actors

California effect, 256
capital, 60, 140–142, 249–251,
    263–264, 265, 304–305
capitalism. *See* economic *entries*;
    financial *entries*; neo-Marxism
Cardosa, Fernando Henrique, 155
centrifugal security models, defection
    dynamics, 221–225, 238–239
centripetal security models, defection
    dynamics, 221–225
Chandler, Alfred D., 45
China, 35, 173, 200
civil association, 163
civil society groups, in power
    dynamics, 77–78
Civil War, U.S., 44
Clark, Ian, 215
classical liberalism, traditional
    meaning, 131–132
class power, traditional theories,
    271–272
class systems
    and democratization, 199, 200–201,
    204
    as social dimension complexity,
    35–36
Clinton, Bill (and administration), 143,
    144, 158
coalition pathway, stable democracy,
    203, 205–206
coalitions. *See* actor sets
coalitions rearticulation stage, in
    structuration change model, 94–95
cold war, 17, 50, 79–80, 197, 225–226,
    234–235

collective goods problem, 13, 85,
    97–103
Competition State, 37–39, 85–86,
    157–161, 169–174
    See also economic *entries*
consumers, 121–122 , 170, 173, 191,
    232, 281
contest factor, state organization,
    162–163
convergence/divergence arguments. *See*
    globalization
corporate actors
    and democratization success, 211
    globalization effects
        summarized, 11–17
    institutional entrepreneur
        hypothesis, 293–294
    as social dimension complexity,
        32–33
    See also economic *entries*
corporatism pathway, stable
    democracy, 204–206
Coser, Lewis, 14
Cox, Christopher, 257
Cox, Robert, 35
credit. *See* financial globalization
Crozier, Michel, 88
cultural postmodernism dimension,
    security dilemma, 230–231,
    236–239

death of ideology dimension, security
    dilemma, 230, 234–236
defection pathways, in security
    dilemma, 221–230
Delaware effect, 256
democratization
    as cultural enclosure, 48
    global governance problem, 213–215
    in globalized
        governmentalization, 185–186
    historical trajectories problem,
        198–201
    and pluralization, 20, 195–198, 201
    process *vs.* outcome problem,
        207–210
    role of actor sets, 210–213

and security dilemma, 235–236
    stability problem, 201–206
diasporas, as social dimension
    complexity, 35, 54–55
distinctiveness factor, state
    organization, 161–162
distribution condition, public
    goods, 98, 100–101
distribution stage, in structuration
    change model, 93–94
divergence/convergence arguments. *See*
    globalization
divisibility, in security dilemma
    and defection pathways, 221–230
    dimensions of, 230–240
divisibility factor, public goods, 98–103
domestic politics
    globalization effects
        summarized, 12–14, 28–29
    interdependence theory, 30–31
    in traditional world politics
        perspectives, 3, 5–7
    See also power dynamics; public
        policy processes
Donaldson, William, 257
Durkheim, Emile, 13

Easton, David, 28
economic actors
    and democratization success, 211
    in flexible pentangles, 116–117
    globalization effects
        summarized, 11–17
    in globalization meanings, 26
    institutional entrepreneur
        hypothesis, 291, 292–295
    in iron triangle concept, 114–116
    structuration alternatives
        summarized, 304
economic dimensions
    boundary-setting processes, 46–47,
        49–50, 52–54, 56–62
    in contested state category, 162
    democratization, 199–201, 204–205
    as fundamental state
        reorientation, 85–87
    in globalization, 31–33, 37–39

interdependence theory, 30
    in neoliberalism consensus
        trend, 136–148, 149–152, 154–155
    in neoliberalism meanings, 134–136
    in power dynamic
        reconfigurations, 78–79
    public goods problem, 85, 97–103
    in public policy process
        changes, 118–119, 120–127
    of security dilemma, 221–227, 230,
        231–234
    of state organizational change,
        169–171
    See also Competition State; financial
        entries; neo-Marxism
The Eighteenth Brumaire of Louis
    Bonaparte (Marx), 10, 274, 289
electricity industry, 250
embedded liberalism, 37
empires, and border-setting
    processes, 43–44, 48–50
environmentalism, 77–78, 127, 187–188
epistemic communities, as social
    dimension complexity, 35
ethnicity
    as divisibility dimension, 236–239
    as social dimension complexity,
        34–35
European Union, 75–76, 138, 144
Evans, Mark G., 146
exchange rate systems, 253–255
excludability criterion, public
    goods, 99–100

Ferguson, Adam, 183
feudalism, transitions from, 29, 41,
    90–97
financial globalization
    overview, 21, 245–249, 268–269
    capital sources, 249–254
    regulatory approaches, 254–260
    regulatory limitations, 260–268
financial market actors
    overview, 247–248
    and democratization success, 211
    globalization effects
        summarized, 11–17

financial market actors (*continued*)
institutional entrepreneur
hypothesis, 291, 294
and issue-area boundaries, 60–61
financial orthodoxy dimension
in flexible pentangles, 116–117
of neoliberalism, 142–144
First Industrial Revolution, 45
flexible pentangles, 116–117
force dimension, domestic *vs.*
international power, 71–72, 79–81
Fordism. *See* Second Industrial
Revolution
Foucault, Michel (writing on)
biopolitics, 42
bureaucratic institutions, 176
economic competition, 158
governmentality, 5, 157, 159, 173,
179, 181–184
fragmegration, 170
France, 45, 49, 91, 138, 145, 196, 205
Friedberg, Erhard, 88
Frieden, Jeffry, 122
Friedman, Thomas, 112
functional differentiation dimension.
See sociocultural dimensions

Gaebler, Ted, 284
Gallarotti, Giulio, 80
Gelpern, Anna, 266
General Agreement on Tariffs and
Trade (GATT), 133, 141
geographical dimensions, borders
overview, 40–41, 43–44
and functional boundaries, 53–54
issue-area boundaries, 57–58, 59–60
in rescaling of state, 281–283
Germany, 45–46, 47, 138, 199–200, 205
Gill, Stephen, 35, 72, 304
global *agora*, 213
global governance
authority vacuum, 66–67
capacity questions, 15–16
as democratization problem, 213–215
from functional boundaries, 51–52
global governmentalization
compared, 186–191

as incomplete architecture, 175–177
and liberal internationalism
tradition, 132–133
and neoliberalism consensus,
149–150, 153, 155–156
as power dynamics dimension,
66–67, 72–78
states system assumptions, 6–7, 28
in structuration change model, 97
See also security dilemma
globalization
actor set hypothesis, 7–8
economic complexity
dimension, 31–33
feudalism transition
comparison, 90–97
and interdependence theory, 28–31
meanings of, 24–28, 39
political complexity dimension, 37–39
social complexity dimension,
33–36
structuration alternatives
summarized, 302–306
See also specific topics, e.g., actor sets;
border forms; economic
dimensions
Globalization (Robertson), 24
glocalization of culture, 55–56
governmentality
as actor set engagement
capacity, 177–179, 183–184
change summarized, 5, 20, 176–177,
191–192
of Competition State, 157–161
interactive requirement, 177–178
as key to globalization process,
184–191
multiple aspect, 169–172
as totalization-individualization
tension management, 175–176,
178–184
transnational typologies, 187–191
See also global governance
Granovetter, Mark, 29
Grant, James, 263
Greenspan, Alan, 39
group theory, 4, 9

Halperin, Sandra, 200
Hardt, Michael, 36
hegemony and class power, 272
Helleiner, Eric, 122
hierarchy control pathway, stable
    democracy, 204, 205–206
Hirst, Paul, 27, 113
Hobbes, Thomas, 67
Hobsbawm, Eric, 45
Höpner, Martin, 263
horizontal dimension, borders. See
    sociocultural dimensions
human rights, in power dynamics,
    77–78
Huntington, Samuel, 202

ideology dimension
    in globalization hypothesis, 8
    in security dilemma, 230, 234–236
incremental adaptation typology,
    structuration processes, 89–90
individualization-totalization tensions.
    See governmentality
indivisibility factor, public goods,
    98–103
Industry and Empire (Hobsbawm), 45
inflation, 142–144
inside/outside distinctions
    and interdependence theory, 29–31
    nation-state concept, 42
    power dimensions, 66–73
    sovereignty dimensions, 163–164
    and states' organizational
        capacities, 164–167
institutional selection stage,
    structuration change model, 96–97
institutional strategies, actor sets,
    overview of globalization
    effects, 11–17, 289–292
interdependence theme,
    globalization, 28–31
interest groups. See actor sets
interest rate examples, 30, 33, 143
intermediaries factors, in transnational
    effectiveness, 106–110
inter-nationalization, 27, 113
International Monetary Fund, 144, 147,

256
international politics. See world politics
    discipline
intervention dimension,
    neoliberalism, 144–147
Iraq War, 168
iron triangles, 114–116
Italy, 199–200

Jacoby, Sanford, 173
Janus comparison, 66
Japan, 32, 45, 138, 199–200, 205
Jessop, Bob, 42, 106, 135, 146,
    273–280, 284–285
Johnson, Samuel, 67
jointness of supply, public goods,
    99–100
Jolly, Richard, 36
Joseph, Keith, 143
justice dimension, political science
    traditions, 5–6

Kahler, Miles, 264
Kaldor, Mary, 44
Kant, Immanuel, 6
Kaplan, Robert D., 36
Kennedy, Paul, 166
Keohane, Robert O., 14, 30, 133–134, 215
Kerry, John, 143
Key, V. O., 14–15, 69
Kindleberger, Charles P., 253
King, Anthony, 114
Klein, Naomi, 123
knowledge-based economy, in Jessop's
    neo-Marxism perspective, 280–281
Kotkin, Joel, 35
Kurki, Milja, 207, 208–209
Kyoto Protocol, 214

labor
    and democratization success, 211
    institutional entrepreneur
        hypothesis, 291, 293
    and neoliberalism, 138, 143
    in neo-Marxism, 275–278
    as social dimension complexity, 36
Lagendijk, Arnoud, 174

Lake, David A., 76, 190, 264
Lefebvre, Henri, 281
Levitt, Arthur, 257
liberal internationalism tradition,
    132–133
liberalism, contradictory
    meanings, 131–132
limited liability company, 251
Luckmann, Thomas, 88
Lula da Silva, Luiz Inácio, 155

Macdonald, Kate, 215–216
Marx, Karl, 10, 273, 274
    See also neo-Marxism
McFarland, Andrew S., 105
Mead, Walter Russell, 199
methodological nationalism, 274–275
Modern Capitalism (Shonfield), 252
modernism, in governmentality,
    179–181
money, 246–247, 253–255
    See also financial entries
Moore, Barrington, Jr., 44, 95
moral hazard problem, 263, 265–266
Moran, Michael, 146, 256
Moravcsik, Andrew, 134
Morgenthau, Hans J., 68
Mouffe, Chantal, 207
multiculturalism dimensions. See social
    actors; sociocultural dimensions
multinodal politics framework,
    overview, 85–87, 302
    See also structuration processes

national economy requirement,
    boundary-setting process, 46–47
national identity pathway, stable
    democracy, 205–206
nationalism
    as dimension in security
        dilemma, 231, 234–236
    methodological approach, 274–275
Negri, Antonio, 36
neoconservative movement, 10
neo-Gramscian theory, 272
neoliberal institutionalism, 30,
    133–134

neoliberalism doctrine
    consensus dimensions, 140–148
    consensus trend, 136–140, 156
    as contested concept, 130–136
    evolutionary nature, 19,
        128–130, 156
    role of actor sets, 148–156
    See also Competition State
neo-Marxism
    overview, 10, 21–22, 270–274,
        287–288
    structural change arguments,
        279–287
    value exchange depictions, 274–279
neopluralism, structuration
    processes, 105–106, 109–110
neorealism theory, 28–31, 133
New Security Dilemma. See security
    dilemma
Nye, Joseph S., Jr., 14, 80

Oakeshott, Michael, 163
Obama, Barack, 143
organization dimension, domestic vs.
    international power, 68–70, 78–79
Osborne, David, 284
outcome-oriented intervention,
    144–147
Overseas Chinese, 35
owners/managers. See corporate actors

Parsons, Talcott, 25
patriotism pathway, stable
    democracy, 205–206
Peace of Westphalia, 41, 47, 68
pentangles, flexible, 116–117
Pitt, Harvey, 257
pluralism paradigm, 3, 8–11, 13–14,
    103–106, 109–110
pluralization
    and democratization, 20, 195–198,
        201
    and Marxism, 271–274
Polanyi, Karl, 181
political actors
    and democratization success,
        210–211, 212

in flexible pentangles, 116–117
institutional entrepreneur
    hypothesis, 291, 295–298
in iron triangle concept, 114–116
and nation-state contradictions, 42
in neoliberalism consensus, 152–153
See also public policy processes;
    structuration processes
political dimension
    boundary-setting processes, 46,
        48–49, 51–53, 56–57
    in contested state category, 163
    globalization, 37–39, 51–53
Political Order in Changing Societies
    (Huntington), 202
Politics (Aristotle), 6
post-Fordism, 33, 54, 58, 124, 232, 253,
    280, 285–286
Poulantzas, Nicos, 270–271
poverty-reduction strategy, World
    Bank, 155, 188, 190–191
power dynamics, international relations
    overview, 64–66, 82
    reconfigurations, 12, 73–81, 292
    in territorial borders history, 43–44
    traditional perspectives, 5–6, 66–72
power dynamics, issue-area
    effects, 105–106
precondition stage, in structuration
    change model, 92–93
Preston, P. W., 63
privatization, 147–148, 190
proactive strategy stage, in structuration
    change model, 95–96
procedural democracy, 207–209
The Process of Government (Bentley), 3,
    8–9
production condition, public
    goods, 98–100
Project for the New American
    Century, 10
protectionism, 121–125, 137, 140–142,
    150
public choice theory, 10
public goods problem, 13, 85, 97–103
public policy processes
    change characteristics, 117–120

flexible pentangle model, 116–117,
    127
globalizing world hypotheses,
    120–127
issue boundary implications, 58
and neoliberalism consensus,
    149–150
and power dynamics
    reconfigurations, 78–79
public goods problem, 85, 97–103
traditional analysis approaches,
    111–116
See also regulatory policy
punctuated equilibrium typology,
    structuration processes, 89–90
Putin, Vladimir, 70, 173

quango-like regimes, 37
quantitative approaches, 10

raison d'État, shift from, 5, 20, 157
raison du monde, shift towards, 5, 20,
    157, 159
raw power dimension, domestic vs.
    international power, 71–72, 79–81
Reagan, Ronald (and
    administration), 138, 143–144
rearticulation of coalitions stage, in
    structuration change model,
    94–95
recession of 1970s, role in
    neoliberalism consensus, 136–139
redistributive collective goods, 100, 101
regulatory policy
    arm's-length model, 145–147, 148,
        155
    and power dynamics
        reconfigurations, 78–79
    in process changes, 118–119, 121,
        125–126
    public goods, 99–100
    See also governmentality; public
        policy processes
religion, 47, 68, 236
rescaling, 21, 272–274, 279–287
Rhodes, R. A. W., 147
Robertson, Roland, 24, 237

Rogowski, Ronald, 122
Roosevelt, Franklin D. (and
    administration), 253
Rosenau, James N., 70, 170
routine adjustment typology,
    structuration processes, 89–90
Ruggie, John, 37, 133, 250, 253
Russia, 70, 173, 200

Santayana, George, 198
Sarbanes-Oxley Act, 155
Saudi Arabia, 185
Second Industrial Revolution
    convergence patterns, 33
    and divisibility factors, 231
    and financial system
        development, 249–250
    as states system reinforcer, 12
    and territorial borders, 45, 47
Securities and Exchange Commission
    (SEC), 257, 258
securitization, financial market,
    258–259
security dilemma
    overview, 20–21, 217–220, 240–244
    defection pathways, 80, 221–227
    divisibility dimensions, 230–240
    new vs. traditional, 217–220,
        227–230
Sheehan, James, 166
Shonfield, Andrew, 252
Simmel, Georg, 13
Sklair, Leslie, 36
Skocpol, Theda, 95
Slaughter, Anne-Marie, 121, 152, 170
social actors
    as complex globalization
        dimension, 33–36
    and democratization success,
        210–211, 212–213
    in financial sector, 248–249
    in flexible pentangles, 116–117
    globalization effects
        summarized, 11–17
    in globalization meanings, 26
    institutional entrepreneur
        hypothesis, 292, 298–302

in iron triangle concept, 114–116
and issue-area boundaries, 59–60
in neoliberalism consensus,
    150–151, 153
structuration alternatives
    summarized, 303–304
social harmony dimension, political
    science traditions, 6
Social Origins of Dictatorship and
    Democracy (Moore), 95
sociocultural dimensions
    boundary-setting process, 40–41,
        44–45, 47–48, 54–57
    in contested state category, 162–163
    in security dilemma, 230–231,
        236–239
sovereignty dimensions, states, 163–164
Soviet Union, 45, 199–200, 225–226,
    270
spatio-temporal fix, 272–273, 282–283,
    286–287
Speth, James Gustave, 36
Spitzer, Eliot, 257
Spruyt, Hendrik, 14, 49, 90–97
state legitimacy dimension, domestic vs.
    international power, 67–68, 76–78
states
    globalization effects
        summarized, 12–17, 19–20,
            22–23, 28–29, 85–87
    in globalization meanings, 26
    interdependence theory, 29–31
    in neoliberalism consensus, 152–153
    in new institutionalism theory, 10
    organizational capacities, 164–169
    organizational changes, 169–172
    organizational characteristics, 161–164
    as political dimension
        complexity, 37–39
    as social dimension complexity, 33–34
    traditional system perspective, 6–7,
        24–25, 28
    See also specific topics, e.g., border
        forms; political actors; security
        dilemma
States and Social Revolutions
    (Skocpol), 95

steel industry, 99, 124
Stone, Diane, 213
Stopford, John, 38, 151
Strange, Susan, 35, 38, 151, 157
Strauss, Leo, 9–10
structural change, neo-Marxism
    perspectives, 279–284
structuration processes
    overview, 19, 86, 87–90
    neopluralism perspectives, 105–106,
        109–110
    pluralism perspectives, 103–106,
        109–110
    potential transnational scenarios
        summarized, 302–306
    public goods problem, 97–103
    stages, 90–97
    transition effectiveness factors,
        106–110
    typologies, 88–90
supply factor, public goods, 99–100
suzerainty as border management, 43
Sweden, 205

tax policy, 121, 143–144
territorial dimension. *See* geographical
    dimensions, borders
terrorism, 81, 150, 236
Tet Offensive, 168
Tett, Gillian, 265
Thatcher, Margaret, 138, 139–140
Third Industrial Revolution, 33, 54, 58,
    124, 232, 253, 280, 285–286
Thompson, Grahame, 27, 113
Thucydides, 6
totalization-individualization tensions.
    See governmentality
trade/production dimension,
    neoliberalism, 140–142
Traditional Security Dilemma. *See*
    security dilemma
transgovernmental networks, in
    globalization hypothesis, 7–8
    See also global governance; security
        dilemma; states
transnational neopluralism,
    overview, 3–8, 20, 106–110, 289

See also specific topics, e.g., actor sets;
    economic *entries*; governmentality
transnational opportunity
    structures, 15, 300–301
transnational structuration, potential
    scenarios summarized, 302–306
triangular diplomacy, 38
Truman, David, 9

United Nations, 97, 132, 155, 188
United States, 45–46, 138, 143–144,
    158, 196, 253
    See also Bush, G. W.; financial
        entries

value exchange depictions, in
    neo-Marxism, 274–279
value group category. *See* social actors
Vandenberg, Arthur, 6
van der Pijl, Kees, 35–36
van Houtum, Henk, 174
Vegetius, 68
Venezuela, 200–201
vertical dimensions, borders. *See*
    geographical dimensions,
    borders
Vietnam War, 168
Vogel, David, 256

Waltz, Kenneth, 30, 67, 70, 133
war
    as cultural enclosure, 47–48, 54
    and democratization processes,
        196–197, 199–200
    effectiveness perspectives, 166,
        168–169, 233, 245
    from nation-building
        complexities, 34, 44
    and power dynamics, 68, 80–81
    See also security dilemma
Warner, Charles Dudley, 95
Weber, Max, 69
welfare state, 37–38, 44–46, 191,
    274–275
Willetts, Peter, 188
Williams, William Appleman,
    186

Williamson, Oliver E., 57, 264
Wolin, Sheldon, 9
World Bank, 144, 147, 155, 188,
    190–191, 256–257
world politics discipline, overview
    change questions, 7
    globalization effects, 12–14, 22–23,
        28–29
    interdependence theory, 29–31

paradigm shifts, 3, 5–7, 18, 24–25
    See also specific topics, e.g., border
        forms; economic dimensions;
        public policy processes; states
World Trade Organization, 74–75, 147,
    214

Zimbabwe, 201
Znaniecki, Florian, 237